ATHENAZE

ATHENAZE

An Introduction to Ancient Greek

Revised Edition
Book I

Maurice Balme
and
Gilbert Lawall
with drawings by Catherine Balme

New York   Oxford
OXFORD UNIVERSITY PRESS
1990

Oxford University Press

Oxford   New York   Toronto
Delhi   Bombay   Calcutta   Madras   Karachi
Petaling Jaya   Singapore   Hong Kong   Tokyo
Nairobi   Dar es Salaam   Cape Town
Melbourne   Auckland

and associated companies in
Berlin   Ibadan

Copyright © 1990 by Oxford University Press, Inc.

Published by Oxford University Press, Inc.,
198 Madison Avenue, New York, New York 10016-4314

Oxford is a registered trademark of Oxford University Press

Library of Congress Cataloging-in-Publication Data
Balme, M. G.
Athenaze / Maurice Balme and Gilbert Lawall.
p.   cm.   English and Ancient Greek.
ISBN 0-19-505621-3 (pbk.).
ISBN 0-19-506384-8   (teacher's handbook)
1. Greek language—Grammar—1950
2. Greek language—Readers.
I. Lawall, Gilbert.   II. Title.
PA258.B325   1990   488.82′421—dc20
89-22967   CIP

14   15   16   17   18   19

Printed in the United States of America
on acid-free paper

PREFACE

This book is a revised and expanded version of *Athenaze*, written ten years ago by Maurice Balme. That original edition was used quite widely in English schools and also in a few universities. Gilbert Lawall used it with his students at the University of Massachusetts at Amherst and suggested some years ago that we revise it and look for a publisher in the United States. At that time we were both fully committed to other tasks, but eventually we decided to undertake the project. Oxford University Press agreed to publish it, and since then we have cooperated closely in a root and branch revision.

The original version was skeletal; it consisted of a narrative in Greek, followed by minimal explanations of grammar and syntax and some exercises at the end of the book. We have kept the framework of the old narrative, expanding it where this seemed desirable, but everything else has been changed. Full explanations of grammar and syntax are given at every stage; short essays on relevant aspects of ancient Greek history, social life, and culture have been added in the middle of the chapters; the exercises have been almost entirely rewritten; and an extensive teacher's handbook has been added.

The revised course was piloted during 1988/1989 in schools and universities by the following teachers and professors:

Sean Smith, Amherst Regional High School, Amherst, Massachusetts
Charles Briody, Ballou Senior High School, Washington, D.C.
Peter Brush, Deerfield Academy, Deerfield, Massachusetts
Mark Greenstock, Harrow School, Harrow-on-the-Hill, England
Joel Kelly, Kent School, Kent, Connecticut
Phyllis B. Katz, Miss Porter's School, Farmington, Connecticut
Carl E. Krumpe, Jr., Phillips Academy, Andover, Massachusetts
Reginald Hannaford, Portland High School, Portland, Maine
Whitney Blair, Rye Country Day School, Rye, New York
Christopher Wilson, Tonbridge School, Tonbridge, England

Anthony Gini, Geoff Bakewell, and William F. Wyatt, Jr., Brown University, Providence, Rhode Island
Douglas Domingo-Forasté and Conrad Barrett, California State University, Long Beach, California
Catharine P. Roth, University of Dayton, Dayton, Ohio
Nancy Felson-Rubin and Timothy Gantz, University of Georgia, Athens, Georgia
Jeanne Kurtz, University of New Hampshire, Durham, New Hampshire
Z. Philip Ambrose, University of Vermont, Burlington, Vermont
Cynthia King, Wright State University, Dayton, Ohio

We wish to thank all of these teachers and professors most sincerely for their cooperation in the pilot project and for their innumerable corrections and suggestions that have helped make this a better book. We also wish to thank Catherine Balme for her numerous drawings based on Greek vase paintings that introduce the reading passages. We are also grateful to Allotype Typographics of Ann Arbor, Michigan, for creating the software necessary to add macrons to the Kadmos font, and we are grateful to Stephen G. Daitz of The City University of New York for his help with the guide to pronunciation and the placement of macrons over appropriate vowels throughout the student's book and teacher's handbook. We also thank Douglas Domingo-Forasté of California State University, Long Beach, California, for his final proofreading of both the student's book and the teacher's handbook, and Marjorie Dearworth Keeley, West Springfield High School, West Springfield, Massachusetts, for typing the greater part of these books into the computer, preparation of the end vocabularies and index, proofreading, and innumerable suggestions for improvement of layout and format. The authors themselves bear responsibility for any errors remaining.

Maurice Balme
Gilbert Lawall

CONTENTS

INTRODUCTION

Part I:
About This Course

The aim of *Athenaze* is to teach you to read ancient Greek as quickly, thoroughly, and enjoyably as possible, and to do so within the context of ancient Greek culture. This means within the context of the daily life of the ancient Greeks as it was shaped and given meaning by historical developments, political events, and the life of the mind as revealed in mythology, religion, philosophy, literature, and art. The stories that you will read in Greek provide the basic cultural context within which you will learn the Greek language, and most of the chapters contain essays in English with illustrations drawn from ancient works of art and with background information to deepen your understanding of some aspects of the history and culture of the Greeks.

The course begins with the story of an Athenian farmer named Dicaeopolis and his family; they live in a village called Cholleidae about twelve miles south-east of Athens. The events are fictitious, but they are set in a definite historical context—autumn 432 B.C. to spring 431. The Athenian democracy, led by Pericles, is at its height; the Athenians rule the seas and control an empire, but their power has aroused the fears and jealousy of Sparta and her allies in the Peloponnesus, especially Corinth. By spring 431, Athens and the Peloponnesian League are engaged in a war, which leads twenty-seven years later to the defeat and downfall of Athens.

The story begins with life in the country, but with Chapter 6 a sub-plot of mythical narrative begins with the story of Theseus and the Minotaur. This mythological sub-plot continues in Chapter 7 with the story of Odysseus and the Cyclops and runs through Chapter 10 with further tales from the *Odyssey* briefly told at the end of each chapter. The main plot continues in Chapter 8 as the family visits Athens for a festival, and the tempo quickens.

A terrible misfortune that strikes the family in Athens in Chapter 10 precipitates a plot that is interwoven with narratives of the great battles of the Persian Wars, based on the accounts of the historian Herodotus. As the main plot reaches its resolution in Chapters 18–20, at the beginning of Book II, the family becomes embroiled in the tensions between Athens and Corinth that triggered the Peloponnesian War, and this sets the stage for the remaining chapters.

The experiences of the family of Dicaeopolis at the beginning of the Peloponnesian War in Chapters 21–23 are based on the accounts of the war written by the historian Thucydides. When the son Philip is left behind in Athens to further his education, we hear something of Plato's views on education (Chapter 24) and then read stories from a book of Herodotus' histories that Philip's teacher gives to him (Chapters 25–28). These are some of the most

famous tales from Herodotus, including those dealing with Solon the Athenian and his encounter with Croesus, king of Lydia.   In Chapter 28 you will
read the account by the lyric poet Bacchylides of Croesus' miraculous rescue
from the funeral pyre.   Chapters 29 and 30 return us to the Peloponnesian War
with Thucydides' descriptions of naval battles and the brilliant victories of
the Athenian general Phormio.   The course concludes with extracts from
Aristophanes showing us Dicaeopolis the peacemaker.   From there you will
be ready to go on to read any Greek author of your choice with considerable
confidence in your ability to comprehend what the ancient Greeks had to say.

The Greek in much of the main story line has been made up to serve the
instructional purposes of this book.   Most of the sub-plots, however, are based
on the ancient Greek writings of Homer, Herodotus, and Thucydides.   They
move steadily closer to the Greek of the authors themselves.   The extracts
from Bacchylides and Aristophanes are unaltered except for cuts.

The readings in the early chapters are simple in content and grammatical structure.   They are so constructed that with knowledge of the vocabulary
that is given before the reading passage and with help from the glosses that
are given beneath each paragraph, you can read and understand the Greek
before studying the formal elements of the grammar.   After you have read the
story out loud and understood it, you should study the formal presentations of
grammar that usually incorporate examples from the reading passage.
There are then exercises of various sorts to help you consolidate your understanding of the grammar and give you skill in manipulating the new forms
and structures of the language as you learn them.

Grammar is introduced in small doses to start with and should be re-
viewed constantly.   We also recommend frequent rereading of the stories
themselves—preferably out loud—as the best way to reinforce your fluency of
pronunciation, your knowledge of the grammar, and your skill in reading
new Greek at sight—which is the main goal of any course in Greek.

At the beginning of each section of the narrative is a picture with a caption
in Greek.   From the picture you should be able to deduce the meaning of the
Greek caption.   Pay particular attention to these captions, since each has been
carefully written to include and reinforce a basic grammatical feature or
features of the Greek language that you will be learning in that particular
chapter.   It may help even to memorize the captions!

The vocabulary given in the lists before the reading passages is meant to
be learned thoroughly, both from Greek to English and from English to
Greek.   Learning the vocabulary will be easier if the words are always studied aloud, combining the advantages of sight *and* sound.   The words given in
glosses beneath the paragraphs in the readings are not meant to be mastered
actively, but you should be able to recognize the meaning of these words when
you see them again in context.   Fluency of reading depends on acquiring a
large, working vocabulary as soon as possible.

Important words are continually reintroduced in the readings in this
course to help you learn them.   Your skill in recognizing the meaning of
Greek words that you have not met will be greatly enhanced by attention to

some basic principles of word building. We have therefore laid out some of these basic principles and incorporated a coherent set of word building exercises in this course.

One of the widely recognized goals of classical language study is attainment of a better understanding of English. With regard to the study of Greek, this means largely a knowledge of Greek roots, prefixes, and suffixes that appear in English words. The influence of Greek on English has been especially notable in scientific and medical terminology, but it is also evident in the language of politics, philosophy, literature, and the arts. We have accordingly incorporated word study sections in the chapters of this course, highlighting the influence of Greek on English vocabulary and providing practice in deciphering the meaning of English words derived from Greek elements.

Myrrhine, Melissa, and Argus

Part II:
The Greek Alphabet,
Pronunciation, Punctuation, and
Transliteration

The Greek Alphabet

Many of the letters of the Greek alphabet will already be familiar to you.
The pronunciation given at the right attempts to approximate the way the letters were pronounced in classical times.

Letter		*Name*		*Pronunciation**
A	α	ἄλφα	alpha	ă (as in *top*), ā (as in *father*)
B	β	βῆτα	bēta	b
Γ	γ	γάμμα	gamma	g (before γ, κ, μ, ξ, or χ = Eng. *ng*)
Δ	δ	δέλτα	delta	d
E	ε	ἒ ψῑλόν	epsilon	ĕ (as in *get*)
Z	ζ	ζῆτα	zēta	sd (as in *wis_d_om*)
H	η	ἦτα	ēta	ē (as in *hair*)
Θ	θ	θῆτα	thēta	t-h** (as in *top*, emphatically pronounced)
I	ι	ἰῶτα	iōta	ĭ (as in *peep*), ī (as in *keen*)
K	κ	κάππα	kappa	k
Λ	λ	λάμβδα	lambda	l
M	μ	μῦ	mu	m
N	ν	νῦ	nu	n
Ξ	ξ	ξῖ	xi	x (= ks)
O	o	ὂ μῑκρόν	omicron	ŏ (as in *but*)
Π	π	πῖ	pi	p
P	ρ	ῥῶ	rhō	r (rolled or trilled *r*)
Σ	σ, ς	σίγμα	sigma	s (as in *sing*, but as *z* before β, γ, δ, and μ) (usually written ς when last letter of word)
T	τ	ταῦ	tau	t
Y	υ	ὒ ψῑλόν	upsilon	ŭ (as in French *tu*), ū (as in French *pur*)
Φ	φ	φῖ	phi	p-h** (as in *pot*, emphatically pronounced)
X	χ	χῖ	chi	k-h** (as in *kit*; emphatically pronounced)
Ψ	ψ	ψῖ	psi	ps
Ω	ω	ὦ μέγα	ōmega	ō (as in *paw*)

*In the following list and throughout this book, the symbol ˘ over a vowel indicates a vowel of short quantity, and the symbol ¯ indicates a vowel of long quantity. The symbol for a long vowel ¯ is generally referred to as a macron (Greek μακρόν "long"). A long vowel is held approximately twice as long as a short vowel. The vowels η (*ēta*) and ω (*ōmega*) are always long; therefore these vowels will not be marked with any symbol. The vowels α (*alpha*), ι (*iōta*), and υ (*upsilon*) are sometimes long and sometimes short. In the case of these three vowels, only the long vowels will be marked (ᾱ, ῑ, and ῡ). If there is no marking (i.e., if written simply α, ι, and υ), the vowel is to be considered short.

All vowels marked with a circumflex accent (see page x) or with an iota subscript (see below) are always long and therefore will usually not be marked.

**In emphatic English pronunciation of *top*, *pot*, and *kit*, the initial consonants are clearly aspirated; the pronunciation of θ, φ, and χ was similar to this.

Diphthongs

Diphthongs	*Words*	*Pronunciation*
αι	αἰγίς	ai (as in *high*)
αυ	αὐτοκρατής	au (as in *how*)
ει	εἴκοσι	ei (as in *they*)
ευ	εὐγενής	eü (= e + u)
ηυ	ηὔρηκα	ēü (= ē + u)
οι	οἰκονομίᾱ	oi (as in *foil*)
ου	οὔτις	ou (as in *fool*)
υι	υἱός	ui (as in French u + y)

Sometimes the letter ι (*iōta*) is written under a vowel, e.g., ᾳ, ῃ, and ῳ (these combinations are referred to as *long* diphthongs); when so written it is called iota subscript. In classical Greek this iota was written on the line after the vowel and was pronounced as a short iota. Its pronunciation ceased in post-classical Greek. When it appears in a word that is written entirely in capital letters (as in the titles to the readings in this book), it is written on the line as a capital iota. Thus πρὸς τῇ κρήνῃ > ΠΡΟΣ ΤΗΙ ΚΡΗΝΗΙ. Accents and breathing marks (see below) are not used when all letters are capitalized.

Double Consonants

Double consonants such as λλ, μμ, ππ, and ττ should be held approximately twice as long as the single consonant.

An exception is γγ; see γ in the alphabet on page viii.

Note that the *gamma* in the following combinations is also pronounced as an *ng*: γκ, γμ, γξ, and γχ.

Breathings

There is no letter *h* in the Greek alphabet, but this sound occurs at the beginning of many Greek words. It is indicated by a mark called a *rough breathing* or *aspiration*, written over the first vowel of a word (over the second vowel of a diphthong), e.g.:

ἑν (pronounced *hen*)   οὑ (pronounced *hou*)

When an *h* sound is not to be pronounced at the beginning of a word begin-ning with a vowel or diphthong, a *smooth breathing* mark is used, e.g.:

ἐν (pronounced *en*)   οὐ (pronounced *ou*)

Punctuation

The period and the comma are written as in English. A dot above the line (·) is the equivalent of an English semicolon. A mark equivalent to an En-glish semicolon (;) is used at the end of a sentence as a question mark.

Accents

Nearly every word in Greek bears an accent mark: an acute (τίς), a grave (τὸ), or a circumflex (ὁρῶ). These marks seldom affect the sense. They were invented as symbols to provide written aid for correct pronunciation; origi-nally they indicated a change in *pitch*, e.g., the acute accent showed that the syllable on which it fell was pronounced at a higher pitch than the preceding or following syllables. Later *stress* replaced pitch, and now ancient Greek is often pronounced with stress on the accented syllables (with no distinction among the three kinds of accents) instead of varying the pitch of the voice. For those who wish to use the pitch accent, we recommend the recording of Stephen Daitz, mentioned below.

Note that the grave accent stands only on the final syllable of a word. It replaces an acute accent on the final syllable of a word when that word is fol-lowed immediately by another word with no intervening punctuation, e.g.: instead of τό δῶρον, we write τὸ δῶρον. Exceptions to this rule and further in-formation about accents are given at the beginning of the Reference Gram-mar at the end of this book.

Transliteration

Note the following standard transliteration of Greek into English letters:

α = a	η = ē	ν = n	τ = t
β = b	θ = th	ξ = x	υ = u *or* y
γ = g	ι = i	ο = o	φ = ph
δ = d	κ = k	π = p	χ = ch
ε = e	λ = l	ρ = r	ψ = ps
ζ = z	μ = m	σ, ς = s	ω = ō

Remember the following: γγ = ng; γκ = nk; γξ = nx, and γχ = nch (but γμ is transliterated as gm); αυ, ευ, ηυ, ου, υι = au, eu, ēu, ou, ui, but when υ is not in a diphthong it is usually transliterated as y. And note that ᾳ, ῃ, and ῳ are transliterated āi, ēi, and ōi, to distinguish them from the short diphthongs, αι, ει, and οι, transliterated ai, ei, and oi.

[The recommendations for pronunciation given above (the *restored* pronun-ciation) are based on W. Sidney Allen, *Vox Graeca: A Guide to the Pronunci-ation of Classical Greek*, Cambridge University Press, 3rd ed., 1988, pages

177–179. For demonstration of the restored pronunciation, including the
pitch accents, students should consult the cassette recording of Stephen G.
Daitz, *The Pronunciation and Reading of Ancient Greek: A Practical Guide*,
2nd ed., 1984, Audio Forum, Guilford, CT 06437 (U.S.A.).]

Part III:
Practice in Writing and Pronunciation

Practice pronouncing the following words, imitating your teacher. Then
copy the Greek words onto a sheet of paper; write the English transliteration of
each Greek word, and give an English derivative of each.

1.	αἴνιγμα	11.	δόγμα	21.	μάθημα	31.	ῥεῦμα
2.	ἀξίωμα	12.	δρᾶμα	22.	μίασμα	32.	στίγμα
3.	ἄρωμα	13.	ἔμβλημα	23.	νόμισμα	33.	σύμπτωμα
4.	ἄσθμα	14.	ζεῦγμα	24.	ὄνομα	34.	σύστημα
5.	γράμμα	15.	θέμα	25.	πλάσμα	35.	σχῆμα
6.	δέρμα	16.	θεώρημα	26.	πνεῦμα	36.	σχίσμα
7.	διάδημα	17.	ἰδίωμα	27.	πρᾶγμα	37.	σῶμα
8.	διάφραγμα	18.	κῖνημα	28.	ποίημα	38.	φλέγμα
9.	δίλημμα	19.	κλίμα	29.	πρίσμα	39.	χάσμα
10.	δίπλωμα	20.	κόμμα	30.	πρόβλημα	40.	χρῶμα

Copy the following names, practice pronouncing the Greek, imitating
your teacher, and write the standard English spelling of each name:

The Twelve Olympians

Ζεύς	Ἄρτεμις	Ἥφαιστος
Ἥρᾱ	Ποσειδῶν	Ἄρης
Ἀθήνη	Ἀφροδίτη	Διόνῡσος
Ἀπόλλων	Ἑρμῆς	Δημήτηρ

The Nine Muses

Κλειώ	Μελπομένη	Πολύμνια
Εὐτέρπη	Τερψιχόρᾱ	Οὐρανίᾱ
Θάλεια	Ἐρατώ	Καλλιόπη

The Three Graces

Ἀγλαΐᾱ	Εὐφροσύνη	Θάλεια

The Three Fates

Κλωθώ	Λάχεσις	Ἄτροπος

Practice reading the following passage of Greek, imitating your teacher, and then copy the first two sentences. In writing the Greek, it will be helpful always to insert the macron over the vowel to which it belongs. As with the accent and breathing mark, the macron should be considered an integral part of the spelling of the word.

ὁ Δικαιόπολις Ἀθηναῖός ἐστιν· οἰκεῖ δὲ ὁ Δικαιόπολις οὐκ ἐν ταῖς Ἀθήναις ἀλλὰ ἐν τοῖς ἀγροῖς· αὐτουργὸς γάρ ἐστιν. γεωργεῖ οὖν τὸν κλῆρον καὶ πονεῖ ἐν τοῖς ἀγροῖς. χαλεπὸς δέ ἐστιν ὁ βίος· ὁ γὰρ κλῆρός ἐστι μῑκρός, μακρὸς δὲ ὁ πόνος. αἰεὶ οὖν πονεῖ ὁ Δικαιόπολις καὶ πολλάκις στενάζει καὶ λέγει· "ὦ Ζεῦ, χαλεπός ἐστιν ὁ βίος· ἀτέλεστος γάρ ἐστιν ὁ πόνος, μῑκρὸς δὲ ὁ κλῆρος καὶ οὐ πολὺν σῖτον παρέχει." ἀλλὰ ἰσχῡρός ἐστιν ὁ ἄνθρωπος καὶ ἄοκνος· πολλάκις οὖν χαίρει· ἐλεύθερος γάρ ἐστι καὶ αὐτουργός· φιλεῖ δὲ τὸν οἶκον. καλὸς γάρ ἐστιν ὁ κλῆρος καὶ σῖτον παρέχει οὐ πολὺν ἀλλὰ ἱκανόν.

Part IV:
Date Chart

BRONZE AGE
   Minos, king of Crete; Theseus, king of Athens
   Ca. 1220 B.C., sack of Troy by Agamemnon of Mycenae
DARK AGE
   Ca. 1050 B.C., emigration of Ionians to Asia Minor.
RENAISSANCE
   Ca. 850 B.C., formation of city states (Sparta, Corinth, etc.)
   776 B.C., first Olympic Games
   Ca. 750–500 B.C., trade and colonization
   Ca. 725 B.C., composition of *Iliad* and *Odyssey* by Homer (Ionia)
   Ca. 700 B.C., composition of *Works and Days* by Hesiod (Boeotia)
   Ca. 657–625 B.C., Cypselus, tyrant of Corinth
   Solon's reforms in Athens
PERSIAN INVASIONS
   546 B.C., defeat of Croesus of Lydia and Greeks in Asia Minor by Cyrus of
      Persia
   507 B.C., foundation of democracy in Athens by Cleisthenes
   490 B.C., expedition sent against Athens by Darius of Persia; battle of
      Marathon
   480 B.C., invasion of Greece by Xerxes: Thermopylae (480), Salamis (480),
      Plataea (479)
   Simonides, poet

IMPERIAL ATHENS

478 B.C., foundation of Delian League, which grows into Athenian Empire

472 B.C., Aeschylus' *Persians*

461–429 B.C., Pericles dominant in Athens: radical democracy and empire

War between Athens and Sparta

446 B.C., Thirty Years Peace with Sparta

Parthenon and other buildings

Herodotus, *History*

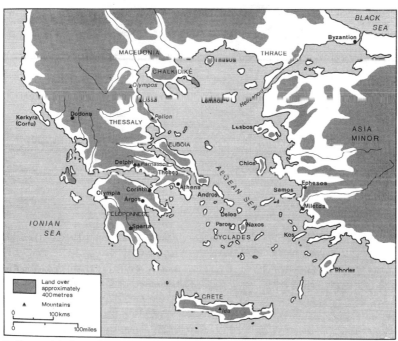

1.1 Greece and the Aegean Sea.

PELOPONNESIAN WAR

431 B.C., outbreak of war between Athens and the Peloponnesian League

430–429 B.C., plague at Athens; death of Pericles

426 B.C., Aristophanes' *Acharnians*

421 B.C., temporary peace between Athens and Sparta

415 B.C., Athenian expedition to Sicily

413 B.C., Sicilian expedition defeated; war between Athens and Sparta

404 B.C., surrender of Athens

Thucydides, *Histories*

1

Ο ΔΙΚΑΙΟΠΟΛΙΣ (α)

ὁ Δικαιόπολις αὐτουργός ἐστιν· φέρει δὲ τὸν μόσχον.

Vocabulary

Verbs
  ἐστί(ν) he/she/it is
  λέγει he/she says, tells, speaks
  οἰκεῖ he/she lives, dwells
  πονεῖ he/she works
  φιλεῖ he/she loves
  χαίρει he/she rejoices

Nouns
  ὁ ἀγρός field
  ὁ ἄνθρωπος man, human
    being, person
  ὁ αὐτουργός farmer
  ὁ οἶκος house, home, dwelling
  ὁ πόνος toil, work
  ὁ σῖτος grain, food

Adjectives
  καλός beautiful
  μακρός long, large
  μῑκρός small
  πολύς much, (plural) many

Prepositional Phrase
  ἐν ταῖς ᾿Αθήναις in Athens
Adverb
  οὐ, οὐκ, οὐχ* not
Conjunctions and Particles
  ἀλλά but
  γάρ (postpositive**) for
  δέ (postpositive**) and, but
  καί and, also, too
  οὖν (postpositive**) and so
Proper Names and Adjectives
  ᾿Αθηναῖος Athenian
  ὁ Δικαιόπολις Dicaeopolis

  *οὐ before consonants, οὐκ before
    vowels, and οὐχ before aspirated
    vowels or diphthongs (e.g., οὐχ
    αἱρεῖ "he/she does not take")
  **These words are always "placed
    after" and never occur first in
    their clause.

ὁ Δικαιόπολις Ἀθηναῖός ἐστιν· οἰκεῖ δὲ ὁ Δικαιόπολις οὐκ ἐν ταῖς Ἀθήναις ἀλλὰ ἐν τοῖς ἀγροῖς· αὐτουργὸς γάρ ἐστιν. γεωργεῖ οὖν τὸν κλῆρον καὶ πονεῖ ἐν τοῖς ἀγροῖς. χαλεπὸς δέ ἐστιν ὁ βίος· ὁ γὰρ κλῆρός ἐστι μῑκρός, μακρὸς δὲ ὁ πόνος. αἰεὶ οὖν πονεῖ ὁ Δικαιόπολις καὶ πολλάκις στενάζει καὶ λέγει· "ὦ Ζεῦ, χαλεπός ἐστιν ὁ βίος· ἀτέλεστος γάρ ἐστιν ὁ πόνος, μῑκρὸς δὲ ὁ κλῆρος καὶ οὐ πολὺν σῖτον παρέχει." ἀλλὰ ἰσχῡρός ἐστιν ὁ ἄνθρωπος καὶ ἄοκνος· πολλάκις οὖν χαίρει· ἐλεύθερος γάρ ἐστι καὶ αὐτουργός· φιλεῖ δὲ τὸν οἶκον. καλὸς γάρ ἐστιν ὁ κλῆρος καὶ σῖτον παρέχει οὐ πολὺν ἀλλὰ ἱκανόν. 5

[ἐν τοῖς ἀγροῖς in the country (lit., fields)   γεωργεῖ he farms, cultivates   τὸν κλῆρον the (= his) farm   χαλεπός hard   ὁ βίος the (= his) life   αἰεί always   πολλάκις often   στενάζει groans   ὦ Ζεῦ O Zeus!   ἀτέλεστος endless   παρέχει provides   ἰσχῡρός strong   ἄοκνος energetic   ἐλεύθερος free   ἱκανόν enough]

Word Study

Many English words are derived from Greek. Often these derivatives are scientific and technical terms formed in English from Greek roots because the precision of the Greek language makes it possible to express a complex concept in a single word.

What Greek words from the story at the beginning of this chapter do you recognize in the following English words? Define the words, using your knowledge of the Greek:

1. anthropology
2. polysyllabic
3. philosophy
4. microscope

English words such as those above often contain more than one Greek root. Which of the words above contain roots of the following Greek words?

1. σκοπεῖ he/she looks at, examines
2. σοφίᾱ wisdom
3. λόγος word, study

Grammar

1. Verb Forms: Endings

Greek verbs have *endings* that show such things as person and number:

Number:		*Singular*	*Plural*
Person:	*1st*	I	we
	2nd	you	you
	3rd	he, she, it	they

This chapter introduces only the third person singular of the present tense, e.g., "he/she/it is."

The Greek verb for "loosen" will serve as an example of a regular Greek verb; the verb for "love" will serve as an example of a contract verb (a type of verb in which the vowel at the end of the stem contracts with the initial vowel of the ending). The common irregular verb for "be" is also given.

λῡ- loosen
3rd singular   λῡ́-ει   he/she loosens, is loosening, does loosen

φιλε- love
3rd singular   φιλέ-ει> φιλεῖ   he/she loves, is loving, does love

ἐσ- be
3rd singular   ἐστί(ν)*   he/she/it is

*ἐστίν is used when followed by a vowel or coming as the last word in a sentence. The -ν is called *movable* ν. The word ἐστί(ν) is enclitic; for the rules governing the accents of enclitics and the words that precede them, see the Reference Grammar at the end of this book, section 1. You will need to be familiar with these rules when you begin to write Greek sentences.

2. Nouns: Gender, Case, and Agreement

a. Grammatical Gender

Greek nouns are usually *masculine* or *feminine* or *neuter* (neither masculine nor feminine) in gender. In learning vocabulary, always learn the article with the noun; this will tell you its gender: ὁ for masculine; ἡ for feminine; and τό for neuter. In this chapter all the nouns listed in the Vocabulary are masculine and are therefore accompanied by the masculine definite article, ὁ.

b. Case

Greek nouns have a *stem* and a variable *ending*. The function of the noun in the sentence is conveyed by the ending, while the stem conveys the meaning of the word. The endings of nouns, pronouns, and adjectives are called *cases*.

There are five cases in Greek; in this chapter we focus on the use of two of them—the *nominative* and the *accusative*.

Nominative: ὁ κλῆρο-ς. This case indicates the subject of the verb and forms the complement after the verb "is."

Accusative: τὸν κλῆρο-ν. This case indicates the object of the verb, e.g.:

subject	verb	complement
ὁ κλῆρός	ἐστι	μῑκρός.
The farm	is	small.

subject	verb	object
ὁ ἄνθρωπος	γεωργεῖ	τὸν κλῆρον.
The man	cultivates	the farm.

Note that it is the endings of the words and not the order in which they are placed in the sentence that builds the meaning of the sentence. The first sentence above could be written μῑκρός ἐστιν ὁ κλῆρος (the definite article marks ὁ κλῆρος as the subject). The second sentence could be written τὸν κλῆρον γεωργεῖ ὁ ἄνθρωπος, with a change in emphasis but no change in basic meaning.

c. Agreement

The definite article and adjectives agree with the nouns they go with in gender, number (singular or plural), and case, e.g.:

ὁ καλὸς ἀγρός: masculine singular nominative
τὸν μῑκρὸν οἶκον: masculine singular accusative

N.B. The definite article is sometimes used in Greek where it is not used in English, e.g., with proper names: ὁ Δικαιόπολις (Dicaeopolis).

Exercise 1a

Translate the following pairs of sentences:

1. ὁ πόνος ἐστὶ μακρός.
   The house is small.
2. καλός ἐστιν ὁ οἶκος.
   The man is strong.
3. ὁ Δικαιόπολις τὸν οἶκον φιλεῖ.
   The man provides the food.
4. πολὺν σῖτον παρέχει ὁ κλῆρος.
   The farm provides much work.
5. ὁ ἄνθρωπος οὐ πονεῖ ἐν τοῖς ἀγροῖς.
   Dicaeopolis does not live in Athens.

The Athenian Farmer

Scenes of plowing and sowing on a Greek vase

Dicaeopolis lives in a village in Attica called Cholleidae, about twelve miles southeast of Athens. Although Athens and its port, the Piraeus, formed a very large city by ancient standards, the majority of the Athenian people lived and worked in the country. The historian Thucydides (2.14) says that when Attica had to be evacuated before the Peloponnesian invasion of 431 B.C. "the evacuation was difficult for them since the majority had always been accustomed to living in the country."

Most of these people were farmers like Dicaeopolis. Their farms were small; ten to twenty acres would be the average size. What they grew on their farms would depend partly on the district in which they lived. On the plain near Athens no doubt the staple products would have been vegetables and grain, but most of Attica is hilly; this poorer land would be more suitable for grape vines, olive trees, sheep, and goats (cows were not kept for milk). All farmers aimed at self-sufficiency, but few would have attained it (two-thirds of the grain consumed by the Athenians was imported). If they had a surplus, e.g., of olive oil or wine, they would take it to the market in Athens for sale and buy what they could not produce themselves.

For purposes of administration, the Athenian citizens were divided into four classes, based on property. The top class, the *pentacosiomedimnoi* or "millionaires," a very small class, were those whose estates produced five hundred *medimnoi* of grain a year (a *medimnos* = about one and a half bushels). The second class, also small, were the *hippeis,* knights, whose estates could support a horse (ἵππος); these provided the cavalry for the army (see illustration, page 114). The third and largest class were the farmers like Dicaeopolis, called the *zeugitai,* who kept a team of oxen (ζεῦγος). These provided the heavy infantry of the army. The fourth class were the *thetes,* hired laborers, who owned no land or not enough to support a family.

Our sources represent the farmers as the backbone of the Athenian democracy—sturdy, industrious, thrifty, and simple—but shrewd. In the comedies of Aristophanes they are often contrasted with self-seeking politicians, decadent knights, and grasping traders. The name of our main character, Dicaeopolis, contains the concepts δίκαιο- "just" and πόλις "city," and therefore means something like "just to the city" or "living in a just city." He is taken from a comedy of Aristophanes called the *Acharnians;* the play was produced in 426 B.C., and at the end of this course you will read extracts from it.

A farmer in contemporary Greece, carrying a kid

Ο ΔΙΚΑΙΟΠΟΛΙΣ (β)

ὁ Δικαιόπολις μέγαν λίθον αἴρει καὶ ἐκ τοῦ ἀγροῦ φέρει.

Vocabulary

Verbs
  αἴρει he/she lifts
  βαδίζει he/she walks, goes
  καθίζει he/she sits
  φέρει he/she carries
Nouns
  ὁ ἥλιος sun
  ὁ χρόνος time

Pronoun
  αὐτόν him
Adjectives
  ἰσχῡρός strong
  χαλεπός difficult
Preposition
  πρός (+ *acc*.) to, toward

ὁ Δικαιόπολις ἐν τῷ ἀγρῷ πονεῖ· τὸν γὰρ ἀγρὸν σκάπτει. μακρός
ἐστιν ὁ πόνος καὶ χαλεπός· τοὺς γὰρ λίθους ἐκ τοῦ ἀγροῦ φέρει.
μέγαν λίθον αἴρει καὶ φέρει πρὸς τὸ ἕρμα. ἰσχῡρός ἐστιν ὁ ἄνθρωπος
ἀλλὰ πολὺν χρόνον πονεῖ καὶ μάλα κάμνει. φλέγει γὰρ ὁ ἥλιος καὶ
κατατρίβει αὐτόν. καθίζει οὖν ὑπὸ τῷ δένδρῳ καὶ ἡσυχάζει οὐ   5
πολὺν χρόνον. δι᾽ ὀλίγου γὰρ αἴρει ἑαυτὸν καὶ πονεῖ. τέλος δὲ
καταδύνει ὁ ἥλιος. οὐκέτι οὖν πονεῖ ὁ Δικαιόπολις ἀλλὰ πρὸς τὸν
οἶκον βαδίζει.

[**ἐν τῷ ἀγρῷ** in the field　　**σκάπτει** he is digging　　**τοὺς . . . λίθους** the stones
ἐκ τοῦ ἀγροῦ out of the field　　**μέγαν** big　　**τὸ ἕρμα** the stone heap　　**πολὺν
χρόνον** for a long time　　**μάλα κάμνει** he is very tired　　**φλέγει** is blazing
κατατρίβει wears out　　**ὑπὸ τῷ δένδρῳ** under the tree　　**ἡσυχάζει** he rests　　**δι᾽
ὀλίγου** soon　　**αἴρει ἑαυτόν** he lifts himself, gets up　　**τέλος** finally
καταδύνει sets　　**οὐκέτι** no longer]

Word Building

What is the relationship between the words in the following sets? You have not yet met two of these words (φίλος and γεωργός). Try to deduce their meanings (they both refer to people) from studying the relationship between the words in each set:

1. οἰκεῖ   ὁ οἶκος
2. πονεῖ   ὁ πόνος
3. γεωργεῖ   ὁ γεωργός
4. φιλεῖ   ὁ φίλος

Olive groves and vineyards

*   *   *

Ο ΚΛΗΡΟΣ

Read the following passage and answer the comprehension questions:

μακρός ἐστιν ὁ πόνος καὶ χαλεπός. ὁ δὲ αὐτουργὸς οὐκ ὀκνεῖ ἀλλ' αἰεὶ γεωργεῖ τὸν κλῆρον. καλὸς γάρ ἐστιν ὁ κλῆρος καὶ πολὺν σῖτον παρέχει. χαίρει οὖν ὁ ἄνθρωπος· ἰσχῡρὸς γάρ ἐστι καὶ οὐ πολλάκις κάμνει.

[ὀκνεῖ shirks]

1. What is the man not doing? What does he always do?
2. What does the farm provide?
3. Why does the man rejoice?

Exercise 1b

Translate into Greek:

1. Dicaeopolis is a farmer.
2. He always works in the field.
3. And so he is often tired; for the work is long.
4. But he does not shirk; for he loves his home.

2

Ο ΞΑΝΘΙΑΣ (α)

ὁ μὲν Δικαιόπολις ἐλαύνει τὸν βοῦν, ὁ δὲ δοῦλος φέρει τὸ ἄροτρον.

Vocabulary

Verbs
  ἐκβαίνει he/she steps out, comes out
  ἐλαύνει he/she drives
  ἐλθέ come!
  καθεύδει he/she sleeps
  καλεῖ he/she calls
  λαμβάνει he/she takes
  πάρεστι(ν) he/she/it is present, is here, is there
  σπεύδει he/she hurries
Nouns
  τὸ ἄροτρον plow

  ὁ δοῦλος slave
Pronoun
  ἐγώ I
Adverbs
  οὕτω so, thus
  μή don't
Conjunctions and Particles
  μέν . . . δέ . . . on the one hand . . . on the other hand . . .
Expressions
  διὰ τί; why?
Proper Name
  ὁ Ξανθίᾱς Xanthias

ὁ Δικαιόπολις ἐκβαίνει ἐκ τοῦ οἴκου καὶ καλεῖ τὸν Ξανθίᾱν. ὁ Ξανθίᾱς δοῦλός ἐστιν, ἰσχῡρὸς μὲν ἄνθρωπος, ῥᾴθῡμος δέ· οὐ γὰρ πονεῖ, εἰ μὴ πάρεστιν ὁ Δικαιόπολις. νῦν δὲ καθεύδει ἐν τῷ οἴκῳ. ὁ οὖν Δικαιόπολις καλεῖ αὐτὸν καὶ λέγει· "ἐλθὲ δεῦρο, ὦ Ξανθίᾱ. διὰ τί καθεύδεις; μὴ οὕτω ῥᾴθῡμος ἴσθι ἀλλὰ σπεῦδε." ὁ οὖν Ξανθίᾱς βραδέως ἐκβαίνει ἐκ τοῦ οἴκου καὶ λέγει· "διὰ τί εἶ οὕτω χαλεπός, ὦ δέσποτα; οὐ γὰρ ῥᾴθῡμός εἰμι ἀλλὰ ἤδη σπεύδω." ὁ δὲ Δικαιόπολις 5

λέγει· "ἐλθὲ δεῦρο καὶ βοήθει· λάμβανε γὰρ τὸ ἄροτρον καὶ φέρε
αὐτὸ πρὸς τὸν ἀγρόν. ἐγὼ γὰρ ἐλαύνω τοὺς βοῦς. ἀλλὰ σπεῦδε·
μῑκρὸς μὲν γάρ ἐστιν ὁ ἀγρός, μακρὸς δὲ ὁ πόνος."   10

[ἐκ τοῦ οἴκου out of the house   ῥᾴθῡμος lazy   εἰ μή unless   νῦν now   ἐν
τῷ οἴκῳ in the house   δεῦρο here   μή . . . ἴσθι don't be!   βραδέως slowly
δέσποτα master   ἤδη already   βοήθει help!   αὐτό it   τοὺς βοῦς the oxen]

Word Study

1. What do *despotic* and *chronology* mean? What Greek words do you find
   embedded in these English words?
2. What does a *dendrologist* study?
3. Explain what a *heliocentric* theory of the universe is.
4. What is a *chronometer*? What does τὸ μέτρον mean?

Grammar

1. Verb Forms: Indicative Mood; First, Second, and Third Persons Singular

The *moods* indicate whether an action is viewed as being real or
ideal. The *indicative* mood is used to express statements and questions
about reality or fact:

ἐλαύνω τοὺς βοῦς. I am driving the oxen.
διὰ τί καθεύδεις; Why are you sleeping?

The different endings of the verb show not only who or what is
performing the action (I; you; he/she/it; we; you; they) but also how the
action is being viewed (mood). In the following examples we give only
the singular possibilities (I; you; he/she/it) in the indicative mood:

λῡ- loosen

1st singular	λῡ́-ω	I loosen, am loosening, do loosen
2nd singular	λῡ́-εις	you loosen, are loosening, do loosen
3rd singular	λῡ́-ει	he/she loosens, is loosening, does loosen

φιλε- love

1st singular	φιλέ-ω > φιλῶ	I love, am loving, do love
2nd singular	φιλέ-εις > φιλεῖς	you love, are loving, do love
3rd singular	φιλέ-ει > φιλεῖ	he/she loves, is loving, does love

ἐσ- be

1st singular	εἰμί*	I am
2nd singular	εἶ	you are
3rd singular	ἐστί(ν)*	he/she/it is
*enclitic		

Since the endings differ for each person, subject pronouns need not be expressed in Greek, e.g.:

ἐλαύνω = I drive.
ἐλαύνεις = you drive.
ἐλαύνει = he/she drives.

But they are expressed if they are emphatic, e.g.:

ἐγὼ μὲν πονῶ, σὺ δὲ καθεύδεις.   I am working, but you are sleeping.

Exercise 2a

Read aloud and translate into English:

1. τὸν δοῦλον καλῶ.
2. ὁ δοῦλος ἐν τῷ οἴκῳ πονεῖ.
3. διὰ τί οὐ σπεύδεις;
4. οὐκ εἰμι ῥᾴθῡμος.
5. ἰσχῡρὸς εἶ.
6. τὸ ἄροτρον φέρει.
7. πρὸς τὸν ἀγρὸν σπεύδω.
8. διὰ τί καλεῖς τὸν δοῦλον;
9. ὁ δοῦλός ἐστι ῥᾴθῡμος.
10. ὁ δοῦλος ἐκβαίνει ἐκ τοῦ οἴκου.

Exercise 2b

Translate into Greek:

1. He/she is not hurrying.
2. Why are you not working?
3. I am carrying the plow.
4. You are hurrying to the field.
5. He is lazy.
6. I am not strong.
7. You are not a slave.
8. The slave is not working.
9. The slave is carrying the plow to the field.
10. I am lazy.

2. The Imperative

The *imperative* mood is used to express commands:

σπεῦδ-ε hurry!   φίλε-ε > φίλει love!   ἴσθι be!

In prohibitions (negative commands), μή + the imperative is used:

μὴ λάμβανε τὸ ἄροτρον. Don't take the plow!
μὴ ῥᾴθῡμος ἴσθι. Don't be lazy!

Exercise 2c

Read aloud and translate into English:

1. ἔκβαινε ἐκ τοῦ οἴκου, ὦ Ξανθίᾱ, καὶ ἐλθὲ δεῦρο.
2. μὴ κάθευδε, ὦ δοῦλε, ἀλλὰ πόνει.
3. μὴ οὕτω χαλεπὸς ἴσθι, ὦ δέσποτα.
4. λάμβανε τὸ ἄροτρον καὶ σπεῦδε πρὸς τὸν ἀγρόν.
5. κάλει τὸν δοῦλον, ὦ δέσποτα.

Slavery

A farmer on his way to market; he is followed by a slave carrying
two baskets of produce and accompanied by a pig and a piglet.

The adult male population of the city-state of Athens in 431 B.C. has been calculated as follows: citizens 50,000, resident foreigners 25,000, slaves 100,000. The resident foreigners (*metics*) were free men who were granted a distinct status; they could not own land in Attica or contract marriages with citizens, but they had the protection of the courts, they served in the army, they had a role in the festivals, and they played an important part in commerce and industry.

Slaves had no legal rights and were the property of the state or individuals. The fourth-century philosopher Aristotle describes them as "living tools." They were either born into slavery or came to the slave market as a result of war or piracy. They were nearly all barbarians, i.e., non-Greek (a document from 415 B.C. records the sale of fourteen slaves—five were from Thrace, two from Syria, three from Caria, two from Illyria, and one each from Scythia and Colchis). It was considered immoral to enslave Greeks, and this very rarely happened.

The whole economy of the ancient world, which made little use of machines, was based on slave labor. Slaves were employed by the state, e.g., in the silver mines; they worked in factories (the largest we know of was a shield factory, employing 120 slaves); and individual citizens owned one or more slaves in proportion to their wealth. Every farmer hoped to own a slave to help in the house and fields, but not all did. Aristotle remarks that for poor men "the ox takes the place of the slave."

It would be wrong to assume that slaves were always treated inhumanely. A fifth-century writer of reactionary views says:

> Now as to slaves and metics, in Athens, they live a most undisciplined life. One is not permitted to strike them, and a slave will not stand out of the way for you. Let me explain why. If the law permitted a free man to strike a slave or metic or a freedman, he would often find that he had mistaken an Athenian for a slave and struck him, for, as far as clothing and general appearance go, the common people look just the same as slaves and metics. (Pseudo-Xenophon 1.10)

Slaves and citizens often worked side by side and received the same wage, as we learn from inscriptions giving the accounts of public building works. Slaves might save enough money to buy their freedom from their masters, though this was not as common in Athens as in Rome.

In the country, the slaves of farmers usually lived and ate with their masters. Aristophanes' comedies depict them as lively and cheeky characters, by no means downtrodden. We have given Dicaeopolis one slave, named Xanthias, a typical slave name meaning "fair-haired."

Slaves working in a clay pit

Women picking apples—slave and free

Ο ΞΑΝΘΙΑΣ (β)

ὁ Δικαιόπολις λέγει· "σπεῦδε, ὦ Ξανθίᾱ, καὶ φέρε μοι τὸ ἄροτρον."

Vocabulary

Verbs
ἄγω I lead, take
  εἰσάγω I lead in, take in
βαίνω I step, walk, go
βλέπω I look, see
βοηθέω I help

Nouns
  ὁ βοῦς ox
  τὸ δένδρον tree

ὁ δεσπότης master
Preposition
  εἰς (+ *acc.*) into, to, at
Adverbs
  βραδέως slowly
  ἔπειτα then
  ἤδη already, now

ὁ μὲν οὖν Δικαιόπολις ἐλαύνει τοὺς βοῦς, ὁ δὲ Ξανθίᾱς ὄπισθεν βαδίζει καὶ φέρει τὸ ἄροτρον. δι' ὀλίγου δὲ ὁ Δικαιόπολις εἰσάγει τοὺς βοῦς εἰς τὸν ἀγρὸν καὶ βλέπει πρὸς τὸν δοῦλον· ὁ δὲ Ξανθίᾱς οὐ πάρεστιν· βραδέως γὰρ βαίνει. ὁ οὖν Δικαιόπολις καλεῖ αὐτὸν καὶ λέγει· "σπεῦδε, ὦ Ξανθίᾱ, καὶ φέρε μοι τὸ ἄροτρον." ὁ δὲ Ξανθίᾱς λέγει· "ἀλλ' ἤδη σπεύδω, ὦ δέσποτα· διὰ τί οὕτω χαλεπὸς εἶ;" βραδέως δὲ φέρει τὸ ἄροτρον πρὸς αὐτόν. ὁ οὖν Δικαιόπολις ἄγει τοὺς βοῦς ὑπὸ τὸ ζυγὸν καὶ προσάπτει τὸ ἄροτρον. ἔπειτα δὲ πρὸς τὸν δοῦλον βλέπει· ὁ δὲ Ξανθίᾱς οὐ πάρεστιν· καθεύδει γὰρ ὑπὸ τῷ δένδρῳ.

[**ὄπισθεν** behind   **δι' ὀλίγου** soon   **μοι** (to) me   **ὑπὸ τὸ ζυγόν** under the yoke   **προσάπτει** attaches]

ὁ οὖν Δικαιόπολις καλεῖ αὐτὸν καὶ λέγει· "ἐλθὲ δεῦρο, ὦ
κατάρᾱτε. μὴ κάθευδε ἀλλὰ βοήθει. λάμβανε γὰρ τὸ σπέρμα καὶ
ὄπισθεν βάδιζε." ὁ μὲν οὖν δοῦλος τὸ σπέρμα λαμβάνει καὶ ὄπισθεν
βαδίζει, ὁ δὲ δεσπότης καλεῖ τὴν Δημήτερα καὶ λέγει· "ἵλᾱος ἴσθι, ὦ
Δήμητερ, καὶ πλήθῡνε τὸ σπέρμα." ἔπειτα δὲ τὸ κέντρον λαμβάνει   15
καὶ κεντεῖ τοὺς βοῦς καὶ λέγει· "σπεύδετε, ὦ βόες· ἕλκετε τὸ ἄροτρον
καὶ ἀροτρεύετε τὸν ἀγρόν."

[ὦ **κατάρᾱτε** you cursed creature   **τὸ σπέρμα** the seed   **τὴν Δημήτερα**
Demeter (goddess of grain)   **ἵλᾱος** gracious   **πλήθῡνε** multiply!   **τὸ κέντρον**
the goad   **κεντεῖ** goads   **ἕλκετε** drag!]

Word Building

In the readings you have met the following prepositions: εἰς "into"; ἐκ "out
of"; ἐν "in"; and πρός "to," "toward." These prepositions may be prefixed to
verbs to form compound verbs, e.g.:

βαίνει he/she walks, steps   ἐκβαίνει he/she steps out

Deduce the meaning of the following compound verbs:

1. προσφέρει
2. ἐκφέρει
3. προσελαύνει
4. προσβαίνει
5. ἐκκαλεῖ

Note: You can easily deduce the meanings of many more compound verbs of
this sort, which are very frequent in Greek. Right from the start of your study
of Greek you should begin to recognize the meaning of many new words from
your knowledge of ones with which you are already familiar. To encourage
you to develop and use this skill, the meaning of compound verbs will not be
given in the chapter vocabularies when the meaning is clear from the
separate parts of the word. When compound verbs have *special* meanings,
they will be given in the vocabulary lists.

Grammar

3. Articles, Adjectives, and Nouns; Singular, All Cases:

	Masculine			**Neuter**		
Nominative	ὁ	καλὸς	ἀγρός	τὸ	καλὸν	δένδρον
Genitive	τοῦ	καλοῦ	ἀγροῦ	τοῦ	καλοῦ	δένδρου
Dative	τῷ	καλῷ	ἀγρῷ	τῷ	καλῷ	δένδρῳ
Accusative	τὸν	καλὸν	ἀγρόν	τὸ	καλὸν	δένδρον
Vocative	ὦ	καλὲ	ἀγρέ	ὦ	καλὸν	δένδρον

N.B. The endings for the neuter nominative, accusative, and vocative cases are the same.

The subject of the sentence and the complement of the verb "to be" are in the *nominative* case, e.g., **ὁ ἀγρὸς καλός** ἐστιν = *"The field* is *beautiful."*

The *genitive* case is at present used only after certain prepositions, including those that express motion from a place, e.g., ἐκβαίνει **ἐκ τοῦ οἴκου** = "He/She steps/comes *out of the house."*

The *dative* case is also at present used only after certain prepositions, including those that indicate the *place where* someone or something is or something happens, e.g., καθεύδει **ἐν τῷ οἴκῳ** = "He/She sleeps *in the house."*

The *accusative* case indicates the object of a transitive verb (e.g., καλεῖ **αὐτόν**) and is used after certain prepositions, including those that indicate motion toward someone or something, e.g., **πρὸς τὸν οἶκον** βαδίζει = "He/She walks *toward the house."*

The *vocative* case is used when addressing a person, e.g., ἐλθὲ δεῦρο, **ὦ δοῦλε** = "Come here, *slave!"* It is usually preceded by ὦ, which need not be translated.

Exercise 2d

Give the correct form of the article to complete the following phrases:

1. ___ δοῦλον
2. ἐν ___ ἀγρῷ
3. ___ ἄνθρωπος
4. ἐκ ___ οἴκου
5. ___ ἄροτρον
6. ὑπὸ ___ δένδρῳ
7. ἐν ___ οἴκῳ

Exercise 2e

Complete the following sentences by giving correct endings to the verbs, nouns, and adjectives, and then translate the sentences into English:

1. ὁ δοῦλος σπεύδ— πρὸς τὸν ἀγρ—.
2. ὁ Δικαιόπολις τὸν ῥάθῡμ— δοῦλον καλ—.
3. ἐλθ— δεῦρο καὶ βοήθ—.
4. ἐγὼ ἐλαύν— τοὺς βοῦς ἐκ τοῦ ἀγρ—.
5. μὴ χαλεπ— ἴσθι, ὦ δοῦλ—, ἀλλὰ πόν—.

Exercise 2f

Translate the following pairs of sentences:

1. ὁ δοῦλος οὐκ ἔστιν Ἀθηναῖος.
   Xanthias is not strong.
2. ὁ Δικαιόπολις ἐκβαίνει ἐκ τοῦ οἴκου καὶ καλεῖ τὸν δοῦλον.
   The slave hurries to the field and carries the plow.
3. ὁ δοῦλος οὐ βοηθεῖ ἀλλὰ καθεύδει ὑπὸ τῷ δένδρῳ.
   The man is not working but walking to the house.
4. εἴσελθε εἰς τὸν οἶκον, ὦ Ξανθίᾱ, καὶ φέρε τὸν σῖτον.
   Hurry, slave, and drive out (ἐξελαύνω) the oxen.
5. μὴ κάθευδε, ὦ Ξανθίᾱ, ἀλλὰ βοήθει.
   Don't come here, man, but work in the field.

*   *   *

Ο   ΔΟΥΛΟΣ

Read the following passage and answer the comprehension questions:

ὁ αὐτουργὸς σπεύδει εἰς τὸν ἀγρὸν καὶ καλεῖ τὸν δοῦλον.   ὁ δὲ δοῦλος οὐ
πάρεστιν· καθεύδει γὰρ ὑπὸ τῷ δένδρῳ.   ὁ οὖν δεσπότης βαδίζει πρὸς αὐτὸν καὶ
λέγει· "ἐλθὲ δεῦρο, ὦ δοῦλε ῥᾴθυμε, καὶ βοήθει."   ὁ οὖν δοῦλος βαδίζει πρὸς αὐτὸν
καὶ λέγει· "μὴ χαλεπὸς ἴσθι, ὦ δέσποτα· ἤδη γὰρ πάρειμι ἐγὼ καὶ φέρω σοι τὸ
ἄροτρον."   ὁ οὖν δεσπότης λέγει· "σπεῦδε, ὦ Ξανθίᾱ· μῑκρὸς μὲν γάρ ἐστιν ὁ ἀγρός,   5
μακρὸς δὲ ὁ πόνος."
[σοι to you]

1. What is the man doing?
2. What is the slave doing?
3. When told to come and help, what does the slave do?
4. Why is the slave urged to hurry?

Exercise 2g

Translate into Greek:

1. Dicaeopolis no longer (οὐκέτι) works but loosens the oxen.
2. And then he calls the slave and says, "Don't work any longer
   (μηκέτι) but come here and take the plow. For I on the one hand am
   driving the oxen to the house, you (σύ) on the other hand carry the
   plow!"
3. And so Dicaeopolis drives the oxen out of the field, and the slave takes
   the plow and carries it toward the house.

3
Ο ΑΡΟΤΟΣ (α)

ὁ μὲν Δικαιόπολις ἐλαύνει τοὺς βοῦς, οἱ δὲ βόες τὸ ἄροτρον ἕλκουσιν.

Vocabulary

Verbs
μένω I stay, wait, wait for
πίπτω I fall
προσχωρέω (+ *dat.*) I go
   toward, approach
φησί(ν) (*postpositive enclitic*)
   he/she says
Noun
ὁ λίθος stone
Pronouns
αὐτό it
αὐτόν him, it
Adjectives
αἴτιος responsible, to blame

δυνατός possible
μέγας big
Preposition
ἐκ (+ *gen.*) out of
Adverbs
αὖθις again
δεῦρο here
ἔτι still
οὐκέτι no longer
Conjunctions
τε . . . καί *or* **τε καί** both . .
   . and
Expression
ὦ Ζεῦ O Zeus!

ὁ μὲν Δικαιόπολις ἐλαύνει τοὺς βοῦς, οἱ δὲ βόες ἕλκουσι τὸ
ἄροτρον, ὁ δὲ Ξανθίᾱς σπείρει τὸ σπέρμα. ἀλλὰ ἰδού—μένουσιν οἱ
βόες καὶ οὐκέτι ἕλκουσι τὸ ἄροτρον. ὁ μὲν οὖν Δικαιόπολις τοὺς
βοῦς καλεῖ καί, "σπεύδετε, ὦ βόες," φησίν· "μὴ μένετε." οἱ δὲ βόες ἔτι
μένουσιν. ὁ οὖν Δικαιόπολις, "διὰ τί μένετε, ὦ βόες;" φησὶ καὶ βλέπει   5
πρὸς τὸ ἄροτρον, καὶ ἰδού— λίθος ἐμποδίζει αὐτό. ὁ οὖν
Δικαιόπολις λαμβάνει τὸν λίθον ἀλλ' οὐκ αἴρει αὐτόν· μέγας γὰρ

ἐστιν. καλεῖ οὖν τὸν δοῦλον καί, "ἐλθὲ δεῦρο, ὦ Ξανθίᾱ," φησίν, "καὶ
βοήθει· λίθος γὰρ μέγας τὸ ἄροτρον ἐμποδίζει, οἱ δὲ βόες μένουσιν."

[ἕλκουσι (they) drag   σπείρει sows   τὸ σπέρμα the seed   ἰδού look!
ἐμποδίζει obstructs]

ὁ οὖν Ξανθίᾱς βραδέως προσχωρεῖ ἀλλ' οὐ βοηθεῖ· βλέπει γὰρ   10
πρὸς τὸν λίθον καί, "μέγας ἐστὶν ὁ λίθος, ὦ δέσποτα," φησίν· "ἰδού—
οὐ δυνατόν ἐστιν αἴρειν αὐτόν." ὁ δὲ Δικαιόπολις, "μὴ ῥάθῡμος ἴσθι,"
φησίν, "ἀλλὰ βοήθει. δυνατὸν γάρ ἐστιν αἴρειν τὸν λίθον." ἅμα οὖν
ὅ τε δεσπότης καὶ ὁ δοῦλος αἴρουσι τὸν λίθον καὶ φέρουσιν αὐτὸν ἐκ
τοῦ ἀγροῦ.   15

[ῥᾴθῡμος lazy   ἅμα together]

ἐν ᾧ δὲ φέρουσιν αὐτόν, πταίει ὁ Ξανθίᾱς καὶ καταβάλλει τὸν
λίθον· ὁ δὲ λίθος πίπτει πρὸς τὸν τοῦ Δικαιοπόλεως πόδα. ὁ οὖν
Δικαιόπολις στενάζει καί, "ὦ Ζεῦ," φησίν, "φεῦ τοῦ ποδός. λάμβανε
τὸν λίθον, ὦ ἀνόητε, καὶ αἶρε αὐτὸν καὶ μὴ οὕτω σκαιὸς ἴσθι." ὁ δὲ
Ξανθίᾱς, "διὰ τί οὕτω χαλεπὸς εἶ, ὦ δέσποτα;" φησίν· "οὐ γὰρ αἴτιός   20
εἰμι ἐγώ· μέγας γάρ ἐστιν ὁ λίθος καὶ οὐ δυνατόν ἐστιν αὐτὸν φέρειν."
ὁ δὲ Δικαιόπολις, "μὴ φλυᾱρει, ὦ μαστῑγίᾱ, ἀλλ' αἶρε τὸν λίθον καὶ
ἔκφερε ἐκ τοῦ ἀγροῦ." αὖθις οὖν αἴρουσι τὸν λίθον καὶ μόλις
ἐκφέρουσιν αὐτὸν ἐκ τοῦ ἀγροῦ. ἔπειτα δὲ ὁ μὲν Δικαιόπολις ἐλαύνει
τοὺς βοῦς, οἱ δὲ βόες οὐκέτι μένουσιν ἀλλὰ ἕλκουσι τὸ ἄροτρον.   25

[ἐν ᾧ while   πταίει stumbles   καταβάλλει drops   πρὸς τὸν τοῦ
Δικαιοπόλεως πόδα   upon Dicaepolis's foot   στενάζει groans   φεῦ τοῦ ποδός
oh, my poor foot!   ὦ ἀνόητε fool!   σκαιός clumsy   φλυᾱρει talk nonsense   ὦ
μαστῑγίᾱ jailbird!   μόλις with difficulty]

Word Study

1. What does *lithograph* mean? What does γράφω mean?
2. What is a *monolith*? What does μόνος mean?
3. What does *megalithic* mean?
4. What is a *megaphone*? What does ἡ φωνή mean?

Grammar

1. Verb Forms: Plurals and Infinitives

a. In Chapter 2 you learned the 1st, 2nd, and 3rd person singular forms of λύω, φιλέω, and εἰμί. Here are the 3rd person plural forms:

λῡ- loosen
3rd plural λῡ́-ουσι(ν)   they loosen, are loosening, do loosen

φιλε- love
3rd plural φιλέ-ουσι(ν) > φιλοῦσι(ν)   they love, are loving, do love

ἐσ- be
3rd plural εἰσί(ν)*   they are

*enclitic

Locate twelve 3rd person plural verb forms in the reading passage at the beginning of this chapter.

b. In Chapter 2 you learned some forms of the *imperative* mood. These were the singular forms, used to address a command to one person:

σπεῦδε   (You, *singular*) hurry!
φίλει   (You, *singular*) love!
ἴσθι   (You, *singular*) be!
ἐλθέ   (You, *singular*) come! go!

In the reading at the beginning of this chapter you have met plural forms of the imperative, used to address a command to more than one person (or animal!). The plurals of the imperatives given above are:

σπεύδετε
φιλεῖτε (< φιλέ-ετε)
ἔστε
ἐλθέτε

Locate two plural imperatives in the reading passage at the beginning of this chapter. To whom (or what) are the commands addressed?

c. The *infinitive* is the form of the verb that we create in English by using the word *to*. Greek forms the infinitive by use of an ending:

λῡ- loosen
Infinitive   λῡ́-ειν   to loosen, to be loosening

φιλε- love
Infinitive   φιλέ-ειν> φιλεῖν   to love, to be loving

ἐσ- be
Infinitive   εἶναι   to be

Exercise 3a

Find three infinitives in the reading passage at the beginning of this chapter.

Exercise 3b

Read aloud and translate:

1. οἱ βόες οὐκέτι ἕλκουσι τὸ ἄροτρον.
2. ὅ τε Δικαιόπολις καὶ ὁ δοῦλος προσχωροῦσι καὶ βλέπουσι πρὸς τὸ ἄροτρον.
3. ὁ Δικαιόπολις, "ἰδού," φησίν· "λίθος μέγας τὸ ἄροτρον ἐμποδίζει."
4. αἶρε τὸν λίθον καὶ ἔκφερε ἐκ τοῦ ἀγροῦ.
5. ὁ δὲ δοῦλος, "ἰδού," φησίν· "μέγας ἐστὶν ὁ λίθος· οὐ δυνατόν ἐστιν αἴρειν αὐτόν."
6. ὅ τε Δικαιόπολις καὶ ὁ δοῦλος τὸν λίθον αἴρουσι καὶ ἐκφέρουσιν ἐκ τοῦ ἀγροῦ.
7. μὴ μένετε, ὦ βόες, ἀλλὰ σπεύδετε.
8. οἱ βόες οὐκέτι μένουσιν ἀλλὰ τὸ ἄροτρον αὖθις ἕλκουσιν.

Exercise 3c

Translate into Greek:

1. The oxen are sleeping in the field.
2. Come here and drive out (ἐξελαύνω) the oxen, slaves (ὦ δοῦλοι)
3. They take the goad (τὸ κέντρον) and slowly approach the oxen (τοῖς βουσίν).
4. Hurry, oxen; don't sleep in the field.
5. It is not possible to drive out the oxen; for they are strong (ἰσχῡροί).

The Deme and the Polis

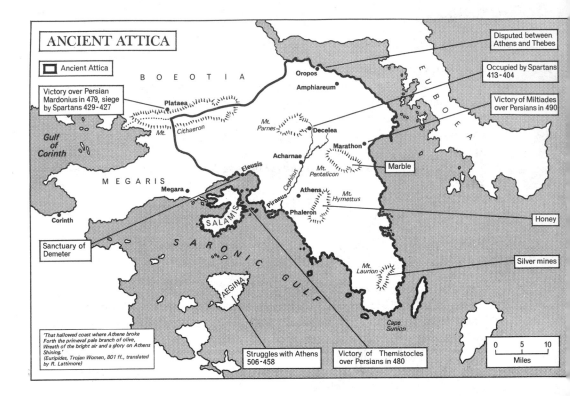

Attica and surroundings

    As we have seen, Dicaeopolis lives in a village about twelve miles south-east of Athens called Cholleidae. Such districts were called demes, and there were 170 of them in Attica, differing greatly in size and population. Each deme had its own assembly, to which all adult male citizens belonged. This assembly elected a demarch (mayor or sheriff) and passed decrees on local affairs, both secular and religious. It kept a record of all births; a man's rights as a citizen depended on his being registered in a deme when he reached adulthood. In all official contexts a man gave his name together with that of his father and deme, e.g., Περικλῆς Ξανθίππου Χολαργεύς (Pericles, son of Xanthippus, of the deme of Cholargus).

    The houses that composed these villages were mostly small and unpretentious, as far as our evidence goes. A typical house would consist of a courtyard surrounded by single-story rooms, and in one corner a storage-tower with an upper floor; this upper floor would form the women's quarters, to which women would retire, if strangers called. There would be no source of water within the house itself; it had to be fetched every day from a public fountain. Light would be provided by clay lamps fired by olive oil, which was also used for cooking and washing. We may assume that the majority of the farmers lived in the village and went out to work on their farms every day, as farmers still do in parts of Greece and Italy today, where houses are as a general rule not in the fields but clustered together in hilltop villages.

The men worked most of the day in the fields, and no doubt in the evenings they spent their time in the wineshop in the agora, discussing farming and politics with their friends. Life was enlivened by a succession of religious festivals. An inscription from the deme of Ercheia records a list of over fifty public sacrifices performed annually, and a public sacrifice usually entailed a public feast. In the winter, at the festival of the Rural Dionysia, touring companies from Athens even brought plays out to the demes. There were also private functions performed with traditional rituals, especially celebrations of birth, marriage, and death.

The farmer's horizon was by no means bounded by the deme. When he produced a surplus of any product such as wine or olives, he would go to Athens to sell it and to buy necessities he could not produce himself. There were religious festivals at regular intervals throughout the year at Athens (see Chapter 10), which he could attend with his wife and family; these included musical, dramatic, and athletic competitions.

There were important political functions that, as an Athenian citizen, the farmer was bound to perform. Forty times a year there were regular meetings of the Athenian Assembly, attended by all adult male citizens. The farmer would in fact have been prevented by his work from attending all of these, but he would certainly have gone to some of them. Every year the assembly of the deme chose representatives for the Council of 500, which was the executive committee of the Assembly. Councilors had to be over thirty years old, and no man could serve more than twice in his life time. It has been calculated that sooner or later nearly every farmer would have to take his turn in this office. This might involve residence in the city, since the Council met every day.

Lastly, the farmers provided the heavy armed infantry of the army (the hoplites). On reaching manhood they would have to do military training, since fighting in hoplite line involved much practice and good discipline. In the fourth century every citizen did two years military service from the age of eighteen and thereafter was liable to be called up in an emergency.

At the end of the first year of the great war between Athens and Sparta (about a year after our story begins), the Athenian leader Pericles made a funeral oration over those who had been killed in the war. Most of his speech was devoted to praise of the ideals of Athenian democracy, for which they had died. In the course of this he says: "The same people [i.e., the whole citizen body] are concerned not only with their domestic affairs but also with politics [i.e., the affairs of the city]; and although employed in different occupations, they are adequately informed on political matters. We alone consider a man who plays no part in these not as one who minds his own business but as useless" (Thucydides 2.40). The farmer's life under the Athenian democracy, despite primitive physical conditions, was far from drab.

Ο ΑΡΟΤΟΣ (β)

"οὐ δυνατόν ἐστιν, ὦ δέσποτα, τοσούτους λίθους ἐκφέρειν."

Vocabulary

Verbs
   ἀροτρεύω I plow
   λείπω I leave
   λύω I loosen
Nouns
   τὸ δεῖπνον dinner
   ὁ or **ἡ παῖς (ὦ παῖ)** boy, girl,
    child
   ὁ πατήρ (τὸν πατέρα, ὦ
    πάτερ) father
Pronoun
   σύ you (*singular*)

Adjectives
   ἀνδρεῖος brave
   πολλοί many
   τοσοῦτος so great, (*plural*) so
    many
Preposition
   ἐν (+ *dat.*) in, on
Adverb
   μηκέτι don't . . . any longer
Conjunction
   ἐπεί when
Proper Name
   ὁ Φίλιππος Philip

    ἐν δὲ τούτῳ προσχωρεῖ ὁ Φίλιππος· ὁ Φίλιππός ἐστιν ὁ τοῦ
Δικαιοπόλεως υἱός, παῖς μέγας τε καὶ ἀνδρεῖος· φέρει δὲ τὸ δεῖπνον
πρὸς τὸν πατέρα. ἐπεὶ δὲ εἰς τὸν ἀγρὸν εἰσβαίνει, τὸν πατέρα καλεῖ
καὶ λέγει· "ἐλθὲ δεῦρο, ὦ πάτερ· ἰδού—τὸ δεῖπνον φέρω. μηκέτι οὖν
πόνει ἀλλὰ κάθιζε καὶ δείπνει."   5

[**ἐν . . . τούτῳ** meanwhile   **ὁ τοῦ Δικαιοπόλεως υἱός** Dicaeopolis's son
δείπνει eat!]

ὁ οὖν πατὴρ λείπει τὸ ἄροτρον καὶ καλεῖ τὸν δοῦλον.
καθίζουσιν οὖν ἅμα καὶ δειπνοῦσιν.   μετὰ δὲ τὸ δεῖπνον ὁ
Δικαιόπολις, "μένε, ὦ παῖ," φησίν, "καὶ βοήθει. λάμβανε τὸ σπέρμα
καὶ σπεῖρε ἐν τῷ πέδῳ. σὺ δέ, ὦ Ξανθίᾱ, σκάπτε τοὺς λίθους καὶ
ἔκφερε ἐκ τοῦ ἀγροῦ. πολλοὶ γάρ εἰσιν οἱ λίθοι καὶ μόλις δυνατόν   10
ἐστιν ἀροτρεύειν." ὁ δὲ Ξανθίᾱς, "ἀλλ᾽ οὐ δυνατόν ἐστι τοσούτους
λίθους ἐκφέρειν." ὁ δὲ Δικαιόπολις, "μὴ φλυᾱρει, ὦ Ξανθίᾱ, ἀλλὰ
πόνει." πονοῦσιν οὖν ὅ τε πατὴρ καὶ ὁ παῖς καὶ ὁ δοῦλος. τέλος δὲ
καταδύνει μὲν ὁ ἥλιος, οἱ δὲ ἄνθρωποι οὐκέτι πονοῦσιν ἀλλὰ λύουσι
μὲν τοὺς βοῦς, τὸ δὲ ἄροτρον λείπουσιν ἐν τῷ ἀγρῷ καὶ πρὸς τὸν   15
οἶκον βραδέως βαδίζουσιν.

[μετά after   τῷ πέδῳ the ground   σκάπτε dig!   μόλις with difficulty, scarcely
τέλος finally   καταδύνει sets]

Word Building

Here are more verbs with prepositional prefixes. Give the meaning of each:

1. εἰσπίπτω   2. ἐκπίπτω   3. εἰσάγω   4. προσάγω   5. προσβλέπω

Grammar

2. Articles, Adjectives, and Nouns; Singular and Plural, All
   Cases:

   In Chapter 2 you learned the singular forms of masculine and neuter
   articles, adjectives, and nouns. Here are the singulars and plurals:

	Masculine			*Neuter*		
Nominative	ὁ	καλὸς	ἀγρός	τὸ	καλὸν	δένδρον
Genitive	τοῦ	καλοῦ	ἀγροῦ	τοῦ	καλοῦ	δένδρου
Dative	τῷ	καλῷ	ἀγρῷ	τῷ	καλῷ	δένδρῳ
Accusative	τὸν	καλὸν	ἀγρόν	τὸ	καλὸν	δένδρον
Vocative	ὦ	καλέ	ἀγρέ	ὦ	καλὸν	δένδρον
Nominative	οἱ	καλοὶ	ἀγροί	τὰ	καλὰ	δένδρα
Genitive	τῶν	καλῶν	ἀγρῶν	τῶν	καλῶν	δένδρων
Dative	τοῖς	καλοῖς	ἀγροῖς	τοῖς	καλοῖς	δένδροις
Accusative	τοὺς	καλοὺς	ἀγρούς	τὰ	καλὰ	δένδρα
Vocative	ὦ	καλοὶ	ἀγροί	ὦ	καλὰ	δένδρα

Note:

1. In the neuter singular the nominative, accusative, and vocative all
   end in -ov; in the plural these cases all end in -α. The other neuter
   case endings are the same as for the masculine.

2. The genitive and dative, singular and plural, of the definite article have circumflex accents.
3. When adjectives and nouns of the type seen above are accented on the final syllable in the nominative case (e.g., καλός and ἀγρός), they change that accent to a circumflex in the genitive and dative, singular and plural.
4. The masculine nominative plural ending -οι is counted as short in determining the accent, thus the plural of ἄνθρωπος is ἄνθρωποι.

Exercise 3d

Give the correct form of the article to complete the following phrases:

1. ___ ἀνθρώπους
2. ___ δοῦλοι
3. ἐν ___ οἴκοις
4. ἐκ ___ ἀγρῶν
5. πρὸς ___ δένδρα
6. ___ ᾿Αθηναίων
7. ___ ἄροτρον
8. ___ χρόνον
9. ___ πόνοι
10. ___ δούλους

Exercise 3e

Complete the following sentences by giving correct endings to the verbs and nouns, and then translate:

1. οἱ δοῦλ__ πον__ ἐν τοῖς ἀγρ__.
2. οἱ ἄνθρωπ__ σπεύδ__ πρὸς τὸν οἶκ__.
3. ὅ τε Δικαιόπολις καὶ ὁ δοῦλ__ μέν__ ἐν τ__ ἀγρῷ.
4. λείπ__ τὰ ἄροτρ__, ὦ δοῦλοι, ἐν τῷ ἀγρ__.
5. αἴρ__ τοὺς λίθ__, ὦ δοῦλοι, καὶ ἐκφέρ__ ἐκ τῶν ἀγρ__.
6. οὐ δυνατόν ἐστι τοὺς λίθους αἴρ__ καὶ ἐκφέρ__.

Exercise 3f

Translate the following pairs of sentences:

1. ὁ μὲν Δικαιόπολις ἐλαύνει τοὺς βοῦς, οἱ δὲ βόες οὐκέτι ἕλκουσι τὸ ἄροτρον.
    The master calls the slaves, but the slaves do not drive the oxen.
2. μὴ καθίζετε ἐν τῷ οἴκῳ, ὦ παῖδες, ἀλλὰ ἔλθετε δεῦρο καὶ βοηθεῖτε.
    Don't stay in the fields, boys, but walk to the house and sleep.
3. οἱ παῖδες ἰσχῡροί εἰσιν· λίθους γὰρ μεγάλους φέρουσιν.
    The slaves are lazy; for they are no longer working.
4. λαμβάνετε τὰ ἄροτρα, ὦ φίλοι, καὶ σπεύδετε πρὸς τοὺς ἀγρούς.
    Loosen the oxen, slaves, and leave the plows in the field.
5. διὰ τί φεύγετε (*are you fleeing*), ὦ παῖδες; ἀνδρεῖοι ἔστε.
    Why are you waiting, boys? Don't be lazy.

ΟΙ ΒΟΕΣ

Read the following passage and answer the comprehension questions:

ὅ τε δεσπότης καὶ ὁ δοῦλος βαδίζουσι πρὸς τὸν ἀγρόν. ὁ μὲν δοῦλος τὸ ἄροτρον
φέρει, ὁ δὲ δεσπότης ἐλαύνει τοὺς βοῦς. ἐπεὶ δὲ τῷ ἀγρῷ προσχωροῦσιν, οἱ βόες
οὐκέτι βαίνουσιν. ὁ οὖν δεσπότης καλεῖ αὐτοὺς καί, "μὴ μένετε, ὦ βόες," φησίν,
"ἀλλὰ σπεύδετε εἰς τὸν ἀγρόν." οἱ δὲ βόες ἔτι μένουσιν. ὁ οὖν δεσπότης τὸν δοῦλον
καλεῖ καί, "ἐλθὲ δεῦρο, ὦ Ξανθίᾱ," φησίν, "καὶ βοήθει. οἱ γὰρ βόες μένουσι καὶ οὐ   5
δυνατόν ἐστιν ἐλαύνειν αὐτοὺς εἰς τὸν ἀγρόν." ὁ μὲν οὖν δοῦλος προσχωρεῖ καί,
"ἀλλὰ δυνατόν ἐστιν," φησίν· "ἰδού," καὶ κεντεῖ τοὺς βοῦς. οἱ δὲ οὐκέτι μένουσιν
ἀλλὰ σπεύδουσιν εἰς τὸν ἀγρόν.

[αὐτούς them   κεντεῖ he goads   οἱ δέ and they]

1. What are the master and slave doing?
2. What happens when they approach the field?
3. What does the master do and with what result?
4. What does the master do in his helplessness?
5. What does the slave do that the master did not do? With what result?

Exercise 3g

Translate into Greek:

1. The master hurries into the field.
2. He looks at (toward) the field and says, "So many stones are in the
   field! It is not possible to plow. Come here, slave, and carry the stones
   out of the field."
3. But the slave says, "It is not possible to carry so many stones out of the
   field. *You* help!"

4
ΠΡΟΣ ΤΗΙ ΚΡΗΝΗΙ (α)

αἱ κόραι πληροῦσι τὰς ὑδρίας πρὸς τῇ κρήνη

Vocabulary

Verbs

ἀκούω (+ *gen.* of person, *acc.* of thing) I listen, hear

ἐθέλω I wish, am willing

οὐκ ἐθέλω I refuse

ἔχω I have, hold

ποιέω I make, do

χαῖρε, (*plural*) χαίρετε greetings!

Nouns

ὁ ἄγγελος messenger

ὁ ἀνήρ (τὸν ἄνδρα, ὦ ἄνερ) man, husband

ἡ γυνή (ὦ γύναι, αἱ γυναῖκες, τὰς γυναῖκας) woman, wife

ἡ ἑορτή festival

ἡ θυγάτηρ (ὦ θύγατερ) daughter

ὁ καιρός time, right time

ἡ κρήνη spring

ἡ μήτηρ mother

ἡ ὑδρίᾱ water jar

ὁ χορός dance, chorus

Adjectives

ῥᾴθῡμος, ῥᾴθῡμον lazy

φίλος, φίλη, φίλον dear, (*as noun*, e.g., ὁ φίλος) friend

Prepositions

ἀπό (+ *gen.*) from

πρός (+ *dat.*) at, near, by, (+ *acc.*) to, toward

Adverbs

ἰδού look!

μάλα very

μόλις with difficulty, scarcely, reluctantly

πρῶτον first

ταχέως quickly

Particle

ἆρα (*introduces a question*)

Expression

ἐν νῷ ἔχω (+ *infinitive*) I have in mind, intend

Proper Names

ἡ Μέλιττα Melissa, daughter of Dicaeopolis and Myrrhine

ἡ Μυρρίνη Myrrhine, wife of Dicaeopolis

τῇ δὲ ὑστεραίᾳ ἐπεὶ πρῶτον ἀνατέλλει ὁ ἥλιος, ἡ γυνὴ τὸν ἄνδρα
καλεῖ καί, "ἔπαιρε σεαυτόν, ὦ ἄνερ," φησίν· "ὁ γὰρ ἥλιος ἀνατέλλει, ὁ
δὲ δοῦλος ἤδη ἄγει τοὺς βοῦς πρὸς τὸν ἀγρόν, ἐγὼ δὲ καὶ ἡ θυγάτηρ
ἐν νῷ ἔχομεν βαδίζειν πρὸς τὴν κρήνην. ἔπαιρε σεαυτόν· καιρὸς γάρ
ἐστι βαδίζειν πρὸς τὸν ἀγρόν." ὁ δὲ Δικαιόπολις μάλα κάμνει καὶ   5
οὐκ ἐθέλει ἐπαίρειν ἑαυτόν· λέγει οὖν· "μὴ χαλεπὴ ἴσθι, ὦ γύναι·
μάλα γὰρ κάμνω καὶ ἐθέλω καθεύδειν." ἡ δὲ γυνή, "ἀλλ’ οὐ δυνατόν
ἐστιν," φησίν, "ἔτι καθεύδειν· καιρὸς γάρ ἐστι πονεῖν. ἔπαιρε σεαυτόν,
ὦ ῥᾴθῡμε."

[τῇ . . . ὑστεραίᾳ the next day   ἀνατέλλει rises   ἔπαιρε σεαυτόν lift
yourself! – get up!   κάμνει is tired   ἑαυτόν himself]

ὁ μὲν οὖν Δικαιόπολις μόλις ἐπαίρει ἑαυτὸν καὶ βαδίζει πρὸς τὸν   10
ἀγρόν, ἡ δὲ Μυρρίνη καὶ ἡ Μέλιττα πρὸς τὴν κρήνην βαδίζουσι (ἡ
Μέλιττα θυγάτηρ ἐστίν, κόρη μάλα καλή). ἥ τε οὖν μήτηρ καὶ ἡ
θυγάτηρ βραδέως βαδίζουσιν· τὰς γὰρ ὑδρίᾱς φέρουσιν· μεγάλαι δ’
εἰσὶν αἱ ὑδρίαι, ὥστε οὐ δυνατόν ἐστι σπεύδειν.

[κόρη girl   μεγάλαι (fem. of μέγας) big   ὥστε so that]

ἐπεὶ δὲ τῇ κρήνῃ προσχωροῦσιν, ἰδού—ἄλλαι γυναῖκες ἤδη   15
πάρεισι καὶ τὰς ὑδρίᾱς πληροῦσιν. ἡ οὖν Μυρρίνη τὰς γυναῖκας
καλεῖ καί, "χαίρετε, ὦ φίλαι," φησίν· "ἆρα ἤδη πληροῦτε τὰς ὑδρίᾱς;"
αἱ δὲ λέγουσιν· "χαῖρε καὶ σύ· ναί, ἤδη πληροῦμεν τὰς ὑδρίᾱς· πρωὶ
γὰρ πάρεσμεν. ἀλλ’ ἐλθὲ δεῦρο ταχέως καὶ ἄκουε· ἄγγελος γὰρ ἥκει
ἀπὸ τοῦ ἄστεως· λέγει δὲ ὅτι οἱ Ἀθηναῖοι ἑορτὴν ποιοῦσιν. ἡμεῖς οὖν   20
ἐν νῷ ἔχομεν βαδίζειν πρὸς τὸ ἄστυ· τοὺς γὰρ χοροὺς ἐθέλομεν
θεωρεῖν καὶ τοὺς ἀγῶνας. ἆρα ἐθέλεις καὶ σὺ τὴν ἑορτὴν θεωρεῖν;"

[ἄλλαι other   πληροῦσιν are filling   πληροῦτε are you (plural) filling?   αἱ
δέ and they   ναί yes   πρωί early   ἥκει has come   τοῦ ἄστεως the city   ὅτι
that   ἡμεῖς we   θεωρεῖν to see   τοὺς ἀγῶνας the contests]

Word Study

*Identify the Greek roots in the English words below and give the meanings of the
English words:*

1. acoustics
2. angel
3. gynecology
4. choreographer

5. tachometer
6. philanthropist
7. polyandry
8. misogynist

Grammar

1. Verb Forms: All Persons, Singular and Plural

You have now met verbs in all persons, singular and plural. Be sure to learn all of the following forms thoroughly:

	Singular		*Plural*	
λ ῡ-	loosen			
1st	λ ῡ́-ω		λῡ́-ομεν	
2nd	λ ῡ́-εις		λῡ́-ετε	
3rd	λ ῡ́-ει		λῡ́-ουσι(ν)	
φιλε-	love			
1st	φιλέ-ω >	φιλῶ	φιλέ-ομεν >	φιλοῦμεν
2nd	φιλέ-εις >	φιλεῖς	φιλέ-ετε >	φιλεῖτε
3rd	φιλέ-ει >	φιλεῖ	φιλέ-ουσι(ν) >	φιλοῦσι(ν)
ἐσ-	be			
1st	εἰμί*		ἐσμέν*	
2nd	εἶ		ἐστέ*	
3rd	ἐστί(ν)*		εἰσί(ν)*	

*enclitic

N.B. Verbs with stems ending in -ε (e.g., φιλε-) are called contract verbs, because the vowel of the stem contracts with the vowel or diphthong of the ending. You have observed this with verbs such as φιλέω from the beginning of the course. The following three rules for contractions may be observed:

1. ε + ε > ει.
2. ε + ο > ου.
3. ε followed by a long vowel or a diphthong is elided or drops out.

Exercise 4a

Locate six 1st and 2nd person plural verb forms in the reading passage at the beginning of this chapter.

2. Articles, Adjectives, and Nouns; Feminine Gender

You have seen charts of masculine and neuter nouns in Chapters 2 and 3, with accompanying articles and adjectives in agreement with them. In the reading passage at the beginning of this chapter are a number of feminine nouns that are declined like κρήνη, the declension of which we show in the following chart with accompanying articles and adjectives:

	Singular			Plural		
Nom.	ἡ	καλὴ	κρήνη	αἱ	καλαὶ	κρῆναι
Gen.	τῆς	καλῆς	κρήνης	τῶν	καλῶν	κρηνῶν
Dat.	τῇ	καλῇ	κρήνῃ	ταῖς	καλαῖς	κρήναις
Acc.	τὴν	καλὴν	κρήνην	τὰς	καλὰς	κρήνᾱς
Voc.	ὦ	καλὴ	κρήνη	ὦ	καλαὶ	κρῆναι

Note:

1. The genitive and dative, singular and plural, of the feminine definite article have circumflex accents, just as do those forms of the masculine and neuter (see page 27).
2. When adjectives and nouns of the type seen above are accented on the final syllable in the nominative case (e.g., καλή), they change that accent to a circumflex in the genitive and dative, singular and plural (again, see page 27 for the same thing with masculine and neuter adjectives and nouns).
3. The nominative plural ending -αι is counted as short in determining the accent, thus κρῆναι has a circumflex accent.
4. The genitive plural of all first declension nouns (see next paragraph) has a circumflex accent on the final syllable.

The noun κρήνη is said to belong to the first group or *declension* of nouns, the stems of which end in -ᾱ (this group of nouns is thus called the *alpha declension*). In nouns like κρήνη, the original ᾱ of the stem has been changed to η in the singular in Attic Greek.

The nouns ἀγρός and δένδρον, which were shown in the charts in Chapters 2 and 3, are said to belong to the second or *omicron declension* of nouns.

Nouns such as ἀνήρ, γυνή, θυγάτηρ, and μήτηρ, which you have met in the reading at the beginning of this chapter, are said to belong to the third declension. (The endings of third declension nouns will be presented later; for the time being you can identify their case and number by observing the article that accompanies them.)

Feminine nouns of the first declension show nominative singular forms ending in -η or -ᾱ or -ᾰ. The full declension of a typical noun ending in -η is shown above (κρήνη).

After ε, ι, or ρ, the original -ᾱ of the stem was retained in Attic Greek, as in the word οἰκίᾱ "house":

Nom.	ἡ	οἰκίᾱ	αἱ	οἰκίαι
Gen.	τῆς	οἰκίᾱς	τῶν	οἰκιῶν
Dat.	τῇ	οἰκίᾳ	ταῖς	οἰκίαις
Acc.	τὴν	οἰκίᾱν	τὰς	οἰκίᾱς
Voc.	ὦ	οἰκίᾱ	ὦ	οἰκίαι

The word κόρη "girl" is an exception to this rule.

A third group consists of nouns ending in -ᾰ, as θάλαττᾰ "sea":

Nom.	ἡ	θάλαττᾰ	αἱ	θάλατται
Gen.	τῆς	θαλάττης	τῶν	θαλαττῶν
Dat.	τῇ	θαλάττῃ	ταῖς	θαλάτταις
Acc.	τὴν	θάλαττᾰν	τᾱς	θαλάττᾱς
Voc.	ὦ	θάλαττᾰ	ὦ	θάλατται

Note the forms with η in the genitive and dative. If the -ᾰ is preceded by ε, ι, or ρ, long α appears in the genitive and dative, as in μάχαιρᾰ "knife":

Nom.	ἡ	μάχαιρᾰ	αἱ	μάχαιραι
Gen.	τῆς	μαχαίρᾱς	τῶν	μαχαιρῶν
Dat.	τῇ	μαχαίρᾳ	ταῖς	μαχαίραις
Acc.	τὴν	μάχαιρᾰν	τᾱς	μαχαίρᾱς
Voc.	ὦ	μάχαιρᾰ	ὦ	μάχαιραι

Note that all first declension nouns decline alike in the plural.

Exercise 4b

Give the genitive of the following phrases:

1. ἡ Μυρρίνη
2. ἡ Μέλιττα
3. ἡ καλὴ οἰκίᾱ
4. ἡ καλὴ ἑορτή
5. ἡ καλὴ κρήνη
6. ὁ μακρὸς πόνος
7. ἡ μῑκρὰ θάλαττα
8. τὸ καλὸν δένδρον

Exercise 4c

Supply the correct form of the definite article in the following phrases:

1. ___ καλαὶ γυναῖκες
2. ἐν ___ ἀγρῷ
3. παρὰ ___ κρήνῃ
4. ___ ἄλλων ἀνδρῶν
5. ἐκ ___ γῆς (*earth*)
6. ἐν ___ οἰκίαις
7. ___ μεγάλα δένδρα
8. ___ ἄγγελοι

Exercise 4d

Put into the plural and translate:

1. ἡ κόρη ἄγει τὴν φίλην ἐκ τοῦ ἀγροῦ.
2. ἡ δούλη τὴν ὑδρίαν φέρει πρὸς τὴν κρήνην.
3. καλή ἐστιν ἡ κόρη· ἆρ' οὐκ ἐθέλεις αὐτὴν (*her*) καλεῖν;
4. χαῖρε, ὦ κόρη· ἆρα βαδίζεις πρὸς τὴν οἰκίαν;
5. ἐν νῷ ἔχω λείπειν τὴν ὑδρίαν ἐν τῇ οἰκίᾳ καὶ βοηθεῖν.

Exercise 4e

Put into the singular and translate:

1. αἱ φίλαι μένουσι πρὸς ταῖς κρήναις.
2. οἱ ἄνθρωποι φέρουσι τὰ ἄροτρα ἐκ τῶν ἀγρῶν.
3. ἀκούετε, ὦ φίλοι· ἐν νῷ ἔχομεν βαδίζειν πρὸς τὰς οἰκίας.
4. τί (*what*) ποιεῖτε, ὦ δοῦλοι; μὴ οὕτω σκαιοὶ (*clumsy*) ἔστε.

Women

Two girls, one holding a writing tablet

When Pericles drew to the end of his funeral oration, he finally had a word for the widows of the dead: "If I should say a word on the duties of the wives who will now be widows, I will sum up the whole in a short piece of advice: your great glory is not to fall beneath the nature you have been given, and hers is the greatest glory who is least talked about among the men for praise or for blame." Women lived in the shadows of their men. This is clearly seen from their legal position; they were treated in law as minors, being under the tutelage of their father or guardian until they were married and thereafter under the tutelage of their husbands. They could not own property in their own right; they had no place in public life, no vote in the Assembly, and no seat on the juries.

Their life centered on the *oikos*, and here they were important and respected figures. The fourth century Athenian writer Xenophon in a work called *Oikonomikos* (which means "management of the *oikos*," not "economics" in its modern sense) gives this advice to a young bride:

Your business will be to stay indoors and help to dispatch the servants who work outside, while supervising those who work indoors. You will re-

ceive incoming revenue and allocate it to any necessary expenditure; you
will be responsible for any surplus and see that the allocation for the
year's expenses is not spent in a month. When wool is delivered to you,
you will see that garments are made for those who need them, and you
will take care that the dried grain is kept fit for consumption. And there
is another of your duties that I'm afraid may seem to you rather thank-
less—you will have to see that any of the servants who is ill gets proper
treatment. (*Oikonomikos* 7.35–37)

The duties of a farmer's wife were similar, though instead of organizing
slaves she had to do the work herself. The work was endless and gave women
little leisure.

Marriages took place early; a girl might be betrothed at five and married
at fifteen, and marriages were arranged by parents, often with considera-
tions of property in mind.

Nevertheless, Athenian art shows us many scenes of contented domestic
life, and inscriptions testify to happy marriages: "In this tomb lies Chaere-
strate: her husband loved her while she was alive and grieved for her when
she died" (*EG* 44, 2–3, Piraeus, fourth or third century B.C.). The husband
was his wife's protector and kept her safe from the dangers of life that lay
outside the *oikos*. Even in the house she had no contact with men outside the
family; if strangers called, she would retire to the women's quarters. In the
opening scene of Euripides' tragedy, *Electra,* Electra is talking to women of
the village outside her house, when two strange men appear. She immediately says to the women: "You flee down the path and I will take refuge in the
house." Later her husband, a farmer, appears when she is talking to the men
who claim to have brought news of her brother; he says: "Who are these
strangers at our door? Why have they come to our country dwelling? Do they
want me? (*to Electra*) It's a disgrace, you know, for a woman to stand around
with young men."

But women's lives were not as confined as we have so far suggested.
They attended the religious festivals in both deme and city, including,
probably, the dramatic festivals. They had important functions in religious
rites; they were priestesses in more than forty public cults, and they formed
choirs and played a leading role in processions. Some of the most powerful
figures in Greek tragedy are women, and all three of the great tragedians,
especially Euripides, show deep insight into the character of women and por-
tray them sympathetically. Despite the restrictions that hedged her around,
the Athenian woman was no cipher. The sixth-century poet Semonides writes
of the good woman:

The gods made her of honey, and blessed is the man who gets her. His
property flourishes and is increased by her. She grows old with a husband
she loves and who loves her, the mother of a handsome and reputable
family. She stands out among all women, and a godlike beauty plays
around her. She takes no pleasure in sitting among women where they
tell stories about love. (*Anthologia Lyrica Graeca*, I.7.83–93).

ΠΡΟΣ ΤΗΙ ΚΡΗΝΗΙ (β)

ἡ Μέλιττα, "οὐκ αἰτία ἐγώ," φησίν· "μεγάλη γάρ ἐστιν ἡ ὑδρία."

Vocabulary

Verbs
πείθω I persuade
στενάζω I groan

Noun
ἡ γῆ land, earth, ground
ἡ ὁδός road, way, journey

Adjectives
ἄλλος, ἄλλη, ἄλλο other,
  another

ῥᾴδιος, ῥᾳδίᾱ, ῥᾴδιον easy
Adverbs
αἰεί always
μάλιστα very much,
  especially
οἴκαδε homeward, to home
Expression
τί; what?

ἡ δὲ Μυρρίνη, "τί λέγετε, ὦ φίλαι; ἆρα ἀληθῶς ἑορτὴν ποιοῦσιν οἱ
Ἀθηναῖοι; ἐγὼ μὲν μάλιστα ἐθέλω αὐτὴν θεωρεῖν· σὺ δέ, ὦ Μέλιττα,
ἆρα καὶ σὺ ἐθέλεις θεωρεῖν; ἀλλ' οὐ δυνατόν ἐστιν· χαλεπὸς γάρ
ἐστιν ὁ ἀνήρ· αἰεὶ γὰρ πονεῖ καὶ σπανίως ἐθέλει ἰέναι πρὸς τὸ ἄστυ."

[ἀληθῶς truly, really   αὐτήν it   σπανίως rarely   ἰέναι to go]

ἡ δὲ Μέλιττα, "ἀλλ' οὐ μάλα χαλεπός ἐστιν ὁ πατήρ· ῥᾴδιον γάρ   5
ἐστι πείθειν αὐτόν." ἡ δὲ Μυρρίνη, "μὴ οὕτω φλυᾱρει ἀλλὰ τὴν
ὑδρίᾱν ταχέως πλήρου· καιρὸς γάρ ἐστιν οἴκαδε ἐπανιέναι."

[φλυᾱρει talk nonsense   πλήρου fill!   ἐπανιέναι to come back, return]

ἥ τε οὖν μήτηρ καὶ ἡ θυγάτηρ τὰς ὑδρίᾱς ταχέως πληροῦσι καὶ
οἴκαδε βαδίζουσιν. ἐν δὲ τῇ ὁδῷ πταίει ἡ Μέλιττα καὶ καταβάλλει

τὴν ὑδρίᾱν πρὸς τὴν γῆν καὶ θραύει αὐτήν. στενάζει οὖν καί, "οἴμοι,"   10
φησίν, "οὐκ αἰτίᾱ εἰμὶ ἐγώ· μεγάλη γάρ ἐστιν ἡ ὑδρίᾱ καὶ οὐ δυνατόν
ἐστι φέρειν αὐτήν."   ἡ δὲ μήτηρ, "τί λέγεις, ὦ θύγατερ; μὴ φλυᾱρει
ἀλλὰ οἴκαδε σπεῦδε καὶ ἄλλην ὑδρίᾱν φέρε."

[πταίει stumbles   καταβάλλει drops   θραύει breaks   αὐτήν it   οἴμοι
alas!]

ἡ μὲν οὖν Μέλιττα οἴκαδε σπεύδει, ἡ δὲ Μυρρίνη βραδέως
βαδίζει· μεγάλη γάρ ἐστιν ἡ ὑδρίᾱ καὶ οὐκ ἐθέλει καταβάλλειν   15
αὐτήν.

Word Building

*Describe the relationship between the words in each of the following pairs.
Deduce the meaning of the words at the right from your knowledge of those at
the left:*

1. ὁ χορός   χορεύω
2. ὁ δοῦλος   δουλεύω
3. τὸ ἄροτρον   ἀροτρεύω
4. ὁ ἵππος (horse) ἱππεύω

Grammar

3. Masculine Nouns of the First Declension

Some nouns of the first declension are masculine in gender and end
in -ης or -ᾱς in the nominative singular, in -ου in the genitive singular,
and in -ᾰ or -ᾱ in the vocative singular. Otherwise they have the same
endings as κρήνη and οἰκίᾱ. As examples, we give ὁ δεσπότης in the
singular and plural and ὁ Ξανθίᾱς in the singular:

	Singular		*Plural*		*Singular*	
Nom.	ὁ	δεσπότης	οἱ	δεσπόται	ὁ	Ξανθίᾱς
Gen.	τοῦ	δεσπότου	τῶν	δεσποτῶν	τοῦ	Ξανθίου
Dat.	τῷ	δεσπότῃ	τοῖς	δεσπόταις	τῷ	Ξανθίᾳ
Acc.	τὸν	δεσπότην	τοὺς	δεσπότᾱς	τὸν	Ξανθίᾱν
Voc.	ὦ	δέσποτα	ὦ	δεσπόται	ὦ	Ξανθίᾱ

Note that all first declension nouns have a circumflex accent on the
final syllable of the genitive plural.

4. Adjectives

Many Greek adjectives have first and second declension endings, e.g.,
the adjective καλός, καλή, καλόν, "beautiful," which we have shown along
with the nouns ἀγρός, δένδρον, and κρήνη on pages 17, 27, and 33. Here are
all of the forms of this typical first and second declension adjective:

	Singular			Plural		
	M.	*F.*	*N.*	*M.*	*F.*	*N.*
Nom.	καλός	καλή	καλόν	καλοί	καλαί	καλά
Gen.	καλοῦ	καλῆς	καλοῦ	καλῶν	καλῶν	καλῶν
Dat.	καλῷ	καλῇ	καλῷ	καλοῖς	καλαῖς	καλοῖς
Acc.	καλόν	καλήν	καλόν	καλούς	καλάς	καλά
Voc.	καλέ	καλή	καλόν	καλοί	καλαί	καλά

Note that adjectives with ε, ι, or ρ preceding -ος have feminine endings that show ᾱ instead of η in the singular (like the noun ἡ οἰκίᾱ), e.g., ῥᾴδιος, ῥᾳδίᾱ, ῥᾴδιον:

Nom.	ῥᾴδιος	ῥᾳδίᾱ	ῥᾴδιον	ῥᾴδιοι	ῥᾴδιαι	ῥᾴδια
Gen.	ῥᾳδίου	ῥᾳδίᾱς	ῥᾳδίου	ῥᾳδίων	ῥᾳδίων	ῥᾳδίων
Dat.	ῥᾳδίῳ	ῥᾳδίᾳ	ῥᾳδίῳ	ῥᾳδίοις	ῥᾳδίαις	ῥᾳδίοις
Acc.	ῥᾴδιον	ῥᾳδίᾱν	ῥᾴδιον	ῥᾳδίους	ῥᾳδίᾱς	ῥᾴδια
Voc.	ῥᾴδιε	ῥᾳδίᾱ	ῥᾴδιον	ῥᾴδιοι	ῥᾴδιαι	ῥᾴδια

In future vocabulary lists adjectives with first and second declension endings will be given in abbreviated form, e.g., καλός, -ή, -όν or ῥᾴδιος, -ᾱ, -ον.

Two common Greek adjectives show slight irregularities: μέγας, μεγάλη, μέγα "big," and πολύς, πολλή, πολύ "much," (plural) "many":

Nom.	<u>μέγας</u>	μεγάλη	<u>μέγα</u>	μεγάλοι	μεγάλαι	μεγάλα
Gen.	μεγάλου	μεγάλης	μεγάλου	μεγάλων	μεγάλων	μεγάλων
Dat.	μεγάλῳ	μεγάλῃ	μεγάλῳ	μεγάλοις	μεγάλαις	μεγάλοις
Acc.	<u>μέγαν</u>	μεγάλην	<u>μέγα</u>	μεγάλους	μεγάλᾱς	μεγάλα
Voc.	<u>μέγας</u>	μεγάλη	<u>μέγα</u>	μεγάλοι	μεγάλαι	μεγάλα
Nom.	<u>πολύς</u>	πολλή	<u>πολύ</u>	πολλοί	πολλαί	πολλά
Gen.	πολλοῦ	πολλῆς	πολλοῦ	πολλῶν	πολλῶν	πολλῶν
Dat.	πολλῷ	πολλῇ	πολλῷ	πολλοῖς	πολλαῖς	πολλοῖς
Acc.	<u>πολύν</u>	πολλήν	<u>πολύ</u>	πολλούς	πολλάς	πολλά
Voc.	none					

5. Formation of Adverbs

Many adverbs may be formed in Greek by changing the last letter of the genitive plural of the corresponding adjective from ν to ς, e.g.:

καλῶν   καλ-ῶς beautifully, well

Exercise 4f

Find five adverbs ending in -ως in the reading passage on pages 37–38.

6. The Definite Article as Case Indicator

Along with your study of first and second declension nouns on pages 27 and 33 you have learned all of the forms of the definite article. Review them in the following chart:

	Singular			*Plural*		
	M	**F**	**N**	**M**	**F**	**N**
Nom.	ὁ	ἡ	τό	οἱ	αἱ	τά
Gen.	τοῦ	τῆς	τοῦ	τῶν	τῶν	τῶν
Dat.	τῷ	τῇ	τῷ	τοῖς	ταῖς	τοῖς
Acc.	τόν	τήν	τό	τούς	τάς	τά

In your reading of Greek you should take full advantage of the definite article as a case indicator, which enables you to determine the case of nouns that you have not yet learned to decline. For example in the phrase τοῦ ἀνδρός the definite article τοῦ tells you that ἀνδρός is genitive singular. Remember that the vocative, which is not accompanied by the definite article, is usually preceded by ὦ.

Exercise 4g

Give the case and number of each of the following phrases:

1. τοὺς ἄνδρας
2. τῇ μητρί
3. τῷ παιδί
4. τὴν ναῦν
5. ὦ πάτερ
6. τὸν βασιλέᾱ
7. τῆς πόλεως
8. τοῦ δεσπότου
9. ταῖς γυναιξί
10. τοῦ κυνός
11. οἱ κύνες
12. τῆς μητρός
13. τοῖς παισί
14. τὸν πατέρα
15. ὦ βασιλεῦ

* * *

ΑΙ ΓΥΝΑΙΚΕΣ ΤΟΥΣ ΑΝΔΡΑΣ ΠΕΙΘΟΥΣΙΝ

Read the following passage and answer the comprehension questions:

πολλαὶ γυναῖκες ἥκουσιν εἰς τὴν κρήνην. ἐν ᾧ δὲ πληροῦσι τὰς ὑδρίας, ἄγγελος προσχωρεῖ. ἐπεὶ δὲ πάρεστιν, "ἀκούετε, γυναῖκες," φησίν· "οἱ γὰρ Ἀθηναῖοι ἑορτὴν ποιοῦσιν. ἆρ' οὐκ ἐθέλετε αὐτὴν θεωρεῖν; πείθετε οὖν τοὺς ἄνδρας ὑμᾶς ἐκεῖσε ἄγειν." αἱ δὲ γυναῖκες χαίρουσι καὶ λέγουσιν, "μάλιστα ἐθέλομεν θεωρεῖν καὶ ἐν νῷ ἔχομεν τοὺς ἄνδρας πείθειν." τὰς οὖν ὑδρίας ταχέως   5
πληροῦσι καὶ οἴκαδε σπεύδουσιν. ἐπεὶ δὲ ἥκουσιν οἱ ἄνδρες ἐκ τῶν ἀγρῶν, ἑκάστη ἡ γυνὴ λέγει· "ἄκουε, ὦ φίλε ἄνερ· ἄγγελος γὰρ πάρεστι καὶ λέγει ὅτι οἱ Ἀθηναῖοι ἑορτὴν ποιοῦσιν. ἆρ' οὐκ ἐθέλεις με ἐκεῖσε ἄγειν;" καὶ ῥᾳδίως πείθουσιν αὐτούς· οἱ γὰρ ἄνδρες αὐτοὶ ἐθέλουσι τὴν ἑορτὴν θεωρεῖν.

[ἐν ᾧ while   ὑμᾶς you (*acc. pl.*)   ἐκεῖσε there   ἑκάστη each   ὅτι that   με me   αὐτούς them   αὐτοί themselves]

1. What are the women doing when the messenger approaches?
2. What are the Athenians doing?
3. What does the messenger tell the women to do?
4. How do the women react to the messenger's announcement?
5. What do the women do with haste?
6. What do the women do when their husbands return from the fields?
7. Why do they succeed in persuading their husbands?

Two women are folding up a finished piece of cloth over a stool, on which lies another finished piece. On either side a woman stands spinning (on page 82 there is a scene of weaving from the same vase).

Exercise 4h

Translate into Greek:

1. Dicaeopolis approaches Myrrhine and says, "Greetings, dear wife (γύναι). What are you doing?"
2. "I am hurrying to the spring. For I wish to carry water (τὸ ὕδωρ) to the house. What are *you* doing?
3. "The slave and I are hurrying to the field. But listen."
4. "The Athenians are holding a festival. Do you wish to see it?"
5. "I very much wish to see it. And so don't go (μὴ ἴθι) to-the field but take me to the city (τὸ ἄστυ)."

5

Ο ΛΥΚΟΣ (α)

ὁ Φίλιππος λαγὼν ὁρᾷ ἐν τῷ ἀγρῷ καὶ βοᾷ, "ἴθι δή, Ἄργε, δίωκε."

Vocabulary

Verbs
   ἄπειμι I am away
   βοάω I shout
   διώκω I pursue
   ζητέω I seek, look for
   ἴθι, (*plural*) ἴτε go!
   ὁράω I see
   τρέχω I run
   φεύγω I flee, escape
   φυλάττω I guard
Nouns
   ὁ *or* ἡ κύων (τὸν *or* τὴν κύνα,
      ὦ κύον), dog
   ὁ λαγώς hare
   ὁ λύκος wolf
   τὰ μῆλα (*plural*) flocks
   ἡ οἰκίᾱ house, home, dwelling
   τὸ ὄρος (τοῦ ὄρους, τοῖς ὄρεσι)
      mountain, hill
   ὁ πάππος grandfather

Adjective
   ἄκρος, -ᾱ, -ον, top (of)
      ἄκρον τὸ ὄρος, the top of the
      mountain/hill
Prepositions
   ἀνά (+ *acc.*) up
   κατά (+ *acc.*) down
Adverb
   ποῦ where?
Conjunctions
   οὐδέ and . . . not, nor, not even
   οὔτε . . . οὔτε neither . . . nor
   ὥστε so that, that
Expression
   δι' ὀλίγου soon
   ἴθι δή go on!
Proper Name
   ὁ Ἄργος Argus (name of a
      dog)

ἐν ᾧ δὲ ἄπεισιν ἥ τε Μυρρίνη καὶ ἡ Μέλιττα, ὁ μὲν πάππος πονεῖ
ἐν τῷ κήπῳ, ὁ δὲ παῖς καὶ ὁ Ἄργος βαδίζουσι πρὸς τὸ αὔλιον· ὁ
Ἄργος κύων ἐστὶ μέγας τε καὶ ἰσχῡρός· τήν τε οἰκίᾱν φυλάττει καὶ τὰ
μῆλα. ἐπεὶ δὲ βαδίζουσιν ὅ τε παῖς καὶ ὁ κύων ἀνὰ τὴν ὁδόν, ὁ
Φίλιππος λαγὼν ὁρᾷ ἐν τῷ ἀγρῷ· λύει οὖν τὸν κύνα καί, "ἴθι δή,   5
Ἄργε," φησίν· "δίωκε." ὁ μὲν οὖν Ἄργος ὑλακτεῖ καὶ διώκει τὸν
λαγών, ὁ δὲ λαγὼς φεύγει ἀνὰ τὸ ὄρος. οὕτω δὲ ταχέως τρέχουσιν
ὥστε δι' ὀλίγου οὐ δυνατόν ἐστιν ὁρᾶν οὔτε τὸν κύνα οὔτε τὸν
λαγών.

[ἐν ᾧ while   τῷ κήπῳ the garden   τὸ αὔλιον the sheepfold   ὑλακτεῖ barks]

ὁ οὖν Φίλιππος σπεύδει μετὰ αὐτοὺς καὶ βοᾷ, "ἐλθὲ δεῦρο, Ἄργε·   10
ἐπάνελθε, ὦ κύον κατάρᾱτε." ἀλλ' ἔτι διώκει ὁ κύων. τρέχει οὖν ὁ
Φίλιππος εἰς ἄκρον τὸ ὄρος ἀλλ' οὐχ ὁρᾷ τὸν κύνα. μέγα οὖν βοᾷ
καὶ καλεῖ, ἀλλ' οὐκ ἀκούει ὁ Ἄργος. τέλος δὲ ἀθῡμεῖ ὁ παῖς καὶ
καταβαίνει τὸ ὄρος.

[μετὰ αὐτούς after them   ἐπάνελθε come back!   κατάρᾱτε cursed   μέγα
loudly   τέλος finally   ἀθῡμεῖ despairs]

ἐπεὶ δὲ προσχωρεῖ τῷ κήπῳ, ὁρᾷ αὐτὸν ὁ πάππος καί, "τί ποιεῖς, ὦ   15
παῖ;" φησίν· "πόθεν ἥκεις καὶ ποῦ ἐστιν ὁ Ἄργος;" ὁ δὲ Φίλιππος,
"ἀπὸ τοῦ αὐλίου ἥκω, ὦ πάππε· ὁ δὲ Ἄργος ἐστί που ἐν τοῖς ὄρεσιν·
λαγὼν γὰρ διώκει." ὁ δὲ πάππος, "ἴθι δή, ὦ παῖ· διὰ τί οὐ ζητεῖς αὐτόν;
μὴ οὕτω ῥᾴθῡμος ἴσθι." ὁ δὲ Φίλιππος, "οὐ ῥᾴθῡμός εἰμι, ὦ πάππε,
οὐδὲ αἴτιος ἐγώ. μέγα γὰρ βοῶ καὶ καλῶ, ἀλλ' οὐκ ἀκούει ὁ κύων."   20
ὁ δὲ πάππος, "ἐλθὲ δεῦρο, ὦ παῖ," φησίν. οὕτω λέγει καὶ τὸ βάκτρον
λαμβάνει καὶ σπεύδει ἅμα τῷ παιδὶ ἀνὰ τὴν ὁδόν.

[πόθεν ἥκεις from where have you come?   που somewhere   τὸ βάκτρον his
stick   ἅμα (+ dat.) together with]

Word Study

*Identify the Greek roots in the English words below and give the meanings of the
English words:*

1. geology
2. geography
3. geometry (what was the original meaning of geometry?)
4. geocentric

Grammar

1. Contract Verbs in -α-

In this chapter you have seen several contract verbs with stems in -α- instead of in -ε-, as were the contract verbs you saw in earlier chapters. Contract verbs in -α- show their endings as follows:

τῑμα- honor

Indicative:

	Singular		**Plural**	
1st	τῑμά-ω >	τῑμῶ	τῑμά-ομεν >	τῑμῶμεν
2nd	τῑμά-εις >	τῑμᾷς	τῑμά-ετε >	τῑμᾶτε
3rd	τῑμά-ει >	τῑμᾷ	τῑμά-ουσι(ν) >	τῑμῶσι(ν)

Imperative:

τίμα-ε >	τίμᾱ	τῑμά-ετε >	τῑμᾶτε

Infinitive: τῑμά-ειν > τῑμᾶν

The following rules for these contractions may be observed:

1. α + ω, ο, or ου > ω.
2. α + ει or ε > ᾱ, with the iota becoming a subscript (the infinitive is an exception to this rule).

Exercise 5a

Locate seven -α- contract verb forms in the reading passage at the beginning of this chapter.

2. Agreement of Subject and Verb

Note that in Greek neuter plural subjects are followed by singular verbs, e.g.:

τὰ ἄροτρα μῑκρά ἐστιν.
τὰ μῆλα ἐν τῷ ἀγρῷ μένει.

Translate the examples above.

3. Article at the Beginning of a Clause

The article + δέ is often used at the beginning of a clause to indicate a change of subject; the article is translated as a pronoun, e.g.:

ὁ δεσπότης τὸν δοῦλον καλεῖ· **ὁ δὲ** οὐ πάρεστιν.
The master calls the slave, *but he* is not present.

ὁ πατὴρ τὴν κόρην καλεῖ· **ἡ δὲ** ταχέως προσχωρεῖ.
The father calls the girl, *and she* approaches quickly.

Exercise 5b

Read and translate the following forms and then give the corresponding singular forms:

1. τῑμᾶτε
2. φιλοῦσι
3. ὁρῶμεν
4. οἰκεῖτε

5. ποιοῦμεν
6. βοῶσιν
7. ὁρᾶτε
8. πονοῦσιν

Exercise 5c

Read and translate the following forms and then give the corresponding plural forms:

1. τῑμᾷ
2. φιλεῖς
3. ζητῶ
4. ὁρῶ

5. βοᾷς
6. οἰκεῖ
7. φίλει
8. τῑμᾱ

Exercise 5d

Translate the following pairs of sentences:

1. ὁ κύων τὸν λαγὼν ὁρᾷ καὶ διώκει πρὸς ἄκρον τὸ ὄρος.
   Father shouts loudly and calls the slave out of the house.
2. ἆρ᾽ ὁρᾶτε τὸν λαγών; διὰ τί οὐ λύετε τὸν κύνα;
   What are you doing, friends? Why are you silent (σῑγάω)?
3. οὕτω κωφός (deaf) ἐστιν ὁ ἀνὴρ ὥστε αἰεὶ μέγα βοῶμεν.
   The boy is so brave that we honor him greatly (μέγα).
4. ἐν νῷ ἔχομεν πρὸς τὸ ἄστυ (the city) βαδίζειν καὶ τοὺς χοροὺς ὁρᾶν.
   We wish to walk to the temple (τὸ ἱερόν) and honor the god (ὁ θεός).
5. μὴ οὕτω ῥᾴθῡμος ἴσθι, ὦ παῖ· ἴθι πρὸς τὸ ὄρος καὶ ζήτει τὸν κύνα.
   Don't be so difficult, grandfather. I am not to blame.

4. Elision

If a word ends in a short vowel, this vowel may be elided (cut off) when the following word starts with a vowel, e.g., δι᾽ ὀλίγου = διὰ ὀλίγου. Note that the elision is marked by an apostrophe. Further examples are ἆρ᾽ ἐθέλεις = ἆρα ἐθέλεις and ἀλλ᾽ ἰδού = ἀλλὰ ἰδού.

If the following word begins with an aspirated vowel (i.e., a vowel with a rough breathing), the consonant left after elision is itself aspirated if possible, i.e., κ becomes χ, π becomes φ, and τ becomes θ. Thus, κατὰ ἡμέρᾱν ("daily") becomes καθ᾽ ἡμέρᾱν.

Elision always occurs when a compound verb is formed by prefixing a preposition that ends in a vowel to a verb that begins with a vowel, e.g.:

ἀνα- + αἴρω > ἀναίρω	ἀπο- + ἐλαύνω > ἀπελαύνω
ἐπι- + αἴρω > ἐπαίρω	ἀπο- + αἱρέω > ἀφαιρέω
παρα- + εἰμί > πάρειμι	κατα- + ὁράω > καθοράω

Gods and Men

Life-size bronze statue of Zeus hurling a thunderbolt

When Dicaeopolis was about to start plowing, he first made a prayer to Demeter, goddess of grain. When he is about to take his family to Athens to the festival of Dionysus, god of wine, he first goes to the altar in the courtyard of his house and pours a libation (drink offering) to Zeus, father of gods and men. Religion permeated Greek life; prayer and offerings were daily obligations. Hesiod, the eighth-century poet, says:

> Appease the immortal gods with libations and sacrifices, when you go to bed and when the holy light returns, that so they may have a kindly heart and spirit toward you, and you may buy other people's land and not have someone else buy yours. (*Works and Days,* 338–341).

The Greeks were polytheists (that is, they worshiped many gods), and their religion was an amalgam of many elements. For instance, when Greek speakers first entered Greece from the north about 2,000 B.C., they brought with them as their principal deity Zeus the Father (Ζεὺς πατήρ = Latin *Juppiter*). The religion of the older inhabitants of Greece centered around a goddess, the Earth Mother, worshiped under various names, including Demeter. Eventually the various deities of different localities and different origins were united into the family of the twelve Olympian gods. They were called Olympian because they were thought to live on the top of the heavenly mountain Olympus, and each god had his (or her) special sphere of influence. Zeus was lord of the thunderbolt and father of gods and men; Hera was his wife and the patron goddess of women; Athena was his daughter and the goddess of wisdom and crafts; Apollo was the god of light, prophecy, and healing; Artemis, his sister, was a virgin huntress and goddess of the moon; Poseidon, Zeus' brother, was god of the sea; Aphrodite was goddess of love; Hermes was the messenger of the gods and bringer of good luck; Hephaestus was the god of fire and smiths; Ares was the god of war; Dionysus was the god of wine; and Demeter was the goddess of grain (for the Greek names, see page xi). Besides the great Olympians, there were many lesser gods, such as Pan and the nymphs, and many foreign gods whose worship was introduced to Greece at various times and who joined the pantheon.

There were in Greek religion no church, no dogma, and no professional full-time priests. Temples were built as the homes of the deity to which they were dedicated; no services were held inside, and the altar at which offerings were made stood in the open outside the temple. The gods were worshiped with prayer and offerings, both privately by the family and publicly by the deme and state at regular festivals recurring throughout the year. The usual offering in private worship was a libation of wine poured over the altar or a pinch of incense burnt in the altar fire. Public ritual culminated in animal sacrifice by the priest of the cult, often on a large scale, followed by a public banquet.

The gods were conceived in human form, and human characteristics were attributed to them. They were immortal, all powerful, and arbitrary. They were primarily interested not in the behavior of humans toward each other (morality) but in the maintenance of the honors due to themselves, and in this respect they were demanding and jealous. If you gave the gods the honors and offerings that were their due, you could expect them to repay you with their help and protection. At the beginning of Homer's *Iliad*, Chryses, whose daughter the Greeks have captured and refuse to return for ransom, prays to Apollo:

> Hearken to me, God of the Silver Bow, protector of Chryse and holy Cilla, mighty ruler of Tenedus, Smintheus, if ever I have built a temple pleasing to you, if ever I have burnt the rich thighs of a bull or a goat for you, fulfill now my prayers: may the Greeks pay for my tears through your arrows.

Chryses prays to Apollo by two of his cult titles (the meaning of the second, Smintheus, is not known for certain) and three of the centers of his worship (the gods were not omnipresent, and Apollo might be resident in any one of these places). Chryses reminds Apollo of past services and only then makes his request, that Apollo may punish the Greeks by striking them down with disease (Apollo's arrows brought sickness and death—since he was the god of healing, he was also the god who sent sickness). The prayer was answered, and the Greeks were struck by plague.

Ο ΛΥΚΟΣ (β)

ὁ Ἄργος ὁρμᾷ ἐπὶ τὸν λύκον.

Vocabulary

Verbs
γιγνώσκω I get to know, learn
ἥκω I have come
θαυμάζω I wonder at, am
   amazed, admire
πάσχω I suffer, experience

Noun
ὁ μῦθος story

Pronouns
ἡμεῖς we
ὑμεῖς you (*plural*)

Adjectives
ἀγαθός, -ή, -όν good
ἄγριος, -ᾱ, -ον savage, wild,
   fierce
πρῶτος, -η, -ον first

Intensive Adjective/Pronoun
αὐτός, -ή, -ό (*intensive
   adjective*) -self, -selves;
   (*pronoun*) him, her, it, them

Prepositions
ἐπί (+ *dat.*) upon, on, (+ *acc.*) at,
   against
ὑπό (+ *dat.*) under

Adverbs
ἐνταῦθα then, there, here
νῦν now

Conjunctions and Particles
καί . . . καί both . . . and
ὅτι that

Expression
ἐνταῦθα δή at that very
   moment, then

ἐπεὶ δὲ τῷ αὐλίῳ προσχωροῦσι ὅ τε Φίλιππος καὶ ὁ πάππος,
πολὺν ψόφον ἀκούουσιν· ὑλακτεῖ γὰρ ἀγρίως ὁ Ἄργος, τὰ δὲ μῆλα
πολὺν θόρυβον ποιεῖ. σπεύδουσιν οὖν· ἐθέλουσι γὰρ γιγνώσκειν τί
πάσχει τὰ μῆλα. πρῶτος οὖν πάρεστιν ὁ παῖς καὶ ἰδού—ὁ μὲν
Ἄργος μένει πρὸς τῇ ὁδῷ καὶ ἀγρίως ὑλακτεῖ, καταβαίνει δὲ ἐκ τοῦ   5

ὄρους πρὸς τὸ αὔλιον λύκος μέγας. ὁ μὲν οὖν Φίλιππος μέγα βοᾷ
καὶ λίθους λαμβάνει καὶ βάλλει τὸν λύκον· ὁ δὲ Ἄργος ὁρμᾷ ἐπ᾿
αὐτὸν καὶ οὕτως ἀγρίως ἐμπίπτει ὥστε ἀναστρέφει ὁ λύκος καὶ
ἀποφεύγει. διώκει μὲν οὖν ὁ κύων, ὁ δὲ Φίλιππος σπεύδει μετὰ αὐτόν.

[ψόφον noise   θόρυβον uproar   βάλλει pelts   ὁρμᾷ rushes   ἐμπίπτει falls
upon, attacks   ἀναστρέφει turns back   μετὰ αὐτόν after him]

ὁ δὲ πάππος ἤδη εἰς ἄκρον τὸ ὄρος ἥκει καὶ τὸν λύκον ὁρᾷ καὶ   10
βοᾷ, "ἐλθὲ δεῦρο, Φίλιππε· μὴ δίωκε ἀλλ᾿ ἐπάνελθε." νῦν δὲ ὁ
Ἄργος τὸν λύκον λαμβάνει καὶ ὅδαξ ἔχει, ὁ δὲ Φίλιππος ἤδη
πάρεστι καὶ τὴν μάχαιραν λαμβάνει καὶ τύπτει τὸν λύκον. ὁ δὲ
ἀσπαίρει καὶ καταπίπτει πρὸς τὴν γῆν.

[ὅδαξ with his teeth   τὴν μάχαιραν his knife   τύπτει strikes   ἀσπαίρει
shudders]

ἐνταῦθα δὴ προσχωρεῖ ὁ πάππος καὶ τὸν λύκον ὁρᾷ ἐπὶ τῇ γῇ   15
κείμενον. θαυμάζει οὖν καί, "εὖ γε, ὦ παῖ," φησίν· "μάλα ἀνδρεῖος εἶ.
μέγας γάρ ἐστιν ὁ λύκος καὶ ἄγριος. σὺ δέ, ὦ Ἄργε, ἀγαθὸς εἶ κύων·
εὖ γὰρ τὰ μῆλα φυλάττεις. νῦν δέ, Φίλιππε, οἴκαδε σπεῦδε· ἡ γὰρ
μήτηρ δήπου ἐθέλει γιγνώσκειν ποῦ εἶ καὶ τί πάσχεις."

[ἐνταῦθα δή at that very moment   κείμενον lying   εὖ γε well done!   δήπου
I suppose]

ἐπεὶ δὲ τῇ οἰκίᾳ προσχωροῦσιν, τὴν μητέρα ὁρῶσιν. ὁ μὲν οὖν   20
πάππος σπεύδει πρὸς αὐτὴν καὶ πάντα λέγει. ἡ δέ, "ἆρα ἀληθῆ
λέγεις;" φησίν. "εὖ γε, ὦ παῖ· μάλα ἀνδρεῖος εἶ. ἀλλ᾿ ἰδού—προσχωρεῖ
ἡ Μέλιττα ἀπὸ τῆς κρήνης. ἐλθὲ δεῦρο, ὦ Μέλιττα, καὶ ἄκουε· ὁ γὰρ
Φίλιππος λύκον ἀπέκτονεν." ὁ μὲν οὖν πάππος πάντα αὖθις λέγει, ἡ
δὲ Μέλιττα μάλιστα θαυμάζει καὶ λέγει ὅτι καὶ ὁ Ἄργος καὶ ὁ   25
Φίλιππος μάλα ἀνδρεῖοί εἰσι καὶ ἰσχυροί.

[πάντα everything   ἀληθῆ the truth   ἀπέκτονεν has killed]

ἔπειτα δὲ ἡ μήτηρ, "νῦν δὲ ἐλθὲ δεῦρο, ὦ φίλε," φησίν, "καὶ κάθιζε
μεθ᾿ ἡμῶν ὑπὸ τῷ δένδρῳ· μάλα γὰρ κάμνεις. σὺ δέ, Μέλιττα, κάθιζε
καὶ σύ. ἀκούετε οὖν· ἐγὼ γὰρ ἐθέλω καλὸν μῦθον ὑμῖν εἰπεῖν."

[μεθ᾿ ἡμῶν with us   κάμνεις you are tired   ὑμῖν to you   εἰπεῖν to tell]

ὁ μὲν οὖν πάππος καθεύδει—μάλα γὰρ κάμνει—οἱ δὲ παῖδες   30
καθίζουσιν ὑπὸ τῷ δένδρῳ καὶ ἀκούουσιν· ἐθέλουσι γὰρ ἀκούειν
τὸν μῦθον.

Word Building

From your knowledge of the verbs at the left, deduce the meaning of the nouns at the right:

1. βοάω   ἡ βοή
2. τῑμάω   ἡ τῑμή
3. ὁρμάω (I rush)   ἡ ὁρμή
4. νῑκάω (I defeat, win)   ἡ νίκη
5. τελευτάω (I end, die)   ἡ τελευτή

Grammar

5. Personal Pronouns

In previous chapters you have met the personal pronouns ἐγώ "I" and σύ "you" (nominative singular) and αὐτόν "him" or "it" (accusative singular) and αὐτό "it" (accusative singular). Forms of the personal pronouns in the dative case (μοι and ὕμῖν) appear in the reading passage above. The full declensions of the personal pronouns are given below:

	1st Person Singular			*1st Person Plural*	
Nom.	ἐγώ		I	ἡμεῖς	we
Gen.	ἐμοῦ	μου	of me	ἡμῶν	of us
Dat.	ἐμοί	μοι	to *or* for me	ἡμῖν	to *or* for us
Acc.	ἐμέ	με	me	ἡμᾶς	us

	2nd Person Singular			*2nd Person Plural*	
Nom.	σύ		you	ὑμεῖς	you
Gen.	σοῦ	σου	of you	ὑμῶν	of you
Dat.	σοί	σοι	to *or* for you	ὑμῖν	to *or* for you
Acc.	σέ	σε	you	ὑμᾶς	you

Note: the unaccented forms are unemphatic and enclitic.

There is no 3rd person pronoun, but in the genitive, dative, and accusative cases forms of αὐτός "self" are used in its place.

	Masculine		*Feminine*		*Neuter*	
Singular						
Nom.	αὐτός	himself	αὐτή	herself	αὐτό	itself
Gen.	αὐτοῦ	of him *or* it	αὐτῆς	of her *or* it	αὐτοῦ	of it
Dat.	αὐτῷ	to *or* for him *or* it	αὐτῇ	to *or* for her *or* it	αὐτῷ	to it
Acc.	αὐτόν	him *or* it	αὐτήν	her *or* it	αὐτό	it

Plural

Nom.	αὐτοί	themselves	αὐταί	themselves	αὐτά	themselves
Gen.	αὐτῶν	of them	αὐτῶν	of them	αὐτῶν	of them
Dat.	αὐτοῖς	to or for them	αὐταῖς	to or for them	αὐτοῖς	to or for them
Acc.	αὐτούς	them	αὐτάς	them	αὐτά	them

The words αὐτός, αὐτή, and αὐτό (nominative) are *intensive adjectives* meaning "-self," "-selves," e.g.: **αὐτὸς** αἴρει τὸν λίθον, "He *himself* lifts the stone" (note that the "he" is implied in the 3rd person singular verb). They are used only for emphasis. In the other cases these words serve as a 3rd person pronoun and are translated "him," "her," "it," etc.

Note also that the 3rd person pronouns can refer to either persons or things. When they refer to things, the gender of the pronoun depends on the gender of the noun to which it refers, e.g.: ὁ Ξανθίας αἴρει τὸν λίθον. αἴρει **αὐτόν** ("He lifts *it*"). The word αὐτόν is translated "it," but it is masculine because it refers to the masculine noun λίθον.

Exercise 5e

Look back through story α in Chapter 3 and story β in Chapter 5 and locate at least eight examples of personal pronouns and forms of αὐτός in each story.

6. Possessive Adjectives

The following possessive adjectives correspond to the personal pronouns above:

1st Person Singular
ἐμός, -ή, -όν my, mine

1st Person Plural
ἡμέτερος, -ᾱ, -ον our

2nd Person Singular
σός, -ή, -όν your

2nd Person Plural
ῡμέτερος, -ᾱ, -ον your

There is no possessive adjective for the 3rd person, but instead the genitive of αὐτός is used:

Masculine	αὐτοῦ	of him, his, of it, its
Feminine	αὐτῆς	of her, her, of it, its
Neuter	αὐτοῦ	of it, its
M, F, N (plural)	αὐτῶν	of them, their

These possessive genitives stand outside the article-noun group to which they belong, and they refer to someone other than the subject of the verb (they are not reflexive), e.g.:

ὁ πάππος τῷ παιδὶ βοηθεῖ· ὁ δὲ τὴν μάχαιραν **αὐτοῦ** λαμβάνει.
Grandfather comes to help the boy; and he (the boy) takes *his* (the grandfather's) knife.

These genitives are said to be in the predicate position (see below, Grammar 7) with respect to the article-noun group to which they belong.

Note that Greek frequently does not use possessives if the possessor is the same as the subject of the verb, e.g.:

ὁ Φίλιππος τὴν μάχαιραν λαμβάνει καὶ τύπτει τὸν λύκον.
Philip takes his knife and strikes the wolf.

7. Attributive and Predicate Position

a. Attributive Position

Note the position of the adjective in the following phrases:

ἡ καλὴ οἰκίᾱ or ἡ οἰκίᾱ ἡ καλή

Both phrases mean "the beautiful house." The adjective is said to be in the *attributive* position in these examples, in which it is placed either between the article and the noun or after the repeated article.

b. Predicate Position.

In the following examples the adjective stands outside the article-noun group. The following examples constitute complete sentences (note that the verb "to be" may be omitted in simple sentences of this sort), and the adjective is said to be in the *predicate* position:

καλὴ ἡ οἰκίᾱ. or ἡ οἰκίᾱ καλή. = The house is beautiful.

The possessive genitives of αὐτός occupy this predicate position with respect to their article-noun group, that is, they always stand outside of it: e.g., ἡ μάχαιρα αὐτοῦ.

8. Feminine Nouns of the Second Declension

Some nouns of the second declension decline like ἀγρός but are feminine in gender: e.g., ἡ ὁδός.

Exercise 5f

Read aloud and translate:

1. ἐλθὲ δεῦρο, ὦ παῖ· ὁ γὰρ ἡμέτερος δεσπότης ἡμᾶς καλεῖ.
2. τί ποιεῖτε, ὦ δοῦλοι; ἐγὼ μὲν γὰρ ὑμᾶς καλῶ, ὑμεῖς δὲ οὐκ ἀκούετε.
3. ἆρ' οὐκ ἀκούετέ μου; φέρετέ μοι τὸ ἄροτρον.
4. ἀλλ', ὦ δέσποτα, νῦν φέρομεν αὐτό σοι.
5. κάθιζε μεθ' ἡμῶν, ὦ παῖ, καὶ λέγε μοι τί πάσχεις.
6. τὸν ἐμὸν κύνα ζητῶ, ὦ πάτερ· ὁ δὲ φεύγει ἀνὰ τὴν ὁδὸν καὶ οὐκ ἐθέλει ἐπανιέναι (*to come back*).
7. θάρσει (*cheer up*), ὦ παῖ· ἐγὼ γὰρ τὴν φωνὴν (*voice*) αὐτοῦ ἀκούω. ζήτει οὖν αὐτόν.
8. ὁρῶ αὐτὸν ἐπὶ ἄκρῳ τῷ ὄρει· ἰδού, νῦν τρέχει πρὸς ἡμᾶς.

9. ἄγριος μὲν ὁ λύκος καὶ μέγας, ὁ δὲ παῖς τὴν μάχαιραν λαμβάνει καὶ τύπτει αὐτόν.

10. ὁ μὲν πάππος ἤδη πάρεστιν, ὁ δὲ Φίλιππος τὴν μάχαιραν αὐτοῦ λαμβάνει καὶ ἀποκτείνει (*kills*) τὸν λύκον.

* * *

Ο ΑΡΓΟΣ ΤΑ ΜΗΛΑ ΣΩΙΖΕΙ

Read the following passages and answer the comprehension questions:

ὅ τε Φίλιππος καὶ ὁ πατὴρ βραδέως βαδίζουσιν ἀνὰ τὴν ὁδόν· ζητοῦσιν γὰρ τὰ μῆλα. ἐπεὶ δὲ εἰς ἄκρον τὸ ὄρος ἥκουσιν, τὰ μῆλα ὁρῶσιν· μένει γὰρ πρὸς τῇ ὁδῷ καὶ πολὺν θόρυβον ποιεῖ. ὁ οὖν Δικαιόπολις, "τί πάσχει τὰ μῆλα;" φησίν· "σπεῦδε κατὰ τὴν ὁδόν, ὦ παῖ, καὶ γίγνωσκε διὰ τί τοσοῦτον θόρυβον ποιεῖ." ὁ οὖν Φίλιππος σπεύδει κατὰ τὴν ὁδόν. ἐπεὶ δὲ τοῖς μήλοις προσχωρεῖ, μέγαν λύκον ὁρᾷ· τὸν οὖν   5
πατέρα καλεῖ καὶ βοᾷ· "ἐλθὲ δεῦρο, ὦ πάτερ, καὶ βοήθει· μέγας γὰρ λύκος πάρεστι καὶ μέλλει τοῖς μήλοις ἐμπίπτειν."

[μένει . . . ποιεῖ they are staying . . . they are making (*note the neuter plural subject of these singular verbs*)   μέλλει is about to   ἐμπίπτειν (+ *dat.*) to fall upon, attack]

1. What are Philip and his father seeking?
2. Where do they see the flocks? What are the flocks doing?
3. What does Philip see when he approaches the flocks?
4. What does he urge his father to do?

ὁ οὖν Δικαιόπολις τὸν κύνα λύει καί, "ἴθι δή, Ἄργε," φησίν· "τὸν λύκον δίωκε· σὺ δέ, ὦ παῖ, μένε ἐνταῦθα." ὁ μὲν οὖν Φίλιππος μένει πρὸς τῇ ὁδῷ, ὁ δὲ Ἄργος ὑλακτεῖ καὶ οὕτως ἀγρίως ὁρμᾷ ἐπὶ τὸν λύκον ὥστε ὁ λύκος ἀποφεύγει. ὁ δὲ   10
Φίλιππος καὶ ὁ πατὴρ τρέχουσι μετ' αὐτοὺς καὶ βοῶσι καὶ λίθους βάλλουσιν. ἐνταῦθα δὴ τὸν κύνα καλοῦσι καὶ τὰ μῆλα οἴκαδε ἐλαύνουσιν.

[μετ' αὐτούς after them   βάλλουσιν throw]

5. What does Dicaeopolis do?
6. Does Philip obey his father?
7. What does Argus do? With what result?
8. What do Philip and his father do at the end of the story?

Exercise 5g

Translate into Greek:

1. We do not see many wolves in the hills now, and they rarely (σπανίως) come down into the fields.
2. And so we are amazed that Philip has killed (ἀπέκτονε) a wolf.
3. He is a good boy and guards the flocks well (εὖ), but he does not always speak (say) the truth (τὰ ἀληθῆ).
4. And so we intend to hurry to the hill and look for the body (ὁ νεκρός).

6
Ο ΜΥΘΟΣ (α)

ὅ τε Θησεὺς καὶ οἱ ἑταῖροι ἀφικνοῦνται εἰς τὴν Κρήτην.

Vocabulary

Verbs
ἀποκτείνω I kill
ἀφικνέομαι I arrive, arrive at
  (+ εἰς + *acc.*)
βασιλεύω I rule
βοηθέω (+ *dat.*) I help
βούλομαι I want, wish
γίγνομαι I become
  γίγνεται he, she, it becomes;
  it happens
δέχομαι I receive
ἔρχομαι I come, go
  ἀπέρχομαι I go away
πείθομαι (+ *dat.*) I obey
πέμπω I send
πλέω I sail
σῴζω I save
φοβέομαι I fear, am afraid of
  (something or someone), am
  frightened, am afraid

Nouns
ὁ βασιλεύς king
ὁ ἑταῖρος comrade, companion

ἡ ἡμέρᾱ day
ὁ λαβύρινθος labyrinth
**ἡ ναῦς (τῆς νεώς, τῇ νηΐ, τὴν
  ναῦν)** ship
ἡ νῆσος island
ἡ νύξ night
ὁ πάππας (ὦ πάππα) father,
  papa
ἡ παρθένος maiden, girl
Adjective
δεινός, -ή, -όν terrible
Preposition
μετά (+ *gen.*) with
Adverb
ἐκεῖ there
Proper Names
αἱ Ἀθῆναι Athens
ὁ Αἰγεύς Aegeus, king of
  Athens
ἡ Ἀριάδνη Ariadne, daughter
  of King Minos
**ὁ Θησεύς (τὸν Θησέᾱ, ὦ
  Θησεῦ)** Theseus, son of King
  Aegeus

ἡ Κνωσσός Knossos
ἡ Κρήτη Crete
ὁ Μῑνώταυρος Minotaur

ὁ Μίνως (τοῦ Μίνωος)
Minos, king of Crete

"ὁ Μίνως οἰκεῖ ἐν τῇ Κρήτῃ· βασιλεὺς δέ ἐστι τῆς νήσου. καὶ ἐν τῇ
τοῦ Μίνωος οἰκίᾳ ἐστὶν ὁ λαβύρινθος· ἐκεῖ δ' οἰκεῖ ὁ Μῑνώταυρος,
θηρίον τι δεινόν, τὸ μὲν ἥμισυ ἄνθρωπος, τὸ δ' ἥμισυ ταῦρος. ὁ δὲ
Μῑνώταυρος ἐσθίει ἀνθρώπους. ὁ οὖν Μίνως ἀναγκάζει τοὺς
Ἀθηναίους ἑπτά τε νεᾱνίᾱς πέμπειν καὶ ἑπτὰ παρθένους κατ' ἔτος   5
πρὸς τὴν Κρήτην καὶ παρέχει αὐτοὺς τῷ Μῑνωταύρῳ ἐσθίειν.

[θηρίον τι a certain beast   τὸ . . . ἥμισυ half   ταῦρος bull   ἐσθίει eats
ἀναγκάζει compels   ἑπτά seven   νεᾱνίᾱς youths   κατ' ἔτος each year
παρέχει gives   τῷ Μῑνωταύρῳ to the Minotaur]

"ἐν δὲ ταῖς Ἀθήναις βασιλεύει ὁ Αἰγεύς· ἔστι δὲ αὐτῷ παῖς τις
ὀνόματι Θησεύς. ὁ δὲ ἐπεὶ πρῶτον ἡβᾷ, τοὺς ἑταίρους οἰκτίρει καὶ
βούλεται βοηθεῖν αὐτοῖς. προσχωρεῖ οὖν τῷ πατρὶ καί, 'πάππα
φίλε,' φησίν, 'τοὺς ἑταίρους οἰκτίρω καὶ βούλομαι σῴζειν. πέμπε με   10
οὖν μετὰ τῶν ἑταίρων πρὸς τὴν Κρήτην.' ὁ δ' Αἰγεὺς μάλιστα
φοβεῖται ἀλλ' ὅμως πείθεται αὐτῷ.

[ἔστι . . . αὐτῷ there is for him, he has   παῖς τις a child   ὀνόματι by name
ἡβᾷ grows up   οἰκτίρει pities   ὅμως nevertheless]

"ὁ οὖν Θησεὺς εἰς τὴν ναῦν εἰσβαίνει μετὰ τῶν ἑταίρων καὶ πλεῖ
πρὸς τὴν Κρήτην. ἐπεὶ δὲ εἰς τὴν νῆσον ἀφικνοῦνται, ὅ τε βασιλεὺς
καὶ ἡ βασίλεια καὶ ἡ θυγάτηρ αὐτῶν, ὀνόματι Ἀριάδνη, δέχονται   15
αὐτοὺς καὶ ἄγουσι πρὸς τὴν Κνωσσόν (οὕτω γὰρ τὴν τοῦ Μίνωος
πόλιν ὀνομάζουσιν) καὶ φυλάττουσιν ἐν τῷ δεσμωτηρίῳ.

[ἡ βασίλεια the queen   τὴν . . . πόλιν the city   ὀνομάζουσιν they call   τῷ
δεσμωτηρίῳ the prison]

ἡ δ' Ἀριάδνη, ἐπεὶ πρῶτον ὁρᾷ τὸν Θησέᾱ, ἐρᾷ αὐτοῦ καὶ
βούλεται σῴζειν. ἐπεὶ οὖν γίγνεται ἡ νύξ, σπεύδει πρὸς τὸ
δεσμωτήριον καὶ τὸν Θησέᾱ καλεῖ καί, 'σῑγᾱ, ὦ Θησεῦ,' φησίν· 'ἐγώ,   20
Ἀριάδνη, πάρειμι. ἐρῶ σοῦ καὶ βούλομαι σῴζειν. ἰδού—παρέχω
γάρ σοι τοῦτο τὸ ξίφος καὶ τοῦτο τὸ λίνον. μὴ οὖν φοβοῦ ἀλλὰ
ἀνδρείως εἴσβαινε εἰς τὸν λαβύρινθον καὶ ἀπόκτεινε τὸν
Μῑνώταυρον. ἔπειτα δὲ ἔκφευγε μετὰ τῶν ἑταίρων καὶ σπεῦδε πρὸς
τὴν ναῦν. ἐγὼ γὰρ ἐν νῷ ἔχω πρὸς τῇ νηῒ μένειν· βούλομαι γὰρ ἀπὸ   25
τῆς Κρήτης ἀποφεύγειν καὶ μετὰ σοῦ πρὸς τὰς Ἀθήνᾱς πλεῖν.' οὕτω

λέγει καὶ ταχέως ἀπέρχεται πρὸς τὴν πόλιν. ὁ δὲ Θησεὺς μάλα μὲν θαυμάζει, δέχεται δὲ τὸ ξίφος καὶ μένει τὴν ἡμέρᾱν."

[ἐρᾷ αὐτοῦ loves him   σίγα be quiet   τοῦτο τὸ ξίφος this sword   τοῦτο τὸ λίνον this thread   μὴ . . . φοβοῦ don't be afraid!]

Word Study

Identify the Greek roots in the English words below and give the meanings of the English words:

1. phobia
2. acrophobia
3. agoraphobia
4. entomophobia
5. triskaidekaphobia
6. Anglophobia

Grammar

1. Verb Forms: Middle Voice

You have met many verbs that are *active* in voice and take direct objects, e.g.:

ὁ Μῑνώταυρος **ἐσθίει** ἀνθρώπους.
The Minotaur *eats* men.

Sentences of this sort can be turned around so that the direct object becomes the subject, e.g.:

Men *are eaten* by the Minotaur.

The verb is now said to be *passive* in voice, and the subject of the sentence is acted on rather than being the actor. The passive voice will be presented later in this course.

In Greek, verbs may be in a third voice termed *middle*. There are many Greek verbs that occur *only* in the middle voice; they are said to be *deponent*, as if they had "put aside" (Latin *dēpōnere*) or lost their active forms. In the vocabulary list and the first reading passage in this chapter you have met the following deponent verbs:

ἀφικνέομαι (+ εἰς + *acc.*) I arrive (at)
βούλομαι I wish
γίγνομαι I become, happen
δέχομαι I receive
ἔρχομαι I come, go
ἀπέρχομαι I go away

The verbs πείθομαι and φοβέομαι do not belong in this list because they may be used in the active voice. Deponent verbs do not have active forms.

Most active verbs also have middle voice forms.   One frequent difference between the active and middle voices of a verb is that the middle voice makes the verb intransitive.   In the active voice it is transitive and will take a direct object, e.g.,

ἐγείρω τὸν παῖδα. = "I wake the child."

In the middle voice it is intransitive and will not take a direct object , e.g.,

ἐγείρομαι. = "I wake up."

In this case the subject is thought of as acting *on* itself, and the verb in the middle voice is said to be *reflexive* ("I wake *myself*" = "I wake up").

Some verbs in the middle voice, however, are transitive and take direct objects, e.g., in the middle voice the verb λύω becomes λύομαι, and it means "I loosen or release (someone) for myself," "I secure the release of (someone)," or "I ransom (someone)," e.g.:

λύομαι τὸν αἰχμάλωτον, = "I ransom the captive."

Here the subject is thought of as acting *for* itself.

Verbs in the middle voice can easily be recognized from their endings, which are different from the endings of the active voice that you have learned in Chapters 1–5. Almost any verb can be used in the middle voice, and as samples of verbs in the middle, we will use our familiar λύω and φιλέω. In the case of the verb φιλέω there is no real difference in meaning between the active and middle voices; they both mean "I love."

In the following sets of forms note the *thematic* or *variable* vowels (o or ε) between the verb stem and the endings. In the second person singular indicative and the singular imperative, the σ at the beginning of the personal ending drops out between the vowels, and the vowels then contract. For the rules of contraction, see Chapter 4, Grammar 1, page 32:

Indicative:

	Singular	*Plural*
1st	λύ-ο-μαι	λῡ-ό-μεθα
2nd	λύ-ε-σαι > λύῃ *or* λύει	λύ-ε-σθε
3rd	λύ-ε-ται	λύ-ο-νται

Imperative:

	λύ-ε-σο > λύου	λύ-ε-σθε

Infinitive: λύ-ε-σθαι

Indicative:

1st	φιλέ-ο-μαι > φιλοῦμαι	φιλε-ό-μεθα > φιλούμεθα
2nd	φιλέ-ε-σαι > φιλῇ *or* φιλεῖ	φιλέ-ε-σθε > φιλεῖσθε
3rd	φιλέ-ε-ται > φιλεῖται	φιλέ-ο-νται > φιλοῦνται

Imperative:

φιλέ-ε-σο > φιλοῦ   φιλέ-ε-σθε > φιλεῖσθε

Infinitive:

φιλέ-ε-σθαι > φιλεῖσθαι

Exercise 6a

Locate twelve verbs in the middle voice in the reading passage at the beginning of this chapter, and translate the sentences in which they occur.

Exercise 6b

For practice, write out the forms of γίγνομαι *and* ἀφικνέομαι. *Write out only the contracted forms. Write translations of each form.*

Exercise 6c

Read aloud and translate the following sets of sentences containing verbs in the active and middle voices:

1. τὸν κύνα λούω (*wash*).
   ἡμεῖς λουόμεθα.
2. ἡ μήτηρ τὸν παῖδα ἐγείρει (*wakes*).
   ὁ παῖς ἐγείρεται.
3. ὁ δεσπότης τὸν δοῦλον τοῦ πόνου παύει (*stops from* + *gen.*).
   τοῦ πόνου παύομαι.
4. ὁ δοῦλος τοὺς λίθους αἴρει.
   ὁ δοῦλος ἐγείρεται καὶ αἴρει ἑαυτόν (*himself*).
5. οἱ παῖδες τὸν τρόχον (*the wheel, hoop*) τρέπουσιν (*turn*).
   ὁ δοῦλος πρὸς τὸν δεσπότην τρέπεται.

Exercise 6d

Change the following forms to their corresponding plurals:

1.	λύομαι	3.	δέχῃ	5.	ἀφικνεῖται
2.	βούλεται	4.	φοβοῦμαι	6.	γίγνομαι

Exercise 6e

Change the following forms to their corresponding singulars:

1.	λύεσθε	3.	βούλονται	5.	φοβούμεθα
2.	πειθόμεθα	4.	ἀφικνεῖσθε	6.	ἀφικνοῦνται

Exercise 6f

Read aloud and translate:

1. οἴκαδε βαδίζειν βουλόμεθα.
2. οὔ σε φοβοῦνται.
3. ῥᾴθῡμος γίγνῃ, ὦ δοῦλε.
4. εἰς τὴν Κρήτην ἀφικνούμεθα.
5. ὁ βασιλεὺς ἡμᾶς δέχεται.

Exercise 6g

Translate into Greek:

1. We want to stay.
2. I am not afraid of you.
3. They arrive at the island.
4. Don't be frightened, friends.
5. They are becoming lazy.

Myth

Athena decks out Pandora before sending her to Epimetheus

The Greek word μῦθος means "story," and the Greeks were great story-tellers. Many of the stories were of immemorial antiquity, told to all children at their mothers' knees. There were stories about the times before man existed at all, about times when men and gods were on much closer terms than they are today, and about the gods and the heroes of old. The myths included stories of widely differing types. Some, like the creation myths, were concerned exclusively or primarily with the gods. For instance, Hesiod (*Works and Days* 42–105) relates how the demigod Prometheus, in pity for mankind, stole fire from heaven and gave it to man:

Zeus the Cloud-gatherer, angry with Prometheus, said to him: "Prometheus, wise beyond all others, you are very pleased to have stolen fire and to have deceived me, but it shall be a cause of suffering both to you and to men to come. In return for the theft of fire, I shall give them a great evil, in which they shall all rejoice, hugging to themselves their own trouble." So spoke the Father of men and gods and laughed aloud. He ordered Hephaestus with all speed to mix earth and water, to put in it the speech and strength of a human, and in face to give it the fair, delightful form of a young girl like the immortal goddesses. He told Athena to teach it crafts to enable it to weave the rich web on the loom; he told golden Aphrodite to pour over its head grace and troublesome desire and pains that melt the limbs; but he bade Hermes put in it the mind of a dog and a deceitful character.

The gods and goddesses did as they were told, and Hermes called the woman Pandora, "because all (πάντες) the gods who live on Olympus gave (ἐδώρησαν) her a gift (δῶρον) for men who eat bread."

The Father sent the swift messenger of the gods, who took the gift to Epimetheus (Prometheus' brother). Epimetheus did not reflect on how Prometheus had told him never to accept a gift from Olympian Zeus but to send it back, lest it bring some evil to mortals. After he had received the evil, he remembered.

Before this men lived on earth free from troubles and hard toil and the grievous diseases that bring destruction.

But the woman took the lid off the great jar and scattered the contents, and so she brought suffering on the people. Hope alone remained inside in her indestructible home beneath the rim of the jar and did not fly out, for Pandora put the lid back before Hope could escape, through the will of Zeus the Cloud-gatherer. Countless troubles roam among the people. The earth is full of evils, and full is the sea. Diseases come upon men in the day and others come at night, bringing suffering to mortals, silently, since Zeus has taken from them the power of speech. It is impossible to escape the will of Zeus.

This myth offers an explanation of why men suffer diseases and other troubles. (Why, for instance, should men have to work for their food? In the Golden Age earth produced all manner of food spontaneously.) The story is told in allusive style: Pandora takes the lid off a great jar, from which all troubles fly out, but we are told nothing about this jar or about how it got there and why Pandora took the lid off. Hesiod's audience presumably knew the story, and he had no need to tell them. Nor is it clear why Hope is said to remain in the jar. Is the human condition hopeless?

Other myths are based on history or what the Greeks believed to be history. The story of Theseus and the Minotaur falls into this class. Theseus was an early king of Athens around whom a whole cycle of myths crystalized. He belonged to the generation before the Trojan War and was thought to be responsible for the unification of Attica. Minos, king of Knossos in Crete, was also believed to be a historical figure. Thucydides discusses the extent of his sea-power in the introduction to his history. *Labyrinthos* means in the ancient Cretan language "House of the Double Axe," which may have been the name of the great palace at Knossos, where the double axe frequently appears as a religious symbol. The large size and complicated plan of this palace may account for the change in meaning of the word *labyrinth* to its later sense of "maze."

Bull-jumping played an important part in Cretan ritual and is often portrayed in works of Cretan art. The bull-jumpers may well have been young captives taken from Athens and other places. We thus find in the myth of Theseus historical elements strangely transmuted in the course of time.

The myth of Odysseus and the Cyclops (Chapter 7) is taken from Homer's *Odyssey,* which is mainly concerned with the adventures of Odysseus during his journey home to Ithaca from Troy. It illustrates a third strand often found in Greek myth: folk tale. The story of the little man who outwits a one-eyed man-eating giant is found in the folk tales of many other peoples, and the whole structure of the story as told by Homer shows the symmetry common in folk tales.

The making of myths seems to be a universal human activity, and myths are said to enshrine the corporate wisdom of primitive peoples. Their interpretation remains a vexed question, on which no two scholars agree. The strands that go to form the corpus of Greek myth are so many and various that any attempt to form general rules for their interpretation seems doomed to failure. However we look at them, they are stories that have caught the imagination of Western man throughout recorded history.

Knossos, the throne room in the palace of Min

Ο ΜΥΘΟΣ (β)

ὁ Θησεὺς οὐ φοβεῖται ἀλλὰ ἀνδρείως μάχεται καὶ τὸν Μῑνώταυρον ἀποκτείνει.

Vocabulary

Verbs

ἐξέρχομαι (+ ἐκ + *gen.*) I go out of, come out of

ἡγέομαι (+ *dat.*) I lead

μάχομαι I fight

παρέχω I provide, give

πορεύομαι I go, walk, march, journey

προχωρέω I go forward, come forward, advance

τῑμάω I honor

τύπτω I strike

φᾱσί(ν) (*postpositive enclitic*) they say

Noun

αἱ πύλαι (*plural*) double gates

Adverbs

οὕτως = οὕτω so, thus

οὐχί (*an emphatic form of* οὐ, οὐκ, οὐχ) not, no!

πολλάκις many times, often

ὡς how

Particles

γε (*postpositive enclitic*) at least, indeed (*restrictive or intensive*)

δή (*postpositive*) indeed, in fact (*emphasizes that what is said is obvious or true*)

"ἐπεὶ δὲ γίγνεται ἡ ἡμέρᾱ, ὁ Μίνως ἔρχεται πρὸς τὸ δεσμωτήριον καὶ καλεῖ τόν τε Θησέᾱ καὶ τοὺς ἑταίρους καὶ ἄγει αὐτοὺς πρὸς τὸν λαβύρινθον. ἐπεὶ δὲ ἀφικνοῦνται, οἱ δοῦλοι ἀνοίγουσι τὰς πύλᾱς καὶ τοὺς Ἀθηναίους εἰσελαύνουσιν. ἔπειτα δὲ τὰς πύλᾱς κλείουσι καὶ ἀπέρχονται· οὕτω γὰρ τῷ Μῑνωταύρῳ σῖτον παρέχουσιν εἰς πολλὰς   5
ἡμέρᾱς. οἱ μὲν οὖν ἑταῖροι μάλιστα φοβοῦνται, ὁ δὲ Θησεύς, 'μὴ φοβεῖσθε, ὦ φίλοι,' φησίν· 'ἐγὼ γὰρ ῡμᾶς σώσω. ἕπεσθέ μοι οὖν ἀνδρείως.' οὕτω λέγει καὶ ἡγεῖται αὐτοῖς εἰς τὸν λαβύρινθον.

[ἀνοίγουσι open   κλείουσι they shut   εἰς for   σώσω I will save   ἕπεσθέ μοι follow me!]

"ὁ μὲν οὖν Θησεὺς ἐν μὲν τῇ ἀριστερᾷ ἔχει τὸ λίνον, ἐν δὲ τῇ δεξιᾷ τὸ ξίφος καὶ προχωρεῖ εἰς τὸν σκότον. οἱ δὲ ἑταῖροι μάλιστα 10 φοβοῦνται ἀλλ' ὅμως ἕπονται· ἡ γὰρ ἀνάγκη αὐτοὺς ἔχει. μακρὰν οὖν ὁδὸν πορεύονται καὶ πολλάκις μὲν τρέπονται, πολλάκις δὲ ψόφους δεινοὺς ἀκούουσιν· ὁ γὰρ Μῑνώταυρος διώκει αὐτοὺς ἐν τῷ σκότῳ καὶ μάλα δεινῶς βρῡχᾶται. ἐνταῦθα δὴ τὸν τῶν ποδῶν ψόφον ἀκούουσι καὶ τὸ τοῦ θηρίου πνεῦμα ὀσφραίνονται, καὶ ἰδού—ἐν τῇ 15 ὁδῷ πάρεστιν ὁ Μῑνώταυρος. δεινῶς δὴ βρῡχᾶται καὶ ἐπὶ τὸν Θησέα ὁρμᾶται.

[τῇ ἀριστερᾷ the left hand   τῇ δεξιᾷ the right hand   τὸν σκότον the darkness   ἡ . . . ἀνάγκη necessity   τρέπονται they turn   ψόφους noises βρῡχᾶται roars   τῶν ποδῶν of feet   τὸ τοῦ θηρίου πνεῦμα the breath of the beast   ὀσφραίνονται they smell   ὁρμᾶται rushes]

ὁ δὲ Θησεὺς οὐ φοβεῖται ἀλλὰ μάλα ἀνδρείως μάχεται· τῇ μὲν γὰρ ἀριστερᾷ λαμβάνεται τῆς κεφαλῆς τοῦ θηρίου, τῇ δὲ δεξιᾷ τὸ στῆθος τύπτει. ὁ δὲ Μῑνώταυρος δεινῶς κλάζει καὶ καταπίπτει πρὸς 20 τὴν γῆν. οἱ δὲ ἑταῖροι ἐπεὶ ὁρῶσι τὸ θηρίον ἐπὶ τῇ γῇ κείμενον, χαίρουσι καί, 'ὦ Θησεῦ,' φᾱσίν, 'ὡς ἀνδρεῖος εἶ· ὡς θαυμάζομέν σε καὶ τῑμῶμεν. ἀλλὰ νῦν γε σῷζε ἡμᾶς ἐκ τοῦ λαβυρίνθου καὶ ἡγοῦ πρὸς τὰς πύλᾱς. μακρὰ γάρ ἐστιν ἡ ὁδὸς καὶ πολὺς ὁ σκότος· τὴν δ' ὁδὸν ἀγνοοῦμεν.' 25

[λαμβάνεται τῆς κεφαλῆς takes hold of the head   τὸ στῆθος its breast κλάζει shrieks   κείμενον lying   ἀγνοοῦμεν we do not know]

"ὁ δὲ Θησεὺς οὐ φοβεῖται ἀλλὰ τὸ λίνον λαμβάνει—οὕτω γὰρ τὴν ὁδὸν γιγνώσκει—καὶ ἡγεῖται τοῖς ἑταίροις πρὸς τὰς πύλᾱς. ἐπεὶ δ' ἀφικνοῦνται, τὸν μόχλον διακόπτουσι καὶ μένουσιν ἐκεῖ· ἔτι γὰρ ἡμέρᾱ ἐστίν. ἐπεὶ δὲ γίγνεται ἡ νύξ, ἐξέρχονται ἐκ τοῦ λαβυρίνθου καὶ σπεύδουσι πρὸς τὴν ναῦν. ἐκεῖ δὲ τὴν Ἀριάδνην ὁρῶσιν· μένει 30 γὰρ πρὸς τῇ νηί. ταχέως οὖν εἰσβαίνουσι καὶ ἀποπλέουσι πρὸς τὰς Ἀθήνᾱς. οὕτως οὖν ὁ Θησεὺς τόν τε Μῑνώταυρον ἀποκτείνει καὶ τοὺς ἑταίρους σῷζει εἰς τὰς Ἀθήνᾱς."

[τὸν μόχλον the bolt   διακόπτουσι they cut through   σῷζει εἰς brings . . . safely to]

οὕτω περαίνει τὸν μῦθον ἡ Μυρρίνη, ἡ δὲ Μέλιττα, "καὶ ἡ Ἀριάδνη," φησίν· "ἆρα χαίρει; ἆρα φιλεῖ αὐτὴν ὁ Θησεύς;" ἡ δὲ

Μυρρίνη, "οὐχί· οὐ χαίρει ἡ Ἀριάδνη οὐδὲ φιλεῖ αὐτὴν ὁ Θησεύς." ἡ δὲ Μέλιττα, "διὰ τί οὐ φιλεῖ αὐτὴν ὁ Θησεύς; τί γίγνεται;" ἡ δὲ μήτηρ, "ἐκεῖνον τὸν μῦθον οὐκ ἐθέλω σοι εἰπεῖν νῦν γε."

[περαίνει ends   ἐκεῖνον that   εἰπεῖν to tell]

Word Building

Describe the relationship between the words in the following sets. From your knowledge of the words at the left, deduce the meaning of those on the right:

1. ὁ δοῦλος   ἡ δούλη
2. ὁ φίλος   ἡ φίλη
3. ὁ θεός   ἡ θεά
4. ὁ ἑταῖρος   ἡ ἑταίρᾱ
5. ὁ οἶκος   ἡ οἰκίᾱ

Grammar

2. Some Uses of the Dative Case

a. The *indirect object* of a verb is in the dative case, e.g., οὕτω γὰρ τῷ **Μῑνωταύρῳ** σῖτον παρέχουσιν = "In this way they give *the Minotaur* food" or "In this way they give food *to the Minotaur*." Here the word σῖτον is the direct object of the verb παρέχουσιν, and the words τῷ Μῑνωταύρῳ are the indirect object.

b. The dative case may be used to indicate the person who *possesses* something, e.g., ἔστιν **αὐτῷ** παῖς τις ὀνόματι Θησεύς, literally, "there is *for him* a child. . . . " (= "he has a child").

c. The Greek sentence in b above shows another use of the dative case, the dative of *respect*: **ὀνόματι** Θησεύς literally, "Theseus *with respect to his name*" (= "called Theseus").

d. The dative case may be used to indicate the *means* or *instrument* by which an action is carried out, e.g., τῇ μὲν γὰρ **ἀριστερᾷ** λαμβάνεται τῆς κεφαλῆς τοῦ θηρίου, τῇ δὲ **δεξιᾷ** τὸ στῆθος τύπτει = "*with his left hand* he takes hold of the head of the beast, and *with his right hand* he strikes its chest."

e. The dative case may be used to indicate the *time when* an action takes place, e.g., τῇ **ὑστεραίᾳ** "*on the next day*." Note that the Greek does not use a preposition here.

f. The dative case is used after certain prepositions, especially those that indicate the *place where* someone or something is or something happens, e.g., ἐν **τῇ ἀριστερᾷ** and πρὸς **τῇ νηΐ**.

g. The dative case is used with *certain verbs*, e.g.: οἱ βόες τῷ ἀγρῷ προσχωροῦσιν = "the oxen approach *the field*"; ὁ Αἰγεὺς πείθεται αὐτῷ = "Aegeus obeys *him*"; ἕπεσθέ μοι ἀνδρείως = "follow *me* bravely"; and ἡγεῖται αὐτοῖς εἰς τὸν λαβύρινθον = "he leads *them* into the labyrinth."

3. Prepositions

While, as seen above, prepositions that take the dative case usually refer to the *place where* someone or something is or *where* some action takes place, prepositions that take the genitive often express ideas of *place from which*, and prepositions that take the accusative often express ideas of *place to which*. Observe the following examples that have been given in the vocabulary lists so far:

With genitive: ἀπό from; ἐκ out of; μετά with (with this last example there is no sense of motion from a place)
With dative: ἐν in; ἐπί upon, on; πρός at, near, by; ὑπό under
With accusative: ἀνά up; εἰς into; ἐπί at, against; κατά down; πρός to, toward; παρά to the side of

Exercise 6h

Write out the following sentences, putting the nouns in the correct case, and then translate the sentences:

1. πρὸς (ὁ ἀγρός) ἐρχόμεθα.
2. πρὸς (ἡ ὁδός) καθίζουσιν.
3. ἐκ (ἡ οἰκία) σπεύδει.
4. ἀπὸ (ἡ νῆσος) πλέουσιν.
5. κατὰ (ἡ ὁδός) πορεύονται.
6. μετὰ (οἱ ἑταῖροι) φεύγει.
7. ἐν (ὁ λαβύρινθος) μένετε.
8. ἡγεῖσθε ἡμῖν πρὸς (ἡ κρήνη).
9. οἱ παῖδες τρέχουσιν ἀνὰ (ἡ ὁδός).
10. αἱ παρθένοι καθίζουσιν ὑπὸ (τὸ δένδρον).
11. ὁ κύων ὁρμᾶται ἐπὶ (ὁ λύκος).
12. οἱ ἑταῖροι εἰς (ὁ λαβύρινθος) εἰσέρχονται.

Exercise 6i

Read aloud, translate, and identify the uses of the dative case:

1. ὁ ἀνὴρ ὑμῖν οὐ πείθεται.
2. πείθεσθέ μοι, ὦ παῖδες.
3. πάρεχέ μοι τὸ ἄροτρον.
4. τὸν μῦθον τῷ παιδὶ λέγω.
5. ἔστι τῷ αὐτουργῷ ἄροτρον.
6. ὁ αὐτουργός, Δικαιόπολις ὀνόματι, τοῖς βουσὶν εἰς τὸν ἀγρὸν ἡγεῖται.
7. ὁ παῖς τὸν λύκον λίθοις βάλλει (*pelts*).

8.   ἡ γυνὴ τῷ ἀνδρὶ πολὺν σῖτον παρέχει.
9.   ὁ δεσπότης τοὺς δούλους τοσαύτῃ βοῇ καλεῖ ὥστε φοβοῦνται.
10. ἔστι τῷ παιδὶ καλὸς κύων.

Exercise 6j

Translate into Greek:

1.   Aren't you willing to obey me, boy?
2.   Tell (**εἰπέ**) me the story.
3.   I give you the plow.
4.   The farmer has a big ox. (*Use dative case.*)
5.   The young man (**ὁ νεᾱνίᾱς**), called Theseus, leads his comrades bravely.
6.   The boy strikes the wolf with a stone.
7.   The girl gives her friend food.
8.   The slave strikes the oxen with a goad (**τὸ κέντρον**).
9.   The girl approaches the gates.
10. On the next day the Athenians flee out of the labyrinth.

Exercise 6k

Translate the following pairs of sentences:

1.   ὁ Θησεὺς βούλεται τοὺς ἑταίρους σῴζειν.
     Aegeus is very afraid but obeys him.
2.   οἱ μὲν Ἀθηναῖοι ἀφικνοῦνται εἰς τὴν νῆσον, ὁ δὲ βασιλεὺς δέχεται αὐτούς.
     The comrades are very afraid, but Theseus leads them bravely.
3.   μὴ μάχεσθε, ὦ φίλοι, μηδὲ (*and don't*) βοᾶτε ἀλλὰ σῑγᾶτε (*be quiet*).
     Don't fear the Minotaur, friends, but be brave.
4.   ἐπεὶ γίγνεται ἡ νύξ, ἡ παρθένος ἔρχεται πρὸς τὰς πύλᾱς.
     When day comes (becomes), the ship arrives at the island.
5.   ἐπεὶ ὁ Θησεὺς ἀποκτείνει τὸν Μῑνώταυρον, ἑπόμεθα αὐτῷ ἐκ τοῦ λαβυρίνθου.
     When we are journeying to Crete, we see many islands.

Theseus deserts Ariadne.

Ο ΘΗΣΕΥΣ ΤΗΝ ΑΡΙΑΔΝΗΝ
ΚΑΤΑΛΕΙΠΕΙ

Read the following passages and answer the comprehension questions:

οὕτως οὖν ὁ Θησεὺς τοὺς ἑταίρους σῴζει καὶ ἀπὸ τῆς Κρήτης ἀποφεύγει. πρῶτον μὲν οὖν πρὸς νῆσόν τινα, Νάξον ὀνόματι, πλέουσιν. ἐπεὶ δὲ ἀφικνοῦνται, ἐκβαίνουσιν ἐκ τῆς νεὼς καὶ ἀναπαύονται. ἐπεὶ δὲ γίγνεται ἡ νύξ, οἱ μὲν ἄλλοι καθεύδουσιν· ὁ δὲ Θησεὺς οὐ καθεύδει ἀλλὰ ἥσυχος μένει· οὐ γὰρ φιλεῖ Ἀριάδνην οὐδὲ βούλεται φέρειν αὐτὴν πρὸς τὰς Ἀθήνας. δι' ὀλίγου οὖν, ἐπεὶ καθεύδει ἡ   5
Ἀριάδνη, ὁ Θησεὺς ἐγείρει τοὺς ἑταίρους καί, "σῑγᾶτε, ὦ φίλοι," φησίν· "καιρός ἐστιν ἀποπλεῖν. σπεύδετε οὖν πρὸς τὴν ναῦν." ἐπεὶ οὖν εἰς τὴν ναῦν ἀφικνοῦνται, ταχέως λύουσι τὰ πείσματα καὶ ἀποπλέουσιν· τὴν δ' Ἀριάδνην λείπουσιν ἐν τῇ νήσῳ.

[τινα a certain   Νάξον Naxos, an island in the middle of the Aegean Sea, north of Crete   ἀναπαύονται they rest   ἥσυχος quiet(ly)   ἐγείρει wakes up   σῑγᾶτε be quiet!   τὰ πείσματα the cables]

1. Where do Theseus and his men sail first?
2. What do they do first when they arrive there?
3. Why does Theseus not sleep?
4. What does Theseus say to his men when he awakens them?

ἐπεὶ δὲ γίγνεται ἡ ἡμέρᾱ, ἀνεγείρεται ἡ Ἀριάδνη καὶ ὁρᾷ ὅτι οὔτε Θησεὺς οὔτε   1
οἱ ἑταῖροι πάρεισιν. τρέχει οὖν πρὸς τὸν αἰγιαλὸν καὶ βλέπει πρὸς τὴν θάλατταν· τὴν δὲ ναῦν οὐχ ὁρᾷ. μάλιστα οὖν φοβεῖται καὶ βοᾷ· "ὦ Θησεῦ, ποῦ εἶ; ἆρά με καταλείπεις; ἐπάνελθε καὶ σῷζέ με."

[ἀνεγείρεται wakes up   τὸν αἰγιαλόν the shore   τὴν θάλατταν the sea   ἐπάνελθε come back!]

5. What does Ariadne see when she wakes up?
6. What does she shout?

Exercise 6l

Translate into Greek:

1. While (ἐν ᾧ) Ariadne is calling, the god (ὁ θεός) Dionysus (ὁ Διόνῡσος) looks from heaven (ὁ οὐρανός) toward earth; he sees Ariadne and loves her.
2. And so he flies (πέτεται) from heaven to earth. And when he arrives at the island, he approaches her and says, "Ariadne, don't be afraid. I, Dionysus, am here. I love you and want to save you. Come with me to heaven."
3. Ariadne rejoices and goes to him.
4. And so Dionysus carries her up (ἀναφέρει) to heaven; and Ariadne becomes a goddess (θεά) and stays forever (εἰσαεί) in heaven.

7

Ο ΚΥΚΛΩΨ (α)

ὁ Ὀδυσσεὺς τὸ ῥόπαλον ἐλαύνει εἰς τὸν ἕνα ὀφθαλμὸν τοῦ Κύκλωπος.

Vocabulary

Verbs
αἱρέω I take
εἰπέ, (*plural*) εἰπέτε tell!
   εἰπεῖν to say, tell
εὑρίσκω I find
ἰέναι to go
κελεύω I order, tell (someone
   to do something)
παρασκευάζω I prepare

Nouns
ἡ θάλαττα s e a
τὸ ὄνομα name
   ὀνόματι by name, called
ἡ πόλις city

Interrogative Pronoun / Adjective
τίς (*nom. pl.* τίνες) (*pronoun*)
   who? (*adjective*) which . . . ?
   what . . . ?

Indefinite Pronoun / Adjective
τις (*acc. sing.* τινα) (*enclitic
   pronoun*) someone,
   something, anyone, anything;

(*enclitic adjective*) a certain, a,
   some

Pronoun / Adjective
οὐδείς, οὐδεμία, οὐδέν (*masc.
   acc. sing.* οὐδένα) (*pronoun*)
   no one, nothing; (*adjective*) no

Reflexive Pronoun
ἐμαυτοῦ, σεαυτοῦ, ἑαυτοῦ of
   myself, of yourself, of him-,
   her-, itself, etc.

Adjective
μέγιστος, -η, -ον very big,
   biggest

Prepositions
περί (+ *acc.*) around

Proper Names
ὁ Ἀγαμέμνων (τοῦ
   Ἀγαμέμνονος)
   Agamemnon
οἱ Ἀχαιοί Achaeans, Greeks
ὁ Ὀδυσσεύς (τοῦ Ὀδυσσέως)
   Odysseus
ἡ Τροίᾱ Troy

ἐπεὶ δὲ περαίνει τὸν μῦθον ἡ Μυρρίνη, ἡ Μέλιττα, "ὡς καλός
ἐστιν ὁ μῦθος," φησίν· "εἰπὲ ἡμῖν ἄλλον τινὰ μῦθον, ὦ μῆτερ." ἡ δὲ
Μυρρίνη, "οὐχί," φησίν· "νῦν γὰρ ἐν νῷ ἔχω τὸ δεῖπνον
παρασκευάζειν." ἡ μὲν οὖν Μέλιττα δακρύει, ὁ δὲ Φίλιππος, "μὴ
δάκρῡε, ὦ Μέλιττα," φησίν· "ἐγὼ γὰρ ἐθέλω σοι μῦθον καλὸν εἰπεῖν   5
περὶ ἀνδρὸς πολυτρόπου, ὀνόματι Ὀδυσσέως.

[περαίνει finishes   δακρύει cries   περὶ ἀνδρός about a man   πολυτρόπου
much-traveled]

"ὁ γὰρ Ὀδυσσεὺς ἐπὶ τὴν Τροίᾱν πλεῖ μετὰ τοῦ τ' Ἀγαμέμνονος
καὶ τῶν Ἀχαιῶν. δέκα μὲν οὖν ἔτη περὶ Τροίᾱν μάχονται, τέλος δὲ
τὴν πόλιν αἱροῦσιν. ὁ οὖν Ὀδυσσεὺς τοὺς ἑταίρους κελεύει εἰς τὰς
ναῦς εἰσβαίνειν, καὶ ἀπὸ τῆς Τροίᾱς οἴκαδε ἀποπλέουσιν. ἐν δὲ τῇ   10
ὁδῷ πολλὰ καὶ δεινὰ πάσχουσιν. πολλάκις μὲν γὰρ χειμῶνας
ὑπέχουσιν, πολλάκις δὲ εἰς ἄλλους κινδύνους μεγίστους ἐμπίπτουσιν.

[δέκα . . . ἔτη for ten years   τέλος finally   χειμῶνας storms   ὑπέχουσι
they undergo   κινδύνους dangers   ἐμπίπτουσιν = ἐν- + πίπτουσιν]

"πλέουσί ποτε εἰς νῆσόν τινα μῑκρᾱ́ν, ἐκβαίνουσι δὲ ἐκ τῶν νεῶν
καὶ δεῖπνον ποιοῦσιν ἐν τῷ αἰγιαλῷ. ἔστι δὲ ἐγγὺς ἄλλη νῆσος·
καπνὸν ὁρῶσι καὶ φθογγὴν ἀκούουσιν οἰῶν τε καὶ αἰγῶν. τῇ οὖν   15
ὑστεραίᾳ ὁ Ὀδυσσεὺς τοὺς ἑταίρους κελεύει εἰς τὴν ναῦν εἰσβαίνειν·
βούλεται γὰρ εἰς τὴν νῆσον πλεῖν καὶ γιγνώσκειν τίνες ἐκεῖ οἰκοῦσιν.

[ποτε at one time   νεῶν the ships   τῷ αἰγιαλῷ the beach   ἐγγύς near
καπνόν smoke   φθογγήν the sound   οἰῶν of sheep   αἰγῶν of goats
τῇ . . . ὑστεραίᾳ on the next day]

"δι' ὀλίγου οὖν ἀφικνοῦνται εἰς τὴν νῆσον. ἐγγὺς τῆς θαλάττης
ἄντρον μέγα ὁρῶσι καὶ πολλούς τε οἷς καὶ πολλοὺς αἶγας. ὁ οὖν
Ὀδυσσεὺς τοῖς ἑταίροις, 'ὑμεῖς μέν,' φησίν, 'πρὸς τῇ νηὶ̀ μένετε. ἐγὼ δὲ   20
ἐν νῷ ἔχω εἰς τὸ ἄντρον εἰσιέναι.' δώδεκα οὖν τῶν ἑταίρων κελεύει
ἑαυτῷ ἕπεσθαι. οἱ δὲ ἄλλοι πρὸς τῇ νηὶ̀ μένουσιν. ἐπεὶ δὲ εἰς τὸ
ἄντρον ἀφικνοῦνται, οὐδένα ἄνθρωπον εὑρίσκουσιν ἔνδον. οἱ οὖν
ἑταῖροι, 'ὦ Ὀδυσσεῦ,' φασίν, 'οὐδεὶς ἄνθρωπός ἐστιν ἔνδον. ἔλαυνε
οὖν τούς τ' οἷς καὶ τοὺς αἶγας πρὸς τὴν ναῦν καὶ ἀπόπλει ὡς   25
τάχιστα.'

[ἄντρον cave   δώδεκα twelve   ἑαυτῷ ἕπεσθαι to follow him   ἔνδον inside
ὡς τάχιστα as quickly as possible]

"ὁ δὲ Ὀδυσσεὺς οὐκ ἐθέλει τοῦτο ποιεῖν· βούλεται γὰρ γιγνώσκειν
τίς ἐν τῷ ἄντρῳ οἰκεῖ. οἱ δὲ ἑταῖροι μάλα φοβοῦνται· ὅμως δὲ τῷ
Ὀδυσσεῖ πείθονται καὶ μένουσιν ἐν τῷ ἄντρῳ."

[τοῦτο this   ὅμως nevertheless]

Word Study

*Identify the Greek roots in the English words below and give the meanings of the
English words:*

1. myth
2. mythology
3. polytheist (what does ὁ θεός mean?)
4. pantheist (what does πᾶν mean?)
5. monotheist (what does μόνος mean?)
6. atheist (what does ἀ- mean?)
7. theology

Grammar

1. Nouns: Declensions

As you have seen, Greek nouns are divided into three large groups or
declensions. You have already studied nouns of the first or ᾱ declension
(e.g., ἡ κρήνη, ἡ θάλαττα, ἡ οἰκίᾱ, ὁ δεσπότης, and ὁ Ξανθίᾱς) and of the
second or o declension (e.g., ὁ ἀγρός and τὸ δένδρον). Nouns of the first
declension are feminine, except for those whose nominatives end in -ης
or -ᾱς, such as ὁ δεσπότης and ὁ Ξανθίᾱς; most nouns of the second
declension are masculine (e.g., ὁ ἀγρός), a few are feminine (e.g., ἡ ὁδός, ἡ
νῆσος, and ἡ παρθένος), and some are neuter (e.g., τὸ δένδρον).

The third declension has many nouns of all three genders, and it is
not easy to predict the gender from the ending of the nominative singular,
as it is with first and second declension nouns. Some third declension
nouns can be either masculine or feminine, such as ὁ or ἡ παῖς "child,"
"boy," or "girl."

The third declension is made up of nouns the stems of which end in a
consonant or (less commonly) in the vowels ι or υ. Third declension
nouns can be recognized by the ending -ος or -ως in the genitive singular,
e.g., παιδός and πόλεως. By removing the ending, you find the stem, e.g.,
παιδ-.

To help you identify the declension to which a noun belongs and
determine the stem of third declension nouns, we will henceforth list
nouns in the vocabulary lists with their nominative and genitive forms,
as follows:

First Declension:	ἡ κρήνη, τῆς κρήνης spring
(stems in ᾱ)	ἡ οἰκίᾱ, τῆς οἰκίᾱς house, home
	ἡ θάλαττα, τῆς θαλάττης sea
	ὁ δεσπότης, τοῦ δεσπότου master
	ὁ Ξανθίᾱς, τοῦ Ξανθίου Xanthias
Second Declension:	ὁ ἀγρός, τοῦ ἀγροῦ field
(stems in o)	ἡ ὁδός, τῆς ὁδοῦ road, way, journey
	τὸ δένδρον, τοῦ δένδρου tree
Third Declension:	ὁ or ἡ παῖς, τοῦ or τῆς παιδός child, boy, girl
	ἡ πόλις, τῆς πόλεως city

2. Third Declension Nouns: ὁ παῖς and τὸ ὄνομα

Many third declension nouns are declined like παῖς:

Stem: παιδ-

	Singular		*Plural*	
Nom.	ὁ	παῖς	οἱ	παῖδ-ες
Gen.	τοῦ	παιδ-ός	τῶν	παίδ-ων
Dat.	τῷ	παιδ-ί	τοῖς	παιδ-σί(ν) > παισί(ν)
Acc.	τὸν	παῖδ-α	τοὺς	παῖδ-ας
Voc.	ὦ	παῖ	ὦ	παῖδ-ες

If one were using the above word with reference to a girl rather than a boy, one would use the feminine definite article.

The following is an example of a neuter noun of the third declension. Note the ways in which it is similar to and different from the masculine/feminine noun above:

Stem: ὀνοματ- name

	Singular		*Plural*	
Nom.	τὸ	ὄνομα	τὰ	ὀνόματ-α
Gen.	τοῦ	ὀνόματ-ος	τῶν	ὀνομάτ-ων
Dat.	τῷ	ὀνόματ-ι	τοῖς	ὀνόματ-σι(ν) > ὀνόμασι(ν)
Acc.	τὸ	ὄνομα	τὰ	ὀνόματ-α
Voc.	ὦ	ὄνομα	ὦ	ὀνόματ-α

Note that in neuter nouns the nominative, accusative, and vocative singular forms are identical, as are the corresponding plural forms.

Exercise 7a

Locate the following third declension nouns in the reading passage at the beginning of this chapter. Identify the case and number of each, and explain why that particular case is being used:

1. ἀνδρός
2. ὀνόματι
3. Ἀγαμέμνονος
4. χειμῶνας

5. οἰῶν
6. αἰγῶν
7. αἶγας

Exercise 7b

The following third declension nouns have been given in the vocabulary lists (Chapters 2–7, in the following order):

ὁ βοῦς, τοῦ βοός
ὁ or ἡ παῖς, τοῦ or τῆς παιδός
ὁ πατήρ, τοῦ πατρός
ὁ ἀνήρ, τοῦ ἀνδρός
ἡ γυνή, τῆς γυναικός
ἡ θυγάτηρ, τῆς θυγατρός
ἡ μήτηρ, τῆς μητρός
ὁ or ἡ κύων, τοῦ or τῆς κυνός
ὁ βασιλεύς, τοῦ βασιλέως
τὸ ὄρος, τοῦ ὄρους

ἡ ναῦς, τῆς νεώς
ἡ νύξ, τῆς νυκτός
ὁ Αἰγεύς, τοῦ Αἰγέως
ὁ Θησεύς, τοῦ Θησέως
ὁ Μίνως, τοῦ Μίνωος
τὸ ὄνομα, τοῦ ὀνόματος
ἡ πόλις, τῆς πόλεως
ὁ Ἀγαμέμνων, τοῦ Ἀγαμέμνονος
ὁ Ὀδυσσεύς, τοῦ Ὀδυσσέως

Using the information supplied in the charts and lists above, give the correct definite article to accompany each of the following third declension nouns:

1. κυνί (2 possibilities)
2. πατράσι
3. ἄνδρα
4. Ὀδυσσεῖ
5. ὀνόματα
6. μητέρες
7. θυγατράσιν
8. γυναῖκας
9. ἀνδρῶν
10. νυκτί

11. νύκτα
12. Μίνωϊ
13. Αἰγέᾱ
14. ἄνδρας
15. βόες
16. ναυσί
17. Ἀγαμέμνονι
18. κύνα (2 possibilities)
19. γυναιξί (γυναικ-σί)
20. παισί (2 possibilities)

3. Reflexive Pronouns

In Chapter 4 Myrrhine says to Dicaeopolis ἔπαιρε σεαυτόν, ὦ ἄνερ = "Lift yourself, husband!" or "Get up, husband!" Later ὁ Δικαιόπολις μόλις ἐπαίρει ἑαυτόν "Dicaeopolis reluctantly lifts himself (= gets up)."

The pronouns σεαυτόν "yourself" and ἑαυτόν "himself" are called *reflexive* since they are used to refer to or reflect the subject of the verb. In the first and second persons the reflexive pronouns have masculine and feminine forms only; in the third person there are neuter forms as well. There are no nominatives.

First Person

	Masculine	Feminine
G.	ἐμαυτοῦ	ἐμαυτῆς
D.	ἐμαυτῷ	ἐμαυτῇ
A.	ἐμαυτόν	ἐμαυτήν
G.	ἡμῶν αὐτῶν	ἡμῶν αὐτῶν
D.	ἡμῖν αὐτοῖς	ἡμῖν αὐταῖς
A.	ἡμᾶς αὐτούς	ἡμᾶς αὐτάς

Second Person

	Masculine	Feminine
G.	σεαυτοῦ	σεαυτῆς
D.	σεαυτῷ	σεαυτῇ
A.	σεαυτόν	σεαυτήν
G.	ὑμῶν αὐτῶν	ὑμῶν αὐτῶν
D.	ὑμῖν αὐτοῖς	ὑμῖν αὐταῖς
A.	ὑμᾶς αὐτούς	ὑμᾶς αὐτάς

Third Person

	Masculine	Feminine	Neuter
G.	ἑαυτοῦ	ἑαυτῆς	ἑαυτοῦ
D.	ἑαυτῷ	ἑαυτῇ	ἑαυτῷ
A.	ἑαυτόν	ἑαυτήν	ἑαυτό
G.	ἑαυτῶν	ἑαυτῶν	ἑαυτῶν
D.	ἑαυτοῖς	ἑαυταῖς	ἑαυτοῖς
A.	ἑαυτούς	ἑαυτάς	ἑαυτά

Exercise 7c

Read aloud and translate (fill in appropriate reflexive pronouns where missing):

1. ὁ παῖς ἑαυτὸν ἐπαίρει καὶ πρὸς τὸν ἀγρὸν σπεύδει.
2. οἱ παῖδες _____ ἐπαίρουσι καὶ πρὸς τὸν ἀγρὸν σπεύδουσιν.
3. ἔπαιρε σεαυτὴν, ὦ γύναι, καὶ ἐλθὲ δεῦρο.
4. ἐπαίρετε _____, ὦ γυναῖκες, καὶ ἔλθετε δεῦρο.
5. οὐκ ἐθέλω ἐμαυτὴν ἐπαίρειν· μάλα γὰρ κάμνω (I am tired).
6. οὐκ ἐθέλομεν _____ ἐπαίρειν· μάλα γὰρ κάμνομεν.
7. τίνι λέγει ἡ παρθένος τὸν μῦθον; ἆρ' ἑαυτῇ λέγει;
8. ὁ πατὴρ τὴν θυγατέρα μεθ' ἑαυτοῦ καθίζει (makes . . . sit down).
9. οἱ πατέρες τὰς θυγατέρας μεθ' _____ καθίζουσιν.
10. ὁ παῖς τὸν τοῦ πατρὸς κύνα ὁρᾷ ἀλλ' οὐχ ὁρᾷ τὸν ἑαυτοῦ.
11. μὴ εἴσιτε εἰς τὸ ἄντρον, ὦ φίλοι· αὐτοὶ γὰρ ὑμᾶς αὐτοὺς εἰς μέγιστον κίνδῡνον ἄγετε.
12. βοήθει ἡμῖν, ὦ Ὀδυσσεῦ· οὐ γὰρ δυνάμεθα (we cannot) ἡμᾶς αὐτοὺς σῴζειν.

Homer

Homer

The earliest poems in Western literature (and according to some, the greatest) are the *Iliad* and the *Odyssey*. These are epics, that is to say long narrative poems; each of the poems contains 24 books, the books varying in length from 450 to 900 lines. They tell stories about the age of the heroes, and both center upon the Trojan War.

The *Iliad* tells the story of the wrath of Achilles, the greatest of the Greek heroes who fought at Troy. Achilles and Agamemnon, leader of the Greek host, quarrel at an assembly of the army before Troy. Agamemnon takes away Achilles' prize, a captive girl whom he loves. Thus insulted, Achilles refuses to fight any longer and stays by his ships, with disastrous consequences for both himself and the rest of the Greeks.

Without his help the Greeks suffer heavy losses and are driven back to their ships. Achilles still refuses to fight but is at last persuaded to allow his closest friend, Patroclus, to lead his men into battle. Only when Patroclus has been killed by Hector, the greatest of the Trojan heroes, does Achilles turn his anger from Agamemnon and fight against the Trojans. To avenge the death of Patroclus, he leads his men into battle, causing terrible carnage. He sweeps the Trojans back into the city and kills Hector in single combat before the walls of Troy. He then ties the corpse of Hector behind his chariot and drags it around the walls before the eyes of Hector's father, Priam, and his mother and wife.

Achilles' anger does not cease until the aged Priam, alone and at night, makes his way through the Greek camp to Achilles' tent and begs him to return the body of Hector for burial. Achilles, overcome by pity for the old man, consents and allows a truce for his burial.

The *Odyssey* tells the story of the return of Odysseus from Troy to his home in Ithaca. The plot is more complex than that of the *Iliad*. It starts in Ithaca, where Penelope, Odysseus' wife, has been waiting for twenty years for her husband's return (Odysseus was fighting before Troy for ten years and spent another ten on the journey home). She is beset by suitors who are competing for her hand and the kingdom. Her son, Telemachus, sets out to look for his father, who he believes is still alive.

Odysseus, meanwhile, is held captive by a nymph, Calypso, on a far-off island. She is at last persuaded by the gods to let him go and helps him build a raft. He sails off, only to be wrecked on the island of Phaeacia. Here the king receives him kindly, and at a banquet given in his honor Odysseus recounts the adventures he has undergone since he left Troy. The Phaeacians load him with gifts and take him home to Ithaca, where they leave him sleeping on the shore. The second half of the *Odyssey* tells how he returned to his palace disguised as a beggar and with the help of Telemachus and a faithful servant slew the suitors and was reunited with Penelope.

The Greeks attributed both of these great poems to Homer. Scholars have shown that the poems are in fact the culmination of a long tradition of oral poetry, that is of poetry composed without the aid of writing. The tradition probably originated in the Bronze Age, and in every succeeding generation poets retold and embroidered the stories about the heroes. Finally, Homer composed these two great poems, which are on a far larger scale than oral epic usually is, in an age when writing had just been reintroduced to Greece.

The internal evidence of the *Iliad* suggests that it was composed between 750 and 700 B.C. in Ionia. Modern scholars are not agreed on whether the *Odyssey* was composed by the same poet; there are considerable differences in style and tone between the two poems. Both poems show characteristics of oral epic that make them very different from literary poetry. They were composed to be recited or sung aloud to the accompaniment of the lyre. The stories themselves, the recurrent themes, and a large proportion of the actual lines are traditional, but the structure of the poems, the clear and consistent characterization of the leading figures, and the atmosphere of each poem, tragic in the *Iliad,* romantic in the *Odyssey,* are the creation of a single poetic genius.

A rhapsode recites Homer.

Ο ΚΥΚΛΩΨ (β)

ὁ Ὀδυσσεὺς ἐκ τοῦ ἄντρου τοῦ Κύκλωπος ἐκφεύγει.

Vocabulary

Verbs

ἀποκρῑνομαι I answer

βάλλω I throw, put, pelt

μέλλω (+ *infinitive*) I am about to, am destined to, intend to

ὁρμάω I set in motion, set out, start, rush; (*middle, intransitive*) I set out, start, rush

παύω I stop; (*middle, intransitive*) I stop (+ *participle*), cease from (+ *gen.*)

Nouns

ὁ ξένος, τοῦ ξένου foreigner

ὁ οἶνος, τοῦ οἴνου wine

ὁ ὀφθαλμός, τοῦ ὀφθαλμοῦ eye

τὸ πῦρ, τοῦ πυρός fire

ὁ χειμών, τοῦ χειμῶνος storm, winter

Adjectives

δύο two

εἷς, μία, ἕν (*acc. sing. masc.* **ἕνα**) one

πᾶς, πᾶσα, πᾶν (*nom. pl. masc.* **πάντες**, *gen. pl.* **πάντων**, *acc. pl. masc.* **πάντας**, *nom.* and *acc. pl. neuter* **πάντα**) all, every

σώφρων, σῶφρον wise, prudent, well-behaved

Adverbs

ἐνθάδε here, to this place

πόθεν from where?

πῶς; how?

Proper Names

ὁ Κύκλωψ, τοῦ Κύκλωπος Cyclops (one-eyed monster)

"δι᾽ ὀλίγου δὲ ψόφον μέγιστον ἀκούουσι καὶ εἰσέρχεται γίγᾱς φοβερός· πελώριος γάρ ἐστιν· εἷς ὀφθαλμὸς ἐν μέσῳ τῷ μετώπῳ ἔνεστιν. ὅ τ᾽ οὖν Ὀδυσσεὺς καὶ οἱ ἑταῖροι μάλιστα φοβοῦνται καὶ εἰς τὸν τοῦ ἄντρου μυχὸν φεύγουσιν. ὁ δὲ γίγᾱς πρῶτον μὲν τὰ μῆλα εἰς τὸ ἄντρον εἰσελαύνει, ἐπεὶ δὲ πάντα ἔνδον ἐστίν, λίθον μέγιστον αἴρει   5 καὶ εἰς τὴν τοῦ ἄντρου εἴσοδον βάλλει. ἐνταῦθα δὴ πρῶτον μὲν τὰ μῆλα ἀμέλγει, ἔπειτα δὲ πῦρ καίει. οὕτω δὴ τόν τ' Ὀδυσσέα καὶ τοὺς ἑταίρους ὁρᾷ καί, 'ὦ ξένοι,' βοᾷ, 'τίνες ἐστὲ καὶ πόθεν πλεῖτε;'

[ψόφον noise   γίγᾱς φοβερός a terrifying giant   πελώριος monster   μέσῳ τῷ μετώπῳ the middle of his forehead   τὸν τοῦ ἄντρου μυχόν the far corner of the cave   ἔνδον inside   τὴν . . . εἴσοδον the entrance   ἀμέλγει milks   καίει lights]

"ὁ δ' Ὀδυσσεύς, 'ἡμεῖς Ἀχαιοί ἐσμεν,' φησίν, 'καὶ ἀπὸ τῆς Τροίας οἴκαδε πλέομεν. χειμὼν δὲ ἡμᾶς ἐνθάδε ἐλαύνει.'   10

"ὁ δὲ Κύκλωψ οὐδὲν ἀποκρίνεται ἀλλὰ ὁρμᾶται ἐπὶ τοὺς Ἀχαιούς· τῶν ἑταίρων δὲ δύο ἁρπάζει καὶ κόπτει πρὸς τὴν γῆν· ὁ δὲ ἐγκέφαλος ἐκρεῖ καὶ δεύει τὴν γῆν."

[ἁρπάζει he seizes   κόπτει he strikes, bashes   πρὸς τὴν γῆν onto the ground ὁ . . . ἐγκέφαλος ἐκρεῖ their brains flow out   δεύει wet]

ἡ δὲ Μέλιττα, "παῦε, ὦ Φίλιππε," φησίν, "παῦε· δεινὸς γάρ ἐστιν ὁ μῦθος. ἀλλ' εἰπέ μοι, πῶς ἐκφεύγει ὁ Ὀδυσσεύς; ἆρα πάντας τοὺς   15 ἑταίρους ἀποκτείνει ὁ Κύκλωψ;"

ὁ δὲ Φίλιππος, "οὐχί," φησίν· "οὐ πάντας ἀποκτείνει ὁ Κύκλωψ. ὁ γὰρ Ὀδυσσεύς ἐστιν ἀνὴρ πολύμητις. πρῶτον μὲν οὖν πολὺν οἶνον τῷ Κύκλωπι παρέχει, ὥστε δι' ὀλίγου μάλα μεθύει. ἐπεὶ δὲ καθεύδει ὁ Κύκλωψ, ῥόπαλον μέγιστον ὁ Ὀδυσσεὺς εὑρίσκει καὶ τοὺς ἑταίρους   20 κελεύει θερμαίνειν αὐτὸ ἐν τῷ πυρί. ἐπεὶ δὲ μέλλει ἅψεσθαι τὸ ῥόπαλον, ὁ Ὀδυσσεὺς αἴρει αὐτὸ ἐκ τοῦ πυρὸς καὶ ἐλαύνει εἰς τὸν ἕνα ὀφθαλμὸν τοῦ Κύκλωπος.

[πολύμητις cunning   μεθύει is drunk   ῥόπαλον stake   θερμαίνειν to heat ἅψεσθαι to catch fire]

"ὁ δὲ ἀναπηδᾷ καὶ δεινῶς κλάζει. ὁ δὲ Ὀδυσσεὺς καὶ οἱ ἑταῖροι εἰς τὸν τοῦ ἄντρου μυχὸν φεύγουσιν. ὁ δὲ Κύκλωψ οὐ δύναται   25 αὐτοὺς ὁρᾶν. τυφλὸς γάρ ἐστιν."

[ἀναπηδᾷ leaps up   κλάζει shrieks   οὐ δύναται is not able, cannot   τυφλός blind]

ἡ δὲ Μέλιττα, "ὡς σοφός ἐστιν ὁ Ὀδυσσεύς. ἀλλὰ πῶς ἐκφεύγουσιν ἐκ τοῦ ἄντρου;"

[σοφός clever]

ὁ δὲ Φίλιππος, "τῇ ὑστεραίᾳ ἐπεὶ πρῶτον ἀνατέλλει ὁ ἥλιος, ὁ Κύκλωψ τὸν λίθον ἐξαίρει ἐκ τῆς τοῦ ἄντρου εἰσόδου καὶ πάντα τὰ μῆλα ἐκπέμπει. ὁ οὖν Ὀδυσσεὺς τοὺς ἑταίρους κρύπτει ὑπὸ τῶν οἰῶν. οὕτω δὴ ὁ Κύκλωψ ἐκπέμπει τοὺς Ἀχαιοὺς μετὰ τῶν οἰῶν, οἱ δὲ τοὺς οἷς πρὸς τὴν ναῦν ἐλαύνουσι καὶ ἀποπλέουσιν."

[τῇ ὑστεραίᾳ on the next day   ἀνατέλλει rises   ἐξαίρει lifts out   κρύπτει hides   ὑπὸ τῶν οἰῶν under the sheep]

Word Building

From the meanings of the words in boldface, deduce the meaning of the other word in each pair:

1. ἡ παρασκευή   **παρασκευάζω**
2. **τὸ ὄνομα**   ὀνομάζω
3. τὸ θαῦμα   **θαυμάζω**
4. **τὸ ἔργον** (work) ἐργάζομαι

Grammar

4. Another Third Declension Noun: ὁ χειμών

    Stem: χειμων- storm, winter

	Singular		Plural	
Nom.	ὁ	χειμών	οἱ	χειμῶν-ες
Gen.	τοῦ	χειμῶν-ος	τῶν	χειμών-ων
Dat.	τῷ	χειμῶν-ι	τοῖς	χειμῶν-σι(ν) > χειμῶσι(ν)
Acc.	τὸν	χειμῶν-α	τοὺς	χειμῶν-ας
Voc.	ὦ	χειμών	ὦ	χειμῶνες

5. A Third Declension Adjective: σώφρων

    Stem: σώφρον- wise, prudent, well-behaved

	Singular		Plural	
	M. & F.	**N.**	**M. & F.**	**N.**
Nom.	σώφρων	σῶφρον	σώφρον-ες	σώφρον-α
Gen.	σώφρον-ος	σώφρον-ος	σωφρόν-ων	σωφρόν-ων
Dat.	σώφρον-ι	σώφρον-ι	σώφρον-σι > σώφροσι(ν)	σώφρον-σι > σώφροσι(ν)
Acc.	σώφρον-α	σῶφρον	σώφρον-ας	σώφρον-α
Voc.	σῶφρον	σῶφρον	σώφρον-ες	σώφρον-α

6. The Interrogative Pronoun and Adjective

When the Cyclops asks Odysseus and his men τίνες ἐστὲ καὶ πόθεν πλεῖτε; he uses the interrogative pronoun τίνες ("Who . . . ?"). The same word may be used as an interrogative adjective, e.g.:

εἰς τίνα νῆσον πλέομεν;
To *what* island are we sailing?

This pronoun/adjective has third declension endings, and its masculine and feminine forms are the same. It always receives an acute accent on the first syllable. Its forms are as follows:

Stem: τιν-

	Singular		**Plural**	
	M. & F.	**N.**	**M. & F.**	**N.**
Nom.	τίς	τί	τίν-ες	τίν-α
Gen.	τίν-ος	τίν-ος	τίν-ων	τίν-ων
Dat.	τίν-ι	τίν-ι	τίν-σι > τίσι	τίν-σι > τίσι
Acc.	τίν-α	τί	τίν ας	τίν-α

Locate two occurrences of the interrogative pronoun in the reading passage at the beginning of this chapter.

7. The Indefinite Pronoun and Adjective

In the sentence πλέουσί ποτε εἰς νῆσόν τινα μῑκρὰν the word τινα is an indefinite adjective meaning "a certain" or simply "a," "an." This word may also be used as an indefinite pronoun meaning "someone," "something," "anyone," "anything," e.g.:

ἆρ' ὁρᾷς τινα ἐν τῷ ἄντρῳ;
Do you see *anyone* in the cave?

In all of its forms this word is spelled the same as the interrogative pronoun τίς given above, but it is enclitic (see Reference Grammar, pages 209 and 226).

Locate two occurrences of the indefinite adjective in the first two paragraphs of the first reading passage in Chapter 6. Explain their agreement with the nouns they modify and explain the accents.

Exercise 7d

Change the verbs, nouns, pronouns, and adjectives in the following sentences into the plural and then translate the new sentences:

1. ἡ γυνὴ τῑμᾷ τὴν σώφρονα παρθένον.
2. ὁ ἀνὴρ μῦθόν τινα τῇ παιδὶ λέγει.
3. μὴ φοβοῦ τὸν χειμῶνα, ὦ φίλε.

4. βούλομαι γιγνώσκειν τίς ἐν τῷ ἄντρῳ οἰκεῖ.

5. ὁ παῖς οὐ βούλεται ἡγεῖσθαί μοι πρὸς τὴν θάλατταν.

Exercise 7e

Change the verbs, nouns, pronouns, and adjectives in the following sentences into the singular and then translate the new sentences:

1. ἀγνοοῦμεν (we do not know) τὰ τῶν παίδων ὀνόματα.

2. οἱ πατέρες τοὺς παῖδας κελεύουσι τῖμᾶν τοὺς θεούς (the gods).

3. εἰπέτε ἡμῖν τί ποιοῦσιν οἱ ἄνδρες.

4. παῖδές τινες τοὺς κύνας εἰς τοὺς ἀγροὺς εἰσάγουσιν.

5. αἱ μητέρες οὐκ ἐθέλουσι ταῖς θυγατράσι πρὸς τὴν πόλιν ἡγεῖσθαι.

Exercise 7f

Read aloud and translate:

1. τίς ἐν τῷ ἄντρῳ οἰκεῖ; γίγᾱς τις φοβερὸς ἐν τῷ ἄντρῳ οἰκεῖ.

2. τίνα ἐν τῇ οἰκίᾳ ὁρᾷς; γυναῖκά τινα ἐν τῇ οἰκίᾳ ὁρῶ.

3. τίσιν εἰς τὴν πόλιν ἡγῇ; δούλοις τισὶν εἰς τὴν πόλιν ἡγοῦμαι.

4. τίνος ἄροτρον πρὸς τὸν ἀγρὸν φέρεις; φίλου τινὸς ἄροτρον φέρω.

5. τίνι ἐστὶν οὗτος ὁ κύων (this dog); ἔστι τῷ ἐμῷ πατρί.

*   *   *

Ο ΤΟΥ ΘΗΣΕΩΣ ΠΑΤΗΡ ΑΠΟΘΝΗΙΣΚΕΙ

Read the following passages and answer the comprehension questions:

The story of Theseus, concluded. This part of the story begins with a flashback to the time when Theseus left Athens to sail to Crete with the victims to be fed to the Minotaur.

ἐπεὶ δὲ ὁ Θησεὺς πρὸς τὴν Κρήτην μέλλει ἀποπλεῖν, ὁ πατὴρ αὐτῷ λέγει· "ἐγὼ μάλιστα φοβοῦμαι ὑπὲρ σοῦ, ὦ παῖ· ὅμως δὲ ἴθι εἰς τὴν Κρήτην καὶ τόν τε Μῑνώταυρον ἀπόκτεινε καὶ σῷζε τοὺς ἑταίρους· ἔπειτα δὲ οἴκαδε σπεῦδε. ἐγὼ δέ, ἕως ἂν ἄπῃς, καθ᾽ ἡμέρᾱν ἀναβήσομαι ἐπὶ ἄκρᾱν τὴν ἀκτήν, βουλόμενος ὁρᾶν τὴν σὴν ναῦν. ἀλλ᾽ ἄκουέ μου· ἡ γὰρ ναῦς ἔχει τὰ ἱστία μέλανα· σὺ δὲ ἐὰν τόν τε   5 Μῑνώταυρον ἀποκτείνῃς καὶ τοὺς ἑταίρους σώσῃς, οἴκαδε σπεῦδε, καὶ ἐπειδὰν ταῖς Ἀθήναις προσχωρῇς, στέλλε μὲν τὰ μέλανα ἱστία, αἶρε δὲ τὰ ἱστία λευκά. οὕτω γὰρ γνώσομαι ὅτι σῷοί ἐστε."

[ὑπέρ on behalf of, for   ὅμως nevertheless   ἕως ἂν ἄπῃς as long as you are away   καθ᾽ ἡμέρᾱν every day   ἀναβήσομαι I will go up   ἐπί (+ acc.) onto   ἄκρᾱν τὴν ἀκτήν the top of the promontory   βουλόμενος wishing   τὰ ἱστία μέλανα sails (that are) black   ἐάν if   ἀποκτείνῃς you kill   σώσῃς you save

ἐπειδὰν . . . προσχωρῇς when you approach   στέλλε take down   λεῦκα
white   γνώσομαι I will learn   σῶοι safe]

1. Where does Aegeus say he will go every day while Theseus is away?
2. What will he watch for?
3. What does Aegeus tell Theseus to do with the sails of his ship on the
   return voyage?

ὁ οὖν Θησεὺς λέγει ὅτι τῷ πατρὶ ἐν νῷ ἔχει πείθεσθαι καὶ πρὸς τὴν Κρήτην
ἀποπλεῖ. ὁ δ' Αἰγεὺς καθ' ἡμέραν ἐπὶ ἄκραν τὴν ἀκτὴν ἀναβαίνει καὶ πρὸς τὴν   10
θάλατταν βλέπει.

4. What does Theseus promise Aegeus?
5. What does Aegeus do in Theseus' absence?

ἐπεὶ δὲ ὁ Θησεὺς τὴν Ἀριάδνην ἐν τῇ Νάξῳ λείπει καὶ οἴκαδε σπεύδει,
λανθάνεται τῶν τοῦ πατρὸς λόγων, καὶ οὐ στέλλει τὰ μέλανα ἱστία. ὁ οὖν
Αἰγεὺς τὴν μὲν ναῦν γιγνώσκει, ὁρᾷ δὲ ὅτι ἔχει τὰ μέλανα ἱστία. μάλιστα οὖν
φοβεῖται ὑπὲρ τοῦ Θησέως. μέγα μὲν βοᾷ, ῥίπτει δὲ ἑαυτὸν ἀπὸ τῆς ἀκτῆς εἰς τὴν   15
θάλατταν καὶ οὕτως ἀποθνήσκει. διὰ τοῦτο οὖν τὸ ὄνομα τῇ θαλάττῃ ἐστὶν
Αἰγαῖος πόντος.

[λανθάνεται τῶν . . . λόγων he forgets the words   μέγα loudly   ῥίπτει h e
throws   ἀποθνήσκει he dies   διὰ τοῦτο for this reason   πόντος sea]

6. What does Theseus forget to do after abandoning Ariadne?
7. What does Aegeus see when he spots Theseus' ship?
8. What is his emotional reaction?
9. What three things does he do?
10.   How did the Aegean Sea get its name?

Exercise 7g

Translate into Greek:

1. When Theseus arrives at Athens, he learns that his father is dead
   (τέθνηκεν).
2. His mother says to the young man (ὁ νεᾱνίᾱς), "You are to blame; for
   you always forget your father's words."
3. Theseus is very sad (λῡπέομαι) and says, "I am to blame; I intend to
   flee from home."
4. But his mother tells (orders) him not (μή) to go away (ἀπιέναι).
5. Soon he becomes king, and all the Athenians love and honor him.

8
ΠΡΟΣ ΤΟ ΑΣΤΥ (α)

αἱ γυναῖκες διαλεγόμεναι ἀλλήλαις πέπλον ὑφαίνουσιν.

Vocabulary

Verbs
διαλέγομαι (+ *dat.*) I talk to, converse with
ἕπομαι (+ *dat.*) I follow
ἐργάζομαι I work
θεάομαι I see, watch, look at
Nouns
τὸ ἄστυ, τοῦ ἄστεως city
τὸ ἔργον, τοῦ ἔργου work, deed
ἡ ἑσπέρα, τῆς ἑσπέρας evening
ὁ θεός, τοῦ θεοῦ god
ἡ θύρα, τῆς θύρας door
ὁ ποιητής, τοῦ ποιητοῦ poet

Preposition
ἐξ (*before words beginning with vowels*) = **ἐκ** (+ *gen.*) out of
Adverbs
ἐκεῖσε to there
οἴκοι at home
ὥσπερ just as
Conjunctions
ὅμως nevertheless
Expressions
εὖ γε good! well done!
ἐν ᾧ while
Proper Name
ὁ Διόνῡσος, τοῦ Διονῡσου Dionysus

ἐν δὲ τούτῳ ὅ τε Δικαιόπολις καὶ ὁ δοῦλος ἐν τῷ ἀγρῷ ἐργάζονται. ἐπεὶ δὲ γίγνεται ἡ ἑσπέρα, τοὺς βοῦς λύουσι καὶ οἴκαδε ἄγουσιν. οἴκοι δὲ ἥ τε Μυρρίνη καὶ ἡ θυγάτηρ πέπλον ὑφαίνουσιν· ἐν ᾧ δὲ

ὑφαίνουσιν, διαλέγονται ἀλλήλαις. δι᾽ ὀλίγου δὲ ἡ μήτηρ ὁρᾷ τὸν
ἄνδρα εἰς τὴν αὐλὴν εἰσερχόμενον. παύεται οὖν ἐργαζομένη καὶ   5
σπεύδει πρὸς τὴν θύραν καί, "χαῖρε, ὦ ἄνερ," φησίν· "ἐλθὲ δεῦρο καὶ
ἄκουε δή. ὅ τε γὰρ Φίλιππος καὶ ὁ Ἄργος λύκον ἀπεκτόνᾱσιν." ὁ
δέ, "ἆρα ἀληθῆ λέγεις; εἰπέ μοι τί ἐγένετο." ἡ μὲν οὖν Μυρρίνη
πάντα ἐξηγεῖται, ὁ δὲ θαυμάζει καὶ λέγει· "εὖ γε· ἀνδρεῖός ἐστιν ὁ
παῖς καὶ ἰσχῡρός. ἀλλ᾽ εἰπέ μοι, ποῦ ἐστιν; βούλομαι γὰρ τῑμᾶν τὸν   10
λυκοκτόνον." καὶ ἐν νῷ ἔχει ζητεῖν τὸν παῖδα. ἡ δὲ Μυρρίνη, "ἀλλὰ
μένε, ὦ φίλε," φησίν, "καὶ αὖθις ἄκουε. ἄγγελος γὰρ ἥκει ἀπὸ τοῦ
ἄστεως· λέγει δὲ ὅτι οἱ Ἀθηναῖοι τὴν ἑορτὴν ποιοῦνται τῷ Διονύσῳ.
ἆρα ἐθέλεις ἐμέ τε καὶ τοὺς παῖδας πρὸς τὴν ἑορτὴν ἄγειν;" ὁ δέ,
"ἀλλ᾽ οὐ δυνατόν ἐστιν, ὦ γύναι· ἀνάγκη γάρ ἐστιν ἐργάζεσθαι. ὁ   15
γὰρ λῑμὸς τῷ ἀργῷ ἀνδρὶ ἕπεται, ὥσπερ λέγει ὁ ποιητής· ἐξ ἔργων δ᾽
ἄνδρες πολύμηλοί τ᾽ ἀφνειοί τε γίγνονται."

[ἐν ... τούτῳ meanwhile   πέπλον cloth, mantle, robe   ὑφαίνουσιν are
weaving   ἀλλήλαις with one another   τὴν αὐλήν the courtyard
ἀπεκτόνᾱσιν have killed   ἀληθῆ the truth   ἐγένετο happened   ἐξηγεῖται
relates   τὸν λυκοκτόνον the wolf-slayer   ἀνάγκη ... ἐστιν it is necessary
ὁ λῑμός hunger   ἀργῷ lazy   πολύμηλοί τ᾽ ἀφνειοί τε rich in flocks and
wealthy (Hesiod, *Works and Days* 308)]

ἡ δὲ Μυρρίνη, "ἀλλ᾽ ὅμως ἡμᾶς ἐκεῖσε ἄγε, ὦ φίλε ἄνερ. σπανίως
γὰρ πορευόμεθα πρὸς τὸ ἄστυ· καὶ πάντες δὴ ἔρχονται." ὁ δέ, "ἀλλ᾽
ἀδύνατον· ἀργὸς γάρ ἐστιν ὁ δοῦλος· ὅταν γὰρ ἄπω, παύεται   20
ἐργαζόμενος."

[σπανίως rarely   ἀδύνατον (it's) impossible   ὅταν ... ἄπω whenever I'm
away]

ἡ δὲ Μέλιττα, "ἀλλὰ μὴ χαλεπὸς ἴσθι, ὦ πάτερ, ἀλλὰ πείθου
ἡμῖν. ἆρ᾽ οὐκ ἐθέλεις καὶ σὺ τὴν ἑορτὴν θεᾶσθαι καὶ τὸν θεὸν τῑμᾶν;
ὁ γὰρ Διόνῡσος σῴζει ἡμῖν τὰς ἀμπέλους. καὶ τὸν Φίλιππον—ἆρ᾽ οὐ
βούλῃ τῑμᾶν τὸν παῖδα διότι τὸν λύκον ἀπέκτονεν; βούλεται γὰρ   25
τούς τε ἀγῶνας θεᾶσθαι καὶ τοὺς χορούς. ἄγε οὖν ἡμᾶς πάντας
πρὸς τὸ ἄστυ."

[τᾱς ἀμπέλους the vines   διότι because   τοὺς ... ἀγῶνας the contests]

ὁ δὲ Δικαιόπολις, "ἔστω οὖν, ἐπεὶ οὕτως βούλεσθε. ἀλλὰ λέγω
ὑμῖν ὅτι ὁ λῑμὸς ἕπεσθαι ἡμῖν μέλλει—ἀλλ᾽ οὐκ αἴτιος ἔγωγε."

[ἔστω let it be! very well!   ἐπεί (*here*) since   ἔγωγε *an emphatic* ἐγώ]

Word Study

Identify the Greek roots in the English words below and give the meanings of the English words:

1. politics
2. politburo
3. metropolis (*metr-* is not from μέτρον)
4. necropolis (ὁ νεκρός = corpse)
5. cosmopolitan

Grammar

1. Participles: Present Middle

In addition to the indicative mood, the imperative, and the infinitive, which you have studied so far in this course, verbs have adjectival forms known as *participles*. These are often used to modify nouns, e.g.:

ἡ μήτηρ ὁρᾷ τὸν ἄνδρα εἰς τὴν αὐλὴν **εἰσερχόμενον**.
The mother sees her husband *coming into* the courtyard.

Note that the participle agrees with the noun that it modifies in gender, case, and number, i.e., it is masculine accusative singular because it modifies τὸν ἄνδρα.

Participles may also be used to complete the meaning of a verb, e.g.:

παύεται **ἐργαζομένη**. She stops *working*.

Note that the participle here agrees with the implied subject of the verb in gender (feminine), case (nominative), and number (singular).

The sentences above contain participles of deponent verbs, which have their forms in the middle voice. The following charts give the full sets of forms of present middle participles, and it will be noted that the endings are the same as those of first and second declension adjectives such as καλός, -ή, -όν (see page 39).

λῡ-ό-μενος

	Masculine	Feminine	Neuter
Nom.	λῡόμενος	λῡομένη	λῡόμενον
Gen.	λῡομένου	λῡομένης	λῡομένου
Dat.	λῡομένῳ	λῡομένῃ	λῡομένῳ
Acc.	λῡόμενον	λῡομένην	λῡόμενον
Nom.	λῡόμενοι	λῡόμεναι	λῡόμενα
Gen.	λῡομένων	λῡομένων	λῡομένων
Dat.	λῡομένοις	λῡομέναις	λῡομένοις
Acc.	λῡομένους	λῡομένᾱς	λῡόμενα

φιλε-ό-μενος > φιλούμενος

Nom.	φιλούμενος	φιλουμένη	φιλούμενον
Gen.	φιλουμένου	φιλουμένης	φιλουμένου
Dat.	φιλουμένῳ	φιλουμένῃ	φιλουμένῳ
Acc.	φιλούμενον	φιλουμένην	φιλούμενον

Nom.	φιλούμενοι	φιλούμεναι	φιλούμενα
Gen.	φιλουμένων	φιλουμένων	φιλουμένων
Dat.	φιλουμένοις	φιλουμέναις	φιλουμένοις
Acc.	φιλουμένους	φιλουμένας	φιλούμενα

Exercise 8a

Read aloud and translate the following sentences. Then identify and explain the gender, case, and number of each participle:

1. αἱ γυναῖκες παύονται ἐργαζόμεναι.
2. ὁ Φίλιππος τὸν πατέρα ὁρᾷ εἰς τὴν οἰκίαν εἰσερχόμενον.
3. βουλόμενοι τὴν ἑορτὴν θεᾶσθαι, πρὸς τὸ ἄστυ σπεύδομεν.
4. ἆρ' ὁρᾶτε τοὺς παῖδας ταῖς καλαῖς παρθένοις ἑπομένους;
5. αἱ παρθένοι μάλα φοβοῦνται ὡς τάχιστα (*as quickly as possible*) οἴκαδε τρέχουσιν.
6. ἆρ' ἀκούεις τῶν γυναικῶν ἐν τῇ οἰκίᾳ ἀλλήλαις διαλεγομένων;

Exercise 8b

Translate into Greek:

1. Do you see the boys fighting in the road?
2. Dicaeopolis stops working and drives the oxen home.
3. Stop (παῦε) following me and go away (ἄπελθε)!
4. Obeying her father, the girl stays at home.
5. Bravely leading his comrades, Theseus escapes (ἐκφεύγει) out of the labyrinth.
6. The men suffer many terrible things journeying to the island.

2. Verb Forms: Middle Voice of -α- Contract Verbs

In Chapter 6 you were given the middle voice of regular verbs and of -ε- contract verbs (see pages 57–58). You have already studied the active voice of -α- contract verbs in Chapter 5 (see page 44 for the rules of contraction). In the first reading passage in the present chapter you met the deponent verb θεάομαι, "I see," "I watch," "I look at," which may serve as a model for the middle voice of -α- contract verbs. Its forms are as follows:

Indicative:

	Singular			Plural	
1st	θεά-ο-μαι	>	θεῶμαι	θεα-ό-μεθα >	θεώμεθα
2nd	θεά-ε-σαι	>	θεᾷ	θεά-ε-σθε >	θεᾶσθε
3rd	θεά-ε-ται	>	θεᾶται	θεά-ο-ναι >	θεῶνται
Imperative:	θεά-ε-σο >		θεῶ	θεά-ε-σθε >	θεᾶσθε
Infinitive:	θεά-ε-σθαι >		θεᾶσθαι		
Participle:	θεα-ό-μενος >		θεώμενος, -η, -ον		

Exercise 8c

Write out the forms of τῑμάω in the middle voice.

Athens: A Historical Outline

The Acropolis of Athens

1. Bronze Age

Athens grew around the Acropolis, the rocky hill that rises precipitously in the middle of the later city. Archaeologists have shown that in the Bronze Age the Acropolis was fortified and was crowned by a palace, which was no doubt the administrative center of the surrounding district, like the palaces at Mycenae and Pylos. Tradition says that Theseus united Attica in the generation before the Trojan War, but in the *Iliad* there is scant mention of Athenian heroes, and this suggests that Athens was not an important center in the Bronze Age.

2. The Dark Age

Bronze Age civilization collapsed soon after the end of the Trojan War, about 1200 B.C. In the troubles that ensued, the so-called Dorian invasions, Athens, according to tradition, was the only city not sacked. Certainly, in this period Athens grew in size, and we are told that the emigration (ca. 1050 B.C.) that peopled the islands and coast of Asia Minor with Greeks was from Athens, which later claimed to be the mother city of all Ionian settlements.

3. The Renaissance of Greece (ca. 850 B.C.)

As Greece slowly recovered from the Dark Age, population increased, and other states sent out colonies that peopled much of the Mediterranean coast from southern France to the Black Sea (750–500 B.C.). Athens played no part in this movement and seems not to have experienced those problems that led to emigration from other parts of Greece.

4. The Reforms of Solon

Monarchy had been succeeded by the rule of the nobles, who oppressed the farmers until revolution threatened. In this crisis the Athenians chose an arbitrator named Solon (chief archon in 594/593 B.C., but his reforms may date to twenty years later), who worked out a compromise between the conflicting interests of the nobles and farmers. Solon was not only a statesman but a poet, and in a surviving fragment of his poetry he defends his settlement:

To the people I gave as much power as was sufficient,
Neither taking from their honor nor giving them excess;
As for those who held power and were envied for their wealth,
I saw that they too should have nothing improper.
I stood there casting my sturdy shield over both sides
And allowed neither to conquer unjustly.

His settlement included important economic reforms, which gave the farmer a new start, and constitutional reforms, which paved the way for the later democracy. It was he who divided the citizens into four classes according to property qualifications and gave appropriate rights and functions to each; in this way, wealth, not birth, became the criterion for political privilege, and the aristocratic monopoly of power was weakened.

5. Tyranny—Pisistratus

Solon's settlement pleased neither side, and within half a generation, a tyrant, Pisistratus, seized power and ruled off and on for 33 years (561–528 B.C.). Under his rule Athens flourished; the economy improved, the city was adorned with public buildings, and Athens became a greater power in the Greek world. His son, Hippias, succeeded him but was driven out in 510 B.C.

6. Cleisthenes and Democracy

Three years later Cleisthenes put through reforms that made Athens a democracy, in which the Assembly of all male citizens was sovereign. The infant democracy immediately faced a crisis. Hippias had taken refuge with the King of Persia, whose empire now reached the shores of the Aegean and included the Greek cities of Ionia. In 499 the Ionians revolted and asked the mainland cities for help. Athens sent a force, which was highly success-ful for a short time, but the revolt was finally crushed in 494 B.C.

7. The Persian Wars

In 490 B.C. the Persian king Darius sent an expedition by sea to conquer and punish Athens. It landed on the east coast of Attica at Marathon. After an anxious debate, the Athenians sent their army to meet the Persians and won a spectacular victory, driving the Persians back to their ships. Athens alone defeated this Persian expedition; it was a day the Athenians never for-got, and it filled the new democracy with confidence. (See map, page 167.)

Ten years later Darius' son, Xerxes, assembled a vast fleet and army with the intention of conquer-ing all Greece and adding it to his empire. The Greeks mounted a hold-ing operation at Thermopylae (August, 480 B.C.), before abandoning all Greece north of the Peloponnesus, including Attica. Athens was evacu-ated and sacked by the Persians, but in September the combined Greek fleet, inspired by the Athenian gen-eral Themistocles, defeated the Per-sian fleet off the island of Salamis. Xerxes, unable to supply his army without the fleet, led a retreat to Asia, but he left a force of 100,000 men in the north of Greece under the command of Mardonius with orders to subdue Greece the following year. In spring, 479 B.C., the Greek army marched north and met and defeated the Per-sians at Plataea; on the same day, according to tradition, the Greek fleet attacked and destroyed the remains of the Persian navy at Mycale in Asia Minor.

Persian soldiers

8. The Delian League and the Athenian Empire

These victories at the time seemed to the Greeks to offer no more than a respite in their struggle against the might of the Persian empire. Many outlying Greek cities, including the islands and the coasts of the Aegean, were still held by the Persians. In 478 B.C. a league was formed at the island of Delos of cities that pledged themselves to continue the fight against Persia under Athenian leadership.

The Delian League under the Athenian general Cimon won a series of victories and only ceased fighting when the Persians accepted humiliating peace terms in 449 B.C. Meanwhile what had started as a league of free and independent states had gradually developed into an Athenian empire, in which the allies had become subjects. Sparta was alarmed by the growing power of Athens, and these fears led to an intermittent war in which Sparta and her allies (the Peloponnesian League) fought Athens in a series of indecisive actions. This first Peloponnesian war ended in 446 B.C., when Athens and Sparta made a thirty years' peace.

9. Pericles and Radical Democracy

In this period Pericles dominated Athens; from 443 until he died in 429 he was elected general every year. At home he was responsible for the measures that made Athens a radical democracy. In foreign policy he was an avowed imperialist, who reckoned that the Athenian Empire brought positive benefits to its subjects that outweighed their loss of independence.

After the Thirty Years' Peace, Athens embarked on no more imperial ventures. She controlled the seas, kept a tight hand on her empire, and expanded her economic influence westwards. Sparta and its allies had good reason to fear Athenian ambitions, and Corinth, whose prosperity and very existence depended on her trade, was especially alarmed by Athenian expansion into the western Mediterranean. There were dangerous incidents, as when Corfu, a colony of Corinth, made a defensive alliance with Athens and an Athenian naval squadron routed a Corinthian fleet (434 B.C.). In the autumn of 432 B.C. (when our story of Dicaeopolis and his family begins) there was frantic diplomatic activity, as both sides prepared for war.

Pericles

ΠΡΟΣ ΤΟ ΑΣΤΥ (β)

ὁ Δικαιόπολις σπονδὴν ποιούμενος
τὸν Δία εὔχεται σῴζειν πάντας.

Vocabulary

Verbs

ἐγείρω I wake (someone) up;
(*middle, intransitive*) I wake up

εὔχομαι I pray

καθίζω I make someone sit
down; (*intransitive*) I sit;
(*middle, intransitive*) I sit down

Nouns

ἡ ἀγορά, τῆς ἀγορᾶς agora,
city center, market place

ὁ βωμός, τοῦ βωμοῦ altar

ὁ νεᾱνίᾱς, τοῦ νεᾱνίου
young man

ὁ πολίτης, τοῦ πολίτου
citizen

ἡ χείρ, τῆς χειρός hand

Preposition

ὑπέρ (+ *gen.*) on behalf of, for

Adverb

τέλος in the end, finally

Expressions

ἐν . . . τούτῳ meanwhile

τῇ ὑστεραίᾳ on the next day

Proper Names

ἡ Ἀκρόπολις, τῆς
Ἀκροπόλεως Acropolis, the
citadel of Athens

ὁ Ζεύς, τοῦ Διός, τῷ Διί, τὸν
Δία, ὦ Ζεῦ Zeus, king of the
gods

ὁ Παρθενών, τοῦ Παρθενῶνος
the Parthenon, temple of
Athena on the Acropolis in
Athens

τῇ οὖν ὑστεραίᾳ ἐπεὶ πρῶτον γίγνεται ἡ ἡμέρᾱ, ἐγείρεταί τε ἡ
Μυρρίνη καὶ τὸν ἄνδρα ἐγείρει καί, "ἔπαιρε σεαυτόν, ὦ ἄνερ," φησίν·
"οὐ γὰρ δυνατόν ἐστιν ἔτι καθεύδειν· καιρὸς γάρ ἐστι πρὸς τὸ ἄστυ
πορεύεσθαι." ὁ οὖν ἀνὴρ ἐπαίρει ἑαυτόν· καὶ πρῶτον μὲν τὸν

Ξανθίαν καλεῖ καὶ κελεύει αὐτὸν μὴ ἀργὸν εἶναι μηδὲ παύεσθαι
ἐργαζόμενον. ἐν δὲ τούτῳ ἡ Μυρρίνη τόν τε σῖτον φέρει καὶ τόν τε
πάππον ἐγείρει καὶ τοὺς παῖδας. ἔπειτα δὲ ὁ Δικαιόπολις εἰς τὴν
αὐλὴν εἰσέρχεται καὶ τοῖς ἄλλοις ἡγεῖται πρὸς τὸν βωμόν· σπονδὴν
δὲ ποιούμενος τὸν Δία εὔχεται σῴζειν πάντας πρὸς τὸ ἄστυ
πορευομένους. τέλος δὲ τὸν ἡμίονον ἐξάγει, ὁ δὲ πάππος ἀναβαίνει
ἐπ’ αὐτόν. οὕτως οὖν πορεύονται πρὸς τὸ ἄστυ.

[ἔπαιρε σεαυτόν get yourself up!   μηδέ and . . . not   τὴν αὐλήν the courtyard
σπονδήν a libation (drink offering)   τὸν ἡμίονον the mule   ἐπ’ onto]

μακρά δ’ ἐστιν ἡ ὁδὸς καὶ χαλεπή. δι’ ὀλίγου δὲ κάμνει ἡ
Μυρρίνη καὶ βούλεται καθίζεσθαι· κάμνει δὲ καὶ ὁ ἡμίονος καὶ οὐκ
ἐθέλει προχωρεῖν. καθίζονται οὖν πρὸς τῇ ὁδῷ καὶ ἀναπαύονται.
δι’ ὀλίγου δ’ ὁ Δικαιόπολις, "καιρός ἐστι πορεύεσθαι," φησίν· 15
"θάρρει, γύναι· μακρὰ γὰρ ἡ ὁδὸς καὶ χαλεπὴ τὸ πρῶτον, ἐπὴν δ’ εἰς
ἄκρον ἵκηαι, ὥσπερ λέγει ὁ ποιητής, ῥᾳδία δὴ ἔπειτα γίγνεται."

[κάμνει is tired   ἀναπαύονται they rest   θάρρει cheer up!   μακρὰ . . .
γίγνεται (Dicaeoplis is again quoting from Hesiod, Works and Days 290–292)
ἐπὴν . . . ἵκηαι when(ever) you arrive, get]

προχωροῦσιν οὖν ἀνὰ τὸ ὄρος καὶ ἐπεὶ εἰς ἄκρον ἀφικνοῦνται,
τὰς ’Αθήνας ὁρῶσι κάτω κειμένας. ὁ δὲ Φίλιππος τὴν πόλιν θεώμενος,
"ἰδού," φησίν, "ὡς καλή ἐστιν ἡ πόλις. ἆρ’ ὁρᾶτε τὴν ’Ακρόπολιν;" ἡ 20
δὲ Μέλιττα, "ὁρῶ δή. ἆρ’ ὁρᾶτε καὶ τὸν Παρθενῶνα; ὡς καλός ἐστι
καὶ μέγας." ὁ δὲ Φίλιππος, "ἀλλὰ σπεῦδε, πάππα· καταβαίνομεν γὰρ
πρὸς τὴν πόλιν."

[κάτω κειμένᾱς lying below]

ταχέως οὖν καταβαίνουσι καὶ εἰς τὰς πύλᾱς ἀφικόμενοι τὸν
ἡμίονον προσάπτουσι δένδρῳ τινὶ καὶ εἰσέρχονται. ἐν δὲ τῷ ἄστει 25
πολλοὺς ἀνθρώπους ὁρῶσιν ἐν ταῖς ὁδοῖς βαδίζοντας· ἄνδρες γὰρ
γυναῖκες νεᾱνίαι παῖδες, πολῖταί τε καὶ ξένοι, σπεύδουσι πρὸς τὴν
ἀγοράν. ἡ οὖν Μυρρίνη φοβουμένη ὑπὲρ τῶν παίδων, "ἐλθὲ δεῦρο, ὦ
Φίλιππε," φησίν, "καὶ λαμβάνου τῆς χειρός. σὺ δέ—Μέλιτταν λέγω—
μὴ λεῖπέ με ἀλλ’ ἕπου ἅμα ἐμοί· τοσοῦτοι γάρ εἰσιν οἱ ἄνθρωποι ὥστε 30
φοβοῦμαι ὑπέρ σου."

[ἀφικόμενοι upon arriving   προσάπτουσι they tie X (acc.) to Y (dat.)   δένδρῳ
τινί a certain tree   βαδίζοντας walking   λαμβάνου τῆς χειρός take hold of
my hand   ἅμα ἐμοί with me]

Word Building

The following sets contain words expressing ideas of place where, place to which, and place from which. You already know the meanings of the words in boldface; deduce the meanings of the others:

1. **ποῦ**   ποῖ *or* πόσε   **πόθεν**
2. **ἐκεῖ**   ἐκεῖσε   ἐκεῖθεν
3. **οἴκοι**   οἴκαδε   οἴκοθεν
4. **ἄλλοθι**   ἄλλοσε   ἄλλοθεν
5. **πανταχοῦ**   πανταχόσε   πανταχόθεν
6. **᾿Αθήνησι(ν)**   ᾿Αθήναζε   ᾿Αθήνηθεν

Grammar

3. **More Third Declension Nouns: ὁ ἀνήρ, ὁ πατήρ, ἡ μήτηρ, and ἡ θυγάτηρ**

    The endings of these nouns are the same as those you learned for third declension nouns in Chapter 7, but the stems of these nouns undergo some changes:

ὁ	ἀνήρ	ὁ	πατήρ	ἡ	μήτηρ	ἡ	θυγάτηρ
τοῦ	ἀνδρός	τοῦ	πατρός	τῆς	μητρός	τῆς	θυγατρός
τῷ	ἀνδρί	τῷ	πατρί	τῇ	μητρί	τῇ	θυγατρί
τὸν	ἄνδρα	τὸν	πατέρα	τὴν	μητέρα	τὴν	θυγατέρα
ὦ	ἄνερ	ὦ	πάτερ	ὦ	μῆτερ	ὦ	θύγατερ
οἱ	ἄνδρες	οἱ	πατέρες	αἱ	μητέρες	αἱ	θυγατέρες
τῶν	ἀνδρῶν	τῶν	πατέρων	τῶν	μητέρων	τῶν	θυγατέρων
τοῖς	ἀνδράσι(ν)	τοῖς	πατράσι(ν)	ταῖς	μητράσι(ν)	ταῖς	θυγατράσι(ν)
τοὺς	ἄνδρας	τοὺς	πατέρας	τὰς	μητέρας	τὰς	θυγατέρας
ὦ	ἄνδρες	ὦ	πατέρες	ὦ	μητέρες	ὦ	θυγατέρες

4. **The Adjective πᾶς, πᾶσα, πᾶν**

    You have met a number of forms of this adjective in the readings. Here is its complete set of forms. Note that in the masculine and neuter it has third declension endings and that in the feminine it has endings like those of the first declension noun θάλαττα (see Chapter 4, page 34).

    Singular:

Nom.	πᾶς	πᾶσα	πᾶν
Gen.	παντ-ός	πάσης	παντ-ός
Dat.	παντ-ί	πάσῃ	παντ-ί
Acc.	πάντ-α	πᾶσαν	πᾶν

Plural:

	M.	F.	N.
Nom.	πάντ-ες	πᾶσαι	πάντ-α
Gen.	πάντ-ων	πᾱσῶν	πάντ-ων
Dat.	πάντ-σι(ν) >	πᾱσαις	πάντ-σι(ν) >
	πᾶσι(ν)		πᾶσι(ν)
Acc.	πάντ-ας	πᾶσᾱς	πάντ-α

5. Numbers

The Greek numbers from one to ten are:

1	εἷς, μία, ἕν	6	ἕξ
2	δύο	7	ἑπτά
3	τρεῖς, τρία	8	ὀκτώ
4	τέτταρες, τέιταρα	9	ἐννέα
5	πέντε	10	δέκα

The numbers from five to ten are indeclinable; that is, they appear only in the forms given above no matter what gender, case, or number the noun is that they modify. For the number one, there is a full set of forms in the singular, given at the left below, with the masculine and neuter showing third declension endings, and the feminine showing first declension endings like those of οἰκίᾱ (see Chapter 4, page 33). Compare the declension of πᾶς, πᾶσα, πᾶν above. The word οὐδείς, οὐδεμία, οὐδέν or μηδείς, μηδεμία, μηδέν (*pronoun/adjective*) means "no one," "no."

	M.	F.	N.	M.	F.	N.
Nom.	εἷς	μία	ἕν	οὐδείς	οὐδεμία	οὐδέν
Gen.	ἑν-ός	μιᾶς	ἑν-ός	οὐδενός	οὐδεμιᾶς	οὐδενός
Dat.	ἑν-ί	μιᾷ	ἑν-ί	οὐδενί	οὐδεμιᾷ	οὐδενί
Acc.	ἕν-α	μίαν	ἕν	οὐδένα	οὐδεμίαν	οὐδέν

Note the accents of the genitives and datives.

The declensions of δύο, τρεῖς, and τέτταρες are as follows:

M. F. N.	M. F.	N.	M. F.	N.
δύο	τρεῖς	τρία	τέτταρες	τέτταρα
δυοῖν	τριῶν	τριῶν	τεττάρων	τεττάρων
δυοῖν	τρισί(ν)	τρισί(ν)	τέτταρσι(ν)	τέτταρσι(ν)
δύο	τρεῖς	τρία	τέτταρας	τέτταρα

The ordinals ("first," "second," "third," etc.) are as follows:

πρῶτος, -η, -ον	ἕκτος, -η, -ον
δεύτερος, -ᾱ, -ον	ἕβδομος, -η, -ον
τρίτος, -η, -ον	ὄγδοος, -η, -ον
τέταρτος, -η, -ον	ἔνατος, -η, -ον
πέμπτος, -η, -ον	δέκατος, -η, -ον

Exercise 8d

Read aloud and translate:

1. τῷ αὐτουργῷ δύο μὲν υἱοί (*sons*) εἰσιν, μία δὲ θυγάτηρ.
2. ἡ μήτηρ τῇ θυγατρὶ οὐδένα σῖτον παρέχει.
3. τῇ τρίτῃ ἡμέρᾳ ἡ θυγάτηρ τῷ πατρὶ πάντα λέγει.
4. ὁ πατὴρ τήν τε μητέρα καὶ τοὺς παῖδας καλεῖ.
5. τῇ μητρί, "τρεῖς παῖδές σοί εἰσιν," φησίν. "διὰ τί δυοῖν μὲν σῖτον παρέχεις, μιᾷ δὲ οὐδέν;"
6. "δεῖ σε (*you must*) σῖτον πᾶσι παρέχειν."
7. ἡ δὲ γυνὴ τῷ ἀνδρὶ πείθεται καὶ σῖτον πᾶσι τοῖς παισὶ παρέχει.
8. αἱ θυγατέρες τῇ μητρὶ πειθόμεναι τὸν πατέρα ἐγείρουσι καὶ πείθουσιν αὐτὸν Ἀθήναζε πορεύεσθαι.
9. ὁ πατὴρ τοὺς μὲν παῖδας οἴκοι λείπει, ταῖς δὲ θυγατράσιν Ἀθήναζε ἡγεῖται.
10. μακρὰ ἡ ὁδὸς καὶ χαλεπή· τῇ δὲ δευτέρᾳ ἡμέρᾳ ἐκεῖσε ἀφικνοῦνται.
11. πολλοὺς ἀνθρώπους ὁρῶσιν διὰ (*through*) τῶν ὁδῶν πανταχόσε σπεύδοντας.
12. ἐπεὶ δὲ εἰς τὴν ἀγορὰν ἀφικνοῦνται, πολὺν χρόνον μένουσι πάντα θεώμενοι.
13. δύο μὲν ἡμέρας τὰ ἐν τῇ ἀγορᾷ θεῶνται, τῇ δὲ τρίτῃ ἐπὶ τὴν Ἀκρόπολιν ἀναβαίνουσιν.
14. ἐννέα μὲν ἡμέρας Ἀθήνησι μένουσιν, τῇ δὲ δεκάτῃ οἴκαδε ὁρμῶνται.
15. τέτταρας μὲν ἡμέρας ὁδὸν ποιοῦνται, βραδέως πορευόμενοι, τῇ δὲ πέμπτῃ οἴκαδε ἀφικνοῦνται.

*   *   *

Ο ΟΔΥΣΣΕΥΣ ΚΑΙ Ο ΑΙΟΛΟΣ

Read the following passage and answer the comprehension questions:

Odysseus tells how he sailed on to the island of Aeolus, king of the winds, and almost reached home:

ἐπεὶ δὲ ἐκ τοῦ ἄντρου τοῦ Κύκλωπος ἐκφεύγομεν, ἐπανερχόμεθα ταχέως πρὸς τοὺς ἑταίρους. οἱ δέ, ἐπεὶ ἡμᾶς ὁρῶσι, χαίρουσιν. τῇ δὲ ὑστεραίᾳ κελεύω αὐτοὺς εἰς τὴν ναῦν αὖθις εἰσβαίνειν. οὕτως οὖν ἀποπλέομεν.
[τοῦ ἄντρου the cave   ἐπανερχόμεθα we return]

1. What do Odysseus and his men do when they escape from the cave of the Cyclops?
2. What does Odysseus order his men to do the next day?

δι' ὀλίγου δὲ εἰς νῆσον Αἰολίᾱν ἀφικνούμεθα. ἐκεῖ δὲ οἰκεῖ ὁ Αἴολος, βασιλεὺς
τῶν ἀνέμων. ὁ δὲ ἡμᾶς εὐμενῶς δεχόμενος πολὺν χρόνον ξενίζει. ἐπεὶ δὲ ἐγὼ   5
κελεύω αὐτὸν ἡμᾶς ἀποπέμπειν, παρέχει μοι ἀσκόν τινα, εἰς ὃν πάντας τοὺς
ἀνέμους καταδεῖ πλὴν ἑνός, Ζεφύρου πρᾱου.
[Αἰολίᾱν of Aeolus, king of the winds   τῶν ἀνέμων of the winds   εὐμενῶς
kindly   ξενίζει entertains   ἀσκόν bag   ὃν which   καταδεῖ he ties up
πλὴν ἑνός except one   Ζεφύρου Zephyr, the west wind   πρᾱου gentle]

3. Where do Odysseus and his men arrive next?
4. How long do Odysseus and his men stay with Aeolus?
5. What does Aeolus give Odysseus at his departure?
6. What wind was not in the bag?

ἐννέα μὲν οὖν ἡμέρᾱς πλέομεν, τῇ δὲ δεκάτῃ ὁρῶμεν τὴν πατρίδα γῆν.
ἐνταῦθα δὴ ἐγὼ καθεύδω· οἱ δὲ ἑταῖροι, ἐπεὶ ὁρῶσί με καθεύδοντα, οὕτω λέγουσιν·
"τί ἐν τῷ ἀσκῷ ἔνεστιν; πολὺς δήπου χρῡσὸς ἔνεστιν, πολύ τε ἀργύριον, δῶρα τοῦ   10
Αἰόλου. ἄγε δή, λύετε τὸν ἀσκὸν καὶ τὸν χρῡσὸν αἱρεῖτε."
[τὴν πατρίδα γῆν our fatherland   καθεύδοντα sleeping   δήπου surely
χρῡσός gold   ἀργύριον silver   δῶρα gifts   ἄγε δή come on!]

7. How long do Odysseus and his men sail?
8. When they come within sight of their fatherland, what does Odysseus do?
9. What do his comrades think is in the bag?

ἐπεὶ δὲ λύουσι τὸν ἀσκόν, εὐθὺς ἐκπέτονται πάντες οἱ ἄνεμοι καὶ χειμῶνα
δεινὸν ποιοῦσι καὶ τὴν ναῦν ἀπὸ τῆς πατρίδος γῆς ἀπελαύνουσιν. ἐγὼ δὲ ἐγείρομαι
καὶ γιγνώσκω τί γίγνεται. ἀθῡμῶ οὖν καὶ βούλομαι ῥίπτειν ἐμαυτὸν εἰς τὴν
θάλατταν· οἱ δὲ ἑταῖροι σῴζουσί με. οὕτως οὖν οἱ ἄνεμοι ἡμᾶς εἰς τὴν τοῦ Αἰόλου   15
νῆσον πάλιν φέρουσιν.
[εὐθύς at once   ἐκπέτονται fly out   ἀθῡμῶ I despair   ῥίπτειν to throw
πάλιν again]

10. What happens when the men open the bag?
11. How does Odysseus react when he wakes up?
12. Where do the winds carry the ship?

Exercise 8e

Translate into Greek:

1. When we arrive at the island, I go to the house of Aeolus.
2. And he, when he sees me, is very amazed and says: "What is the
   matter (= what are you suffering)? Why are you here again?"
3. And I answer: "My comrades are to blame. For they loosed (ἔλῡσαν)
   the winds. But help us, friend."
4. But Aeolus says: "Go away (ἄπιθι) from the island quickly. It is not
   possible to help you. For the gods surely (δήπου) hate (μῑσέω) you."

9
Η ΠΑΝΗΓΥΡΙΣ (α)

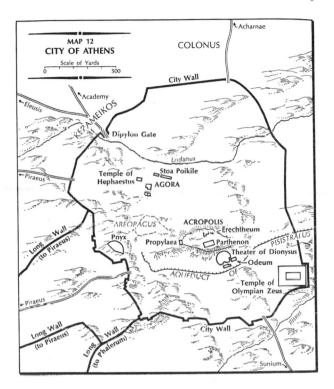

αἱ Ἀθῆναι

ὁρῶσι τὴν εἰκόνα τῆς Ἀθήνης,
ἐνοπλίου οὔσης καὶ Νίκην τῇ δεξιᾷ φερούσης.

Vocabulary

Verbs
ἄγε, (plural) ἄγετε   come on!
ἀναβαίνω I go up, get up; I
   climb, go up onto (+ ἐπί "onto"
   + acc.)
ἐπανέρχομαι I come back,
   return, return to (+ εἰς or πρός +
   acc.)
ἐσθίω I eat
κάμνω I am sick, tired
πίνω I drink
Nouns
ἡ ἀριστερά, τῆς ἀριστερᾶς
   left hand
ἡ δεξιά, τῆς δεξιᾶς right
   hand
ἡ θεός, τῆς θεοῦ goddess
τὸ ἱερόν, τοῦ ἱεροῦ temple
ὁ κίνδῡνος, τοῦ κινδύνου
   danger

Adjective
κάλλιστος, -η, -ον most
   beautiful, very beautiful
Preposition
διά (+ gen.) through
ἐπί (+ dat.) upon, on, (+ acc.) at,
   against, onto
Adverb
πότε when?
Proper Names
ἡ Ἀθήνη, τῆς Ἀθήνης
   Athena, daughter of Zeus
ἡ Νίκη, τῆς Νίκης Nike, the
   goddess of victory
ἡ Παρθένος, τῆς Παρθένου
   the Maiden, the goddess
   Athena
ὁ Φειδίας, τοῦ Φειδίου
   Pheidias, the great Athenian
   sculptor

οὕτως οὖν πορευόμενοι ἀφικνοῦνται εἰς τὴν ἀγοράν. ἐκεῖ δὲ
τοσοῦτός ἐστιν ὁ ὅμιλος ὥστε μόλις προχωροῦσι πρὸς τὴν
Ἀκρόπολιν. τέλος δὲ τῷ Δικαιοπόλει ἑπόμενοι εἰς στοάν τινα
ἀφικνοῦνται καὶ καθιζόμενοι θεῶνται τοὺς ἀνθρώπους σπεύδοντας
καὶ βοῶντας καὶ θόρυβον ποιοῦντας.   5

[ὁ ὅμῑλος the crowd   στοάν colonnade   θόρυβον a din]

ἤδη δὲ μάλα πεινῶσιν οἱ παῖδες. ὁ δὲ Φίλιππος ἀλλαντοπώλην
ὁρᾷ διὰ τοῦ ὁμίλου ὠθιζόμενον καὶ τὰ ὤνια βοῶντα. τὸν οὖν
πατέρα καλεῖ καί, "πάππα φίλε," φησίν, "ἰδού, ἀλλαντοπώλης
προσχωρεῖ. ἆρ' οὐκ ἐθέλεις σῖτον ὠνεῖσθαι; μάλα γὰρ πεινῶμεν." ὁ
οὖν Δικαιόπολις τὸν ἀλλαντοπώλην καλεῖ καὶ σῖτον ὠνεῖται. οὕτως   10
οὖν ἐν τῇ στοᾷ καθίζονται ἄλλαντας ἐσθίοντες καὶ οἶνον πίνοντες.

[πεινῶσιν   are hungry   ἀλλαντοπώλην a sausage-seller   ὠθιζόμενον
pushing   τὰ ὤνια his wares   ὠνεῖσθαι to buy   ἄλλαντας sausages]

μετὰ δὲ τὸ δεῖπνον ὁ Δικαιόπολις, "ἄγετε," φησίν, "ἆρ' οὐ
βούλεσθε ἐπὶ τὴν Ἀκρόπολιν ἀναβαίνειν καὶ τὰ ἱερὰ θεᾶσθαι;" ὁ
μὲν πάππος μάλα κάμνει καὶ οὐκ ἐθέλει ἀναβαίνειν, οἱ δὲ ἄλλοι

λείπουσιν αὐτὸν ἐν τῇ στοᾷ καθιζόμενον καὶ διὰ τοῦ ὁμίλου ὠθι-   15
ζόμενοι ἐπὶ τὴν Ἀκρόπολιν ἀναβαίνουσιν.

[μετά (+ acc.) after]

    ἐπεὶ δὲ εἰς ἄκρᾱν τὴν Ἀκρόπολιν ἀφικνοῦνται καὶ τὰ προπύλαια
διαπερῶσιν, τὸ τῆς Παρθένου ἱερὸν ὁρῶσιν ἐναντίον καὶ τὴν τῆς
Ἀθήνης εἰκόνα, μεγίστην οὖσαν, ἐνόπλιον καὶ δόρυ δεξιᾷ φέρουσαν.
πολὺν οὖν χρόνον ἡσυχάζουσιν οἱ παῖδες τὴν θεὸν θεώμενοι, τέλος   20
δὲ ὁ Δικαιόπολις, "ἄγετε," φησίν, "ἆρ᾽ οὐ βούλεσθε τὸ ἱερὸν
θεᾶσθαι;" καὶ ἡγεῖται αὐτοῖς πόρρω.

[τὰ προπύλαια the gateway   διαπερῶσιν they pass through   ἐναντίον
opposite   τὴν . . . εἰκόνα the statue   οὖσαν being   ἐνόπλιον fully armed
δόρυ spear   ἡσυχάζουσιν stay quiet   πόρρω forward]

    μέγιστόν ἐστι τὸ ἱερὸν καὶ κάλλιστον. πολὺν χρόνον τὰ
ἀγάλματα θεῶνται, ἃ τὸ πᾶν ἱερὸν κοσμεῖ. ἀνεῳγμέναι εἰσὶν αἱ
πύλαι· ἀναβαίνουσιν οὖν οἱ παῖδες καὶ εἰσέρχονται. πάντα τὰ εἴσω   25
σκοτεινά ἐστιν, ἀλλ᾽ ἐναντίᾱν μόλις ὁρῶσι τὴν τῆς Ἀθήνης εἰκόνα,
τὸ κάλλιστον ἔργον τοῦ Φειδίου. ἡ θεὸς λάμπεται χρῡσῷ, τῇ μὲν
δεξιᾷ Νίκην φέρουσα τῇ δὲ ἀριστερᾷ τὴν ἀσπίδα. ἅμα τ᾽ οὖν
φοβοῦνται οἱ παῖδες θεώμενοι καὶ χαίρουσιν. ὁ δὲ Φίλιππος
προχωρεῖ καὶ τὰς χεῖρας ἀνέχων τῇ θεῷ εὔχεται· "ὦ Ἀθήνη   30
Παρθένος, παῖ Διός, πολιοῦχε, ἵλαος ἴσθι καὶ ἄκουέ μου εὐχομένου·
σῷζε τὴν πόλιν καὶ σῷζε ἡμᾶς ἐκ πάντων κινδύνων." ἐνταῦθα δὴ
πρὸς τὴν Μέλιτταν ἐπανέρχεται καὶ ἡγεῖται αὐτῇ ἐκ τοῦ ἱεροῦ.

[τὰ ἀγάλματα the carvings   ἃ which   κοσμεῖ decorate   ἀνεῳγμέναι open
τὰ εἴσω the inside   σκοτεινά dark   λάμπεται gleams   χρῡσῷ with gold
τὴν ἀσπίδα her shield   ἅμα at the same time   ἀνέχων holding up
πολιοῦχε protectress of our city   ἵλαος gracious]

    πολύν τινα χρόνον τοὺς τέκοντας ζητοῦσιν, τέλος δὲ εὑρίσκουσιν
αὐτοὺς ὄπισθεν τοῦ ἱεροῦ καθορῶντας τὸ τοῦ Διονύσου τέμενος. ὁ   35
δὲ Δικαιόπολις, "ἰδού, ὦ παῖδες," φησίν, "ἤδη συλλέγονται οἱ
ἄνθρωποι εἰς τὸ τέμενος. καιρός ἐστι καταβαίνειν καὶ ζητεῖν τὸν
πάππον."·

[τοὺς τέκοντας their parents   ὄπισθεν behind   καθορῶντας looking down on
τὸ . . . τέμενος the sanctuary   συλλέγονται are gathering]

    καταβαίνουσιν οὖν καὶ σπεύδουσι πρὸς τὴν στοάν· ἐκεῖ δὲ
εὑρίσκουσι τὸν πάππον ὀργίλως ἔχοντα· "ὦ τέκνον," φησίν, "τί ποιεῖς;   40
διὰ τί με λείπεις τοσοῦτον χρόνον; διὰ τί τὴν πομπὴν οὐ θεώμεθα;"

ὁ δὲ Δικαιόπολις, "θάρρει, πάππα," φησίν· "νῦν γὰρ πρὸς τὸ τοῦ
Διονύσου τέμενος πορευόμεθα· δι' ὀλίγου γὰρ γίγνεται ἡ πομπή. ἄγε
δή." οὕτω λέγει καὶ ἡγεῖται αὐτοῖς πρὸς τὸ τέμενος.

[ὀργίλως ἔχοντα in a bad temper   τέκνον child   τὴν πομπήν the procession
θάρρει cheer up!]

Word Study

*Identify the Greek roots in the English words below and give the meanings of the
English words (ὁ δῆμος = the people):*

1. democracy (what does τὸ κράτος mean?)
2. demagogue
3. demography
4. endemic
5. epidemic
6. pandemic

Grammar

1. Participles: Present Active

In the last chapter you learned the forms of the present participle in the
middle voice, e.g., λῡόμενος, λῡομένη, λῡόμενον, which has the same
endings as the adjective καλός, καλή, καλόν.

In the reading passage at the beginning of this chapter you have met
many forms of the *present active* participle, e.g., σπεύδοντας "hurrying,"
βοῶντας "shouting," and ποιοῦντας "making." Present active participles
have endings similar, but not exactly identical to those of πᾶς, πᾶσα, πᾶν,
which you learned in the second half of the last chapter (see pages 92–93).
The present participles are declined as follows:

	Masculine	*Feminine*	*Neuter*
The verb εἰμί:			
Nom.	ὤν	οὖσα	ὄν
Gen.	ὄντος	οὔσης	ὄντος
Dat.	ὄντι	οὔσῃ	ὄντι
Acc.	ὄντα	οὖσαν	ὄν
Nom.	ὄντες	οὖσαι	ὄντα
Gen.	ὄντων	οὐσῶν	ὄντων
Dat.	ὄντ-σι(ν) > οὖσι(ν)	οὔσαις	ὄντ-σι(ν) > οὖσι(ν)
Acc.	ὄντας	οὔσᾱς	ὄντα

The verb λύω:

Nom.	λύ-ων	λύ-ουσα	λῦ-ον
Gen.	λύ-οντος	λυ-ούσης	λύ-οντος
Dat.	λύ-οντι	λυ-ούσῃ	λύ-οντι
Acc.	λύ-οντα	λύ-ουσαν	λῦ-ον
Nom.	λύ-οντες	λύ-ουσαι	λύ-οντα
Gen.	λυ-όντων	λυ-ουσῶν	λυ-όντων
Dat.	λύ-ουσι(ν)	λυ-ούσαις	λύ-ουσι(ν)
Acc.	λύ-οντας	λυ-ούσᾱς	λύ-οντα

For the participles of contract verbs, we show how the contractions work in the nominative singular but then give only contracted forms:

The verb φιλέω:

Nom.	φιλέ-ων > φιλῶν	φιλέ-ουσα > φιλοῦσα	φιλέ-ον > φιλοῦν
Gen.	φιλοῦντος	φιλούσης	φιλοῦντος
Dat.	φιλοῦντι	φιλούσῃ	φιλοῦντι
Acc.	φιλοῦντα	φιλοῦσαν	φιλοῦν
Nom.	φιλοῦντες	φιλοῦσαι	φιλοῦντα
Gen.	φιλούντων	φιλουσῶν	φιλούντων
Dat.	φιλοῦσι	φιλούσαις	φιλοῦσι
Acc.	φιλοῦντας	φιλούσᾱς	φιλοῦντα

The verb τῑμάω:

Nom.	τῑμά-ων > τῑμῶν	τῑμά-ουσα > τῑμῶσα	τῑμά-ον > τῑμῶν
Gen.	τῑμῶντος	τῑμώσης	τῑμῶντος
Dat.	τῑμῶντι	τῑμώσῃ	τῑμῶντι
Acc.	τῑμῶντα	τῑμῶσαν	τῑμῶν
Nom.	τῑμῶντες	τῑμῶσαι	τῑμῶντα
Gen.	τῑμώντων	τῑμωσῶν	τῑμώντων
Dat.	τῑμῶσι	τῑμώσαις	τῑμῶσι
Acc.	τῑμῶντας	τῑμώσᾱς	τῑμῶντα

Exercise 9a

Locate twelve present active participles in the reading passage at the beginning of this chapter, identify the gender, case, and number of each, and locate the noun, pronoun, or subject of a verb that each participle modifies.

Exercise 9b

Write the correct form of the present participle of the verb given in parentheses to agree with the following nouns:

1. οἱ παῖδες (τρέχω)
2. τῷ ἀνδρί (βαδίζω)
3. τοὺς νεανίας (τῑμάω)
4. τοῖς παισί (εἰμί)
5. τῶν νεανιῶν (μάχομαι)

6. τὰς γυναῖκας (λέγω)
7. τὸν Δικαιόπολιν (εὔχομαι)
8. τοῦ δούλου (πονέω)
9. αἱ παρθένοι (ἀκούω)
10. τοῦ ἀγγέλου (βοάω)

Exercise 9c

Complete each of the following sentences by adding the correct form of a participle to translate the verb in parentheses, and then translate the sentence:

1. οἱ δοῦλοι ἥκουσι τοὺς βοῦς (leading).
2. ὁ πολίτης ξένον ὁρᾷ πρὸς τῇ ὁδῷ (waiting).
3. αἱ γυναῖκες ἐν τῷ ἀγρῷ καθίζονται τοὺς παῖδας (watching).
4. οἱ παῖδες οὐ παύονται λίθους (throwing).
5. οἱ ἄνδρες θεῶνται τὴν παρθένον εἰς τὸ ἱερόν (coming in).

Exercise 9d

Translate the following pairs of sentences:

1. οἱ παῖδες ἐν τῇ ἀγορᾷ καθίζονται οἶνον πίνοντες.
    The slaves hurry home driving the oxen.
2. ἆρ' ὁρᾷς τὴν παρθένον εἰς τὸ ἱερὸν σπεύδουσαν;
    The foreigner sees the boys running into the agora.
3. πάντες ἀκούουσι τοῦ ἀλλαντοπώλου τὰ ὤνια βοῶντος.
    No one hears the girl calling her mother.
4. οἱ ἄνδρες τὰς γυναῖκας λείπουσιν ἐν τῷ οἴκῳ καθιζούσᾱς.
    The boy finds his father waiting in the agora.
5. ὁ νεανίας τὴν παρθένον φιλεῖ μάλα καλὴν οὖσαν.
    The father honors the boy who is (= *being*) very brave.

The City of Athens

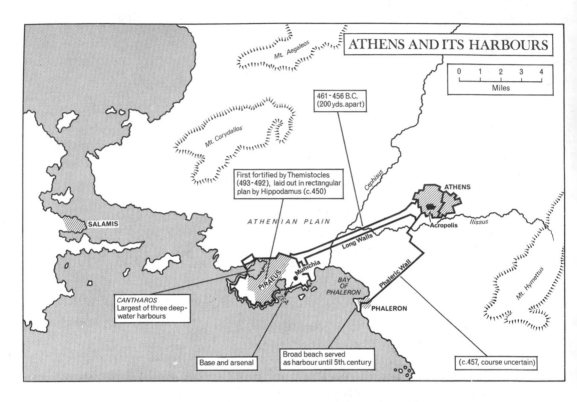

The Piraeus and Athens in the time of Pericles

Reconstruction of the agora at Athens as seen from the southeast, about 400 B.C.

The city to which Dicaeopolis and his family journeyed was largely built after the battle of Salamis, since the earlier city and its temples were destroyed when the Persians occupied and sacked Athens. A visitor coming by sea would arrive at the Piraeus, the greatest port in Greece and perhaps its finest natural harbor. The fortification of the Piraeus was begun by Themistocles in 493–492 B.C. It was completed after the Greek victory at Plataea, when the city of Athens was rebuilt and connected to the Piraeus by the Long Walls, making Athens virtually impregnable as long as she controlled the seas.

Leaving the harbor quarter, visitors would have made their way through the marketplace and town of Piraeus to the road that led between the Long Walls, and then they would have walked the seven miles to Athens through continuous traffic of mules and ox-carts carrying goods to and from the city. From a distance they would have seen the Parthenon dominating the Acropolis and perhaps the spear of the great statue of Athena in full armor, which stood outside the Parthenon.

Entering the city, they would see on their left close to the city wall the Pnyx, a large open slope where the Assembly met (see map, page 96). They would then pass between the Areopagus (Hill of Ares), a bare outcrop of rock of immemorial sanctity, and the Acropolis into the agora. This was the center of Athens. On the left stood the Strategeion or Generals' Headquarters (to the left of and not shown in the model on the facing page) and then (see model) the Tholos (the round magistrates' clubhouse), the Metroon (Archive), the temple of Apollo Patroos, and the stoa of Zeus; behind the Metroon stood the Bouleuterion (Council Chamber); on the right (not shown in the model) were the law courts. On the hill behind the Bouleuterion there still stands the temple of Hephaestus, the best preserved of all Greek temples. In the agora itself were great altars to Zeus and to the ten eponymous heroes of Athens, and there were also fine marble colonnades (stoas), where people could rest and talk in the shade.

The agora was not only the seat of government but also the market and mercantile center of Athens. Here you could buy anything, as a comic poet of this time wrote:

You will find everything sold together in the same place at Athens: figs, witnesses to summonses, bunches of grapes, turnips, pears, apples, givers of evidence, roses, medlars, porridge, honeycombs, chickpeas, lawsuits, puddings, myrtle, allotment-machines, irises, lambs, waterclocks, laws, indictments.

Pushing their way eastwards through the crowds of people conducting business or strolling in conversation, our visitors would reach the Panathenaic Way, which led to the Acropolis (see map, page 96, and illustrations, page 105). As they climbed to the top of the steep road, they would see on their right the little temple of Athena Nike, built to commemorate victory over the Persians (see model, page 105, and photograph, page 207). They would then enter the great monumental gateway, the Propylaea, designed by Mnesicles to balance the Parthenon but never completed, since work was interrupted by the outbreak of war in 431 B.C. Even so, it was a beautiful and impressive building, which included a picture gallery.

On leaving the Propylaea, our visitors face the Parthenon and in front of it the great bronze statue of Athena Promachus. The temple takes the traditional form of a cella, in which stood the statue of the goddess, surrounded by a peristyle of Doric pillars. The architect, Ictinus, incorporated many subtleties in the basically simple design, and these give the temple a unique grace and lightness, despite its great size. The sculptures that adorned the two pediments, the 92 metopes, and the frieze running around the cella were designed by Pericles' friend Pheidias. On the frieze was depicted the great Panathenaic procession, in which every fourth year representatives of the whole people of Athens brought the offering of a new robe to their patron goddess. Inside the cella was the great statue of Athena, standing in full armor, made of ivory and gold, so awe-inspiring that none could look on it without fear and admiration (see illustration, page 96).

To the west of the Parthenon stood the Erechtheum, sacred to Erechtheus, the founder-king of Athens, and to Poseidon and Athena. The temple is irregular in plan, having three porticoes, each in a different style; it stood on the site of the most ancient shrine on the Acropolis. Here could be seen the sacred olive tree that Athena had given to the people of Athens and the sacred serpent, which embodied the spirit of Erechtheus.

Crossing to the eastern edge of the Acropolis, behind the Parthenon, our visitors would look down on the precinct of Dionysus (see illustration, page 108). There was the theater (not built in stone until the following century) and the temple of Dionysus.

All these buildings, and others, were part of Pericles' master program. They were paid for by the tribute of the subject allies. His political opponents said, "The treasure contributed for the necessity of war was being squandered on the city, to gild her all over and adorn her like a harlot, with precious stones and statues and temples." Pericles answered that the people were not obliged to give any account of the money to the allies, provided that Athens maintained their defense and kept off the Persians. His program gave employment to an army of workmen and artists and made Athens a worthy center of her empire, "an education to Greece."

Maidens from the frieze of the Parthenon

Model of the Acropolis

The Parthenon seen from the Propylaea

Η ΠΑΝΗΓΥΡΙΣ (β)

τῶν παρόντων πολλοὶ μεθύοντες κωμάζουσιν.

Vocabulary

Verbs
αὐξάνω I increase
ἐπανιέναι to come back,
    return, return to (+ εἰς *or* πρός +
    acc.)
καίω I kindle, burn; (*middle,
    intransitive*) I burn, am on fire
σῑγάω I am silent
τέρπομαι I enjoy myself, I
    enjoy (+ *dat. or participle*)
Nouns
ὁ γέρων, τοῦ γέροντος old
    man
ὁ δῆμος, τοῦ δήμου the people
τὸ ἱερεῖον, τοῦ ἱερείου
    sacrificial victim

ὁ ἱερεύς, τοῦ ἱερέως priest
ὁ κῆρυξ, τοῦ κήρῡκος herald
ὁ οὐρανός, τοῦ οὐρανοῦ sky,
    heaven
ἡ πομπή, τῆς πομπῆς
    procession
Adjectives
ἄριστος, -η, -ον best, very
    good, noble
ἕτοιμος, -η, -ον ready
ἵλαος, -ον propitious
μέσος, -η, -ον middle (of)
Proper Name
ὁ Βρόμιος, τοῦ Βρομίου
    Thunderer (*an epithet of
    Dionysus*)

ἑσπέρᾱ ἤδη πάρεστιν. δι' ὀλίγου σῑγῶσι πάντες οἱ ἄνθρωποι· ὁ
γὰρ κῆρυξ προσχωρεῖ καὶ βοῶν, "σῑγᾶτε, ὦ πολῖται," φησίν· "ἡ γὰρ
πομπὴ προσχωρεῖ. ἐκποδὼν γίγνεσθε." πάντες οὖν ἐκποδὼν γίγνονται καὶ τὴν πομπὴν μένουσιν.

[ἐκποδών out of the way]

ἐνταῦθα δὴ τὴν πομπὴν ὁρῶσι προσχωροῦσαν. ἡγοῦνται μὲν οἱ 5
κήρῡκες· ἔπειτα δὲ παρθένοι κάλλισται βαδίζουσι κανᾶ φέρουσαι
βοτρύων πλήρη. ἔπονται δὲ αὐταῖς πολλοί τε πολῖται ἀσκοὺς οἴνου
φέροντες καὶ πολλοὶ μέτοικοι σκάφια φέροντες. ἔπειτα δὲ προχωρεῖ ὁ
τοῦ Διονύσου ἱερεὺς καὶ ἅμ' αὐτῷ νεανίαι ἄριστοι τὴν τοῦ Διονύσου
εἰκόνα φέροντες. τελευταῖοι δὲ οἱ ὑπηρέται ἔρχονται τὰ ἱερεῖα 10
ἄγοντες.

[κανᾶ baskets   βοτρύων πλήρη full of grapes   ἀσκοὺς οἴνου skins (full) of
wine   μέτοικοι resident aliens   σκάφια trays (of offerings)   ἅμ' αὐτῷ with
him   τελευταῖοι last   οἱ ὑπηρέται the attendants]

πάντες οὖν χαίροντες τῇ πομπῇ ἔπονται πρὸς τὸ τοῦ θεοῦ
τέμενος. ἐπεὶ δὲ ἀφικνοῦνται, ὁ μὲν ἱερεὺς καὶ οἱ νεανίαι τὴν ιοῦ θεοῦ
εἰκόνα εἰς τὸ ἱερὸν φέρουσιν, οἱ δὲ ὑπηρέται τὰ ἱερεῖα πρὸς τὸν βωμὸν
ἄγουσιν. ἔπειτα δὲ ὁ κῆρυξ τῷ δήμῳ κηρύττων, "εὐφημεῖτε, ὦ 15
πολῖται," φησίν. σῑγᾷ οὖν ὁ πᾶς ὅμῑλος καὶ ἥσυχος μένει.

[κηρύττων proclaiming   εὐφημεῖτε keep holy silence!   ἥσυχος quiet]

ὁ δὲ ἱερεὺς τὰς χεῖρας πρὸς τὸν οὐρανὸν αἴρων, "ὦ ἄναξ
Διόνῡσε," φησίν, "ἄκουέ μου εὐχομένου· Βρόμιε, τήν τε θυσίᾱν δέχου
καὶ ἵλαος ἴσθι τῷ δήμῳ· σὺ γὰρ ἵλαος ὢν τάς τε ἀμπέλους σῴζεις καὶ
αὐξάνεις τοὺς βότρυας ὥστε παρέχειν ἡμῖν τὸν οἶνον." 20

[ἄναξ lord   τήν ... θυσίᾱν the sacrifice   τάς ... ἀμπέλους the vines
τοὺς βότρυας the grapes]

οἱ δὲ παρόντες πάντες βοῶσιν· "ἐλελεῦ, ἴου, ἴου, Βρόμιε, ἵλαος ὢν
τούς τε βότρυας αὔξανε καὶ πάρεχε ἡμῖν τὸν οἶνον." ἔπειτα δὲ ὁ
ἱερεὺς σφάζει τὰ ἱερεῖα· οἱ δὲ ὑπηρέται ἕτοιμοι ὄντες λαμβάνουσιν
αὐτὰ καὶ κατατέμνουσιν. καὶ τὰ μὲν τῷ θεῷ παρέχουσιν ἐν τῷ βωμῷ
καίοντες, τὰ δὲ τοῖς παροῦσι διαιροῦσιν. ἐπεὶ δὲ ἕτοιμά ἐστι πάντα, ὁ 25
ἱερεὺς οἶνον σπένδει καὶ τῷ θεῷ εὔχεται. ἐνταῦθα δὴ πάντες τόν τ'
οἶνον πίνουσι καὶ τὰ κρέα ἐσθίουσι τῷ δαιτὶ τερπόμενοι.

[ἐλελεῦ, ἴου, ἴου untranslatable ritual chants   σφάζει slaughters   κατατέμνουσιν cut up   τὰ μέν ... τὰ δέ some (parts) ... other (parts)   διαιροῦσιν
they divide   σπένδει pours ... as a libation   τὰ κρέα the flesh   τῷ δαιτί the
feast]

μέση νὺξ νῦν ἐστίν, τῶν δὲ παρόντων πολλοὶ μεθύοντες
κωμάζουσιν. ἡ οὖν Μυρρίνη, φοβουμένη ὑπὲρ τῶν παίδων, "ἄγε δή,
ὦ ἄνερ," φησίν, "ὁ πάππος μάλα κάμνει. καιρός ἐστιν ἐπανιέναι

πρὸς τὰς πύλᾱς καὶ καθεύδειν." ὁ δὲ πάππος, "τί λέγεις;" φησίν, "οὐ
κάμνω ἐγώ. βούλομαι κωμάζειν." ὁ δὲ Δικαιόπολις, "γέρων εἶ,
πάππα," φησίν· "οὐ προσήκει σοι κωμάζειν. ἐλθέ." οὕτω λέγει καὶ
ἡγεῖται αὐτοῖς πρὸς τὰς πύλᾱς. ἐπεὶ δὲ ἀφικνοῦνται, τὸν ἡμίονον
εὑρίσκουσι καὶ πάντες χαμαὶ καθεύδουσιν.   35

[μεθύοντες being drunk   κωμάζουσιν are reveling   οὐ προσήκει σοι it is
not suitable for you   τὸν ἡμίονον the mule   χαμαί on the ground]

The theater of Dionysus

Word Building

*Describe the relationship between the words in the following sets. From your
knowledge of the words at the left, deduce the meaning of those to the right:*

1. ἡ πόλις   ὁ πολίτης   πολῑτικός, -ή, -όν
2. ἡ ναῦς   ὁ ναύτης   ναυτικός, -ή, -όν
3. ποιέω   ὁ ποιητής   ποιητικός, -ή, -όν

Grammar

2. Another Third Declension Noun: ὁ βασιλεύς

	Singular		**Plural**	
Nom.	ὁ	βασιλεύ-ς	οἱ	βασιλῆς
Gen.	τοῦ	βασιλέ-ως	τῶν	βασιλέ-ων
Dat.	τῷ	βασιλέ-ι (> εῖ)	τοῖς	βασιλεῦ-σι(ν)
Acc.	τὸν	βασιλέ-ᾱ	τοὺς	βασιλέ-ᾱς
Voc.	ὦ	βασιλεῦ	ὦ	βασιλῆς

The words ὁ Θησεύς and ὁ ἱερεύς are declined the same as ὁ βασιλεύς.

3. Uses of the Genitive Case

a. The genitive is frequently used to show possession, e.g., ὁ τοῦ παιδὸς κύων = the *boy's* dog, the dog *of the boy*. Note that the genitive is usually placed in the *attributive position* between the article and the noun (see Chapter 5, Grammar 7a, page 52).

b. The genitive is used to express the whole of which some part is mentioned; this is the genitive of the whole or the partitive genitive, e.g., τῶν παρόντων πολλοί "many *of those present*."

c. The genitive case is used after certain prepositions, often (but by no means always) expressing ideas of place from which, e.g., ἀπό from; διά through; ἐκ (ἐξ) out of; μετά with; and ὑπέρ on behalf of, for.

d. The genitive is used with certain verbs, e.g.:

ἡ Ἀριάδνη, ἐπεὶ πρῶτον ὁρᾷ τὸν Θησέα, ἐρᾷ αὐτοῦ.
Ariadne, when she first sees Theseus, loves him.

ὁ Θησεὺς τῇ ἀριστερᾷ λαμβάνεται τῆς κεφαλῆς τοῦ θηρίου.
Theseus takes hold of the head of the beast with his left hand.

Exercise 9e

Translate the following:

1. τί ἐστι τὸ τοῦ ξένου ὄνομα;
2. ὁ βασιλεὺς δέχεται τὸν τῶν Ἀθηναίων ἄγγελον.
3. ἀφικνούμεθα εἰς τὸν τοῦ πατρὸς ἀγρόν.
4. ὁ παῖς διὰ τῆς ὁδοῦ βαδίζων τῆς τοῦ πατρὸς χειρὸς ἔχεται.
5. οἱ πολῖται τοῦ ἀγγέλου ἀκούουσι βουλόμενοι γιγνώσκειν τοὺς τοῦ βασιλέως λόγους (*words*).
6. τῶν παρθένων αἱ μὲν πρὸς τῇ κρήνῃ μένουσιν, αἱ δὲ μετὰ τῶν μητέρων ἤδη ἐπανέρχονται.
7. We hear the messenger's words.
8. I am going to the house of the poet.
9. They are looking for the girl's father.
10. The mother hears the girl crying (δακρύω) and hurries out of the house.
11. The citizens seize the messenger and lead him to the king.
12. Many of the women want to go to the city with their husbands.

4. Some Uses of the Article

a. You have already met the following uses of the article (see Chapter 5, Grammar 3, page 44):

ὁ δέ = and/but he	ἡ δέ = and/but she
οἱ δέ = and/but they	αἱ δέ = and/but they

οἱ μέν . . . οἱ δέ = some . . . others
αἱ μέν . . . αἱ δέ = some . . . others
τὰ μέν . . . τὰ δέ = some . . . others

b. The article + a participle form a noun phrase that may be translated by a relative clause in English, e.g.:

οἱ ἐν τῷ ἀγρῷ ἐργαζόμενοι = the in the field working [men] = the men who are working in the field

ὁ ἱερεὺς ὁ τὴν θυσίαν ποιούμενος = the priest who is making the sacrifice

Exercise 9f

Read aloud and translate:

1. ὁ πατὴρ τὸν παῖδα κελεύει ἐν τῇ οἰκίᾳ μένειν· ὁ δὲ οὐ πείθεται αὐτῷ.
2. τῶν πολῑτῶν οἱ μὲν οἴκαδε ἐπανέρχονται, οἱ δὲ μένουσιν τὴν πομπὴν θεώμενοι.
3. αἱ παρθένοι αἱ τὰ κανᾶ (*baskets*) φέρουσαι κάλλισταί εἰσιν.
4. οἱ τοὺς χοροὺς θεώμενοι μάλα χαίρουσιν.
5. ἆρ᾽ ὁρᾷς τοὺς ἐν τῷ ἀγρῷ πονοῦντας;

*   *   *

Ο ΟΔΥΣΣΕΥΣ ΚΑΙ Η ΚΙΡΚΗ

Read the following passages and answer the comprehension questions:

Odysseus comes to the island of Aeaea, where the witch Circe lives:

ἐπεὶ δὲ ἡμᾶς ἀποπέμπει ὁ Αἴολος, ἀποπλέομεν λῡπούμενοι καὶ δι᾽ ὀλίγου ἀφικνούμεθα εἰς τὴν νῆσον Αἰαίᾱν· ἐκεῖ δὲ οἰκεῖ ἡ Κίρκη, θεὸς οὖσα δεινή. ἐγὼ δὲ τοὺς ἑταίρους πρὸς τῇ νηῒ λείπων ἐπὶ ὄρος τι ἀναβαίνω, βουλόμενος γιγνώσκειν εἴ τις ἄνθρωπος ἐν τῇ νήσῳ οἰκεῖ. ἐπεὶ δὲ εἰς ἄκρον τὸ ὄρος ἀφικνοῦμαι, καπνὸν ὁρῶ πρὸς τὸν οὐρανὸν φερόμενον. πρὸς τὴν ναῦν οὖν ἐπανέρχομαι καὶ τῶν ἑταίρων τοὺς 5 μὲν κελεύω πρὸς τῇ νηῒ μένειν, τοὺς δὲ κελεύω πρὸς μέσην τὴν νῆσον πορευομένους γιγνώσκειν τίς ἐκεῖ οἰκεῖ. ὁ δὲ Εὐρύλοχος αὐτοῖς ἡγεῖται.

[λῡπούμενοι grieving   εἴ τις if any   καπνόν smoke   φερόμενον rising
Εὐρύλοχος Eurylochus]

1. With what feelings do Odysseus and his men set sail?
2. How is Circe described?
3. Why does Odysseus climb the hill?
4. What does he see from the top of the hill?
5. With what purpose in mind does Odysseus send some of his men to the middle of the island?
6. Who leads them?

οἱ δὲ τὴν τῆς Κίρκης οἰκίᾶν εὑρίσκουσιν ἐν μέσῃ ὕλῃ οὖσαν· ἐγγὺς δὲ τῆς οἰκίᾶς
πολλούς τε λύκους ὁρῶσι καὶ πολλοὺς λέοντας. τούτους δὲ ὁρῶντες μάλα φοβοῦνται
καὶ ἐπὶ τῇ θύρᾳ μένουσιν. ἔπειτα δὲ τῆς Κίρκης ἀκούουσιν ἔνδον ἀειδούσης.　10
καλοῦσιν οὖν αὐτήν· ἡ δὲ ἐκ τῆς θύρᾱς ἐκβαίνει καὶ εἰσκαλεῖ αὐτούς. οἱ δὲ πάντες
ἕπονται αὐτῇ· μόνος δὲ ὁ Εὐρύλοχος ἔξω μένει, φοβούμενος κίνδῡνόν τινα. ἡ δὲ Κίρκη
τοὺς ἄλλους εἰσάγει καὶ καθίζεσθαι κελεύει καὶ σῖτόν τε αὐτοῖς παρέχει καὶ
οἶνον· φάρμακα δὲ κακὰ τῷ σίτῳ κυκᾷ.

[ὕλη woods　ἐγγύς (+ gen.) near　λέοντας lions　ἐπί (+ dat.) at　ἔνδον inside
ἀειδούσης singing　μόνος only　ἔξω outside　φάρμακα . . . κακά evil
drugs　κυκᾷ she mixes]

7.　What do the men see around Circe's house?
8.　What feeling prompts the men to wait at Circe's door rather than going
in?
9.　What do they hear?
10.　Why does Circe come out of the door?
11.　Who follow her in?
12.　Why does Eurylochus not go in?
13.　What three things does Circe give the men to eat and drink?

ἐπεὶ δὲ οἱ ἑταῖροι ἐσθίουσι τὸν σῖτον, ἡ Κίρκη ῥάβδῳ αὐτοὺς πλήττει καὶ εἰς　15
τοὺς σῦφεοὺς ἐλαύνει· οἱ δὲ εὐθὺς σύες γίγνονται. ἔπειτα δὲ ἡ Κίρκη βαλάνους
αὐτοῖς βάλλει ἐσθίειν καὶ λείπει αὐτοὺς ἐν τοῖς σῦφεοῖς.

[ῥάβδῳ with her wand　πλήττει strikes　τοὺς σῦφεοὺς the pigsties　εὐθύς
straightway　σύες pigs　βαλάνους acorns]

14.　How does Circe change the men into pigs?
15.　What does she now give them to eat and where does she leave them?

Exercise 9g

Translate into Greek:　　　　　Odysseus threatens Circe.

1.　When Eurylochus sees what is happening, he flees and runs to the
ship.
2.　But I, when I hear everything, go to Circe's house, wishing to save my
comrades.
3.　And Circe gives me food and wine; then, striking me with her wand,
she orders (me) to go to the pigsties.
4.　But I do not become a pig (σῦς); and she, being very afraid, is willing
to free (λύειν) my comrades.

10
Η ΣΥΜΦΟΡΑ (α)

ὁ πρῶτος χορὸς προχωρεῖ, τὰ τοῦ Διονύσου ἔργα ὑμνῶν.

Vocabulary

Verb
νῑκάω I defeat, win
Noun
ἡ σπονδή, τῆς σπονδῆς
  libation

Adverb
καλῶς well
Interjection
φεῦ (*often used with gen. of cause*) alas!

τῇ δὲ ὑστεραίᾳ ἐπεὶ πρῶτον ἀνατέλλει ὁ ἥλιος, ὁ Δικαιόπολις τήν τε γυναῖκα καὶ τὸν πάππον καὶ τοὺς παῖδας ἐγείρει καὶ αὐτοῖς ἡγεῖται πρὸς τὸ τοῦ Διονύσου θέατρον. πρῷ οὖν ἀφικνοῦνται ἀλλ' ἤδη πλεῖστοι ἄνθρωποι τὸ θέατρον πληροῦσιν. ὁ οὖν πάππος στενάζει καί, "φεῦ, φεῦ," φησίν, "μεστόν ἐστι τὸ πᾶν θέατρον. ποῦ δυνατόν ἐστι καθίζεσθαι;" ὁ δὲ Δικαιόπολις, "θάρρει, πάππε," φησὶ καὶ ἡγεῖται αὐτοῖς ἄνω καὶ θρᾶνον εὑρίσκει ἐν ἄκρῳ τῷ θεάτρῳ. 5

[**ἀνατέλλει** rises   **τὸ ... θέᾱτρον** the theater   **πρῷ** early   **πλεῖστοι** very many   **πληροῦσιν** are filling   **μεστόν** full   **θάρρει** cheer up!   **ἄνω** upwards   **θρᾶνον** bench]

ἐπεὶ δὲ πρῶτον καθίζονται, ὁ σαλπιγκτὴς προχωρεῖ καὶ σαλπίζει, τοὺς πολίτας κελεύων εὐφημεῖν. ἔπειτα δὲ ὁ τοῦ Διονύσου ἱερεὺς τῷ

βωμῷ προσχωρεῖ καὶ σπονδὴν ποιεῖται, τῷ θεῷ εὐχόμενος· "ὦ ἄναξ   10
Διόνῡσε, τήν τε σπονδὴν ἵλαος δέχου καὶ τοὺς χοροὺς χαίρων θεῶ."

[ὁ σαλπιγκτής the trumpeter   σαλπίζει sounds his trumpet   εὐφημεῖν to keep
silence   ἄναξ lord   θεῶ (from θεάομαι) watch!]

ἐνταῦθα δὴ ὁ πρῶτος χορὸς προχωρεῖ εἰς τὴν ὀρχήστρᾱν, τὰ τοῦ
Διονύσου ἔργα ὑμνῶν. θαυμάζει οὖν ἡ Μέλιττα θεωμένη καὶ χαίρει
ἀκούουσα. οὕτω γὰρ καλῶς χορεύει ὁ χορός. πέντε χοροὶ παίδων
καὶ πέντε ἀνδρῶν ἐφεξῆς ἀγωνίζονται καὶ πάντες ἄριστα χορεύουσιν.   15
ἐπεὶ δὲ παύεται ὁ δέκατος χορός, οἱ νῑκῶντες τοὺς στεφάνους
δέχονται καὶ πάντες οἱ παρόντες σπεύδουσιν ἐκ τοῦ θεάτρου.

[τὴν ὀρχήστρᾱν the dancing circle   ὑμνῶν hymning, praising   χορεύει
dances   ἐφεξῆς in order   ἀγωνίζονται compete   ἄριστα very well   τοὺς
στεφάνους garlands]

Word Study

*Identify the Greek roots in the italicized words below and give the meanings of
the English words:*

1. He found fulfillment in an *agonistic* way of life.
2. She is studying *macroeconomics*.
3. He suffers from *xenophobia*.
4. He is a dangerous *pyromaniac*. What does ἡ μανίᾱ mean?
5. She is an *ophthalmic* surgeon.

Grammar

1. Two More Third Declension Nouns: ἡ πόλις and τὸ ἄστυ

	Singular		**Plural**	
Nom.	ἡ	πόλι-ς	αἱ	πόλε-ες > πόλεις
Gen.	τῆς	πόλε-ως	τῶν	πόλε-ων
Dat.	τῇ	πόλε-ι	ταῖς	πόλε-σι(ν)
Acc.	τὴν	πόλι-ν	τὰς	πόλεις
Voc.	ὦ	πόλι	ὦ	πόλε-ες > πόλεις
Nom.	τὸ	ἄστυ	τὰ	ἄστε-α > ἄστη
Gen.	τοῦ	ἄστε-ως	τῶν	ἄστε-ων
Dat.	τῷ	ἄστε-ι	τοῖς	ἄστε-σι(ν)
Acc.	τὸ	ἄστυ	τὰ	ἄστε-α > ἄστη
Voc.	ὦ	ἄστυ	ὦ	ἄστε-α > ἄστη

Note the -ως ending instead of -ος in the genitive singular and ν instead
of α in the accusative singular of πόλις.

Exercise 10a

Read aloud and translate:

1. ἡμεῖς πρὸς τὸ ἄστυ ἐρχόμεθα, βουλόμενοι τήν τε ἑορτὴν θεᾶσθαι καὶ τὴν πομπήν· ἆρα βούλῃ μεθ' ἡμῶν ἰέναι;

2. ἐγὼ μὲν μάλιστα βούλομαι ἰέναι· ἀλλὰ πότε ἐν νῷ ἔχετε ἀπὸ τοῦ ἄστεως ἐπανιέναι;

3. ἐν νῷ ἔχομεν τὴν μὲν νύκτα ἐν τῷ ἄστει μένειν, αὔριον (*tomorrow*) δὲ ἐπανιέναι.

4. ἤδη ἐν τῇ ἀγορᾷ ἐσμεν· τοσοῦτοί δ' εἰσιν ἄνθρωποι ἐν ταῖς ὁδοῖς ὥστε μόλις ἔξεστι (*it is possible*) προχωρεῖν πρὸς τὴν Ἀκρόπολιν.

5. πάντες μὲν γὰρ οἱ πολῖται πάρεισιν, πάντες δὲ οἱ μέτοικοι (*resident aliens*), πολλοὶ δὲ ξένοι ἥκουσιν ἀπὸ τῶν τῆς ἀρχῆς (*the empire*) πόλεων.

6. ὡς καλαί εἰσιν αἱ παρθένοι αἱ τὰ κανᾶ (*baskets*) φέρουσαι. ἆρ' ὁρᾷς τόν τε ἱερέα καὶ τοὺς νεανίας τὴν τοῦ θεοῦ εἰκόνα (*image*) φέροντας;

7. ἤδη εἰς τὸ τέμενος (*sanctuary*) εἰσέρχονται· ἆρ' οὐ βούλεσθε τῇ πομπῇ ἕπεσθαι εἰς τὸ τέμενος;

Festivals

Knights in the Panathenaic procession on the Parthenon frieze

In the course of his praise of the democracy, Pericles says in his funeral oration: "We provide more recreations for the mind from toil than any other state, with competitions and sacrifices throughout the year." There were in fact over sixty days in the year that were holidays in Athens, when festivals were held in honor of the gods. These involved all members of the population, citizens and metics, men and women, children and slaves. Many festivals entailed processions, and most culminated in public sacrifice, followed by a feast in which all present joined.

The greatest of all the processions is represented on the Parthenon frieze. Here we see all classes of Athenians playing a part. The knights are shown, at first preparing for parade, then moving off, and later entering the procession at a canter. Stewards are portrayed, marshaling the procession. Next comes a group of elders, led by lyre players and flutists. Ahead of them are young men bearing jugs of holy water and others with trays of offerings. Girls carry wine jars, bowls for pouring libations, and incense burners. The victims are led toward the central scene on the east side, where in the middle stand the priestess and a magistrate with the robe that has been offered to Athena. On either side of them are seated larger figures, looking outward toward the procession; these are the twelve Olympian gods, watching and enjoying the procession.

Sacrifice was performed at the altar, which stood outside every shrine, in accordance with a set ritual. Priest and victims wore garlands. There was a call for holy silence. The altar and participants were sprinkled with water. Then the priest scattered sacred grain over the victim's head and cut a lock of hair from it, which he burnt in the altar fire. The victim was lifted up by attendants and stunned with a blow from a club. Then, while music played, the priest cut the victim's throat and caught the blood in a dish; this was poured as an offering over the altar. Next the victim was skinned and cut up. The inedible parts (the thigh bones wrapped in fat) were burned on the altar for the gods, and the rest was cooked and divided among the people to eat. Thus, gods and men shared the sacrificial banquet.

Sacrifice to Apollo

Every festival had its own ritual. Many, perhaps all, were celebrated with music and dancing. At some there were athletic competitions, notably at the Panathenaea. At the most important festival of Dionysus, the Greater Dionysia, the ten tribes into which the Athenian people were divided each put on a chorus, five of men and five of boys, which sang and danced in competition. Later in the festival, which lasted six days in all, there were four days of drama. On each of these days, three tragedies were performed in the morning, followed in the afternoon by a satyr play (an old form of drama in which the chorus consisted of satyrs, half-man, half-goat) and a comedy. The theater held between 17,000 and 20,000 people, so that a large proportion of the citizens could be present.

Η ΣΥΜΦΟΡΑ (β)

ὁ Φίλιππος νεᾱνίᾱς τινὰς ὁρᾷ ἐν τῇ ὁδῷ μαχομένους.

Vocabulary

Verbs

δεῖ (+ *acc. and infinitive*) it is
necessary

δεῖ ἡμᾶς παρεῖναι we must
be there

ἔξεστι(ν) (+ *dat. and infinitive*)
it is allowed, possible

ἔξεστιν ἡμῖν ἐπανιέναι w e
are allowed to return, we
may return, we can return

τρέπω I turn; (*middle,
intransitive*) I turn myself,
turn

Nouns

ἡ βοή, τῆς βοῆς shout

ἡ κεφαλή, τῆς κεφαλῆς head

οἱ τεκόντες, τῶν τεκόντων
(*plural*) parents

τὸ ὕδωρ, τοῦ ὕδατος water

Preposition

πρό (+ *gen.*) before (of time or
place)

Adverbs

εὐθύς immediately

ποτέ (*enclitic*) (at) some time,
ever

ἤδη μεσημβρίᾱ ἐστίν, ὁ δὲ Δικαιόπολις βούλεται εἰς τὸν κλῆρον
ἐπανιέναι. "ἄγε δή," φησίν, "καιρός ἐστιν οἴκαδε σπεύδειν, δεῖ γὰρ
ἡμᾶς πρὸ τῆς νυκτὸς ἐκεῖσε παρεῖναι." ἡ δὲ Μυρρίνη, "ἀλλ', ὦ φίλε
ἄνερ, ἆρ' οὐ βούλῃ τὰς τραγῳδίᾱς θεᾶσθαι; ἆρ' οὐκ ἔξεστιν ἡμῖν
αὔριον ἐπανιέναι;" ὁ δὲ Δικαιόπολις, "οὐχί," φησίν, "ἀλλὰ δεῖ ἡμᾶς   5
εὐθὺς πορεύεσθαι. ἤδη γὰρ πολὺν χρόνον τοῦ κλήρου ἄπεσμεν καὶ
ὁ Ξανθίᾱς ἀμελεῖ οὐδὲν ποιεῖ. οἱ οὖν βόες πεινῶσιν, τὰ δὲ μῆλα
ἀποφεύγει, ὁ δὲ οἶκος κατ' εἰκὸς καίεται. ἄγε. δεῖ σπεύδειν."

[μεσημβρίᾱ midday   τὸν κλῆρον the farm   τὰς τραγῳδίᾱς the   tragedies
αὔριον tomorrow   τοῦ κλήρου from the farm (with ἄπεσμεν)   ἀμελεῖ
certainly   πεινῶσιν are hungry   κατ' εἰκός probably]

οὕτω λέγει καὶ ταχέως ἡγεῖται αὐτοῖς πρὸς τὰς πύλας. ἐν ᾧ δὲ
σπεύδουσι διὰ τῶν ὁδῶν, ὁ Φίλιππος νεᾱνίᾱς τινὰς ὁρᾷ ἐν τῇ ὁδῷ   10
μαχομένους· πολὺν γὰρ οἶνον πεπώκᾱσιν καὶ μεθύουσιν. μένει οὖν
ὁ Φίλιππος τὴν μάχην θεώμενος· τέλος δὲ οἱ ἄλλοι νεᾱνίαι ἕνα τινὰ
καταβάλλουσι καὶ οὐ παύονται τύπτοντες αὐτόν. ὁ δὲ Φίλιππος
φοβούμενος ὑπὲρ αὐτοῦ προστρέχει καί, "παύετε, μὴ τύπτετε αὐτόν,
ὦ ἄνθρωποι," φησίν· "ἀποκτείνετε γὰρ τὸν τλήμονα." τῶν δὲ νεᾱνιῶν   15
τις ἀγρίως βοῶν πρὸς τὸν Φίλιππον τρέπεται καί, "τίς ὢν σύ," φησίν,
"οὕτω πολυπρᾱγμονεῖς;" καὶ τύπτει αὐτόν. ὁ δὲ πρὸς τὴν γῆν
καταπῑπτει καὶ ἀκῑνητος μένει.

[πεπώκᾱσιν (from πῑνω) they have drunk   μεθύουσιν   they are drunk   τὴν
μάχην the fight   τὸν τλήμονα the poor man   πολυπρᾱγμονεῖς do you
interfere?   ἀκῑνητος motionless]

οἱ δὲ τεκόντες τὰς βοὰς ἀκούοντες σπεύδουσι πρὸς τὸν παῖδα καὶ
ὁρῶσιν αὐτὸν ἐπὶ τῇ γῇ κείμενον. αἴρουσιν οὖν αὐτόν, ὁ δὲ ἔτι   20
ἀκῑνητος μένει. ἡ δὲ Μέλιττα, "ὦ Ζεῦ," φησίν, "τί ποτε πάσχει ὁ
τλήμων;" ἡ δὲ μήτηρ, "φέρετε αὐτὸν πρὸς τὴν κρήνην." φέρουσιν
οὖν αὐτὸν πρὸς τὴν κρήνην καὶ τὸ ὕδωρ καταχέουσι τῆς κεφαλῆς.
δι' ὀλίγου οὖν κῑνεῖται καὶ ἀναπνεῖ. ἐπαίρει οὖν ἑαυτὸν καὶ τῆς
μητρὸς ἀκούει λεγούσης. βλέπων δὲ πρὸς αὐτήν, "ποῦ εἶ σύ, μῆτερ;"   25
φησίν· "διὰ τί σκότος ἐστίν;" ἡ δὲ μήτηρ, "ἀλλ' οὐ σκότος ἐστίν, ὦ
παῖ· βλέπε δεῦρο." ἀλλ' οὐδὲν ὁρᾷ ὁ παῖς· τυφλὸς γάρ ἐστιν.

[κείμενον lying   καταχέουσι they pour X (acc.) over Y (gen.)   κῑνεῖται he
moves   ἀναπνεῖ he breathes again, recovers   ἐπαίρει lifts ... up   σκότος
darkness]

Word Building

*Study the relationships between the nouns and verbs in the following sets, and
give definitions of each word:*

1.	μάχομαι	ἡ μάχη	2.	ἡ θέᾱ	θεάομαι
	εὔχομαι	ἡ εὐχή		ἡ βοή	βοάω
	βούλομαι	ἡ βουλή		ἡ νίκη	νῑκάω
	λέγω	ὁ λόγος		ἡ σῑγή	σῑγάω
	πέμπω	ἡ πομπή			
	σπεύδω	ἡ σπουδή			

3. σώφρων   σωφρονέω   ὁ παῖς   παιδεύω
   (σωφρον-)   (παιδ-)
   ἡ νόσος   νοσέω
   (sickness)   5. ὁ χρόνος   χρονίζω
   ὁ φόβος   φοβέομαι   ὁ λόγος   λογίζομαι
                                        (calculation)
4. ὁ βασιλεύς   βασιλεύω   ἡ ὀργή   ὀργίζομαι
   ὁ πολίτης   πολῑτεύω
   ὁ κίνδῡνος   κινδῡνεύω

Grammar

2. Impersonal Verbs

Greek has a number of verbs that are used in the third person singular with an implied impersonal "it" as subject. You have met the following in the reading passage above:

Impersonal verb plus accusative and infinitive:

> δεῖ ἡμᾶς πρὸ τῆς νυκτὸς ἐκεῖσε παρεῖναι.
> It is necessary for us to be there before night.
> We must be there before night.

Impersonal verb plus dative and infinitive:

> ἆρ' ἔξεστιν ἡμῖν αὔριον ἐπανιέναι;
> Is it possible for us to return tomorrow?
> May we return tomorrow?
> Can we return tomorrow?

Exercise 10b

Translate the following pairs of sentences:

1. καιρός ἐστιν ἐπανιέναι· δεῖ ἡμᾶς εὐθὺς ὁρμᾶσθαι.
   Don't wait here; we must hurry.
2. ἆρ' οὐκ ἔξεστιν ἡμῖν τὰς τραγῳδίᾱς θεᾶσθαι;
   May I not stay in the city?
3. οὐ δεῖ σε τύπτειν τὸν νεᾱνίαν.
   We must carry the boy to the spring.
4. δεῖ τὸν Φίλιππον τῷ πατρὶ πείθεσθαι.
   Melissa must stay at home.
5. ἆρ' ἔξεστί μοι γιγνώσκειν τί πάσχει ὁ παῖς;
   We are allowed to go to the city; we must start immediately.

3. Review of Questions

ἆρα; (introduces a question)
ποῖ; where to?
πόθεν; where from?
πότε; when?
ποῦ; where?
πῶς; how?
τίς; τί; who? what?

Exercise 10c

Read aloud and translate:

1. διὰ τί βούλεται ὁ Ὀδυσσεὺς εἰς τὴν νῆσον πλεῖν;
2. βούλεται γιγνώσκειν τίνες ἐν τῇ νήσῳ οἰκοῦσιν.
3. ὁ Κύκλωψ τὸν Ὀδυσσέα ἐρωτᾷ (*asks*) πόθεν ἥκει.
4. πῶς ἐκφεύγουσιν ὅ τε Ὀδυσσεὺς καὶ οἱ ἑταῖροι;
5. ἆρα πάντας τοὺς ἑταίρους σῴζει ὁ Ὀδυσσεύς;
6. ἐπεὶ ἐκφεύγει ὁ Ὀδυσσεύς, ποῖ πλεῖ;
7. ὁ Αἴολος ἰὼν Ὀδυσσέα ἐρωτᾷ τίς ἐστι καὶ πόθεν ἥκει.
8. ὁ Αἴολος τὸν Ὀδυσσέα ἐρωτᾷ πότε ἐν νῷ ἔχει ἀποπλεῖν.

4. Review of Verbs

The following are full sets of the forms of λύω, φιλέω, τῑμάω, and εἰμί that you have met so far in this course:

Indicative	Imperative	Infinitive	Participle
		λύω: Active Voice	
λύω		λύειν	λύων, λύουσα,
λύεις	λῦε		λῦον
λύει			
λύομεν			
λύετε	λύετε		
λύουσι(ν)			
		λύω: Middle Voice	
λύομαι		λύεσθαι	λυόμενος, -η,
λύῃ *or* λύει	λύου		-ον
λύεται			
λυόμεθα			
λύεσθε	λύεσθε		
λύονται			

Indicative	Imperative	Infinitive	Participle

φιλέω: Active Voice

Indicative	Imperative	Infinitive	Participle
φιλῶ		φιλεῖν	φιλῶν, φιλοῦσα,
φιλεῖς	φίλει		φιλοῦν
φιλεῖ			
φιλοῦμεν			
φιλεῖτε	φιλεῖτε		
φιλοῦσι(ν)			

φιλέω: Middle Voice

Indicative	Imperative	Infinitive	Participle
φιλοῦμαι		φιλεῖσθαι	φιλούμενος, -η,
φιλῇ or φιλεῖ	φιλοῦ		-ον
φιλεῖται			
φιλούμεθα			
φιλεῖσθε	φιλεῖσθε		
φιλοῦνται			

τῑμάω: Active Voice

Indicative	Imperative	Infinitive	Participle
τῑμῶ		τῑμᾶν	τῑμῶν, τῑμῶσα,
τῑμᾷς	τίμᾱ		τῑμῶν
τῑμᾷ			
τῑμῶμεν			
τῑμᾶτε	τῑμᾶτε		
τῑμῶσι(ν)			

τῑμάω: Middle Voice

Indicative	Imperative	Infinitive	Participle
τῑμῶμαι		τῑμᾶσθαι	τῑμώμενος, -η,
τῑμᾷ	τῑμῶ		-ον
τῑμᾶται			
τῑμώμεθα			
τῑμᾶσθε	τῑμᾶσθε		
τῑμῶνται			

εἰμί: Active Voice Only

Indicative	Imperative	Infinitive	Participle
εἰμί		εἶναι	ὤν, οὖσα, ὄν
εἶ	ἴσθι		
ἐστί(ν)			
ἐσμέν			
ἐστέ	ἔστε		
εἰσί(ν)			

Ο ΟΔΥΣΣΕΥΣ ΤΟΥΣ ΕΤΑΙΡΟΥΣ ΑΠΟΛΛΥΣΙΝ

Read the following passages and answer the comprehension questions:

ὁ δὲ Ὀδυσσεὺς πολλὰ ἔτι καὶ δεινὰ πάσχει σπεύδων εἰς τὴν πατρίδα γῆν νοστεῖν. τὰς γὰρ Σειρῆνας μόλις φεύγει, καὶ παρὰ τὴν Σικελίαν πλέων εἰς τὸν μέγιστον κίνδῡνον ἐμπίπτει. ἔνθεν μὲν γάρ ἐστιν ἡ Σκύλλη, τέρας δεινόν, ἓξ κεφαλὰς ἔχουσα, ἣ ἐξ ἄντρου τινὸς ὁρμωμένη τοὺς παραπλέοντας ἁρπάζει καὶ ἐσθίει· ἔνθεν δ' ἐστὶν ἡ Χάρυβδις, δῑνη μάλα φοβερά, ἣ πάντα καταπίνει. ὁ δὲ 5
Ὀδυσσεὺς τὴν Χάρυβδιν φεύγων παρὰ τὴν Σκύλλην παραπλεῖ· ἡ δὲ ἐκ τοῦ ἄντρου ὁρμωμένη ἓξ τῶν ἑταίρων ἁρπάζει· τοὺς δ' ἄλλους σῴζει ὁ Ὀδυσσεύς.

[τὴν πατρίδα γῆν the (= his) fatherland   νοστεῖν to return   τὰς . . .
Σειρῆνας the Sirens   παρὰ τὴν Σικελίαν along *or* past Sicily   ἐμπίπτει = ἐν
+ πίπτει   ἔνθεν . . . ἔνθεν on one side . . . on the other side   ἡ Σκύλλη Scylla,
a monster formed of a woman and six dogs   τέρας a monster   ἥ which
ἄντρου cave   ἁρπάζει snatches   ἡ Χάρυβδις Charybdis   δῑνη a whirlpool
φοβερά frightening   καταπίνει drinks *or* gulps down]

1. What does Odysseus continue to experience as he hastens to return home?
2. Where does he fall into the greatest danger?
3. How is Scylla described?
4. How is Charybdis described?
5. What does Scylla do as Odysseus sails by?
6. Why did Odysseus have to sail so close to Scylla?

δι' ὀλίγου εἰς ἄλλην τινὰ νῆσον ἀφικνοῦνται· ἐκεῖ δὲ πολλοὺς βοῦς εὑρίσκουσιν· οἱ δὲ ἑταῖροι βούλονται ἀποκτείνειν αὐτοὺς καὶ ἐσθίειν. ὁ δὲ Ὀδυσσεύς, "μὴ βλάπτετε τοὺς βοῦς," φησίν· "εἰσὶ γὰρ τῷ Ἡλίῳ." οἱ δὲ οὐ πείθονται αὐτῷ ἀλλὰ 10
ἀποκτείνουσι τοὺς βοῦς. ὁ μὲν οὖν Ἥλιος τῷ πατρὶ Διῒ εὐχόμενος, "Ζεῦ πάτερ," φησίν, "οἱ τοῦ Ὀδυσσέως ἑταῖροι τοὺς ἐμοὺς βοῦς ἀποκτείνουσιν. τῑμώρει οὖν αὐτούς. εἰ δὲ μή, οὐδέποτε αὖθις ἐν τοῖς ἀνθρώποις λάμψω."

[βλάπτετε harm   τῷ Ἡλίῳ the Sun God   τῑμώρει punish!   εἰ . . . μή if not
οὐδέποτε never   λάμψω I will shine]

7. What do Odysseus' comrades find on the island, and what do they want to do?
8. Why does Odysseus tell them not to do this?
9. Do they obey?
10. What does the Sun God ask Zeus to do?
11. What threat does the Sun God make?

ὁ δὲ Ζεὺς ἀκούει αὐτοῦ εὐχομένου· ἐπεὶ γὰρ ὅ τε Ὀδυσσεὺς καὶ οἱ ἑταῖροι ἀποπλέοντες τὴν νῆσον λείπουσιν, χειμῶνα δεινὸν πέμπει καὶ τὴν ναῦν κεραύνῳ 15
πλήττει. πάντες οὖν οἱ ἑταῖροι ἐκ τῆς νεὼς ἐκπίπτουσι καὶ ἀποθνήσκουσιν· μόνος δὲ ὁ Ὀδυσσεὺς ἐκφεύγει, τοῦ ἱστοῦ λαμβανόμενος.

[κεραύνῳ with a thunderbolt   πλήττει strikes   ἀποθνῄσκουσιν die   μόνος
only   τοῦ ἱστοῦ the mast]

12. What three things does Zeus do?
13. What happens to Odysseus' comrades? How does Odysseus escape?

The Sirens sing to Odysseus as he sails by.

Exercise 10d

Translate into Greek:

1. For nine days the wind (ὁ ἄνεμος) carries Odysseus (τὸν ᾿Οδυσσέα)
    through the sea, but on the tenth he arrives at another island.
2. The nymph (ἡ νύμφη) Calypso (ἡ Καλυψώ) lives there; she receives
    him kindly (εὐμενῶς).
3. Loving him, she says: "Stay with me always on the island." But
    Odysseus wants to return home and see his wife and child.
4. Finally Zeus sends a messenger and orders the nymph to release
    (λύω) Odysseus.
5. Calypso tells him to make a raft (σχεδίᾱ) and helps him.
6. When the raft is ready, Odysseus sails away rejoicing.

PREVIEW OF NEW VERB FORMS

Most of the verbs in the stories up to now have been in the present tense. In the stories in the following chapters you will meet verbs in the future, imperfect, aorist, and perfect tenses. Forms that you have not met before will be glossed at their first appearance in each of the readings, and the various tenses will be formally explained in appropriate chapters.

The following is a brief overview of the Greek verbal system, which is really quite simple in its general outlines. It will give you a framework within which you will be able to place the various new verb forms that you will meet and learn.

First we give sample forms of λύω, which is typical of many Greek verbs that have past tense formations called *first aorist*:

Present: λύ-ω I loosen, am loosening, do loosen
Future: λύ-σ-ω I will loosen, will be loosening
Imperfect: ἔ-λῡ-**ον** I was loosening, loosened
First aorist: ἔ-λῡ-**σα** I loosened, did loosen
 First aorist infinitive: λῡ-**σαι** to loosen, (*sometimes*) to have loosened
 First aorist participle: λύ-**σᾱς** loosening, (*sometimes*) having
  loosened
Perfect: λέ λυ κα I have loosened

Some verbs have past tense formations called *second aorist*; here are the present and aorist tenses of such a verb (note the different stem in the aorist):

Present: **λαμβάν**-ω I take, am taking, do take
Second aorist: ἔ-**λαβ**-ον I took, did take
 Second aorist infinitive: **λαβ**-εῖν to take, (*sometimes*) to have taken
 Second aorist participle: **λαβ**-ών taking, (*sometimes*) having taken

1. The future tense is usually formed with -σ-.
2. The imperfect is formed from the verb stem used in the present tense + the prefix ἐ-, which shows past time.
3. The first aorist is formed with the suffix -σα and the prefix ἐ-, which shows past time and appears only in the indicative mood. It is absent from other forms such as the infinitive and participle, which usually do not refer to past time.
4. The perfect tense is formed by reduplicating the verb stem used in the present tense and adding the suffix -κα. Reduplicating means prefixing the first consonant of the verb + ε.
5. Some verbs have second rather than first aorists (a few have both). In second aorists there is a change in the stem of the verb and no -σα suffix.

11
Ο ΙΑΤΡΟΣ (α)

ἐπεὶ ἀφίκοντο εἰς τὴν τοῦ ἀδελφοῦ οἰκίᾱν, ὁ Δικαιόπολις ἔκοψε τὴν θύρᾱν.

Vocabulary

Verbs

αἰτέω I ask, ask for

ἀφικνέομαι, ἀφῑκόμην I arrive, arrive at (+ εἰς + *acc.*)

γίγνομαι, ἐγενόμην I become

δακρύω I cry, weep

δοκεῖ (+ *dat. and infinitive*) it seems (good)

   δοκεῖ μοι it seems good to me, I decide, I think it best

εἰσάγω, εἰσήγαγον I lead in, take in

ἔφη he/she said

κομίζω I bring, take

κόπτω, ἔκοψα I strike, knock on (a door)

λαμβάνω, ἔλαβον I take; (*middle + gen.*) I seize, take hold of

μανθάνω, ἔμαθον I learn, understand

πάσχω, ἔπαθον I suffer, experience

σκοπέω I look at, examine, consider

Nouns

ὁ ἀδελφός, τοῦ ἀδελφοῦ, ὦ ἄδελφε brother

ὁ ἰᾱτρός, τοῦ ἰᾱτροῦ doctor

ὁ λόγος, τοῦ λόγου word, story

Adjective

σοφός, -ή, -όν skilled, wise, clever

τυφλός, -ή, -όν blind

Preposition

παρά (+ *acc.*) to

Adverb

αὔριον tomorrow

Conjunction

εἰ if

Expressions

καλῶς ἔχω I am well

πῶς ἔχεις; How are you?

ἡ δὲ Μυρρίνη ἐπεὶ ἔμαθεν ὅτι τυφλός ἐστιν ὁ παῖς, δακρύουσα τῷ
ἀνδρί, "ὦ Ζεῦ," ἔφη, "τί δεῖ ἡμᾶς ποιεῖν; τοῖς θεοῖς εὔχου βοηθεῖν
ἡμῖν." ὁ δὲ Δικαιόπολις, "ἀλλὰ δεῖ ἡμᾶς τὸν παῖδα φέρειν παρὰ
ἰᾱτρόν τινα," ἔφη· "ἀλλ' ἑσπέρᾱ ἤδη γίγνεται. νῦν οὖν δεῖ πρὸς τὴν
τοῦ ἀδελφοῦ οἰκίᾱν σπεύδειν καὶ αἰτεῖν αὐτὸν ἡμᾶς δέχεσθαι.   5
αὔριον δὲ δεῖ ζητεῖν ἰᾱτρόν."

βραδέως οὖν τῷ παιδὶ ἡγούμενοι βαδίζουσιν πρὸς τὴν τοῦ
ἀδελφοῦ οἰκίᾱν. ἐπεὶ δ' ἀφίκοντο, ὁ μὲν Δικαιόπολις ἔκοψε τὴν
θύρᾱν. ὁ δὲ ἀδελφὸς πρὸς τὴν θύρᾱν ἐλθὼν καὶ τὸν Δικαιόπολιν
ἰδών, "χαῖρε, ὦ ἄδελφε," ἔφη· "πῶς ἔχεις; σὺ δέ, ὦ Μυρρίνη, χαῖρε καὶ   10
σύ. ἀλλ' εἴπετέ μοι, τί πάσχετε; διὰ τί οὐκ ἐπανέρχεσθε εἰς τοὺς
ἀγροὺς ἀλλ' ἔτι μένετε ἐν τῷ ἄστει; ἑσπέρᾱ γὰρ ἤδη γίγνεται." ὁ δὲ
Δικαιόπολις, "ἐγὼ μὲν καλῶς ἔχω, ὁ δὲ παῖς—ἰδού—τυφλὸς γὰρ
γέγονεν· οὐδὲν ὁρᾷ. πάρεσμεν οὖν αἰτοῦντές σε ἡμᾶς δέχεσθαι." ὁ δὲ
ἀδελφός ἰδὼν τὸν παῖδα τυφλὸν ὄντα, "ὦ Ζεῦ," ἔφη, "τί ποτε ἔπαθεν ὁ   15
παῖς; εἰσέλθετε καὶ εἴπετέ μοι τί ἐγένετο."

[ἐλθών coming, having come   ἰδών seeing, having seen   γέγονεν has become, is
εἰσέλθετε come in!]

οὕτως εἰπὼν εἰσήγαγεν αὐτοὺς εἰς τὴν οἰκίᾱν· οἱ δὲ πάντα τὰ
γενόμενα αὐτῷ εἶπον. ὁ δὲ τὴν γυναῖκα καλῶν, "ἐλθὲ δεῦρο," ἔφη·
"πάρεισι γὰρ ὅ τε Δικαιόπολις καὶ ἡ Μυρρίνη· ὁ δὲ Φίλιππος δεινὸν
ἔπαθεν· τυφλὸς γὰρ γέγονεν. κόμιζε οὖν αὐτόν τε καὶ τὰς γυναῖκας   20
εἰς τὸν γυναικῶνα. σὺ δέ, ὦ ἄδελφε, ἐλθὲ δεῦρο." ὅ τε οὖν
Δικαιόπολις καὶ ὁ ἀδελφὸς εἰς τὸν ἀνδρῶνα εἰσελθόντες πολλὰ
διαλέγονται σκοποῦντες τί δεῖ ποιεῖν. τέλος δὲ ὁ ἀδελφός, "ἅλις
λόγων," ἔφη· "ἐγὼ σοφὸν ἰᾱτρὸν ἔγνωκα καὶ αὔριον, εἴ σοι δοκεῖ,
κομιῶ ὑμᾶς παρὰ αὐτόν. νῦν δέ—ὀψὲ γάρ ἐστιν—δεῖ ἡμᾶς καθεύδειν."   25

[εἰπών saying, having said   τὰ γενόμενα the things that (had) happened   εἶπον
they told   τὸν γυναικῶνα the women's quarters   τὸν ἀνδρῶνα the men's
quarters   εἰσελθόντες entering, having entered   ἅλις enough (+ gen.)   ἔγνωκα
I know   κομιῶ I will take   ὀψέ late]

Word Study

Identify the Greek roots in the English words below and give the meanings of the English words:

1. logic
2. dialogue
3. monologue

4. prologue
5. eulogy

Grammar

1. Verb Forms: Past Tense: The Aorist

Both English and Greek have several different past tenses, e.g., I was coming, I came, I have come, I had come. The term aorist in Greek means "unlimited," and the aorist expresses simple, undifferentiated action. In the indicative mood, it expresses simple, undifferentiated action, usually in past time, e.g., "I came."

There are two ways of forming the aorist in Greek, corresponding to two ways of forming the simple past tense in English:

1. the first aorist, in which a suffix is added to the verb stem, e.g.:

   present: λύ-ω I loosen
   aorist: ἔ-λῡ-**σα** I loosen*ed*

2. the second aorist, in which the verb stem is changed, e.g.:

   present: **λαμβάν**-ω I *take*
   aorist: ἔ-**λαβ**-ον I *took*

In the aorist indicative an ε is placed before the stem of verbs that begin with consonants. This is called an *augment*, and it indicates past time. Note in the lists of forms on the next page that the augment does not occur in the forms of the imperative, infinitive, and participle.

In this chapter we focus on the second aorist.

The personal endings for the second aorist indicative active are slightly different from those for the present indicative. The second aorist endings are called *secondary*, and they should be memorized as follows:

Secondary: -ν, -ς, —, -μεν, -τε, -ν

The endings for the active and middle second aorist imperative, infinitive, and participle are the same as those you have learned for the present tense.

The aorist middle indicative has different endings from those you have learned for the present middle indicative. The endings for the present are called *primary*, and those for the aorist are called *secondary*. They should be memorized as follows:

Primary: -μαι, -σαι, -ται, -μεθα, -σθε, -νται
Secondary: -μην, -σο, -το, -μεθα, -σθε, -ντο

Second Aorist Active		**Second Aorist Middle**	
Present: λαμβάνω		Present: γίγνομαι	
Aorist stem: λαβ-		Aorist stem: γεν-	

Indicative

ἔ-λαβ-ο-ν	I took	ἐ-γεν-ό-μην	I became
ἔ-λαβ-ε-ς	you took	ἐ-γέν-ε-σο > ἐγένου	you became
ἔ-λαβ-ε(ν)	he/she took	ἐ-γέν-ε-το	he/she/it became
ἐ-λάβ-ο-μεν	we took	ἐ-γεν-ό-μεθα	we became
ἐ-λάβ-ε-τε	you took	ἐ-γέν-ε-σθε	you became
ἔ-λαβ-ο-ν	they took	ἐ-γέν-ο-ντο	they became

Imperative

| λαβ-έ | take! | γενοῦ | become! |
| λαβ-έτε | take! | γέν-ε-σθε | become! |

Infinitive

| λαβ-εῖν | to take *or* to have taken | γεν-έ-σθαι | to become *or* to have become |

Participle

| λαβ-ών, λαβ-οῦσα, λαβ-όν | taking *or* having taken | γεν-ό-μενος, γεν-ο-μένη, γεν-ό-μενον | becoming *or* having become |

Note the accents of the second aorist active infinitive and participles; these are the regular accents for these forms in the second aorist. The accent of the second aorist active imperative of λαμβάνω is irregular; the usual accent of the second aorist active imperative is recessive, e.g., λίπε, λίπετε (from λείπω).

Exercise 11a

In the reading passage at the beginning of this chapter, locate two examples of an aorist of the verb πάσχω and two aorist forms of the verb γίγνομαι.

Exercise 11b

Copy the second aorist active forms of λαμβάνω (as given above) down the left-hand column of a sheet of paper. On the right-hand column of the same sheet write the corresponding present active forms of λαμβάνω. Repeat this exercise by writing the second aorist middle and the present middle forms of γίγνομαι on a second sheet of paper. Carefully compare the present and second aorist forms.

Exercise 11c

Using the chart above as a guide, write the corresponding aorist active forms of πάσχω (aorist ἔ-παθ-ο-ν) and the corresponding aorist middle forms of λαμβάνομαι = "I take hold of" (aorist ἐ-λαβ-ό-μην). Translate each form you write into English.

2. Aspect

Notice that the indicatives in the charts on the previous page are translated "I took," "you took," etc. In the indicative mood the aorist designates *simple, undifferentiated past action.*

Notice, however, that with the imperatives, which have no augment, the translations are the same as those for the present tense. This is because the aorist imperative differs from the present not in *time* but in *aspect,* that is, in the way in which the action of the verb is looked on. The present tense is used of a *process,* the aorist of *simple action,* e.g.:

> Present imperative: ἄκουε τὸν μῦθον. "Listen to the story!"
> (The listening will take place over a period of time.)
> Aorist imperative: λάβου τῆς ἐμῆς χειρός. "Take my hand!"
> (Reference is to the simple action itself.)

Aorist infinitives and participles often designate simple action without reference to time (past, present, or future), e.g.:

> ἀποκρῑνάμενος εἶπεν. "Answering, he said." or "He said *in reply.*"

At other times aorist infinitives and participles may indicate time before that of the main verb, e.g.:

> οἱ δὲ πάντα τὰ **γενόμενα** αὐτῷ εἶπον. "They told him all the things *that (had) happened.*"

Compare the following:

> ὁ δὲ ἀδελφὸς πρὸς τὴν θύρᾱν ἐλθὼν καὶ τὸν Δικαιόπολιν ἰδών, "χαῖρε, ὦ ἀδελφέ," ἔφη.
> And his brother, coming (having come) to the door and seeing (having seen) Dicaeopolis, said, "Greetings, brother."

3. Second Aorist Participles

The second aorist active participle has the same endings as the present active participle (see Chapter 9, Grammar 1), but it differs in accent:

Nom.	λαβ-ών	λαβ-οῦσα	λαβ-όν
Gen.	λαβ-όντος	λαβ-ούσης	λαβ-όντος
Dat.	λαβ-όντι	λαβ-ούσῃ	λαβ-όντι
Acc.	λαβ-όντα	λαβ-οῦσαν	λαβ-όν
Nom.	λαβ-όντες	λαβ-οῦσαι	λαβ-όντα
Gen.	λαβ-όντων	λαβ-ουσῶν	λαβ-όντων
Dat.	λαβ-οῦσι(ν)	λαβ-ούσαις	λαβ-οῦσι(ν)
Acc.	λαβ-όντας	λαβ-ούσᾱς	λαβ-όντα

The second aorist middle participle has the same endings as the present middle participle (see Chapter 8, Grammar 1):

Nom.   γεν-ό-μενος   γεν-ο-μένη   γεν-ό-μενον
etc.

4. Verb Forms: List of Second Aorists

Learn the following list of second aorists, paying particular attention to the difference between the verb stem as it is seen in the present tense and the aorist stem:

Present	Aorist Stem	Aorist Indicative	Aorist Participle	Meaning
ἄγ-ω	ἀγαγ-	ἤγαγ-ο-ν	ἀγαγ-ών	I lead, take
ἀπο-θνῄσκ-ω	θαν-	ἀπ-έ-θαν-ο-ν	ἀπο-θαν-ών	I die
ἀφ-ικνέ-ο-μαι	ἱκ-	ἀφ-ῑκ-ό-μην	ἀφ-ικ-ό-μενος	I arrive
βάλλ-ω	βαλ-	ἔ-βαλ-ο-ν	βαλ-ών	I throw
γίγν-ο-μαι	γεν-	ἐ-γεν-ό-μην	γεν-ό-μενος	I become
εὑρίσκ ω	εὑρ	ηὗρ ο ν	εὑρ ών	I find
ἔχ-ω	σχ-	ἔ-σχ-ο-ν	σχ-ών	I have
λαμβάν-ω	λαβ-	ἔ-λαβ-ο-ν	λαβ-ών	I take
λείπ-ω	λιπ-	ἔ-λιπ-υ-ν	λιπ-ών	I leave
μανθάν-ω	μαθ-	ἔ-μαθ-ο-ν	μαθ-ών	I learn
πάσχ-ω	παθ-	ἔ-παθ-ο-ν	παθ-ών	I suffer
πίπτ-ω	πεσ-	ἔ-πεσ-ο-ν	πεσ-ών	I fall
φεύγ-ω	φυγ-	ἔ-φυγ-ον	φυγ-ών	I flee

Exercise 11d

Read aloud and translate:

1. ἡ γυνὴ μαθοῦσα ὅτι τυφλὸς ἐγένετο ὁ παῖς, τῷ ἀνδρί, "ὦ Ζεῦ," ἔφη, "τί δεῖ ἡμᾶς ποιεῖν;"
2. ἀφικόμενοι εἰς τὴν τοῦ ἀδελφοῦ οἰκίαν εἶπον αὐτῷ τί ἔπαθεν ὁ παῖς.
3. οἱ ἄνδρες τὰς γυναῖκας ἐν τῷ οἴκῳ λιπόντες τὸν παῖδα πρὸς τὸν ἰᾱτρὸν ἤγαγον.
4. ὁ αὐτουργὸς τὸν κύνα πρὸς τὸ ὄρος ἀγαγὼν τὸν λύκον ηὗρε τοῖς μήλοις (*flocks*) ἐμπῑπτειν (ἐν + πῑπτω) μέλλοντα.
5. ἡ μήτηρ τὸν σῖτον τῷ παιδὶ παρασχοῦσα κελεύει αὐτὸν σπεύδειν πρὸς τὸν ἀγρόν.
6. εἰς τὸν ἀγρὸν ἀφικόμενος τῷ πατρὶ τὸ δεῖπνον παρέσχεν.
7. ὁ πατὴρ τὸ ἄροτρον ἐν τῷ ἀγρῷ λιπὼν τὸ δεῖπνον ἔλαβεν.
8. ὁ μὲν παῖς τὸν λύκον ἔβαλεν, ὁ δὲ φοβούμενος ἔφυγεν.
9. οἱ νεᾱνίαι ἀπέθανον ὑπὲρ τῆς πόλεως μαχόμενοι.
10. δεινὰ παθόντες οὐκ ἔφυγον ἀλλὰ ἔπεσον ἀνδρείως μαχόμενοι.

Greek Medicine

Healing divine and secular

The inscription at the bottom of this relief says that it was dedicated by Aeschinus to the hero healer Amphiaraus. On the right, the patient sleeps in the sanctuary and is visited by Amphiaraus and his divine serpent, which licks his wound. On the left a doctor (or the god himself?) operates on the wound.

The beginnings of Greek science are to be found in the speculations of the philosophers who lived in the Ionian city of Miletus in the seventh century B.C.. The first of these thinkers was Thales, whose floruit can be dated confidently, since he predicted an eclipse of the sun that took place on 25 May 585 B.C. He and his successors were primarily interested in questions of physics. They all sought for a unifying principle underlying the multifarious appearances of the physical world; in simple terms, they asked, "What is the ultimate constituent of matter?" Thales answered that this was water. He conceived of the earth as a flat disc floating on water (the ocean), with water above (rain falling from the sky). Water, when rarefied, becomes steam or mist. He speculated that air, when rarefied, becomes fire. Water condensed takes on a solid form, ice or mud; further condensed it becomes earth and stone. The interest in Thales' theory lies not in its truth or falsehood but in the boldness with which he sought for an answer in terms of natural causation to questions that had been traditionally answered in terms of myth.

The speculations of the Ionian philosophers had no practical end in view, and here they differed from Greek medicine, which had developed from early time as an art; the doctor (ἰᾱτρός = healer) was a craftsman. There were already famous doctors before we hear of any theory of medicine. The best known is Democedes, whose story as told by the historian Herodotus is given at the end of this chapter.

The man whom the Greeks looked upon as the founder of medical science belonged to the next century. This was Hippocrates (fl. 430 B.C.), who founded a famous medical school on the little island of Cos (see map, page 199). To him is ascribed a large collection of writings that cover all aspects of medicine including anatomy, physiology, prognostics, dietetics, surgery, and pharmacology. They include a book of precepts on how doctors should behave toward their patients and the famous Hippocratic oath, which was taken by all students of medicine:

> I will pay the same respect to my master in the science as to my parents and share my life with him and pay all my debts to him. I will regard his sons as my brothers and teach them the science, if they desire to learn it, without fee or contract. . . . I will give treatment to help the sick to the best of my ability and judgment. . . . I will not give lethal drugs to anyone if I am asked . . . nor will I give a woman means to procure an abortion. . . . Whatever I see or hear that should not be spoken to any person outside, I will never divulge. . . .

The oath both gives an insight into how the medical schools were organized (a system of apprenticeship) and also shows the ethical principles to which ancient Greek doctors subscribed.

None of the writings can be confidently ascribed to Hippocrates himself, but many, perhaps most, were written in the fifth century and contain some strikingly enlightened features. The case histories recorded in the Hippocratic writings are particularly interesting, showing the close observation and careful recording on which all sound diagnosis must depend. For instance:

> At Thasos, Pythion had a violent rigor and high fever as the result of strain, exhaustion, and insufficient attention to his diet. Tongue parched, he was thirsty and bilious and did not sleep. Urine rather dark, containing suspended matter, which did not settle. Second day: about midday, chilling of the extremities. . . . (*Epidemics* 3.2, case 3)

The patient's condition and symptoms continued to be recorded until the tenth day, when he died.

Greek doctors did not claim to be able to effect cures in many cases. Their remedies were simple. Drugs, usually purgatives, were used sparingly. Surgery made steady advances, although anatomy was held back by reluctance to perform dissection of the human body. Bloodletting was a common remedy, and great importance was attached to diet and exercise. Despite its limitations, Greek medicine was rational in all aspects and rejected the belief that sickness was caused by evil spirits, still current in the Palestine of New Testament times. If a Greek doctor could not cure a patient, the only recourse for the patient was to visit one of the healing sanctuaries, where a combination of medical care and faith healing resulted in some remarkable cures, if the tablets put up by patients are to be believed.

Ο ΙΑΤΡΟΣ (β)

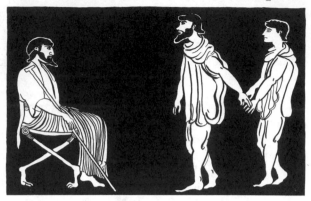

ὁ ἰᾱτρός, "ἐλθὲ δεῦρο, ὦ παῖ," ἔφη· "τί ἔπαθες; πῶς τυφλὸς ἐγένου;"

Vocabulary

Verbs
αἱρέω, εἷλον, ἑλών   I take
ἔρχομαι, ἦλθον, ἐλθών   I come, go
λέγω, εἶπον, εἰπών   I say, tell, speak
νοσέω   I am sick, ill
ὁράω, εἶδον, ἰδών   I see
προσέρχομαι, προσῆλθον, προσελθών (+ *dat. or* πρός + *acc.*) I approach
ὠφελέω   I help, benefit

Nouns
τὸ ἀργύριον, τοῦ ἀργυρίου   silver, money
ἡ δραχμή, τῆς δραχμῆς   drachma

ὁ μισθός, τοῦ μισθοῦ   reward, pay
ὁ ὀβολός, τοῦ ὀβολοῦ   obol

Preposition
πρός (+ *dat.*) at, near, by, (+ *acc.*) to, toward, against

Interjection
οἴμοι   alas!

Expression
κατὰ θάλατταν   by sea

Proper Names
ὁ Ἀσκλήπιος, τοῦ Ἀσκληπίου Asclepius, the god of healing
ἡ Ἐπίδαυρος, τῆς Ἐπιδαύρου Epidaurus
ὁ Πειραιεύς, τοῦ Πειραιῶς, τῷ Πειραιεῖ, τὸν Πειραιᾶ Piraeus, the port of Athens

τῇ οὖν ὑστεραίᾳ ἐπεὶ πρῶτον ἐγένετο ἡ ἡμέρᾱ, τὰς γυναῖκας ἐν τῇ οἰκίᾳ λιπόντες ὅ τε Δικαιόπολις καὶ ὁ ἀδελφὸς τὸν Φίλιππον εἰς τὴν ὁδὸν ἤγαγον. ὁ δὲ τῆς τοῦ πατρὸς χειρὸς ἐλάβετο ἀλλ' ὅμως πρὸς τοὺς λίθους πταίων πρὸς τὴν γῆν κατέπεσεν. ὁ οὖν πατὴρ αἴρει αὐτὸν καὶ φέρει. οὕτως οὖν πορευόμενοι δι' ὀλίγου ἀφίκοντο εἰς τὴν τοῦ ἰᾱτροῦ οἰκίᾱν. ὁ δ' ἀδελφός, "ἰδού," ἔφη· "εἰς τοῦ ἰᾱτροῦ ἥκομεν. ἐλθὲ δεῦρο καὶ κόπτε τὴν θύρᾱν." τοῦτο εἰπὼν ὁ ἀδελφὸς οἴκαδε ἐπανῆλθεν.   5

[πταίων stumbling   εἰς τοῦ ἰᾱτροῦ ιο (the house) of the doctor   ἐπανῆλθεν returned]

ὁ οὖν Δικαιόπολις προσελθὼν ἔκοψε τὴν θύρᾱν, ἀλλ᾽ οὐδεὶς ἦλθεν. ἐπεὶ δ᾽ αὖθις ἔκοψεν, δοῦλός τις ἐξελθών, "βάλλ᾽ εἰς   10 κόρακας," ἔφη· "τίς ὢν σὺ κόπτεις τὴν θύρᾱν;" ὁ δὲ Δικαιόπολις, "ἀλλ᾽, ὦ δαιμόνιε, ἐγώ εἰμι Δικαιόπολις· τὸν δὲ παῖδα κομίζω παρὰ τὸν σὸν δεσπότην· τυφλὸς γὰρ γέγονεν." ὁ δὲ δοῦλος, "ἀλλ᾽ οὐ σχολὴ αὐτῷ." ὁ δὲ Δικαιόπολις, "ἀλλ᾽ ὅμως κάλει αὐτόν. δεινὰ γὰρ ἔπαθεν ὁ παῖς· ἀλλὰ μένε, ὦ φίλε." καὶ οὕτως εἰπὼν δύο ὀβολοὺς τῷ δούλῳ   15 παρέσχεν. ὁ δέ, "μένετε οὖν ἐνταῦθα. ἐγὼ γὰρ τὸν δεσπότην κι.λῶ, εἴ πως ἐθέλει ῡ̔μᾶς δέχεσθαι."

[βάλλ᾽ εἰς κόρακας go to the crows! (= go to hell!)   ὦ δαιμόνιε my dear fellow οὐ σχολὴ αὐτῷ he doesn't have leisure (= he's busy)   καλῶ I will call   εἴ πως if somehow, if perhaps]

ὅ τε οὖν πατὴρ καὶ ὁ παῖς ὀλίγον τινὰ χρόνον μένουσιν ἐπὶ τῇ θύρᾳ. ἔπειτα δ᾽ ὁ δοῦλος ἐξελθών, "εἰσέλθετε," ἔφη· "ὁ γὰρ δεσπότης ἐθέλει ῡ̔μᾶς δέχεσθαι." ὁ οὖν πατὴρ τῷ παιδὶ εἰσηγούμενος τὸν   20 ἰᾱτρὸν εἶδεν ἐν τῇ αὐλῇ καθιζόμενον. προσελθὼν οὖν, "χαῖρε," ἔφη· "ἐγὼ μέν εἰμι Δικαιόπολις Χολλείδης, κομίζω δὲ παρά σε τὸν ἐμὸν παῖδα· δεινὰ γὰρ ἔπαθεν· τυφλὸς γέγονεν." ὁ δὲ ἰᾱτρός, "δεῦρο ἐλθέ, ὦ παῖ. τί ἔπαθες; πῶς τυφλὸς ἐγένου;" ὁ μὲν οὖν Δικαιόπολις πάντα τῷ ἰᾱτρῷ εἶπεν, ὁ δὲ τοὺς τοῦ παιδὸς ὀφθαλμοὺς πολὺν χρόνον   25 σκοπεῖ. τέλος δέ, "ἐγὼ μὲν οὐ δύναμαι αὐτὸν ὠφελεῖν. οὐδὲν γὰρ νοσοῦσιν οἱ ὀφθαλμοί. οὐκ οὖν δύνανται ὠφελεῖν οἱ ἄνθρωποι, ἀλλὰ τοῖς γε θεοῖς πάντα δυνατά. δεῖ οὖν σε κομίζειν τὸν παῖδα πρὸς τὴν Ἐπίδαυρον καὶ τῷ Ἀσκληπιῷ εὔχεσθαι, εἴ πως ἐθέλει αὐτὸν ἰᾶσθαι." ὁ δὲ Δικαιόπολις, "οἴμοι, πῶς γὰρ ἔξεστί μοι πένητι ὄντι πρὸς   30 τὴν Ἐπίδαυρον ἰέναι;" ὁ δὲ ἰᾱτρός, "σὸν ἔργον, ὦ ἄνθρωπε," ἔφη· "χαίρετε."

[ὀλίγον small, short   τῇ αὐλῇ the courtyard   Χολλείδης from Cholleidae (Dicaeopolis's home village or deme)   δύναμαι I am able   ἰᾶσθαι to heal   πένητι a poor man   σὸν ἔργον (that's) your problem]

ὁ οὖν Δικαιόπολις μάλα λῡπούμενος βαδίζει πρὸς τὴν θύρᾱν καὶ τῷ παιδὶ οἴκαδε ἡγεῖται. ἀφικόμενος δὲ πάντα τὰ γενόμενα τῷ ἀδελφῷ εἶπεν. ἡ δὲ Μυρρίνη πάντα μαθοῦσα, "ἔστω· οὐ δυνάμεθα τῇ ἀνάγκῃ   35 μάχεσθαι. δεῖ σε οὖν τὸν παῖδα πρὸς τὴν Ἐπίδαυρον κομίζειν." ὁ δὲ Δικαιόπολις, "ἀλλὰ πῶς ἔξεστί μοι, ὦ γύναι," ἔφη, "τὸν παῖδα ἐκεῖσε

ἄγειν; δεῖ γὰρ κατὰ θάλατταν ἰέναι· οὐ γὰρ δύναται πεζῇ ἰέναι ὁ
παῖς τυφλὸς ὤν. πῶς οὖν ἔξεστι τὸν μισθὸν παρασχεῖν τῷ ναυκλήρῳ;
οὐ γὰρ ἔστι μοι τὸ ἀργύριον."   40

[λυπούμενος grieving   ἔστω all right!   τῇ ἀνάγκῃ necessity   πεζῇ on foot
τῷ ναυκλήρῳ to the ship's captain]

    ὁ δὲ ἀδελφός, "μὴ φρόντιζε, ὦ φίλε," ἔφη. καὶ πρὸς τὴν κυψέλην
ἐλθὼν πέντε δραχμὰς ἐξεῖλε καὶ τῷ Δικαιοπόλιδι παρέσχεν. ὁ δὲ τὸ
ἀργύριον δέχεται καὶ μεγάλην χάριν ἔχων, "ὦ φίλτατ' ἀνδρῶν," ἔφη,
"τοὺς θεοὺς εὔχομαι πάντα ἀγαθά σοι παρέχειν οὕτω εὔφρονι ὄντι."
οὕτως οὖν δοκεῖ αὐτοῖς τῇ ὑστεραίᾳ πρὸς τὸν Πειραιᾶ σπεύδειν καὶ   45
ναῦν τινα ζητεῖν πρὸς τὴν Ἐπίδαυρον μέλλουσαν πλεῖν.

[μὴ φρόντιζε don't worry!   τὴν κυψέλην the chest   χάριν ἔχων having (=
giving) thanks   φίλτατ' dearest   εὔφρονι kind]

Word Building

Three types of nouns are commonly formed from verb stems:

1. First declension masculine nouns ending in -της express the doer of the
    action, e.g., ποιε- make > ὁ ποιη-τής the maker, the poet.
2. Third declension feminine nouns ending in -σις express the action of the
    verb, e.g., ἡ ποίη-σις the making, the creation, the composition.
3. Third declension neuter nouns ending in -μα express the result of the
    action, e.g., τὸ ποίη-μα the thing made, the work, the poem.

Give the meanings of the following:

1. οἰκέω   ὁ οἰκητής   ἡ οἴκησις   τὸ οἴκημα
2. μανθάνω (μαθ-) ὁ μαθητής   ἡ μάθησις   τὸ μάθημα

Grammar

5. Irregular Second Aorists

    A few Greek verbs form their aorists from a completely different root
from that seen in the verb stem used for the present tense, as does English
with, for example, *I go* (present) and *I went* (past). The following are the
most common such verbs in Greek, and you have already seen most of
their aorist imperatives and participles in the readings:

Present	Aorist Stem	Aorist Indicative	Aorist Imperative	Aorist Participle
αἱρέω I take	ἑλ-	εἷλον	ἕλε/ἕλετε	ἑλών
ἔρχομαι I come, go	ἐλθ-	ἦλθον	ἐλθέ/ἐλθέτε	ἐλθών
λέγω I say, tell	εἰπ-	εἶπον	εἰπέ/εἰπέτε	εἰπών
ὁράω I see	ἰδ-	εἶδον	ἰδέ/ἰδέτε	ἰδών

Note that the accents of ἐλθέ, εἰπέ, and ἰδέ are irregular in that they are not recessive (so also εὑρέ and λαβέ).

Note that the accent of the *compound* forms of these imperatives *is* recessive, e.g., ἐπάνελθε (from ἐπανέρχομαι).

6. Augment

To indicate past time in the aorist indicative, as we saw in grammar section 1 above, Greek puts an ε before the stem of verbs beginning with consonants. This is called a *syllabic augment*. If the stem begins with a vowel or diphthong, a syllabic augment is not added, but the initial vowel is lengthened in spelling or sound. This is called *temporal augment*. The following list compares present and aorist indicatives and shows how the stems of verbs beginning with vowels and diphthongs are augmented. A number of these verbs are first aorists and are cited merely as examples of augment.

Present   **Aorist**

Single vowels:

ἀκούω	ἤκουσα	(α lengthens to η)
ἐγείρω	ἤγειρα	(ε also lengthens to η)
ἱκνέομαι	ἱκόμην	(ῐ lengthens to ῑ)
ὁρμάω	ὥρμησα	(ο lengthens to ω)
ὠφελέω	ὠφέλησα	(no change)
ὑβρίζω	ὕβρισα	(ῠ lengthens to ῡ)

Diphthongs:

αἰτέω	ᾔτησα	(α lengthens to η, and ι goes subscript)
αὐξάνω	ηὔξησα	(αυ lengthens to ηυ)
εὔχομαι	ηὐξάμην	(ευ lengthens to ηυ)
οἰκέω	ᾤκησα	(ο lengthens to ω, and ι goes subscript)

Exercise 11e

Augment the following stems:

1. κελευ-	4. ἰᾱτρευ-	7. ἡγε-	10. ὀνομαζ-
2. ἐθελ-	5. ἀρχ-	8. ἀμῡν-	11. ἐλθ-
3. ὀτρῡν-	6. λαβ-	9. εὐχ-	12. μαθ-

Exercise 11f

Turn the following forms into corresponding forms of the aorist and translate each form:

1. λαμβάνομεν	7. λέγε	13. λέγειν
2. μανθάνει	8. ἔχεις	14. ἔρχομαι
3. πάσχουσι	9. ἀφικνεῖσθαι	15. ὁρᾶν
4. λείπεις	10. λείπειν	16. λέγομεν
5. πίπτων	11. λαμβάνουσα	17. ὁρᾷ
6. γιγνόμεθα	12. λείπετε	18. ἔρχεσθαι

Exercise 11g

Read aloud and translate:

1. ὁ αὐτουργὸς εἰς τὸν ἀγρὸν εἰσελθὼν τὴν θυγατέρα εἶδεν ὑπὸ τῷ δένδρῳ καθιζομένην.
2. προσῆλθεν οὖν καὶ εἶπεν· "διὰ τί καθίζῃ ὑπὸ τῷ δένδρῳ δακρῦουσα, ὦ θύγατερ;"
3. ἡ δὲ εἶπεν· "τὸ δεῖπνόν σοι φέρουσα, ὦ πάτερ, ἐν τῇ ὁδῷ κατέπεσον καὶ τὸν πόδα (*foot*) ἔβλαψα (*I hurt*).
4. ὁ δέ, "ἐλθὲ δεῦρο," φησίν, "δεῖ με τὸν σὸν πόδα σκοπεῖν."
5. τὸν οὖν πόδα αὐτῆς σκοπεῖ καί, ἰδὼν ὅτι οὐδὲν νοσεῖ, "θάρρει (*cheer up*), ὦ θύγατερ," ἔφη· "οὐδὲν κακὸν ἔπαθες. πάρασχε οὖν μοι τὸ δεῖπνον καὶ οἴκαδε ἐπάνελθε."
6. ἡ οὖν παρθένος τὸ δεῖπνον τῷ πατρὶ παρασχοῦσα οἴκαδε βραδέως ἀπῆλθεν.

Exercise 11h

Translate into Greek:

1. How did you become blind, boy? Tell me what happened.
2. Where did you see the oxen? Did you leave them in the field?
3. After suffering much (= many things) by sea, they finally arrived at the land.
4. After seeing the dances, the boys went home and told their father (*dative case*) what happened.
5. Falling into the sea, the girls suffered terribly (= terrible things).

Ο ΔΗΜΟΚΗΔΗΣ ΤΟΝ ΒΑΣΙΛΕΑ ΙΑΤΡΕΥΕΙ

Read the following passage (based on Herodotus 3.129–130) and answer the comprehension questions:

ἐπεὶ δὲ ἀπέθανεν ὁ Πολυκράτης, οἱ Πέρσαι τούς τε ἄλλους θεράποντας τοῦ
Πολυκράτους λαβόντες καὶ τὸν Δημοκήδη εἰς Σοῦσα ἐκόμισαν. δι' ὀλίγου δὲ ὁ
βασιλεὺς κακόν τι ἔπαθεν· ἀπὸ τοῦ ἵππου γὰρ πεσὼν τὸν πόδα ἔβλαψεν. οἱ δὲ
ἰατροὶ οὐκ ἐδύναντο αὐτὸν ὠφελεῖν. μαθὼν δὲ ὅτι ἰατρός τις Ἑλληνικὸς πάρεστιν
ἐν τοῖς δούλοις, τοὺς θεράποντας ἐκέλευσε τὸν Δημοκήδη παρ' ἑαυτὸν ἀγαγεῖν. ὁ   5
οὖν Δημοκήδης εἰς μέσον ἦλθεν, πέδας τε ἕλκων καὶ ῥάκεσιν ἐσθημένος. ὁ οὖν
βασιλεὺς ἰδὼν αὐτὸν ἐθαύμασε καὶ ἤρετο εἰ δύναται τὸν πόδα ἰατρεύειν. ὁ δὲ
Δημοκήδης φοβούμενος εἶπεν ὅτι οὐκ ἔστιν ἰατρὸς σοφὸς ἀλλὰ ἐθέλει πειρᾶσθαι.
ἐνταῦθα δὴ Ἑλληνικῇ ἰατρείᾳ χρώμενος τὸν πόδα ταχέως ἰάτρευσεν. οὕτως οὖν
φίλος ἐγένετο τῷ βασιλεῖ, ὁ δὲ πολὺ ἀργύριον αὐτῷ παρέσχε καὶ μεγάλως ἐτίμα.   10

[ὁ Πολυκράτης, τοῦ Πολυκράτους Polycrates, tyrant of Samos (*sixth century* B.C.; *he was captured and put to death by the Persians*)   οἱ Πέρσαι the Persians   θεράποντας servants   ὁ Δημοκήδης, τὸν Δημοκήδη Democedes   Σοῦσα (*neuter acc. pl.*) Susa   ἐκόμισαν brought   κακόν τι something bad   τοῦ ἵππου the horse   τὸν πόδα his foot   ἔβλαψεν he hurt   ἐδύναντο were able   Ἑλληνικός Greek   ἐκέλευσε he ordered   ἀγαγεῖν to lead   πέδας . . . ἕλκων dragging his shackles   ῥάκεσιν ἐσθημένος clothed in rags   ἐθαύμασε was amazed   ἤρετο asked   ἰατρεύειν to heal   πειρᾶσθαι to try   ἰατρείᾳ healing, medicine   χρώμενος (ι *dat.*) using   ἐτίμα was honoring, honored]

1. What happened to the Persian king? Of what help were his doctors?
2. What did the king learn? What did he order his servants to do?
3. In what two ways could Democedes be recognized as a slave?
4. How does the Persian king react to the sight of Democedes?
5. What did Democedes say to the king? How did he heal the king's foot?
6. In what three ways did Democedes benefit?

Exercise 11i

Translate into Greek:

1. When the king fell from his horse, he suffered something bad, but the doctors said that they could not (οὐ δύνανται) help him.
2. Learning that there was another doctor present among the slaves, the servants said, "We must bring this doctor (τοῦτον τὸν ἰατρόν) to you."
3. When the doctor arrived, the king said, "Is it possible to heal my foot?"
4. The doctor said that he was willing (*use present tense*) to try.
5. When the doctor cured (ἰάτρευσε) his foot, the king became very friendly to him.

12
ΠΡΟΣ ΤΟΝ ΠΕΙΡΑΙΑ
(α)

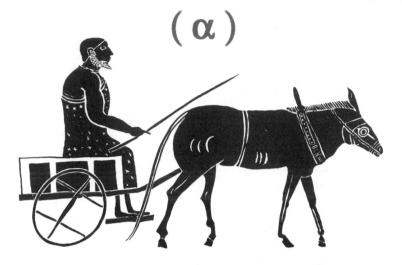

προσεχώρησεν ἀνήρ τις ἅμαξαν ἐλαύνων.

Vocabulary

Verbs
ἀπορέω, ἠπόρησα, ἀπορήσᾱς I
am at a loss
**καταλείπω, κατέλιπον,
καταλιπών** I leave behind,
desert
**φροντίζω, ἐφρόντισα,
φροντίσᾱς** I worry, care
Nouns
ὁ ἡμίονος, τοῦ ἡμιόνου mule
ὁ λιμήν, τοῦ λιμένος harbor
ὁ ὅμῑλος, τοῦ ὁμίλου crowd
τὸ τεῖχος, τοῦ τείχους wall
Adjectives
γεραιός, -ά, -όν old

κακός, -ή, -όν b a d
ὀρθός, -ή, -όν straight, right,
correct
Adverbs
τάχιστα very quickly, most
quickly
ὡς τάχιστα as quickly as
possible
Conjunction
ἤ or
ἤ . . . ἤ either . . . or
καίπερ (+ *participle*) although
Expression
χαίρειν κελεύω I bid farewell

τῇ δ᾽ ὑστεραίᾳ ἐπεὶ πρῶτον ἐγένετο ἡ ἡμέρᾱ, ὁ Δικαιόπολις
πάντας ἐκέλευσε παρασκευάζεσθαι. οἱ μὲν οὖν ἄλλοι εὐθὺς
παρεσκευάσαντο βουλόμενοι ὡς τάχιστα πορεύεσθαι καὶ δι᾽ ὀλίγου
ἕτοιμοι ἦσαν. ὁ δὲ πάππος οὐκ ἠθέλησε πορεύεσθαι· οὕτω γὰρ

γεραιὸς ἦν ὥστε οὐκ ἐδύνατο μακρὰν βαδίζειν· ἡ δὲ Μέλιττα οὕτω 5
μακρὰν τῇ προτεραίᾳ βαδίσασα ὑπέρκοπος ἦν· ἔδοξεν οὖν τῇ μητρὶ
καταλιπεῖν αὐτὴν οἴκοι μετὰ τοῦ πάππου. ἐπεὶ δὲ παρῆσαν οἱ ἄλλοι,
ὁ Δικαιόπολις ἡγησάμενος αὐτοῖς εἰς τὴν αὐλὴν τῷ βωμῷ
προσεχώρησε καὶ σπονδὴν ποιησάμενος τὸν Δία ηὔξατο σῴζειν
πάντας τοσαύτην ὁδὸν ποιοῦντας. 10

[ἐκέλευσε ordered παρεσκευάσαντο prepared themselves ἦσαν they were
οὐκ ἠθέλησε refused ἦν he was ἐδύνατο he was able μακρὰν a long way
τῇ προτεραίᾳ the day before βαδίσασα having walked ὑπέρκοπος
exhausted ἔδοξεν it seemed (good) ἡγησάμενος leading, having led τὴν
αὐλήν the courtyard ποιησάμενος making, having made ηὔξατο (from
εὔχομαι) he prayed]

   τόν τ’ οὖν πάππον καὶ τὴν Μέλιτταν χαίρειν κελεύσαντες
ὥρμησαν καὶ δι’ ὀλίγου εἰς τὰς τῆς πόλεως πύλας ἀφικόμενοι τὴν
πρὸς τὸν λιμένα ὁδὸν εἵλοντο. ὀρθὴ δ’ ἦν ἡ ὁδός, διὰ τῶν μακρῶν
τειχῶν φέρουσα· πολλοὶ δὲ ἄνθρωποι ἐνῆσαν, πολλαὶ δὲ ἅμαξαι,
πολλοὶ δὲ καὶ ἡμίονοι τὰ φορτία φέροντες ἢ πρὸς τὴν πόλιν ἢ ἀπὸ τῆς 15
πόλεως πρὸς τὸν λιμένα. ὁ δὲ Δικαιόπολις σπεύδει διὰ τοῦ ὁμίλου
βουλόμενος ὡς τάχιστα ἀφικέσθαι. ὁ δὲ Φίλιππος καίπερ τῆς τοῦ
πατρὸς χειρὸς ἐχόμενος ἔπταισε καὶ πρὸς τὴν γῆν κατέπεσεν. ἡ δὲ
μήτηρ βοήσασα, "ὦ τλῆμον παῖ," ἔφη, "τί ἔπαθες;" καὶ προσδραμοῦσα ἦρεν αὐτόν. ὁ δὲ οὐδὲν κακὸν παθών, "μὴ φρόντιζε, 20
μῆτερ," ἔφη· "καίπερ γὰρ πεσὼν ἐγὼ καλῶς ἔχω." ἡ δὲ μήτηρ ἔτι
φροντίζει καὶ τὸν παῖδα σκοπεῖ.

[ὥρμησαν they set out εἵλοντο they took, chose τὰ φορτία burdens, cargoes
ἐχόμενος (+ gen.) holding ἔπταισε stumbled τλῆμον wretched, poor
προσδραμοῦσα running, having run toward (him) ἦρεν (from αἴρω) she lifted]

   ἐν ᾧ δὲ πάντες περιμένουσιν ἀποροῦντες τί δεῖ ποιεῖν,
προσεχώρησεν ἀνήρ τις ἅμαξαν ἐλαύνων. ἰδὼν δ’ αὐτοὺς ἐν τῇ ὁδῷ
περιμένοντας καὶ ἀποροῦντας, τὸν ἡμίονον ἔστησε καί, "εἴπετέ μοι, τί 25
πάσχετε, ὦ φίλοι;" ἔφη, "διὰ τί οὕτω περιμένετε; ἆρα κακόν τι ἔπαθεν
ὁ παῖς;" οἱ μὲν οὖν πάντα ἐξηγήσαντο, ὁ δέ, "ἐλθὲ δεῦρο, ὦ παῖ," ἔφη,
"καὶ ἀνάβηθι ἐπὶ τὴν ἅμαξαν. καὶ σύ, ὦ γύναι, εἰ τῷ ἀνδρὶ δοκεῖ,
ἀνάβηθι. καὶ ἐγὼ γὰρ πρὸς τὸν λιμένα πορεύομαι." οἱ δὲ ἐδέξαντο
τὸν λόγον καὶ οὕτω πορευόμενοι δι’ ὀλίγου ἀφίκοντο εἰς τὸν λιμένα. 30

[περιμένουσιν are waiting around ἔστησε he stopped ἐξηγήσαντο related
ἀνάβηθι get up! ἐδέξαντο received, accepted]

Word Study

Identify the Greek roots in the English words below and give the meanings of the English words:

1. mathematics
2. polymath
3. orthodoxy (what must ἡ δόξα mean?)
4. orthodontist (what must ὁ ὀδούς, τοῦ ὀδόντος mean?)
5. orthopedics *or* orthopaedics

Grammar

1. Verb Forms: Past Tense: The First Aorist

Most Greek verbs have first aorists rather than the second aorist formations studied in the last chapter. First aorists are formed by adding the termination -σα to the verb stem, e.g., ἔ-λῡ-σα. (Certain types of verbs add only -α and not -σα; these will be studied in the second half of this chapter.) As with the second aorists, the verb stem is augmented only in the indicative, and secondary endings are used in the middle voice.

First Aorist Active		**First Aorist Middle**	
Indicative			
ἔ-λῡ-σα	I loosened	ἐ-λῡ-σά-μην	I ransomed
ἔ-λῡ-σα-ς	you loosened	ἐ-λύ-σα-σο > ἐλύσω	you ransomed
ἔ-λῡ-σ-ε(ν)	he/she loosened	ἐ-λύ-σα-το	he/she ransomed
ἐ-λύ-σα-μεν	we loosened	ἐ-λῡ-σά-μεθα	we ransomed
ἐ-λύ-σα-τε	you loosened	ἐ-λύ-σα-σθε	you ransomed
ἔ-λῡ-σα-ν	they loosened	ἐ-λύ-σα-ντο	they ransomed
Imperative			
λῦ-σον	loosen!	λῦ-σαι	ransom!
λύ-σα-τε	loosen!	λύ-σα-σθε	ransom!
Infinitive			
λῦ-σαι	to loosen	λύ-σα-σθαι	to ransom
Participle			
λύ-σᾱς, λύ-σᾱσα, λῦ-σαν		λῡ-σά-μενος, λῡ-σα-μένη, λῡ-σά-μενον	
	loosening or		ransoming or
	having loosened		having ransomed

Note the following:

The letter α is characteristic of the first aorist, and it occurs in all forms except in the third person singular of the active indicative (ἔλῡσε) and the singular imperative (λῦσον).

The first aorist active infinitive is always accented on the penult, e.g., λῦσαι and κελεῦσαι (the diphthong -αι is short here).

Note what happens when the stem of the verb ends in a consonant instead of a vowel (as with the stem λῡ- above):

a. If the stem ends in a *labial* (β, π, φ), the labial + σ coalesce to form ψ, e.g.:

βλάπτω (I harm; stem βλαβ-), **ἔβλαψα**
πέμπ-ω, **ἔ-πεμψα**.
ἀλείφ-ω (anoint), **ἤλειψα**

b. If the stem ends in a *guttural* (γ, κ, χ), the combination with the σ of the aorist produces ξ, e.g.:

πρᾱ́ττω (stem πρᾱγ-), **ἔπρᾱξα**
φυλάττω (stem φυλακ-), **ἐφύλαξα**
δέχ-ομαι, **ἐδεξάμην**

c. If the stem ends in a *dental* (δ, ζ, θ, τ), the last consonant of the stem drops out before the σ, e.g.:

δείδ-ω (I fear), **ἔδεισα**
κομίζ-ω, **ἐκόμισα**
πείθ-ω, **ἔπεισα**
ἐρέσσω (I row; stem ἐρετ-), **ἤρεσα**

Contract verbs with stems ending in ε or α lengthen the stem vowel before the σ of the aorist, e.g.:

φιλέ-ω, **ἐφίλη-σα**
ἡγέ-ο-μαι, **ἡγη-σά-μην**
τῑμά-ω, **ἐτῑ́μη-σα**

You will meet a few contract verbs with stems ending in o; the stem vowel of these verbs also lengthens before the σ of the aorist, e.g.:

δηλό-ω, **ἐδήλω-σα**

The verb καλέω is irregular: aorist **ἐκάλεσα**.

Note that in vocabulary lists the aorist indicative and participle are now included in the entry for each verb, to show augmented and unaugmented forms.

Exercise 12a

In the second and third paragraphs of the reading passage at the beginning of this chapter, locate eight first aorist verb forms. Identify each form (mood, person, and number for finite verbs; gender, case, and number for participles).

Exercise 12b

Using the charts on the opposite page as a guide, write the corresponding aorist active forms of ἀκούω and the aorist middle forms of δέχομαι. Translate into English each form you write.

Exercise 12c

Give the aorist indicative, first person singular, of the following verbs:

1. δακρύω
2. βλέπω
3. θαυμάζω
4. ἀκούω
5. δέχομαι

6. διώκω
7. νῑκάω
8. κηρύττω (*I announce*)
9. κομίζω
10. ἡγέομαι

11. βοηθέω
12. δουλόω (*I enslave*)
13. παύω
14. φυλάττω
15. πέμπω

2. First Aorist Participles

The first aorist active participle is declined like the adjective πᾶς, πᾶσα, πᾶν (see Chapter 8, Grammar 4), except for the accent:

Singular:

Nom.	λύσᾱς	λύσᾱσα	λῦσαν
Gen.	λύσαντ-ος	λῡσάσης	λύσαντ-ος
Dat.	λύσαντ-ι	λῡσάσῃ	λύσαντ-ι
Acc.	λύσαντ-α	λύσᾱσαν	λῦσαν

Plural:

Nom.	λύσαντ-ες	λύσᾱσαι	λύσαντ-α
Gen.	λῡσάντ-ων	λῡσᾱσῶν	λῡσάντ-ων
Dat.	λύσαντ-σι(ν) > λύσᾱσι(ν)	λῡσάσαις	λύσαντ-σι(ν) > λύσᾱσι(ν)
Acc.	λύσαντ-ας	λῡσάσᾱς	λύσαντ-α

The first aorist middle participle has the same endings as the present middle participle (see Chapter 8, Grammar 1):

Nom.	λῡ-σά-μενος	λῡ-σα-μένη	λῡ-σά-μενον
etc.			

Exercise 12d

Write the forms of the aorist active participles of ποιέω and βοάω.

3. Verb Forms: Past Tense: The Irregular Verb εἰμί "I am"

This verb does not have an aorist tense. Its past tense expresses a *continuous* state of being in past time, and this tense is called the *imperfect* (not completed). The forms are:

Indicative

ἦν	I was
ἦσθα	you were
ἦν	he/she/it was
ἦμεν	we were
ἦτε	you were
ἦσαν	they were

Exercise 12e

Locate four occurrences of the past tense of εἰμί or its compounds in the first paragraph of the reading passage at the beginning of this chapter.

Exercise 12f

Translate into English:

1. ὁ Δικαιόπολις οὐκ ἠθέλησε τῇ γυναικὶ πρὸς τὸ ἄστυ ἡγήσασθαι.
2. ὁ ξένος εἰσελθὼν εὐθὺς οἶνον ᾔτησεν.
3. ὁ ἱερεὺς σπονδὴν ποιησάμενος τοῖς θεοῖς ηὔξατο.
4. αἱ γυναῖκες, καίπερ τοὺς ἄνδρας ἰδοῦσαι, οὐκ ἐπαύσαντο βοῶσαι.
5. εἴσελθε, ὦ παῖ, καὶ τὸν πατέρα κάλεσον.
6. ἐλθὲ δεῦρο, ὦ παῖ, καὶ εἰπέ μοι τί ἐποίησας.
7. ἡ παρθένος τοὺς χοροὺς θεασαμένη οἴκαδε ἔσπευσεν.
8. ὁ μὲν δεσπότης τοὺς δούλους ἐκέλευσε σῑγῆσαι, οἱ δὲ οὐκ ἐπαύσαντο διαλεγόμενοι.
9. ἡμεῖς μὲν ἀγαθαὶ ἦμεν, ὑμεῖς δὲ κακαί.
10. ὁ γέρων οὕτω γεραιὸς ἦν, ὥστε πάντες αὐτὸν ἐθαυμάσαμεν.

Exercise 12g

Translate into Greek (note that to render the correct aspect of the actions, all verb forms in this exercise—indicatives, imperatives, infinitives, and participles—should be in the aorist):

1. (After) making a libation and praying to the gods, we walked to the city.
2. The father told the boy to send the dog home.
3. I helped you, but you led me into danger.
4. Call your mother, boy, and ask her to receive us.
5. The young man, (after) winning, received a crown (ὁ στέφανος).
6. When we arrived at the city, we saw many men in the roads.

Trade and Travel

In the late Bronze Age the Achaeans traded extensively throughout the eastern Mediterranean. The Dark Age that followed (ca. 1100–800) was generally a period of isolation, in which there was little overseas trade and during which contacts with the East were broken. Early in the eighth century B.C., two Greek settlements were being made specifically for trade, the first in the East at Al Mina at the mouth of the Orontes River in Syria, the second in the West on the island of Ischia outside the Bay of Naples about 775 B.C. Both were probably made for trade in metals, essential for manufacturing arms (copper and tin from the East; copper, tin, and iron from Etruria in the West).

Al Mina was strategically placed to tap trade both inland up the Orontes to Mesopotamia and down the coast to Phoenician cities and Egypt. Its foundation was followed by a flood of Eastern imports into Greece, not only metals and artefacts, but also craftsmen and ideas, notably the alphabet, adapted by Greeks from Phoenician script about 750 B.C. The period was one of rapid change and development in Greece, a kind of renaissance. The *polis* (city-state) developed from unions of villages. Aristocracy replaced monarchy in most states. There was a revolution in warfare: hoplites (heavy armed infantry fighting in close line) replaced cavalry as the main fighting force. Growth in population led to emigrations; cities sent out colonies that peopled the coasts of the Mediterranean wherever there was no strong power to keep them out. These colonies, though founded primarily to provide land for surplus population, soon grew into prosperous, independent cities (e.g., Syracuse, founded in 733 B.C. by Corinth) and further stimulated trade, especially in grain, to supply the increasing population of the mainland. Italy from the Bay of Naples south and almost the entire coast of Sicily were studded with Greek colonies, and the area became known as Greater Greece. The leading states in this movement were Chalcis and Eretria in Euboea, Aegina, and Corinth. Miletus and other East Greek states were active in the north of the Aegean and the Black Sea.

The perils of seafaring
A pirate ship bears down on an unsuspecting merchant ship; it is about to ram the merchant ship with its bronze beak.

The story of Colaeus of Samos, who voyaged out through the Straits of Gibraltar and landed at Tartessus in the Bay of Cadiz, was told by Herodotus and is given at the end of this chapter; it shows the enterprise of these traders. The new market in the West opened up by Colaeus was developed by another Ionian state, Phocaea (see map, page 199). Phocaeans founded Massilia (Marseilles) about 600 B.C. and soon after entered into profitable trade with the king of Tartessus. This western expansion of Greek trade was curtailed

by the Carthaginians, who succeeded in pushing back the Greeks and monop-
olizing the route through the Straits of Gilbratar to Spain, Britanny, and
Britain.

Trade with Egypt developed in the seventh century, encouraged by a
friendly pharaoh, Psammetichus I (664–610 B.C.). From Egypt the Greeks
imported grain; their exports were olive oil, wine, perhaps silver, and certainly mercenary soldiers. Psammetichus employed a regular force of
Greek hoplites, and two reigns later his grandson, Psammetichus II still used
Greek mercenaries. A Greek settlement was made at the mouth of the Nile
and was named Naucratis. It was given a charter by the pharaoh Amasis
(570–526 B.C.). Naucratis developed into the largest port in Egypt, a flourish-
ing center of trade and tourism. Egypt, with a culture of immemorial antiquity, fascinated the Greeks, and many visited it out of curiosity as well as for
trade. When the family members of the poet Sappho were exiled from their
native Lesbos, she went to Sicily, but her brother went to Egypt, where he fell in
love with the most famous courtesan of the day and spent his fortune on her.
Sappho's contemporary, the poet Alcaeus, also went to Egypt during his exile,
but his brother Antimenidas served as a mercenary in the army of Nebuchadnezzar, king of Babylon, and took part in the campaign that culminated
in the capture of Jerusalem (587 B.C.) and the exile of the Jews. Antimenidas
became the army's champion and slew the enemy's Goliath.

At the time of our story, the Piraeus was the greatest port in Greece and,
indeed, in the whole Mediterranean. In Chapter 14 we will explain how
Athens came to take the lead from Corinth as a naval and mercantile power.
The harbor must have been always crowded with ships both Athenian and
foreign, both Greek and barbarian. The most important single item of import
was grain, which came from the great grain producing areas of the ancient
world: Egypt, Sicily, and the steppes of south Russia (Scythia). Athens had
treaties with the princes of Scythia that gave her a monopoly of this trade.
Shipbuilding timber was imported in large quantities both for building mer-
chantmen and for the great Athenian navy (300 triremes). Attica did not produce any metals except for silver from the mines at Laurium. She exported
olive oil, silver, and fine pottery (her black and red figure vases had driven
out all competitors by 550 B.C.).

Although commerce and far-flung trade thrived, we should not forget that
only a minority of the people were involved in it. The farmers stuck to their
farms, and the attitude of Dicaeopolis to seafaring may have been not unlike
that of Hesiod three centuries before. The only voyage he ever made was to
cross the straits between Boeotia and Euboea to take part in a poetry competition. You can only sail safely, he says, in the fifty days following the summer solstice (21 June). You might also, he says, risk a voyage in spring:

> I don't recommend it. It has no attraction for me—it must be snatched,
> and you are unlikely to avoid trouble. But men will do it in the foolish-
> ness of their hearts; for money is life to unhappy mortals. But it is a terri-
> ble thing to die in the waves.

ΠΡΟΣ ΤΟΝ ΠΕΙΡΑΙΑ
(β)

ὁ Δικαιόπολις τὴν γυναῖκα χαίρειν κελεύσᾱς, τῷ Φιλίππῳ πρὸς τὴν ναῦν ἡγήσατο.

Vocabulary

Verbs

δύναμαι I am able, can

ἐξηγέομαι, ἐξηγησάμην, ἐξηγησάμενος I relate

ἐρωτάω, ἠρόμην, ἐρόμενος I ask

φαίνομαι I appear

Nouns

ὁ ἔμπορος, τοῦ ἐμπόρου merchant

ὁ ναύκληρος, τοῦ ναυκλήρου ship's captain

ὁ ναύτης, τοῦ ναύτου sailor

Adjectives

πλείων/πλέων (*alternative forms for either masculine or feminine*), **πλέον** (*neuter*) more

πλεῖστος, -η, -ον most, very great, (*plural*) very many

Adverbs

Ἀθήναζε to Athens

εὖ well

μέγα greatly, loudly

τότε then

Expression

μάλιστά γε certainly, indeed

ἐν δὲ τῷ λιμένι πλεῖστος μὲν ἦν ὅμῑλος, πλεῖστος δὲ θόρυβος. πανταχόσε γὰρ ἔσπευδον οἱ ἄνθρωποι· οἱ μὲν γὰρ ναύκληροι τοὺς ναύτᾱς ἐκάλουν, κελεύοντες αὐτοὺς τὰ φορτία ἐκ τῶν νεῶν ἐκφέρειν, οἱ δὲ ἔμποροι μέγα ἐβόων τὰ φορτία δεχόμενοι καὶ εἰς ἁμάξᾱς εἰσφέροντες· ἄλλοι δὲ τὰ μῆλα ἐξελάσαντες διὰ τῶν ὁδῶν ἦγον. ὁ δὲ Δικαιόπολις πάντα θεώμενος ἠπόρει τί δεῖ ποιῆσαι καὶ ποῦ δεῖ ζητεῖν 5

ναῦν τινα πρὸς τὴν Ἐπίδαυρον μέλλουσαν πλεῖν· πλείστᾱς γὰρ ναῦς
εἶδε πρὸς τῷ χώματι ὁρμούσᾱς. τέλος δὲ πάντες ἐν οἰνοπωλίῳ τινὶ
καθισάμενοι οἶνον ᾔτησαν.

[θόρυβος din   πανταχόσε in all directions   ἔσπευδον were hurrying
ἐκάλουν   were calling   τὰ φόρτια cargoes   ἐβόων were shouting
ἐξελάσαντες having driven out   ἦγον were leading   ἠπόρει was at a loss   τῷ
χώματι the pier   ὁρμούσᾱς lying at anchor   οἰνοπωλίῳ wine-shop, inn]

ἐν ᾧ δὲ τὸν οἶνον ἔπῑνον, προσεχώρησε ναύτης τις γεραιὸς καί,   10
"τίνες ἐστέ, ὦ φίλοι," ἔφη, "καὶ τί βουλόμενοι πάρεστε; ἄγροικοι γὰρ
ὄντες φαίνεσθε ἀπορεῖν. εἴπετέ μοι τί πάσχετε." ὁ δὲ Δικαιόπολις
πάντα ἐξηγησάμενος, "ἆρ' οἶσθα," ἔφη, "εἴ τις ναῦς πάρεστι
μέλλουσα πρὸς τὴν Ἐπίδαυρον πλεῖν;" ὁ δέ, "μάλιστά γε," ἔφη· "ἡ
γὰρ ἐμὴ ναῦς μέλλει ἐκεῖσε πλεῖν. ἔπεσθέ μοι οὖν παρὰ τὸν   15
ναύκληρον. ἀλλ' ἰδού—πάρεστιν αὐτὸς ὁ ναύκληρος εἰς καιρὸν
προσχωρῶν." καὶ οὕτως εἰπὼν ἡγήσατο αὐτοῖς παρὰ νεᾱνίᾱν τινὰ ἐκ
νεώς τινος τότε ἐκβαίνοντα.

[ἔπῑνον they were drinking   ἄγροικοι rustic   ἆρ' οἶσθα do you know?   εἰς
καιρόν at just the right time]

ὁ οὖν Δικαιόπολις προσχωρήσᾱς ἤρετο αὐτὸν εἰ ἐθέλει κομίζειν
αὐτοὺς πρὸς τὴν Ἐπίδαυρον. ὁ δέ, "μάλιστά γε," ἔφη, "ἐθέλω ὑμᾶς   20
ἐκεῖσε κομίζειν. ἀλλὰ εἴσβητε ταχέως· εὐθὺς γὰρ μέλλομεν πλεῖν." ὁ
δὲ Δικαιόπολις, "ἐπὶ πόσῳ;" ὁ δὲ ναύκληρος, "ἐπὶ πέντε δραχμαῖς,"
ἔφη. ὁ δὲ Δικαιόπολις, "ἀλλ' ἄγᾱν αἰτεῖς. ἐγὼ δύο δραχμὰς ἐθέλω
παρασχεῖν." ὁ δέ, "οὐχί· τέτταρας αἰτῶ." ὁ δὲ Δικαιόπολις,
"ἰδού—τρεῖς δραχμάς· οὐ γὰρ δύναμαι πλέον παρασχεῖν." ὁ δέ,   25
"ἔστω· πάρασχέ μοι τὸ ἀργύριον· καὶ εἴσβητε ταχέως."

[εἴσβητε get on board   ἐπὶ πόσῳ; for how much?   ἄγᾱν too much   ἔστω all
right!]

ὁ οὖν Δικαιόπολις τὸ ἀργύριον τῷ ναυκλήρῳ παρέσχε καὶ τήν τε
γυναῖκα καὶ τὸν ἀδελφὸν χαίρειν ἐκέλευσεν. ἡ δὲ Μυρρίνη
δακρύσᾱσα, "τὸν παῖδα," ἔφη, "εὖ φύλαττε, ὦ φίλε ἄνερ, καὶ σπεῦδε
ὡς τάχιστα πάλιν οἴκονδε νέεσθαι. σὺ δέ, ὦ φίλτατε παῖ, θάρρει καὶ   30
σὺν θεῷ δι' ὀλίγου νόστησον ὑγιεῖς ἔχων τοὺς ὀφθαλμούς." οὕτω
εἰποῦσα ἀπετρέψατο· ὁ δὲ ἀδελφὸς αὐτῇ ἡγήσατο Ἀθήναζε
δακρῡούσῃ.

[πάλιν οἴκονδε νέεσθαι to return home again (Iliad 6.189; Odyssey 6.110)
φίλτατε dearest   θάρρει cheer up!   σὺν θεῷ with god's help   νόστησον
return home!   ὑγιεῖς sound, healthy   ἀπετρέψατο she turned herself away]

Word Building

The prefix ἀ- (ἀ-privative) may be attached to the beginning of many verbs, nouns, and adjectives (ἀν- is prefixed to words beginning with vowels) to negate or reverse their meaning or to express a lack or absence, e.g., δυνατός "possible," ἀδύνατος "impossible." Compare *moral* and *amoral* ("without morals"; compare *immoral*) in English.

From the words at the left, deduce the meaning of those to the right:

1. αἴτιος, -ᾱ, -ον   ἀναίτιος, -ον
2. ἄξιος, -ᾱ, -ον (worthy)   ἀνάξιος, -ον
3. δίκαιος, -ᾱ, -ον (just)   ἄδικος, -ον
4. ἀνδρεῖος, -ᾱ, -ον (from ὁ ἀνήρ, τοῦ ἀνδρός)   ἄνανδρος, -ον

Note that adjectives compounded with ἀ-privative have no separate feminine forms; the masculine forms are used with either masculine or feminine nouns.

The Piraeus, from the southeast
The large landlocked harbor to the northwest was Cantharus, the main commercial port; the smaller harbors to the south, Zea (left) and Munychia (right), were for warships.

Grammar

4. Verb Forms: The First Aorist of Liquid Verbs

Verbs with stems ending in liquid consonants (λ, μ, ν, ρ) add -α instead of -σα and show a change in the vowel or diphthong of the stem, e.g.:

μένω	ἔμεινα	(ε lengthens to ει)
φαίνομαι	ἐφηνάμην	(αι changes to η)
ἀποκτείνω	ἀπέκτεινα	(ει remains unchanged)
ἀποκρίνομαι (stem κρῐν-)	ἀπεκρῑνάμην	(ῐ lengthens to ῑ)
ἀμύνω (stem ἀμῠν-)	ἤμῡνα	(ῠ lengthens to ῡ)

Exercise 12h

Give the first person singular, aorist indicative of the following verbs:

1. νέμω (I distribute)
2. ἐγείρω
3. ἀγγέλλω* (I announce)
4. ὀτρύνω (I stir up)
5. σημαίνω (I signal, sign)
6. ἀποκρίνομαι

*The double λ becomes single in the aorist.

5. Irregular First Aorists

Learn the first aorists of the following verbs, which are irregular:

αἴρω (ἀρ-), ἦρα, ἄρᾱς I lift
δοκεῖ (δοκ-), ἔδοξε, δόξαν it seems
ἐθέλω (ἐθελε-), ἠθέλησα, ἐθελήσᾱς I wish, am willing
ἐλαύνω (ἐλα-), ἤλασα, ἐλάσᾱς I drive
καίω (καυ-), ἔκαυσα, καύσᾱς I kindle, burn
καλέω, ἐκάλεσα, καλέσᾱς I call
μάχομαι, ἐμαχεσάμην, μαχεσάμενος I fight
πλέω (πλευ-), ἔπλευσα, πλεύσᾱς I sail

6. Verb Forms: Augment of Compound Verbs

Verbs with prepositional prefixes attach the syllabic augment to the stem of the simple verb. Observe βάλλω (aorist ἔβαλον) with the following prefixes, and note the changes in the spelling of the prefixes for the sake of euphony in the combined forms:

εἰσ- into	εἰσβάλλω, εἰσέβαλον
ἐκ- out	ἐκβάλλω, ἐξέβαλον
προσ- to, toward	προσβάλλω, προσέβαλον
ἀπο- away	ἀποβάλλω, ἀπέβαλον
κατα- down	καταβάλλω, κατέβαλον
συν- together	συμβάλλω, συνέβαλον

Exercise 12i

Give the aorist indicative, first person singular, of the following verbs:

1. προσχωρέω   4. ἀποκρίνομαι   7. εἰσκομίζω
2. ἐκπέμπω   5. εἰσπέμπω   8. συνέρχομαι
3. ἀποφεύγω   6. ἀποκτείνω   9. συλλαμβάνω   (συν-)

Exercise 12j

Read aloud and translate:

1. οἱ δοῦλοι τοὺς λίθους ἄραντες ἐξέβαλον ἐκ τοῦ ἀγροῦ.
2. ὁ δεσπότης τοὺς βοῦς εἰς τὸν ἀγρὸν εἰσελάσᾱς τοὺς δούλους ἐκάλεσεν.
3. ὁ δεσπότης τοὺς μὲν δούλους ἀπέπεμψεν, αὐτὸς δὲ ἐν τῷ ἀγρῷ ἔμεινεν.
4. οἱ δοῦλοι τὸ ἄροτρον ἐν τῷ ἀγρῷ καταλιπόντες ταχέως ἐπανῆλθον.
5. ἡ παρθένος τὸν πατέρα ἰδοῦσα ταχέως προσεχώρησε καὶ ἤρετο διὰ τί οὐκ οἴκαδε ἐπανέρχεται.
6. ὁ δὲ ἀπεκρῑνατο ὅτι δεῖ τὸν ἀγρὸν ἀροτρεύειν.
7. οἱ νεᾱνίαι οὐκ ἀπέφυγον ἀλλὰ ἀνδρείως ἐμαχέσαντο.
8. ὁ ἄγγελος ἤγγειλεν ὅτι πολλοὶ ἐν τῇ μάχῃ (battle) ἀπέθανον.
9. οἱ ναῦται τὴν ναῦν παρασκευασάμενοι ἐκ τοῦ λιμένος ἐξέπλευσαν.
10. τῷ ναυκλήρῳ τὸν χειμῶνα φοβουμέῳ ἔδοξε πρὸς τὸν λιμένα ἐπανελθεῖν.

*   *   *

Ο ΚΩΛΑΙΟΣ ΤΑΡΤΗΣΣΟΝ ΕΥΡΙΣΚΕΙ

Read the following passages (based on Herodotus 4.152) and answer the comprehension questions:

πρῶτοι τῶν Ἑλλήνων εἰς Τάρτησσον ἀφίκοντο οἱ Σάμιοι. ἔμπορος γάρ τις
Κωλαῖος ὀνόματι, ἀπὸ τῆς Σάμου ὁρμώμενος πρὸς τὴν Αἴγυπτον ἔπλει, ἀλλὰ χειμὼν
μέγιστος ἐγένετο καὶ πολλὰς ἡμέρας οὐκ ἐπαύσατο ὁ ἄνεμος αἰεὶ φέρων τὴν ναῦν
πρὸς τὴν ἑσπέρᾱν. τέλος δὲ Ἡρακλείᾱς στήλᾱς διεκπερήσαντες εἰς ὠκεανὸν
εἰσέπλευσαν καὶ οὕτως εἰς Τάρτησσον ἀφίκοντο.   5
[τῶν Ἑλλήνων of the Greeks   Τάρτησσον Tartessus   οἱ Σάμιοι the Samians
Κωλαῖος Colaeus   ἡ Σάμος Samos   τὴν Αἴγυπτον Egypt   ἔπλει was sailing
ὁ ἄνεμος the wind   τὴν ἑσπέρᾱν the evening, the west   Ἡρακλείᾱς στήλᾱς
the Pillars of Hercules   διεκπερήσαντες having passed through   ὠκεανόν the
ocean]

1. Who were the first Greeks to arrive at Tartessus?
2. To what country did Colaeus set out to sail?
3. What happened that made him sail westward?
4. What did he sail through before arriving at Tartessus?

οἱ δὲ ἐπιχώριοι λαβόντες αὐτοὺς ἐκόμισαν παρὰ τὸν βασιλέα, γέροντά τινα
Ἀργαθώνιον ὀνόματι. ὁ δὲ ἤρετο αὐτοὺς τίνες εἰσὶ καὶ πόθεν ἥκουσιν. ὁ δὲ

Κωλαῖος ἀπεκρίνατο· "Ἕλληνές ἐσμεν· καὶ πρὸς τὴν Αἴγυπτον πλέοντας χειμὼν ἡμᾶς εἰς τὴν σὴν γῆν ἤλασεν." ὁ δὲ βασιλεὺς πάντα ἀκούσᾱς ἐθαύμασεν, εὐμενῶς δὲ δεξάμενος αὐτοὺς πλεῖστόν τε ἀργύριον καὶ πλεῖστον κασσίτερον αὐτοῖς   10
παρέσχεν. οἱ δὲ πολύν τινα χρόνον ἐν Ταρτήσσῳ μένοντες ἐμπορίᾱν ἐποιοῦντο. τέλος δὲ τὸν Ἀργαθώνιον χαίρειν κελεύσαντες ἀπέπλευσαν καὶ εἰς τὴν Σάμον ἐπανῆλθον οὐδὲν κακὸν παθόντες.

[οἱ . . . ἐπιχώριοι the natives   Ἀργαθώνιον Argathonius   Ἕλληνες Greeks   εὐμενῶς kindly   κασσίτερον tin   ἐμπορίᾱν ἐποιοῦντο carried on trade]

5. Where did the natives take Colaeus?
6. What did Argathonius ask Colaeus and his men?
7. What did Colaeus answer?
8. How did Argathonius receive Colaeus and his men and what did he give them?
9. What did Colaeus and his men do in Tartessus?
10. Did Colaeus and his men arrive home safely?

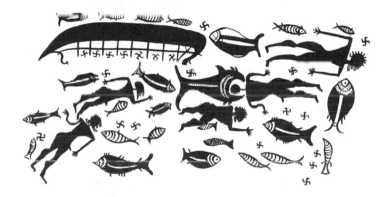

An ancient shipwreck; an overturned ship and men in the sea, one being eaten by a fish

Exercise 12k

Translate into Greek:

1. When Colaeus returned home, he told the Greeks (τοῖς Ἕλλησιν) what happened.
2. All were amazed, and many, having heard that Argathonius was very wealthy (ὄλβιος), wanted (ἐβούλοντο) to sail to Tartessus.
3. They decided to set out immediately; and having prepared four ships they sailed away.
4. (After) suffering many terrible things, they finally arrived at Tartessus.
5. The king received them kindly and gave them much silver and tin.
6. And so the Greeks thus for a long time carried on trade with (πρός) the citizens of Tartessus.

13
ΠΡΟΣ ΤΗΝ ΣΑΛΑΜΙΝΑ
(α)

στρογγύλη ἦν ἡ ναῦς, ἢ σῖτόν τε καὶ οἶνον ἔφερε πρὸς τὰς νήσους.

Vocabulary

Verbs
ἄγω, ἤγαγον, ἀγαγών I
  lead, take
ἐρέσσω, ἤρεσα, ἐρέσᾱς I row
ἡσυχάζω, ἡσύχασα,
  ἡσυχάσᾱς I keep quiet

Nouns
ὁ ἄνεμος, τοῦ ἀνέμου wind
τὰ ἱστία, τῶν ἱστίων sails

Pronoun
ἀλλήλων of one another

Adjectives
βέβαιος, -ᾱ, -ον firm
λαμπρός, -ά, -όν bright,
  brilliant
ταχύς, ταχεῖα, ταχύ quick,
  swift

Proper Name
ἡ Σαλαμίς, τῆς Σαλαμῖνος
  Salamis

ἐν δὲ τούτῳ ὁ ναύτης ὁ γεραιὸς τόν τε Δικαιόπολιν καὶ τὸν παῖδα
εἰς τὴν ναῦν ἀγαγὼν ἐκέλευσε καθίζεσθαι ἐπὶ τῷ καταστρώματι.
ἐνταῦθα δὴ ὁ μὲν ναύκληρος ἐκέλευσε τοὺς ναύτᾱς λῦσαι τὰ
πείσματα, οἱ δὲ ναῦται τὰ πείσματα λύσαντες τὴν ναῦν βραδέως
ἤρεσσον πρὸς τὴν θάλατταν. ἔπειτα δὲ τὴν γῆν καταλιπόντες τὰ
ἱστία ἐπέτασαν.

[ὁ **ναύτης** ὁ **γεραιός** the old sailor   **τῷ καταστρώματι** the deck   **τὰ πείσματα**
the cables   **ἐπέτεσαν** (*from* πετάννυμι) they spread]

ἐπεὶ δὲ ἡ μὲν ναῦς βεβαίως ἔπλει οἱ δὲ ναῦται τῶν ἔργων
παυσάμενοι ἡσύχαζον, ὁ Δικαιόπολις πᾶσαν τὴν ναῦν ἐσκόπει.
στρογγύλη ἦν ἡ ναῦς, οὐ μεγάλη οὐδὲ ταχεῖα ἀλλὰ βεβαία, ἣ φόρτια
ἔφερε πρὸς τὰς νήσους· σῖτός τε γὰρ ἐνῆν καὶ οἶνος καὶ ὕλη καὶ μῆλα.   10
καὶ πολλοὶ ἐνῆσαν ἄνθρωποι, ἄγροικοι ὄντες, οἳ τὰ φόρτια ἐν ταῖς
Ἀθήναις πωλήσαντες οἴκαδε ἐπανῆσαν· ἄλλοι δὲ παρὰ τοὺς
οἰκείους ἐπορεύοντο οἳ ἐν ταῖς νήσοις ᾤκουν. πάντες δὲ ἐτέρποντο
πλέοντες—οὔριος γὰρ ἦν ὁ ἄνεμος καὶ λαμπρὸς ὁ ἥλιος—καὶ ἢ
διελέγοντο ἀλλήλοις ἢ μέλη ᾖδον.   15

[ἣ which   φόρτια cargo   ὕλη timber   ἄγροικοι rustic   οἳ who
πωλήσαντες having sold   ἐπανῆσαν were returning   τοὺς οἰκείους their
relatives   οὔριος favorable   μέλη songs   ᾖδον they were singing]

Word Study

Identify the Greek roots in the English words below and give the meanings of the English words. Give the meanings of the Greek words in parentheses:

1. nautical
2. cosmonaut (ὁ κόσμος, τοῦ κόσμου)
3. aeronaut (ὁ *or* ἡ ἀήρ, τοῦ *or* τῆς ἀέρος)
4. astronaut (τὸ ἄστρον, τοῦ ἄστρου)
5. cosmology
6. astrology

Grammar

1. Verb Forms: The Imperfect Tense

This tense is formed by augmenting the verb stem as found in the present tense and adding the thematic vowels and the secondary personal endings. Compare the formation and endings of the second aorist, which is similar except that it is based on a different stem.

Imperfect Active

ἔ-λῡ-ο-ν	I was loosening, I loosened
ἔ-λῡ-ε-ς	you were loosening, you loosened
ἔ-λῡ-ε(ν)	he/she was loosening, he/she loosened
ἐ-λύ-ο-μεν	we were loosening, we loosened
ἐ-λύ-ε-τε	you were loosening, you loosened
ἔ-λῡ-ο-ν	they were loosening, they loosened

Imperfect Middle

ἐ-λῡ-ό-μην	I was ransoming, I ransomed
ἐ-λύ-ε-σο > ἐλύου	you were ransoming, you ransomed
ἐ-λύ-ε-το	he/she was ransoming, he/she ransomed
ἐ-λῡ-ό-μεθα	we were ransoming, we ransomed
ἐ-λύ-ε-σθε	you were ransoming, you ransomed
ἐ-λύ-ο-ντο	they were ransoming, they ransomed

Contract verbs follow the rules given above for the formation of the imperfect tense and the rules for contraction given on pages 32 and 44:

Active

ἐ-φίλε-ο-ν >	ἐφίλουν		ἐ-τίμα-ο-ν >	ἐτίμων
ἐ-φίλε-ε-ς >	ἐφίλεις		ἐ-τίμα-ε-ς >	ἐτίμᾱς
ἐ-φίλε-ε >	ἐφίλει		ἐ-τίμα-ε >	ἐτίμᾱ
ἐ-φιλέ-ο-μεν >	ἐφιλοῦμεν		ἐ-τῑμά-ο-μεν >	ἐτῑμῶμεν
ἐ-φιλέ-ε-τε >	ἐφιλεῖτε		ἐ-τῑμά-ε-τε >	ἐτῑμᾶτε
ἐ-φίλε-ο-ν >	ἐφίλουν		ἐ-τίμα-ο-ν >	ἐτίμων

Middle

ἐ-φιλε-ό-μην >	ἐφιλούμην		ἐ-τῑμα-ό-μην >	ἐτῑμώμην
ἐ-φιλέ-ε-σο >	ἐφιλοῦ		ἐ-τῑμά-ε-σο >	ἐτῑμῶ
ἐ-φιλέ-ε-το >	ἐφιλεῖτο		ἐ-τῑμά-ε-το >	ἐτῑμᾶτο
ἐ-φιλε-ό-μεθα >	ἐφιλούμεθα		ἐ-τῑμα-ό-μεθα >	ἐτῑμώμεθα
ἐ-φιλέ-ε-σθε >	ἐφιλεῖσθε		ἐ-τῑμά-ε-σθε >	ἐτῑμᾶσθε
ἐ-φιλέ-ο-ντο >	ἐφιλοῦντο		ἐ-τῑμά-ο-ντο >	ἐτῑμῶντο

Exercise 13a

Locate thirteen verbs in the imperfect tense in the second paragraph of the reading passage at the beginning of this chapter. Remember that the past tense forms of εἰμί that you learned in Chapter 12 are imperfect tense forms.

Exercise 13b

In parallel columns on a sheet of paper write the following forms:

Present active indicative of λύω
Imperfect active indicative of λύω
Aorist active indicative of λαμβάνω
Aorist active indicative of λύω

On a second sheet of paper write the corresponding middle forms.

On additonal sheets of paper write the following:

Present, imperfect, and aorist active indicative of φιλέω
Present, imperfect, and aorist middle indicative of φιλέω
Present, imperfect, and aorist active indicative of τῑμάω
Present, imperfect, and aorist middle indicative of τῑμάω

2. Aspect

The imperfect tense looks on the action of the verb as a process, while the aorist looks on the action as an event. The imperfect is used to indicate continuous or incomplete action in past time. It can often be translated by the English imperfect, e.g.:

ἐπεὶ προσεχωροῦμεν, οἱ φύλακες τὰς πύλᾱς ἔκλειον.
When we were approaching, the guards were shutting the gates.

Compare the aorist:

ἐπεὶ εἰσήλθομεν, οἱ φύλακες τὰς πύλᾱς ἔκλεισαν.
When we went (had gone) in, the guards shut the gates.

The imperfect can also be translated by a simple past tense in English, e.g.:

οἱ βόες ἔμενον ἐν τῷ ἀγρῷ.
The oxen stayed (for a long time) in the field.

Exercise 13c

Translate into English:

1. ἡμεῖς μὲν πρὸς τὸ ἄστυ ἐσπεύδομεν, σὺ δὲ ἐν τῇ οἰκίᾳ ἡσύχαζες.
2. ἡ ναῦς τὸν λιμένα καταλιποῦσα πρὸς τὴν νῆσον ἔπλει.
3. ἐπεὶ ἐγένετο νύξ, μείζων (greater, stronger) ἐγίγνετο ὁ ἄνεμος.
4. καίπερ εἰς κίνδῡνον ἐμπεσόντες (ἐν + πίπτω) οὐκ ἐφοβούμεθα.
5. οἱ Ἕλληνες (the Greeks) τοὺς θεοὺς ἐτίμων καὶ τὴν πόλιν ἐφίλουν.
6. αἱ γυναῖκες ἐν τῇ ὁδῷ μένουσαι τοῖς ἀνδράσι διελέγοντο.
7. ἐπεὶ ἐνόσει ὁ παῖς, ὁ πατὴρ ἐκόμισεν αὐτὸν παρὰ τὸν ἰᾱτρόν.
8. οἱ αὐτουργοὶ τοὺς βοῦς λῡσαντες οἴκαδε ἦγον.
9. ἐπεὶ πρὸς τὴν θάλατταν ᾖρεσαν οἱ ναῦται, τὰ ἱστία ᾖραν.
10. οἱ ἔμποροι μέγα βοῶντες τὸν σῖτον ἐκ τῆς νεὼς ἐξέφερον.

Exercise 13d

Change the following forms first into the corresponding forms of the imperfect and then of the aorist:

1. λῡομεν	6. ἀκούετε	11. ἀφικνεῖται
2. λῡονται	7. ἡγῇ	12. νῑκῶμεν
3. ποιοῦσι	8. γιγνόμεθα	13. βοᾷ
4. φιλεῖ	9. πέμπομεν	14. πῑπτει
5. λαμβάνει	10. εὔχονται	15. λείπω

Exercise 13e

Translate into Greek:

1. The young men were running very quickly to the agora.
2. When the boy returned home, the girl was waiting by the door.
3. He was already sailing through the straits (τὰ στενά) to the harbor.
4. I was staying at home, but you were journeying to the city.
5. When we arrived at the island, no one wanted to help us.
6. What were you doing, boy, when I saw you in the harbor?
7. Were you watching the ship sailing out to sea?
8. The captain was shouting loudly, but we were not afraid of him.

The Rise of Persia

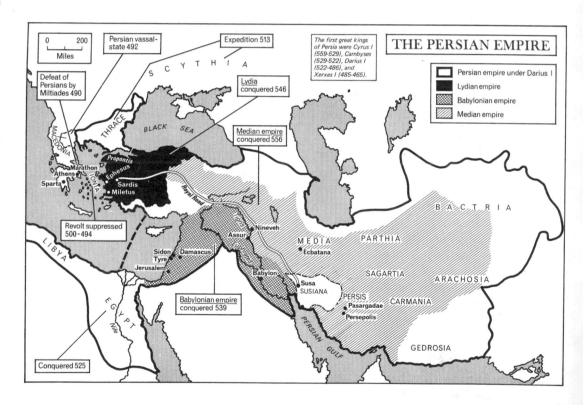

The Persian Empire

The events that led to the sudden emergence of Persia as a world power are complex, involving the fall of three ancient empires in quick succession. Until the sixth century, the Persians were a wandering mountain tribe, whose name occasionally crops up in contemporary records as they gradually worked their way southeast from Russia down the mountains of western Iran. By 550 B.C. they were settled east of the mouth of the Tigris as a vassal kingdom of Media. To understand their rapid rise to power it is necessary to go back to the middle of the seventh century, a turning point in the history of the ancient world.

By 650 B.C. the Assyrian Empire, which had ruled Mesopotamia, Egypt, and Syria, began to crumble. In Egypt Psammetichus led a national revival and threw off the Assyrian yoke with the help of Greek mercenaries (ca. 650 B.C.). The Medes, united under King Phraortes (675–653 B.C.), became a formidable power, extending their kingdom on all sides. In Lydia, Gyges (685–657 B.C.) founded a new dynasty and expanded westward to Ionia, where he defeated some of the Ionian Greeks, and eastward to the river Halys (the northeastern border of the Lydian Empire as marked on the map). Babylon, which a thousand years earlier had ruled all of Mesopotamia, revolted from Assyria about 625 B.C. and made an alliance with the Medes. In 612 B.C. the Babylonians and Medes took the Assyrian capital Nineveh and proceeded to divide up their empire. Babylon took the south; their king, Nebuchadnezzar, controlled all of Mesopotamia. He defeated the Egyptians at the great battle of Carchemish (605 B.C.) and drove them from Syria. When the Jews revolted, he took and destroyed Jerusalem (587 B.C.) and carried the tribes of Judah into captivity in Babylon. Assyria itself and the lands to the west up to the borders of Lydia fell to the Medes. On these borders the Medes fought several battles with Lydians, the last of which (28 May 585 B.C.) was broken off when the eclipse of the sun predicted by Thales occurred.

The stage was now set for the rise of Persia. In 556 B.C. Cyrus, king of the Persians, defeated the Medes and became king of the Medes and Persians, founding the dynasty of the Achaemenids, who were to rule the greatest empire the world had ever seen, until they were overthrown by Alexander the Great two hundred years later.

Croesus, king of Lydia, alarmed by the growing power of Cyrus, decided to make a pre-emptive strike. He consulted the oracle of Apollo at Delphi, which answered that if he crossed the river Halys, he would destroy a great empire. Thus encouraged, he led his army over the river and was met by Cyrus near the city of Pteria, about 60 miles east of the Halys. A bloody but indecisive battle followed, after which Croesus led his troops back to Sardis, intending to invade again the following year with larger forces. Cyrus, however, pursued him hotfoot, defeated him, and took the city of Sardis (546 B.C.). Many of the Greek cities of Asia Minor submitted at once. Those that did not were reduced the following year by the general whom Cyrus left behind when he returned to Persia.

When Cyrus had consolidated his empire in Iran, he was ready to move against Babylon, which was suffering from discord. He came as a liberator, for example, of the Jews: "Comfort ye, comfort ye, my people, saith God. . . . Comfort Jerusalem, for her time of humiliation is ended"—so prophesied Isaiah (xl), welcoming the coming of Cyrus as the savior sent by God. Babylon fell in 539 B.C., and there followed a peaceful and orderly occupation.

Cyrus was proclaimed king of Babylon the following year: "I am Cyrus, king of the world, the Great King, the legitimate king, king of Babylon, king of Sumer and Akkad, king of the four corners of the earth" reads an inscription found on a cylinder at Babylon. One of his first decrees allowed the Jews to return to Jerusalem and rebuild the Temple. He died in 530 B.C., much lamented; he had been no mere conqueror but the father of his people.

His son Cambyses consolidated Persian power in the Levant and invaded and defeated Egypt (525 B.C.). In March of 522 B.C., shortly before he died, there was a rebellion led by a Persian who called himself Bardiya, son of Cyrus. By July most of the empire acknowledged him, but in September a conspiracy was formed by seven great Persian nobles, who maintained that Bardiya was a pretender. They murdered him and set on the throne one of their number: Darius. Darius had to put down revolts all over the empire before his position was secure. He consolidated the empire and extended it in the East from Afghanistan into India (the Punjab) and opened up a sea route from the mouth of the Indus to the Persian Gulf and Egypt.

Darius then turned his attention northwest. In 513 B.C. he led his army into Europe across the Hellespont, subdued most of Thrace, and marched north to the mouth of the Danube. He crossed the river by a bridge of boats, built by his Greek engineers, and he disappeared into the steppes of Russia, to deal with the nomad Scythians, who were harassing the northern borders of his empire. He was gone for over sixty days, and the Greeks who were guarding the bridge discussed whether they should break up the bridge and leave him to his fate but decided it was wiser to remain at their post. Eventually he returned with the survivors of his army, having accomplished little against the hit-and-run tactics of the Scythians. He returned to Persia, leaving a general to complete the conquest of Thrace. This was accomplished in one campaign, which brought the Persians up to the borders of Macedonia. By now most of the islands of the Aegean Sea were held by the Persians. The threat to mainland Greece was uncomfortably close.

In 500 B.C. the Ionian Greeks revolted, expelling the tyrants whom the Persians had installed to control them. The revolt was led by Aristagoras, tyrant of Miletus, who was in trouble with the Persian authorities. Aristagoras visited the mainland to beg for support. At Sparta, King Cleomenes refused, but at Athens the assembly of the newly founded democracy was won over by his appeal and voted to send an expedition of twenty ships. These joined the Ionian forces at Ephesus, and the allies marched up country and took and destroyed Sardis, the capital of the satrapy. When a Persian relief force arrived, they retreated rapidly to the coast. The Athenian contingent, satisfied with their exploit, returned to Athens. The Ionians kept up the struggle for four more years with varying success until the Persians eventually crushed all resistance and took Miletus (494 B.C.).

Darius is said to have ordered one of his officials to say to him every day: "Remember the Athenians." Retribution was assured. In 492 B.C. a large force was dispatched by land and sea. Thrace and Macedonia submitted, but, when the fleet was wrecked off Mount Athos the expedition against Greece was called off. Two years later a second expedition sailed straight across the Aegean, landed near Eretria in Euboea (Eretria had sent five ships to help the Ionians), and took and destroyed the city. They then landed on the coast of Attica at Marathon. After heated debate, the Athenian Assembly at the urging of Miltiades decided to send their army out to meet the Persians at Marathon rather than to shut themselves up in the city. The Athenians, though greatly outnumbered, faced the Persians alone (apart from a small contingent sent by their ally Plataea). Sparta sent a force to help, but it arrived too late for the battle. By brilliant tactics, the Athenians routed the Persian force and pursued them to the sea, inflicting heavy casualties for small losses (490 B.C.). This day was never forgotten. To have fought at Marathon was an Athenian's proudest boast. Aeschylus, the great tragic poet, makes no mention of his poetry in his epitaph; he simply says: "Of his glorious courage the groves of Marathon could speak, and the long-haired Mede, who knew it well." The dead were buried beneath a great mound still to be seen on the site of the battle.

Darius' preparations to take revenge on the Greeks were thwarted first by a revolt in Egypt and then by his death. It was not until 483 B.C. that his successor, Xerxes, began to assemble the vast force that was intended finally to settle Persia's score with Greece.

Darius, the Persian king, holds an audience. His son and successor, Xerxes, stands behind his throne.

ΠΡΟΣ ΤΗΝ ΣΑΛΑΜΙΝΑ (β)

ἰδού, τὰ στενὰ ἐν οἷς πρὸς τοὺς βαρβάρους ἐμαχόμεθα.

Vocabulary

Verbs

ἀμΰνω, ἤμῡνα, ἀμῦνᾱς
(*active*) I ward off X (*acc.*)
from Y (*dat.*); (*middle*) I ward
off, defend myself (against +
acc.)

ὀργίζομαι I grow angry (at +
dat.)

Nouns

ἡ ἀρχή, τῆς ἀρχῆς beginning

ὁ βάρβαρος, τοῦ βαρβάρου
barbarian

ἡ ἐλευθερίᾱ, τῆς ἐλευθερίᾱς
freedom

τὸ κῦμα, τοῦ κΰματος wave

ἡ μάχη, τῆς μάχης battle

τὸ ναυτικόν, τοῦ ναυτικοῦ
fleet

τὰ στενά, τῶν στενῶν
(*plural*) narrows, straits,
mountain pass

ἡ τριήρης, τῆς τριήρους
trireme

Pronoun and Adjective

μηδείς, μηδεμία, μηδέν (*used
instead of* οὐδείς *with
imperatives and infinitives*) no
one, nothing, no

Relative Pronouns

ὅς, ἥ, ὅ who, whose, whom,
which, that

ὅσπερ, ἥπερ, ὅπερ (*emphatic
forms*) who, whose, whom,
which, that

Adjectives

ἀληθής, ἀληθές true

τὰ ἀληθῆ, τῶν ἀληθῶν the
truth

ἐκεῖνος, ἐκείνη, ἐκεῖνο that,
(*plural*) those
Note word order: ἐκείνη ἡ
μάχη *or* ἡ μάχη ἐκείνη

ψευδής, -ές false
  τὰ ψευδῆ, τῶν ψευδῶν
    lies
Preposition
  ἐγγύς (+ gen.) near
Adverbs
  ἅμα together, at the same time
Conjunctions
  ὅτε when
  ὡς as

Expressions
  τῷ ὄντι in truth
  ὡς δοκεῖ as it seems
Proper Names
  ἡ Ἑλλάς, τῆς Ἑλλάδος
    Hellas, Greece
  ὁ Ποσειδῶν, τοῦ Ποσειδῶνος
    Poseidon

ἐπεὶ δὲ ὀλίγον χρόνον ἔπλευσαν, δέκα νῆες μακραὶ ἐφαίνοντο, αἳ
πρὸς τὸν Πειραιᾶ ἐπορεύοντο ἀπὸ τῶν νήσων ἐπανιοῦσαι. πάντες
οὖν τὰς τριήρεις ἐθεῶντο, αἳ ταχέως διὰ τῶν κῡμάτων ἔσπευδον. οἱ
γὰρ ἐρέται τῷ κελευστῇ πειθόμενοι τὴν θάλατταν ἅμα ἔτυπτον. ἐπεὶ
δὲ οὐκέτι ἐφαίνοντο αἱ τριήρεις, μείζων μὲν ἐγίγνετο ὁ ἄνεμος, ἡ δὲ   5
θάλαττα ἐκύμαινεν. οἱ δ' ἄνθρωποι οὐκέτι ἐτέρποντο, ἀλλ' οἱ μὲν
ἄνδρες ἐσίγων αἱ δὲ γυναῖκες ἔκλαζον εὐχόμεναι τὸν Ποσειδῶνα σῴζειν ἑαυτὰς εἰς τὸν λιμένα.

[ὀλίγον small, short   νῆες μακραί long ships = warships   ἐπανιοῦσαι
returning   οἱ ... ἐρέται rowers   τῷ κελευστῇ boatswain (he gave the time to the
rowers)   μείζων greater, larger   ἐκύμαινεν was becoming rough   ἔκλαζον
were shrieking]

ἀνὴρ δέ τις, ὃς ἐγγὺς τοῦ Δικαιοπόλεως ἐκαθίζετο, ἀνέστη καὶ
βοήσᾱς, "ὀργίζεται ἡμῖν," ἔφη, "ὁ Ποσειδῶν, ὡς δοκεῖ. κακὸν γὰρ   10
ἄνθρωπον ἐν τῇ νηὶ φέρομεν, ὃν δεῖ ῥίπτειν εἰς τὴν θάλατταν." καὶ
τοὺς παρόντας ἐπιφθόνως ἐσκόπει. ὁ δὲ γέρων προσελθών, "σίγησον,
ὦ ἄνθρωπε," ἔφη· "οὐδὲν γὰρ λέγεις. ἤδη γὰρ πίπτει ὁ ἄνεμος καὶ
οὐκέτι τοσοῦτο κῡμαίνει ἡ θάλαττα. κάθιζε οὖν καὶ ἥσυχος ἔχε."
τρεψάμενος δὲ πρὸς τὸν Φίλιππον, "μηδὲν φοβοῦ, ὦ παῖ," ἔφη· "δι'   15
ὀλίγου γὰρ εἰς τὴν Σαλαμῖνα ἀφικνούμεθα. ἤδη γὰρ πλέομεν διὰ τῶν
στενῶν πρὸς τὸν λιμένα. ἰδού, ὦ Δικαιόπολι, τὰ στενὰ ἐν οἷς τὸ τῶν
βαρβάρων ναυτικὸν ἐμένομεν ὅτε τῇ Ἑλλάδι αὐτοὺς ἠμῡνόμεν ὑπὲρ
τῆς ἐλευθερίᾱς μαχόμενοι."

[ἀνέστη stood up   ῥίπτειν to throw   ἐπιφθόνως maliciously, malignantly
τοσοῦτο so greatly   ἥσυχος ἔχε keep quiet!]

ὁ δὲ Δικαιόπολις, "τί λέγεις, ὦ γέρον;" ἔφη· "ἆρα σὺ ἐκείνῃ τῇ μάχῃ   20
παρῆσθα;" ὁ δὲ γέρων, "μάλιστά γε," ἔφη, "ἐγὼ παρῆν, νεᾱνίᾱς ὢν καὶ
ἐρέτης ἐν τριήρει Ἀθηναίᾳ." ὁ δὲ Φίλιππος, "ἆρα τὰ ἀληθῆ λέγεις;

μάλα οὖν γεραιὸς εἶ, εἰ τῷ ὄντι ἐκείνῃ τῇ μάχῃ παρῆσθα. ἀλλ’ εἰπὲ
ἡμῖν τί ἐγένετο." ὁ δέ, "μακρός ἐστιν ὁ λόγος," ἔφη, "καὶ εἰ βούλεσθε
τὰ γενόμενα μαθεῖν, δεῖ με πάντα ἐξ ἀρχῆς ἐξηγεῖσθαι. ἐγὼ δέ, ὃς   25
παρῆν, τέρπομαι ἐξηγούμενος. ἀκούετε οὖν."

Word Building

Give the meanings of the words in the following sets:

1. ἡ ναῦς   ὁ ναύτης   ναυτικός, -ή, -όν   τὸ ναυτικόν
2. ναυμαχέω   ἡ ναυμαχίᾱ   ὁ ναύκληρος   ὁ ναύαρχος

Grammar

3. Relative Clauses

You have now seen a number of relative clauses in the reading
passages, e.g.:

a. δέκα νῆες μακραὶ ἐφαίνοντο, **αἳ πρὸς τὸν Πειραιᾶ ἐπορεύοντο.**
   Ten warships appeared, *which were going to the Piraeus.*

b. κακὸν ἄνθρωπον ἐν τῇ νηῒ φέρομεν, **ὃν δεῖ ῥίπτειν εἰς τὴν
   θάλατταν.**
   We are carrying an evil man in the ship, *whom it is necessary to
   throw into the sea.*

Relative clauses are adjectival or descriptive clauses that are
introduced by relative pronouns, of which English has the forms *who,
whose, whom, which,* and *that.* In Greek the relative pronoun may appear
in any of the following forms:

	Singular			**Plural**		
	Masc.	**Fem.**	**Neut.**	**Masc.**	**Fem.**	**Neut.**
Nom.	ὅς	ἥ	ὅ	οἵ	αἵ	ἅ
Gen.	οὗ	ἧς	οὗ	ὧν	ὧν	ὧν
Dat.	ᾧ	ᾗ	ᾧ	οἷς	αἷς	οἷς
Acc.	ὅν	ἥν	ὅ	οὕς	ἅς	ἅ

Note the following rule: the relative pronoun, which introduces the
relative clause, agrees with the word to which it refers in the main clause
(i.e., the *antecedent*) in gender and number, but its case is determined by
its function in the relative clause.

Thus, in sentence a above, the words δέκα νῆες μακραί (*fem. pl.*) are the
antecedent of the relative pronoun, which must accordingly be feminine
and plural. The relative pronoun is the subject of the verb in its own

clause (ἐπορεύοντο) and must accordingly be in the nominative case; the correct form is therefore αἵ (feminine, plural, nominative).

In sentence b above, the words κακὸν ἄνθρωπον are the antecedent of the relative pronoun, which must accordingly be masculine and singular. The relative pronoun is the object of ῥίπτειν in its own clause and must accordingly be accusative; the correct form is therefore ὅν (masculine, singular, accusative).

The suffix -περ may be added to the forms of the relative pronoun given above for emphasis.

Exercise 13f

In the first two paragraphs of reading passage β, locate five relative clauses. Identify the antecedent of each relative pronoun, and explain why the relative pronoun is in its gender, number, and case. (Two of the five examples have already been analyzed above.) Be careful not to confuse relative pronouns with definite articles. You may wish to compare the forms and accents of relative pronouns with those of the definite article (Chapter 4, Grammar 6, page 40). Note that the relative pronoun never begins with the letter τ and that the masculine and feminine nominative singular and plural definite articles do not have accents.

Exercise 13g

Read aloud and translate into English:

1. οἱ ἔμποροι οἳ ἐν ἐκείνῃ τῇ νηὶ ἔπλεον τὰ κύματα οὐκ ἐφοβοῦντο.
2. ὁ ναύτης ᾧ τὸ ἀργύριον παρέσχες ἡμῖν ἡγήσατο εἰς τὴν ναῦν.
3. οἱ ἄνθρωποι οὓς ἐν τῷ ὄρει εἴδετε σῖτον Ἀθήναζε ἔφερον.
4. ἐκεῖνοι οἱ δοῦλοι πάντα ἐποίουν ἅπερ ἐκέλευσεν ὁ δεσπότης.
5. αἱ γυναῖκες αἷς διελεγόμεθα οὐκ ἔλεγον τὰ ἀληθῆ.
6. πάντας ἐτίμων οἵπερ ὑπὲρ τῆς ἐλευθερίας ἐμάχοντο.
7. ἐκείνη ἡ ναῦς ἣν ἐθεῶ ἀποπλέουσαν σῖτον ἔφερεν ἀπὸ τοῦ Πόντου (*the Black Sea*).
8. ὁ ἄγγελος οὗ ἐν τῇ ἀγορᾷ ἠκούετε οὐκ ἔλεγε τὰ ψευδῆ.
9. ἆρ᾽ οὐκ ἐφοβεῖσθε τοὺς βαρβάρους οὓς ὁ Ξέρξης ἐπὶ τὴν Ἑλλάδα ἦγεν;
10. ἆρ᾽ εἶδες ἐκείνην τὴν παρθένον, ᾗ οὕτως ὠργίζετο ὁ γέρων;

4. Third Declension Nouns and Adjectives with Stems in -εσ-

Some third declension nouns and adjectives have stems ending in
-εσ-, from which the σ drops before the endings, allowing the ε of the stem
to contract with the vowels of the endings, e.g., τὸ τεῖχος (stem τειχεσ-).
The usual contractions occur, as follows:

ε + ε > ει   ε + α > η
ε + ο > ου   ε followed by a long vowel disappears

	Singular		*Plural*	
Nom.	τὸ τεῖχος		τὰ τείχε-α >	τείχη
Gen.	τοῦ τείχε-ος >	τείχους	τῶν τειχέ-ων >	τειχῶν
Dat.	τῷ τείχε-ι >	τείχει	τοῖς τείχεσ-σι(ν) >	τείχεσι(ν)
Acc.	τὸ τεῖχος		τὰ τείχε-α >	τείχη

So also τὸ ὄρος, τοῦ ὄρους

Nom.	ἡ	τριήρης		αἱ	τριήρε-ες >	τριήρεις
Gen.	τῆς	τριήρε-ος >	τριήρους	τῶν	τριηρέ-ων >	τριήρων
Dat.	τῇ	τριήρει		ταῖς	τριήρεσ-σι >	τριήρεσι.
Acc.	τὴν	τριήρε-α >	τριήρη	τὰς	τριήρεις	
Voc.	ὦ	τριῆρες		ὦ	τριήρε-ες >	τριήρεις

The adjective ἀληθής (stem ἀληθεσ-) has only two sets of forms, the
first to go with masculine or feminine nouns and the second to go with
neuter nouns. It also drops the σ of the stem before the endings and shows
the same contractions as the noun above:

	Masc./Fem.		*Neut.*	
Nom.	ἀληθής		ἀληθές	
Gen.	ἀληθέ-ος >	ἀληθοῦς	ἀληθέ-ος >	ἀληθοῦς
Dat.	ἀληθέ-ι >	ἀληθεῖ	ἀληθέ-ι >	ἀληθεῖ
Acc.	ἀληθέ-α >	ἀληθῆ	ἀληθές	
Nom.	ἀληθέ-ες >	ἀληθεῖς	ἀληθέ-α >	ἀληθῆ
Gen.	ἀληθέ-ων >	ἀληθῶν	ἀληθέ-ων >	ἀληθῶν
Dat.	ἀληθέσ-σι(ν) >	ἀληθέσι(ν)	ἀληθέσ-σι(ν) >	ἀληθέσι(ν)
Acc.	ἀληθεῖς		ἀληθέ-α >	ἀληθῆ

Exercise 13h

Decline the following noun and adjective:

1. τὸ ὄρος, τοῦ ὄρους mountain   2. ψευδής, -ές false

5. Expressions of Time

To express the *time within which* something happens, the genitive case is used, e.g.:

νυκτός in the night
πέντε ἡμερῶν within five days

To express the *time when* something happens, the dative case is used, e.g.:

τῇ τρίτῃ ἡμέρᾳ ἀφῑκόμεθα. We arrived on the third day.
τῇ ὑστεραίᾳ οἴκαδε ἐσπεύσαμεν. The next day we hurried home.

To express *duration of time*, the accusative case is used, e.g.:

πόσον χρόνον ἐν τῷ ἄστει ἐμείνατε; How long did you stay in the city?
τρεῖς ἡμέρᾱς ἐμείναμεν. We stayed for three days.

Exercise 13i

Read aloud and translate:

1. δύο μὲν ἡμέρᾱς ἐπορευόμεθα, τῇ δὲ τρίτῃ εἰς ἀκρὸν τὸ ὄρος ἀφῑκόμεθα.
2. τῇ ὑστεραίᾳ οἴκαδε ὁρμήσαντες δι' ὀλίγου εἴδομεν τὰ τῆς πόλεως τείχη.
3. πολὺν μὲν χρόνον κατὰ τὸ ὄρος κατεβαίνομεν, τέλος δὲ πρὸς τοῖς τείχεσι καθισάμενοι ἀνεπαυόμεθα (*rested*).
4. ὁ δοῦλος νυκτὸς ἐξελθὼν τὸν τοῦ δεσπότου κύνα ἐζήτει.
5. οἱ ἔμποροι, τῇ ὑστεραίᾳ ἀποπλεύσαντες, τριῶν ἡμερῶν εἰς τὸν Πειραιᾶ ἀφίκοντο.

Exercise 13j

Translate into Greek:

1. Those young men were journeying to friends who live in the city.
2. The young men whom you saw in the mountains were looking for their flocks all day.
3. The captain received the money that I gave him.
4. He was sailing through the straits in which the Greeks defeated the barbarians.
5. That priest to whom we were talking was telling lies.
6. The ship in which he sailed arrived at the harbor in four days.
7. I was listening to the women who were working in the house at night.
8. On the next day the sailors did all that the captain ordered.
9. Weren't you afraid of that old man, who was shouting so loudly?
10. The foreigners, although hurrying, helped the old man who was looking for the oxen.

* * *

Ο ΞΕΡΞΗΣ ΤΟΝ ΕΛΛΗΣΠΟΝΤΟΝ ΔΙΑΒΑΙΝΕΙ

Read the following passages (based on Herodotus 7.33–35 and 44) and answer the comprehension questions:

ὁ δὲ Ξέρξης, τοὺς Ἕλληνας καταστρέφεσθαι βουλόμενος, στρατὸν μέγιστον παρεσκεύασεν. ἐπεὶ δὲ πάντα τὰ ἄλλα ἕτοιμα ἦν, τοὺς στρατηγοὺς ἐκέλευσε γέφυραν ποιῆσαι ἐπὶ τῷ Ἑλλησπόντῳ, τὸν στρατὸν ἐθέλων διαβιβάσαι εἰς τὴν Εὐρώπην. οἱ μὲν οὖν στρατηγοὶ γέφυραν ἐποίησαν, χειμὼν δὲ μέγας γενόμενος πάντα διέφθειρε καὶ ἔλυσεν.   5

[ὁ . . . Ξέρξης Xerxes   τοὺς Ἕλληνας the Greeks   καταστρέφεσθαι to overthrow, subdue   στράτον army   στρατηγούς generals   γέφυραν bridge τῷ Ἑλλησπόντῳ the Hellespont   διαβιβάσαι to take across, transport   τὴν Εὐρώπην Europe   διέφθειρε destroyed]

1. What did Xerxes wish to do?
2. What did he prepare?
2. What did he order his generals to build? With what purpose in mind?
3. What happened?

ἐπεὶ δὲ ἔμαθεν ὁ Ξέρξης τὰ γενόμενα, μάλιστα ὀργιζόμενος, ἐκέλευσε τοὺς δούλους μαστῑγῶσαι τὸν Ἑλλήσποντον καὶ τοὺς τὴν θάλασσαν μαστῑγοῦντας ἐκέλευσε ταῦτα λέγειν· "ὦ πικρὸν ὕδωρ, ὁ δεσπότης σε οὕτω κολάζει· ἠδίκησας γὰρ αὐτὸν οὐδὲν κακὸν πρὸς αὐτοῦ παθόν. καὶ βασιλεὺς Ξέρξης διαβήσεταί σε, εἴτε βούλῃ εἴτε μή."   10

[μαστῑγῶσαι to whip   ταῦτα these things   πικρόν bitter, spiteful, mean κολάζει punishes   ἠδίκησας you wronged   πρὸς αὐτοῦ from him   παθόν (*note that this aorist participle is neuter to agree with* ὕδωρ, *the subject of* ἠδίκασας) διαβήσεται will cross   εἴτε . . . εἴτε whether . . . or]

5. How did Xerxes react to what had happened?
6. What did he order his slaves to do?
7. To what do the slaves address their speech?
8. What justification is cited for the punishment of the Hellespont?
9. What will Xerxes do?

οὕτως μὲν οὖν ἐκόλασε τὴν θάλασσαν, ἐκείνους δὲ οἳ τὴν γέφυραν ἐποίησαν ἀπέκτεινε, τὰς κεφαλὰς ἀποταμών. ἔπειτα δὲ τοὺς στρατηγοὺς ἐκέλευσεν ἄλλην γέφυραν ποιῆσαι, μάλα ἰσχῡράν. ἐπεὶ δὲ ἑτοίμη ἦν ἡ γέφυρα, ὁ Ξέρξης πρὸς τὸν Ἑλλήσποντον προσελθών, πρῶτον μὲν πάντα τὸν στρατὸν ἤθελεν θεᾶσθαι· ἐπὶ ὄχθον οὖν τινα ἀνέβη, ὅθεν πάντα τὸν πεζὸν στρατὸν ἐθεᾶτο καὶ πάσᾱς τὰς ναῦς.   15 ἔπειτα δὲ τοὺς στρατηγοὺς ἐκέλευσε τὸν πεζὸν στρατὸν διαβιβάσαι εἰς τὴν Εὐρώπην. οὕτως οὖν τῷ στρατῷ ἡγεῖτο ἐπὶ τὴν Ἑλλάδα.

[ἀποταμών cutting off   ὄχθον hill   ἀνέβη he went up, ascended   ὅθεν from where   τὸν πεζὸν στρατόν the infantry]

10. What did Xerxes do to those who had built the bridge?
11. What did he order his generals to do?
12. What did Xerxes want to do when he approached the Hellespont?
13. Where did he go and what did he see?
14. What did he order his generals to do?

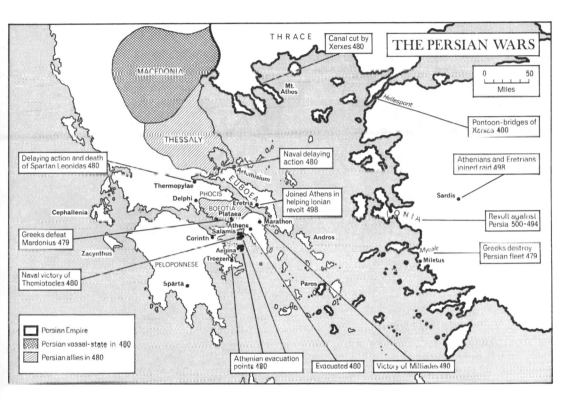

The Persian Wars

Exercise 13k

Translate into Greek:

1. When Philip was sailing to Salamis, the old sailor said that he was present at the battle (*dat. without a preposition*).
2. Philip, who was very amazed, said, "If you are telling the truth, you are very old."
3. The sailor answered: "I was a young man then and rowed in the fleet."
4. "If you wish to listen, I am willing to tell you what happened."
5. "But it's a long story, which I must tell from the beginning."

14

Η ΕΝ ΤΑΙΣ ΘΕΡΜΟΠΥΛΑΙΣ ΜΑΧΗ

(α)

οἱ Ἕλληνες ἀνδρειότατα μαχόμενοι τοὺς βαρβάρους ἤμυνον.

Verbs

ἐλπίζω, ἤλπισα, ἐλπίσᾱς I hope, expect, suppose

ἐπιπέμπω, ἐπέπεμψα, ἐπιπέμψᾱς I send against, send in

πρᾱ́ττω, ἔπρᾱξα, πρᾱ́ξᾱς I do, fare

προσβάλλω, προσέβαλον, προσβαλών (+ *dat.*) I attack

συμβάλλω, συνέβαλον, συμβαλών I join battle with

συνέρχομαι, συνῆλθον, συνελθών I come together

χράομαι, ἐχρησάμην, χρησάμενος (+ *dat.*) I use, enjoy

Nouns

ὁ ὁπλίτης, τοῦ ὁπλίτου hoplite

τὸ πλῆθος, τοῦ πλήθους number, multitude

ὁ στόλος, τοῦ στόλου expedition, army, fleet

ὁ στρατιώτης, τοῦ στρατιώτου soldier

ὁ στρατός, τοῦ στρατοῦ army

Adjectives

ὀλίγος, -η, -ον small, (*plural*) few

οὗτος, αὕτη, τοῦτο this, (*plural*) these

Note the word order: **τοῦτο τὸ ἐπίγραμμα** *or* **τὸ ἐπίγραμμα τοῦτο** this inscription

στενός, -ή, -όν narrow (cf.
τὰ στενά narrows, straits,
mountain pass)
Conjunction
ἤ (*with comparatives*) than
Expressions
ἐν μέσῳ (+ *gen.*) between
κατὰ γῆν by land
Proper Names
ὁ Ἕλλην, τοῦ Ἕλληνος
Greek, (*plural*) the Greeks
ἡ Εὔβοια, τῆς Εὐβοίᾱς Euboea

αἱ Θερμοπύλαι, τῶν
Θερμοπυλῶν Thermopylae
ἡ Κόρινθος, τῆς Κορίνθου
Corinth
οἱ Λακεδαιμόνιοι, τῶν
Λακεδαιμονίων the
Lacedaemonians, Spartans
ὁ Λεωνίδης, τοῦ Λεωνίδου
Leonidas
ὁ Ξέρξης, τοῦ Ξέρξου Xerxes
οἱ Πέρσαι, τῶν Περσῶν the
Persians

"ἐπεὶ ὁ Ξέρξης, βασιλεὺς ὢν τῶν Περσῶν, τὸν στόλον
παρεσκεύαζεν, ἐν νῷ ἔχων πᾶσαν τὴν Ἑλλάδα καταστρέφεσθαι, οἱ
τῶν Ἑλλήνων πρῶτοι συνῆλθον εἰς τὴν Κόρινθον καὶ ἐσκόπουν τί δεῖ
πράττειν. πολὺν δὲ χρόνον ἠπόρουν· μείζονα γὰρ στρατὸν εἶχεν ὁ
Ξέρξης ἢ πάντες οἱ Ἕλληνες καὶ πλέονας ναῦς. τέλος δὲ ἔδοξεν   5
αὐτοῖς τοὺς βαρβάρους ἀμύνειν ἐν ταῖς Θερμοπύλαις· ἐκεῖ γὰρ κατὰ
μὲν γῆν τὰ ὄρη οὕτω πρόσκειται τῇ θαλάττῃ ὥστε ὀλίγοι πρὸς
πολλοὺς δύνανται μάχεσθαι, κατὰ δὲ θάλατταν πόροι εἰσὶ στενοὶ ἐν
μέσῳ τῆς τε Εὐβοίᾱς καὶ τῆς ἠπείρου. μαθόντες οὖν οἱ Ἕλληνες ὅτι
ὁ Ξέρξης ἤδη πρὸς τὴν Ἑλλάδα πορεύεται, τὸν Λεωνίδην ἔπεμψαν,   10
βασιλέα ὄντα τῶν Λακεδαιμονίων, ἑπτάκις χῑλίους ἔχοντα ὁπλίτᾱς.
οὗτοι δὲ ἀφικόμενοι εἰς τὰς Θερμοπύλᾱς παρεσκευάζοντο ἀμύνειν
τοὺς βαρβάρους τῇ Ἑλλάδι.

[καταστρέφεσθαι to subdue   μείζονα bigger, larger   εἶχεν (*irregular imperfect
of* ἔχω)   πρόσκειται (*note neuter plural subject*) lie close to (+ *dat.*)   πόροι straits
τῆς ἠπείρου the mainland   ἑπτάκις χῑλίους seven thousand]

"ὁ δὲ Ξέρξης ἀφικόμενος εἰς τὰ στενὰ στρατὸν ἔχων μέγιστον δή,
τέτταρας μὲν ἡμέρᾱς ἡσύχαζεν· ἤλπιζε γὰρ τοὺς Ἕλληνας   15
ἀποφεύξεσθαι ἰδόντας τὸ πλῆθος τοῦ στρατοῦ. τῇ δὲ πέμπτῃ
ἡμέρᾳ—οἱ γὰρ Ἕλληνες ἔτι ἀκίνητοι ἔμενον—τὸν στρατὸν ἐκέλευσεν
εὐθὺς προσβαλεῖν. οἱ δὲ Ἕλληνες ἀνδρειότατα μαχόμενοι τοὺς
βαρβάρους ἤμῡνον. τέλος δὲ ὁ βασιλεὺς τοὺς Πέρσᾱς ἐπέπεμψεν,
οὓς ἀθανάτους ἐκάλει, ἀνδρειοτάτους ὄντας τῶν στρατιωτῶν,   20
ἐλπίζων τούτους γε ῥᾳδίως νῑκήσειν τοὺς Ἕλληνας. ἐπεὶ δὲ καὶ οὗτοι
συνέβαλον, οὐδὲν ἄμεινον ἔπραττον ἢ οἱ ἄλλοι, ἐν τοῖς στενοῖς
μαχόμενοι καὶ οὐ δυνάμενοι τῷ πλήθει χρῆσθαι. ὁ δὲ βασιλεὺς τὴν

μάχην θεώμενος τρὶς ἀνέδραμεν, ὡς λέγουσιν, ἐκ τοῦ θρόνου, φοβούμενος ὑπὲρ τοῦ στρατοῦ."

[ἤλπιζε . . . τοὺς Ἕλληνας ἀποφεύξεσθαι he hoped that the Greeks would flee ἀκίνητοι unmoved   ἀθανάτους Immortals   νῑκήσειν would conquer ἄμεινον better   χρῆσθαι (*note that this verb has* η *where we would expect* α)   τρίς three times   ἀνέδραμεν (*from* ἀνατρέχω) leaped to his feet   τοῦ θρόνου his throne]

Word Study

Using your knowledge of Greek, explain the meaning of the following forenames:

1. Philip
2. George
3. Theodore (τὸ δῶρον = gift)
4. Sophie
5. Dorothea
6. Ophelia

Grammar

1. Comparison of Adjectives

Adjectives have three *degrees* in English and Greek, e.g., beautiful (*positive*), more beautiful (*comparative*), and most beautiful (*superlative*) or brave (*positive*), braver (*comparative*), and bravest (*superlative*). In Greek the comparative and superlative of adjectives are regularly formed by adding -τερος, -ᾱ, -ον and -τατος, -η, -ον to the stem of the positive:

Positive	*Comparative*	*Superlative*
ἀνδρεῖος, -ᾱ, -ον brave		
ἀνδρειο-	ἀνδρειό-τερος, -ᾱ, -ον braver, rather brave	ἀνδρειό-τατος, -η, -ον bravest, very brave
χαλεπός, -ή, -όν difficult		
χαλεπο-	χαλεπώ-τερος, -ᾱ, -ον more difficult, rather difficult	χαλεπώ-τατος, -η, -ον most difficult, very difficult

Note: as in the example just above, the o at the end of the stem of the positive is lengthened to ω if the syllable preceding it is regarded as short (e.g., contains a short vowel).

ἀληθής, ἀληθές true		
ἀληθεσ-	ἀληθέσ-τερος, -ᾱ, -ον truer, rather true	ἀληθέσ-τατος, -η, -ον truest, very true
σώφρων, σῶφρον wise, prudent		
σωφρον-	σωφρον-έστερος, -ᾱ, -ον wiser, rather wise	σωφρον-έστατος, -η, -ον wisest, very wise

2. Irregular Comparison of Adjectives

Some adjectives are irregular in their formation of comparatives and superlatives and show forms ending in -ῑων or -ων (*masc.* and *fem.*) and -ῑον or -ον (*neuter*) for the comparative and -ιστος, -η, -ον for the superlative. The comparatives are declined like σώφρων, σῶφρον (see page 78), with some alternative forms that will be presented later.

ἀγαθός, -ή, -όν good	ἀμείνων, ἄμεινον better, rather good	ἄριστος, -η, -ον best, very good
κακός, -ή, -όν bad	κακίων, κάκῑον worse, rather bad	κάκιστος, -η, -ον worst, very bad
καλός, -ή, -όν beautiful	καλλίων, κάλλῑον more beautiful, rather beautiful	κάλλιστος, -η, -ον most beautiful, very beautiful
μέγας, μεγάλη, μέγα big	μείζων, μεῖζον bigger, rather big	μέγιστος, -η, -ον biggest, very big
ὀλίγος, -η, ον small, (*plural*) few	ἐλάττων, ἔλαττον smaller, rather small, (*plural*) fewer, rather few	ὀλίγιστος, -η, -ον smallest (in number), (*plural*) fewest, very few
πολύς, πολλή, πολύ much, (*plural*) many	πλείων/πλέων, πλεῖον/πλέον more, rather much, (*plural*) more, rather many	πλεῖστος, η, ον most, very much, (*plural*) most, very many

3. Comparison of Adverbs

As you learned in Chapter 4 (Grammar 5, page 39), the positive degree of an adverb is regularly the same in spelling and accent as the genitive plural of the corresponding adjective, but with ς instead of ν at the end, e.g., adjective καλῶν > adverb καλῶς. The comparative degree is the neuter singular of the adjective, and the superlative degree is the neuter plural of the adjective, e.g.:

Positive	*Comparative*	*Superlative*
ἀνδρείως bravely	ἀνδρειότερον more bravely, rather bravely	ἀνδρειότατα most bravely, very bravely
ἀληθῶς truly	ἀληθέστερον more truly, rather truly	ἀληθέστατα most truly, very truly

εὖ	ἄμεινον	ἄριστα
well =	better, rather well	best, very well

adverb corresponding to ἀγαθός

κακῶς	κάκῑον	κάκιστα
badly	worse, rather badly	worst, very badly

πολύ	πλέον	πλεῖστα
much	more	most

μάλα	μᾶλλον	μάλιστα
very	more, rather	most, very much, especially

4. Constructions Using the Comparatives

Two different constructions may be used in sentences containing comparatives.

a. **μείζονα** στρατὸν εἶχεν ὁ Ξέρξης **ἢ** πάντες οἱ Ἕλληνες.
*Xerxes had a **bigger** army **than** all the Greeks.*

οἱ Ἕλληνες ἐμάχοντο **ἀνδρειότερον ἢ** οἱ Πέρσαι.
*The Greeks fought **more bravely than** the Persians.*

Here the word ἤ "than" is used, and the two things being compared (italicized in the examples above) are in the same case.

b. ὁ ἀνὴρ **μείζων** ἐστὶ *τοῦ παιδός.*
*The man is **bigger** than the boy.*

οἱ ἀθάνατοι **οὐδὲν ἄμεινον** ἔπρᾱττον *τῶν ἄλλων,* ἐν τοῖς στενοῖς μαχόμενοι.
*The Immortals fared **no better** than the others, fighting in the pass.*

Here the *genitive of comparison* (italicized in the examples above) is used instead of ἤ.

A word in the dative case may accompany comparatives to show the *degree of difference,* e.g.:

ὁ ἀνὴρ **πολλῷ** μείζων ἐστὶ τοῦ παιδός.
The man is much bigger (bigger by much) than the boy.

5. Superlatives with ὡς

Note the following:

ὡς τάχιστα as quickly as possible
ὡς ἀνδρειότατα as bravely as possible
ὡς πλεῖστοι as many as possible

Exercise 14a

Locate six comparatives / superlatives in the reading passage at the beginning of this chapter and explain the constructions in which they occur.

Exercise 14b

Translate into English:

1. τῶν Ἑλλήνων πλεῖστοι ἔπεσον ἄριστα μαχόμενοι.
2. οἱ ὁπλῖται, καίπερ ἀνδρειότατα μαχόμενοι, οὐκ ἐδύναντο τοὺς πολεμίους (the enemy) πλέονας ὄντας ἀμύνειν.
3. οἱ Ἕλληνες ἀνδρειότεροι ἦσαν τῶν βαρβάρων καὶ ἄμεινον ἐμάχοντο.
4. τοῖς Ἕλλησι πολλῷ ἐλάττονες νῆες ἦσαν ἢ τοῖς βαρβάροις.
5. ἐν ἐκείνῃ τῇ μάχῃ τῶν μὲν Ἑλλήνων πολλοὶ ἀπέθανον, τῶν δὲ πολεμίων πολλῷ πλέονες.
6. ἡ γυνὴ πολλῷ σωφρονεστέρᾱ οὖσα τοῦ ἀνδρὸς ἀληθέστερα εἶπεν.
7. οἱ Ἕλληνες καίπερ ὀλίγιστοι ὄντες τὰ ὅπλα (their weapons) παρεσκεύαζον, ἐν νῷ ἔχοντες ὡς ἀνδρειότατα ἀποθανεῖν.
8. οἱ βάρβαροι, καίπερ ἀγριώτατα προσβάλλοντες, οὐκ ἐδύναντο τοὺς Ἕλληνας νῑκῆσαι.

Exercise 14c

Translate into Greek:

1. The Persians had a bigger army than we, but we fought more bravely.
2. The best soldiers of Xerxes attacked most fiercely but fared no better than the others.
3. Old men are not always wiser than young men.
4. The hoplites attacked the Persians even (καί) more fiercely.
5. We decided to return home rather than stay in the city.
6. The messenger whom we heard in the agora spoke more truly than you.

The Rise of Athens

Athens played no part in the colonizing movement of the eighth and seventh centuries; she controlled a larger area than any other Greek state except Sparta and so had less need to send out colonies. She was also at this time somewhat backward. An attempt was made to establish a tyranny at Athens by Cylon (632 B.C.), but he failed to win popular support.

Forty years later the discontent of the farmers threatened to lead to civil war in Attica, and Solon was appointed arbitrator to find a solution (see page 87). Although his legislation pleased neither farmers nor nobles and a renewed threat of civil war allowed Pisistratus to establish a tyranny, Solon's

reforms had a lasting and profound effect both constitutionally and economi-
cally. Athens enjoyed a new prosperity. She began to export both olive oil and
fine pottery; Attic black figure pottery began to appear about 600 B.C., gradually drove out Corinthian ware, and achieved a monopoly throughout the
Greek world and beyond.

Athens continued to grow in prosperity and power throughout the tyranny
of Pisistratus and his son, Hippias. Hippias was driven out in 510, and three
years later Cleisthenes put through the reforms that established a democracy.
Immediately Athens was attacked by enemies on every side. The Spartan
king Cleomenes led the army of the Peloponnesian League against her but
turned back at the border, because the Corinthians refused to fight in an un-
just war. Meanwhile the Boeotians had invaded Attica from the north and the
Chalcidians from the east. As soon as Cleomenes had turned back, the Athenian army hurried north, defeated the Boeotians and then crossed to Euboea
and inflicted a crushing defeat on the Chalcidians, taking and destroying
their city.

When Aristagoras arrived in Athens to ask for help in the Ionian revolt
against Persia, the Athenian people were confident enough to accept his appeal (see page 158). Since Hippias had taken refuge with the Persians, their
motives were not entirely disinterested. Less than ten years later, Athens
faced the might of Persia alone at Marathon, and her victory there filled the
democracy with boundless pride and confidence.

Although Athens was now powerful by land, her navy was still inconsid-
erable. The founder of Athenian sea power was Themistocles, the victor of
Salamis, who foresaw that the future of Athens lay by sea and as archon in
493/492 B.C. had begun the fortification of the Piraeus. Ten years later an ex-
ceptionally rich vein of silver was found in the state mines at Laurium. It
was proposed to divide this windfall up among the citizens, but Themistocles
persuaded the Assembly to use the money to build a new fleet. Two years later
at Salamis we find that Athens had a fleet of 200 triremes, more than half the
whole Greek force of 350 ships. Themistocles, as admiral of the Athenian
contingent, had the greatest influence in the allied councils and devised the
tactics that won victory at Salamis in 480 B.C. If Sparta remained the greatest
land power among the Greeks, from now on there could be no doubt that
Athens would take the lead by sea.

Nevertheless, when representatives of the thirty-one loyal Greek states
had met at Corinth in 481 B.C. to plan resistance to Xerxes' imminent invasion, the allies agreed without dispute to give Sparta command by both land
and sea. News of Xerxes' preparations must have reached Greece a good time
before this. He had summoned contingents from all over his empire and
spent the winter of 481/480 at Sardis assembling and preparing his invasion
force. According to Herodotus, his navy consisted of 1,207 ships and his army
of 1,700,000 fighting men. The figure for the navy may be approximately correct, but that for the army is absurd. It may have numbered 200,000. To bring
this great host into Europe, Xerxes' engineers constructed two bridges of boats
across the Hellespont (480 B.C.). When they were destroyed by a storm, two

new and stronger bridges were built, and the army crossed the Hellespont and proceeded along the coast, supplied by the navy. At Mount Athos, off which the Persian fleet had been wrecked in 492 B.C., a canal had been dug across the promontory, one and a half miles long, to forestall a similar disaster (see map, page 167). The invading force continued inexorably through Macedonia and into Thessaly. There was no resistance; the Greeks had abandoned any idea of making a stand anywhere north of Thermopylae, the only place where geography made it possible to hold off the Persians by a combined operation by sea and land. The next defensible point was the Isthmus of Corinth, but withdrawal to this would mean abandoning Attica. Even the wall across the Isthmus would not provide effective defense, if the position could be circumvented by a landing of the Persian fleet south of the Isthmus.

Around the outside of this cup four Athenian warships are being rowed, with dolphins leaping beside their prows. They are not triremes, which with 170 oarsmen were too complicated for any artist to draw on a vase. They are pentecounters, which had fifty oarsmen. Note the helmsmen holding the steering oars, the high platform in the bows where the lookout stood, and the bronze beaks that were used in ramming the enemy.

Η ΕΝ ΤΑΙΣ
ΘΕΡΜΟΠΥΛΑΙΣ ΜΑΧΗ
(β)

οἱ Ἕλληνες μνῆμα ἐποίησαν τῷ Λεωνίδῃ, ὡς ἀνδρὶ ἀρίστῳ γενομένῳ, λέοντα λίθινον.

Vocabulary

Verbs

ἀγγέλλω, ἤγγειλα,
   ἀγγείλᾱς I announce
ἀναχωρέω, ἀνεχώρησα,
   ἀναχωρήσᾱς I retreat,
   withdraw
ἀντέχω, ἀντέσχον, ἀντισχών
   (+ *dat.*) I resist
γράφω, ἔγραψα, γράψᾱς I
   write
διέρχομαι, διῆλθον, διελθών
   I come through, go through
παραγίγνομαι, παρεγενόμην,
   παραγενόμενος I arrive
φράζω, ἔφρασα, φράσᾱς I tell
   (of)

Nouns

οἱ πολέμιοι, τῶν πολεμίων
   the enemy

ὁ πόλεμος, τοῦ πολέμου war
αἱ πύλαι, τῶν πυλῶν
   (*plural*) double gates, pass

Adjectives

ἅπᾱς, ἅπᾱσα, ἅπαν all,
   every, whole
πολέμιος, -ᾱ, -ον hostile,
   enemy

Preposition

μετά (+ *gen.*) with, (+ *acc.*) after

Adverbs

ὅπου where
ὡς how

Conjunctions

ἕως until
ὡς as, when

Expression

τῇ προτεραίᾳ on the day
   before

Proper Names

τὸ ᾿Αρτεμίσιον, τοῦ
   ᾿Αρτεμισίου   Artemisium
ἡ ᾿Αττική, τῆς ᾿Αττικῆς
   Attica
ἡ Βοιωτίᾱ, τῆς Βοιωτίᾱς
   Boeotia
ὁ ᾿Εφιάλτης, τοῦ ᾿Εφιάλτου
   Ephialtes

ἡ Πελοπόννησος, τῆς
   Πελοποννήσου the
   Peloponnesus
ὁ Σπαρτιάτης, τοῦ
   Σπαρτιάτου Spartan
τὸ Φάληρον, τοῦ Φαλήρου
   Phalerum, the old harbor of
   Athens

"τῇ δ᾽ ὑστεραίᾳ οἱ βάρβαροι αὖθις προσβάλλοντες οὐδὲν
ἄμεινον ἔπρᾱττον ἢ τῇ προτεραίᾳ. ὡς οὖν ἠπόρει ὁ Ξέρξης,
προσῆλθε πρὸς αὐτὸν ἀνήρ τις τῶν ῾Ελλήνων, ᾿Εφιάλτης ὀνόματι,
ἔφρασέ τε τὴν ἀτραπὸν τὴν διὰ τοῦ ὄρους φέρουσαν εἰς τὰς
Θερμοπύλᾱς. ταῦτα δὲ μαθὼν ὁ Ξέρξης τοὺς ἀθανάτους ταύτῃ   5
ἔπεμψε, κελεύων αὐτοὺς ἐκ τοῦ ὄπισθεν λαβεῖν τοὺς ῞Ελληνας. οἱ δὲ
῞Ελληνες μαθόντες τί γίγνεται πρῶτον μὲν ἠπόρουν τί δεῖ πρᾶξαι,
τέλος δὲ ἔδοξε τῷ Λεωνίδῃ τοὺς μὲν ἄλλους ἀποπέμψαι πρὸς τὴν
᾿Αττικήν, αὐτὸς δὲ ἔμενεν ἐν ταῖς Θερμοπύλαις τριᾱκοσίους ἔχων
Σπαρτιάτᾱς, ἐν νῷ ἔχων τὰς πύλᾱς φυλάττειν.   10

[τε and   ἀτραπόν (*fem.*) path   φέρουσαν leading   τοὺς ἀθανάτους the
Immortals   ταύτῃ this way   ἐκ τοῦ ὄπισθεν from the rear   τριᾱκοσίους three
hundred]

"οἱ μὲν οὖν βάρβαροι προσέβαλλον, οἱ δὲ Σπαρτιάται ἐμάχοντο
πρὸς πολεμίους πολλαπλασίους ὄντας καὶ πλείστους δὴ ἀπέκτειναν·
τῶν δ᾽ ῾Ελλήνων ἄλλοι τε πολλοὶ ἔπεσον καὶ αὐτὸς ὁ Λεωνίδης, ἀνὴρ
ἄριστος γενόμενος. τέλος δὲ οἱ Πέρσαι οἱ διὰ τοῦ ὄρους διελθόντες
παρεγένοντο καὶ ἐκ τοῦ ὄπισθεν προσέβαλον. τότε δὴ οἱ Σπαρτιάται   15
εἰς τὸ στενὸν τῆς ὁδοῦ ἀνεχώρουν καὶ ἐνταῦθα ἐμάχοντο ἕως
ἅπαντες ἔπεσον. οἱ δὲ ῞Ελληνες μετὰ τὸν πόλεμον τοὺς τριᾱκοσίους
ἔθαψαν ὅπου ἔπεσον καὶ μνῆμα ἐποίησαν τῷ Λεωνίδῃ, λέοντα
λίθινον, ὃν καὶ νῦν ἔξεστιν ἰδεῖν. καὶ τοῦτο τὸ ἐπίγραμμα ἐν στήλῃ
λιθίνῃ ἔγραψαν·   20

ὦ ξεῖν᾽, ἄγγειλον Λακεδαιμονίοις ὅτι τῇδε
   κείμεθα τοῖς κείνων ῥήμασι πειθόμενοι.

[πολλαπλασίους many times their number   ἔθαψαν they buried   ἐπίγραμμα
inscription   στήλη tombstone   ὦ ξεῖν᾽ = ὦ ξένε   τῇδε here   κείμεθα we
lie   τοῖς κείνων ῥήμασι their words]

"ἐν δὲ τούτῳ κατὰ θάλατταν οἱ Ἕλληνες πρὸς τῷ Ἀρτεμισίῳ
μένοντες τὰ στενὰ ἐφύλαττον καὶ ναυμαχοῦντες τοὺς βαρβάρους
ἐνίκησαν καίπερ πλέονας ὄντας καὶ ἤμῡναν. ὡς δὲ οἱ βάρβαροι τὰς   2
Θερμοπύλᾱς εἷλον, οἱ Ἕλληνες οὐκέτι ἐφύλαττον τὰ στενὰ ἀλλὰ
πρὸς τὴν Σαλαμῖνα ταῖς ναυσὶν ἀνεχώρουν. κατὰ δὲ γῆν οὐκέτι
ἐδύναντο ἀντέχειν τοῖς βαρβάροις ἀλλὰ ἔφευγον πρὸς τὴν
Πελοπόννησον, τήν τε Βοιωτίᾱν καὶ τὴν Ἀττικὴν τοῖς πολεμίοις
καταλιπόντες. οὕτως οὖν οἱ βάρβαροι κατὰ μὲν γῆν προχωρήσαντες   3
ταῖς Ἀθήναις προσβαλεῖν ἐν νῷ εἶχον, κατὰ δὲ θάλατταν εἰς τὸ
Φάληρον πλεύσαντες ἐν τῷ λιμένι ὥρμουν."

[ναυμαχοῦντες fighting at sea   ταῖς ναυσίν with their ships   ὥρμουν were
lying at anchor]

Word Building

Deduce the meanings of the words in the following sets:

1. ὁ στρατός   ἡ στρατιᾱ̃   στρατεύω (-ομαι)   τὸ στράτευμα
2. ὁ στρατηγός   στρατηγέω   στρατηγικός, -ή, -όν ὁ στρατιώτης
3. ὁ πόλεμος   πολέμιος, -ᾱ, -ον πολεμικός, -ή, -όν πολεμέω

Grammar

6. Demonstrative Adjectives

Here are three demonstrative adjectives:

οὗτος, αὕτη, τοῦτο this
ἐκεῖνος, ἐκείνη, ἐκεῖνο that
ὅδε, ἥδε, τόδε this here

Note that the demonstrative adjective οὗτος begins with τ everywhere
the definite article does; the feminine has α instead of o everywhere
except in the genitive plural; and the neuter plural nominative and
accusative have αυ:

| | **Singular** | | | **Plural** | | |
	Masc.	*Fem.*	*Neuter*	*Masc.*	*Fem.*	*Neuter*
Nom.	οὗτος	αὕτη	τοῦτο	οὗτοι	αὗται	ταῦτα
Gen.	τούτου	ταύτης	τούτου	τούτων	τούτων	τούτων
Dat.	τούτῳ	ταύτῃ	τούτῳ	τούτοις	ταύταις	τούτοις
Acc.	τοῦτον	ταύτην	τοῦτο	τούτους	ταύτᾱς	ταῦτα

Nom.	ἐκεῖνος	ἐκείνη	ἐκεῖνο	ἐκεῖνοι	ἐκεῖναι	ἐκεῖνα
Gen.	ἐκείνου	ἐκείνης	ἐκείνου	ἐκείνων	ἐκείνων	ἐκείνων
Dat.	ἐκείνῳ	ἐκείνῃ	ἐκείνῳ	ἐκείνοις	ἐκείναις	ἐκείνοις
Acc.	ἐκεῖνον	ἐκείνην	ἐκεῖνο	ἐκείνους	ἐκείνᾱς	ἐκεῖνα

The demonstrative adjective ὅδε is formed from the definite article plus -δε.

Nom.	ὅδε	ἥδε	τόδε	οἵδε	αἵδε	τάδε
Gen.	τοῦδε	τῆσδε	τοῦδε	τῶνδε	τῶνδε	τῶνδε
Dat.	τῷδε	τῇδε	τῷδε	τοῖσδε	ταῖσδε	τοῖσδε
Acc.	τόνδε	τήνδε	τόδε	τούσδε	τάσδε	τάδε

Note that these demonstrative adjectives require the definite article to be used with the noun and that the adjectives stand outside the definite article-noun group, i.e., in the *predicate position* (see Chapter 5, Grammar 7b, page 52), e.g.:

οὗτος ὁ ἀνήρ or ὁ ἀνὴρ **οὗτος** this man
ἐκείνη ἡ γυνή or ἡ γυνὴ **ἐκείνη** that woman
τόδε τὸ ἔργον or τὸ ἔργον **τόδε** this work

The datives ταύτῃ and τῇδε are used as adverbs, meaning "this way."

Exercise 14d

Give the correct form of the demonstrative to fit the following phrases:

1. (οὗτος) αἱ γυναῖκες
2. (ἐκεῖνος) τὸ δένδρον
3. (οὗτος) τὰ ὀνόματα
4. (ὅδε) τῶν νεᾱνιῶν
5. (οὗτος) τῆς παρθένου
6. (οὗτος) οἱ βάρβαροι
7. (ἐκεῖνος) τοῦ στρατοῦ
8. (οὗτος) τῇ πόλει
9. (ὅδε) οἱ γέροντες
10. (οὗτος) τοῦ στρατιώτου

Exercise 14e

Translate:

1. ἐκεῖνο τὸ δένδρον μέγιστόν ἐστιν· οὐδέποτε (*never*) εἶδον δένδρον μεῖζον.
2. ἆρ' ὁρᾷς τούσδε τοὺς παῖδας, οἳ ἐκεῖνον τὸν κύνα διώκουσιν;
3. ταῦτα μαθόντες αἱ γυναῖκες εὐθὺς τοὺς ἄνδρας ἐκάλεσαν.
4. διὰ τί οὐ βούλῃ τῷ ἀρότρῳ τούτῳ χρῆσθαι; ἄμεινον γάρ ἐστιν ἐκείνου.
5. This road is worse than that, but that (one) is longer.
6. (After) seeing these things, that old man grew very angry.
7. These women are wiser than those young men.

7. Interrogatives and Indefinites

In Chapter 7 (Grammar 6 and 7, page 79) you learned the interrogative τίς, τί "who?" "what?" and the corresponding indefinite, meaning "a certain," "a," or "an." The interrogative pronoun always has an acute accent, while the indefinite adjective is enclitic.

Interrogative adverbs also have corresponding indefinite forms:

Interrogative		*Indefinite*	
ποῦ;	where?	που	somewhere, anywhere
πόθεν;	where from?	ποθέν	from somewhere
ποῖ;	where to?	ποι	to somewhere
πότε;	when?	ποτέ	at some time, ever
πῶς;	how?	πως	somehow, in any way

Indefinites cannot stand first in their clause, and for purposes of accentuation they attach themselves to some important word as enclitics.

Exercise 14f

Translate into English:

1. τίνες ἐλαύνουσι τοὺς βοῦς; γέροντές τινες αὐτοὺς ἐλαύνουσιν.
2. ποῖ πορεύεται ὁ βασιλεύς; ὁ βασιλεὺς πορεύεται ποι πρὸς τὰ ὄρη.
3. ποῦ εἰσιν οἱ ναῦται; ἐν τῷ λιμένι πού εἰσιν οἱ ναῦται.
4. τί πάσχετε, ὦ παῖδες; ἆρα κακόν τι πάσχετε;
5. τί ποιεῖς, ὦ πάτερ; ἆρα ταύτῃ τῇ γυναικὶ διαλέγῃ;
6. πότε ἐν νῷ ἔχεις εἰς τὸ ἄστυ ἰέναι; δι' ὀλίγου ποτὲ ἐκεῖσε ἰέναι ἐν νῷ ἔχω.
7. πόθεν ἄγεις ταῦτα τὰ μῆλα; ἄγω αὐτὰ ἀπὸ ἐκείνου τοῦ ὄρους.
8. ποῦ μένει ὁ ἀδελφός; ὁ σὸς ἀδελφὸς μένει που ἐγγὺς τῆς ἀγορᾶς.

*   *   *

ΟΙ ΠΕΡΣΑΙ ΤΑ ΥΠΕΡ ΘΕΡΜΟΠΥΛΩΝ ΣΤΕΝΑ ΑΙΡΟΥΣΙΝ

Read the following passages (based on Herodotus 7.215–219) and answer the comprehension questions:

ὁ δὲ Ξέρξης, μαθὼν ὅτι ἀτραπός ἐστιν ὑπὲρ τὸ ὄρος φέρουσα, μάλιστα χαίρων ἔπεμψε τὸν Ὑδαρνέᾱ, στρατηγὸν ὄντα ἄριστον, καὶ τοὺς ἄνδρας ὧν ἐστρατήγει ὁ Ὑδαρνής. ὡρμῶντο δὲ πρὸς ἑσπέρᾱν ἀπὸ τοῦ στρατοπέδου, ἡγεῖτο δὲ αὐτοῖς ὁ Ἐφιάλτης. αὕτη δὲ ἡ ἀτραπὸς ἄρχεται ἀπὸ τοῦ Ἀσώπου ποταμοῦ. οἱ οὖν Πέρσαι τὸν Ἄσωπον διαβάντες ἐπορεύοντο πᾶσαν τὴν νύκτα. ἡ δὲ ἡμέρᾱ ἐγίγνετο καὶ οἱ 5
Πέρσαι ἀφίκοντο εἰς ἄκρον τὸ ὄρος. κατὰ δὲ τοῦτο τοῦ ὄρους ἐφύλασσον Ἑλλήνων χίλιοι ὁπλῖται.

[ἀτραπός *(fem.)* path   ὑπέρ (+ *acc.*) over   τὸν Ὑδαρνέᾱ Hydarnes
στρατηγόν general   ὧν ἐστρατήγει of whom (he) was in command   τοῦ
στρατοπέδου the camp   ἄρχεται begins   τοῦ Ἀσώπου ποταμοῦ the Asopus
River   διαβάντες having crossed   κατὰ . . . τοῦτο τοῦ ὄρους on this part of
the mountain   χίλιοι a thousand]

1. What had Xerxes learned? Whom did he send?
2. When did they set out? Who led them?
3. Where did the path begin?
4. How long did the Persians march?
5. Who were guarding the top of the mountain?

οὗτοι δὲ οὐκ εἶδον τοὺς Πέρσᾱς ἀναβαίνοντας· πολλὰ γὰρ ἦν δένδρα κατὰ τὸ
ὄρος. ψόφον δὲ ἀκούοντες ἔμαθον ὅτι ἀνέβησαν οἱ Πέρσαι. ἔδραμον οὖν οἱ Ἕλληνες
καὶ ἐνέδῡνον τὰ ὅπλα, καὶ εὐθὺς παρῆσαν οἱ βάρβαροι. ἐπεὶ δὲ οἱ Πέρσαι εἶδον   10
ἄνδρας ἐνδῡνοντας ὅπλα, ἐθαύμαζον· ἐλπίζοντες γὰρ οὐδένα φυλάσσειν τὴν
ἀτραπόν, ἐνεκύρησαν στρατῷ. ὁ μὲν οὖν Ὑδαρνὴς διέταξε τοὺς Πέρσᾱς εἰς μάχην·
οἱ δὲ Ἕλληνες ἐλπίζοντες τοὺς βαρβάρους ἐν νῷ ἔχειν προσβαλεῖν, ἔφυγον εἰς τὸν
τοῦ ὄρους κόρυμβον καὶ παρεσκευάζοντο μαχόμενοι ἀποθανεῖν. οἱ δὲ Πέρσαι τῶν
μὲν Ἑλλήνων οὐδένα λόγον ἐποιοῦντο, κατέβησαν δὲ τὸ ὄρος ὡς τάχιστα.   15
[ψόφον noise   ἀνέβησαν had come up, ascended   ἔδραμον ran   ἐνέδῡνον τὰ
ὅπλα they put on their armor, armed themselves   ἐνεκύρησαν they met, came face
to face with (+ *dat.*)   διέταξε arranged, marshaled   εἰς (+ *acc.*) for   τὸν . . .
κόρυμβον top, peak   οὐδένα λόγον ἐποιοῦντο took no notice of (+ *gen.*)
κατέβησαν they went down]

6. Why didn't the Greeks see the Persians approaching?
7. How did they learn of the Persians' arrival?
8. What did the Greeks do immediately?
9. Why were the Persians surprised to see the Greeks?
10. What did Hydarnes do?
11. What was the response of the Greeks?
12. What did the Persians do?

Exercise 14g

Translate into Greek:

1. When the Persians had taken Thermopylae, they went toward Attica.
2. The Greeks retreated by both land and sea, leaving (behind) Attica to
    the enemy.
3. The Athenians, having sent the women and children and old men to
    the Peloponnesus and Salamis, prepared to fight by sea.
4. And so they asked the other Greeks to sail to Salamis as quickly as
    possible and help.
5. The Peloponnnesians (οἱ Πελοποννήσιοι), who were making a wall
    across (διά + *gen.*) the Isthmus (ὁ Ἰσθμός), did not want to help the
    Athenians, but nevertheless sent their ships to Salamis.

15

Η ΕΝ ΤΗΙ ΣΑΛΑΜΙΝΙ ΜΑΧΗ (α)

οἱ Ἀθηναῖοι εἰς τὰς ναῦς εἰσβάντες παρεσκευάζοντο κατὰ θάλατταν μάχεσθαι.

Vocabulary

Verbs

ἀναγκάζω, ἠνάγκασα, ἀναγκάσᾱς I compel

διαφθείρω, διέφθειρα, διαφθείρᾱς I destroy

εἴκω, εἶξα, εἴξᾱς (+ *dat.*) I yield

Nouns

ἡ ἀπορίᾱ, τῆς ἀπορίᾱς perplexity, difficulty, the state of being at a loss

ὁ ναύαρχος, τοῦ ναυάρχου admiral

ὁ νοῦς, τοῦ νοῦ mind

ὁ στρατηγός, τοῦ στρατηγοῦ general

ἡ φυγή, τῆς φυγῆς flight

Adjective

μόνος, -η, -ον alone, only

Adverb

μηκέτι (+ *imperative*) don't . . . any longer; (+ *infinitive*) no longer

μόνον, only

Conjunctions

οὐ μόνον . . . ἀλλὰ καί not only . . . but also

Proper Name

ὁ Θεμιστοκλῆς, τοῦ Θεμιστοκλέους Themistocles

"οἱ μὲν οὖν Ἀθηναῖοι ἐν ἀπορίᾳ ἦσαν μεγίστῃ· ὁ δὲ Θεμιστοκλῆς ἔπεισεν αὐτοὺς μὴ εἴκειν τοῖς βαρβάροις ἀλλὰ ὑπὲρ τῆς ἐλευθερίας μάχεσθαι. τὰς τ᾽ οὖν γυναῖκας καὶ τοὺς παῖδας καὶ τοὺς γέροντας εἰς τήν τε Πελοπόννησον καὶ τὴν Σαλαμῖνα ἐκόμισαν, τήν τ᾽ Ἀττικὴν καὶ τὴν πόλιν τοῖς πολεμίοις καταλιπόντες. αὐτοὶ δὲ εἰς τὰς ναῦς 5 εἰσβάντες πρὸς τὴν Σαλαμῖνα προσέπλευσαν καὶ παρεσκευάζοντο κατὰ θάλατταν μάχεσθαι.

[εἰσβάντες having gotten into, having embarked upon]

"ἐν δὲ τούτῳ οἱ μὲν τῶν Ἑλλήνων στρατηγοὶ ἐν τῇ Σαλαμῖνι συνελθόντες οὕτως ἐφοβοῦντο ὥστε ἀποφυγεῖν ἐβούλοντο πρὸς τὴν Πελοπόννησον· ὁ δὲ Θεμιστοκλῆς ἐν τῷ συνεδρίῳ ἀναστὰς εἶπεν ὅτι 10 ἔτι καὶ νῦν δύνανται τοὺς πολεμίους νικῆσαι· ἐν γὰρ τοῖς στενοῖς μαχόμενοι οὐ δυνήσονται οἱ βάρβαροι τῷ πλήθει χρῆσθαι· δεῖ οὖν ἀναγκάσαι αὐτοὺς ἐκεῖ συμβαλεῖν.

[τῷ συνεδρίῳ the council   ἀναστὰς having stood up   δυνήσονται would (will) he able]

"οὕτως εἰπὼν οὐ μόνον τοὺς ἄλλους στρατηγοὺς ἔπεισε μάχεσθαι, ἀλλὰ καὶ ἄγγελον παρὰ τὸν Ξέρξην ἔπεμψε λάθρα, λέγοντα ὅτι οἱ 15 Ἕλληνες παρασκευάζονται εἰς φυγήν. ὁ οὖν Ξέρξης, ὡς ἔγνω ὅτι ἀποφυγεῖν ἐν νῷ ἔχουσιν οἱ Ἕλληνες, βουλόμενος αὐτοὺς ὡς τάχιστα διαφθεῖραι, διέγνω αὐτοὺς ἀναγκάσαι ἐν Σαλαμῖνι μάχεσθαι. τῶν οὖν νεῶν τὰς μὲν ἔπεμψε περὶ τὴν νῆσον, κελεύων τοὺς ναυάρχους τοὺς ἔκπλους φυλάττειν, τὰς δὲ ἐκέλευσε φυλάττειν 20 τὰ στενὰ ὥστε μηκέτι ἐξεῖναι τοῖς Ἕλλησιν ἀποπλεῖν."

[λάθρα secretly   ἔγνω he learned   διέγνω decided   τοὺς ἔκπλους the escape routes]

Word Study

Identify the Greek roots in the English words below and give the meanings of the English words:

1. monogamy (what does γαμέω mean?)
2. monologue
3. monochrome (what does τὸ χρῶμα mean?)
4. monosyllable (what does ἡ συλλαβή mean? From what verb is this noun formed?)
5. monograph

Grammar

1. More Second Aorists

The following common verbs form their aorist indicatives, imperatives, and infinitives by adding the appropriate endings directly to the long vowel grade stem without a thematic vowel in between. The participles are formed on the short vowel stem. These are called athematic aorists. The aorist of βαίνω is used only in compounds in Attic Greek:

βαίνω, stems βη-/βα-   γιγνώσκω, stems γνω-/γνο-
I step, walk, go   I get to know, learn

Indic.	*Imper.*	*Infin.*	*Partic.*	*Indic.*	*Imper.*	*Infin.*	*Partic.*
ἔβην		βῆναι	βάς,	ἔγνων		γνῶναι	γνούς,
ἔβης	βῆθι		βᾶσα,	ἔγνως	γνῶθι		γνοῦσα,
ἔβη			βάν	ἔγνω			γνόν
ἔβημεν				ἔγνωμεν			
ἔβητε	βῆτε			ἔγνωτε	γνῶτε		
ἔβησαν				ἔγνωσαν			

stems στη-/στα-
stand

Indic.	*Imper.*	*Infin.*	*Partic.*
ἔστην		στῆναι	στάς,
ἔστης	στῆθι		στᾶσα,
ἔστη			στάν
ἔστημεν			
ἔστητε	στῆτε		
ἔστησαν			

For the declension of the participles, see page 142.
Note the meanings of the words above:

    ἔβην I went
    βῆθι go!
    βῆναι to go
    βάς going *or* having gone

    ἔγνων I learned
    γνῶθι learn! know!
    γνῶναι to learn, know
    γνούς learning, having learned

    ἔστην I stood, stopped
    στῆθι stand! stop!
    στῆναι to stand, stop
    στάς standing, having stood, stopping, having stopped

Exercise 15a

In the reading passage at the beginning of this chapter, locate four instances of the above verbs or compounds of them. Identify each form fully.

Exercise 15b

Read aloud and translate:

1. ἆρ' οὐ βούλεσθε γνῶναι τί εἶπεν ὁ ἄγγελος;
2. οἱ 'Αθηναῖοι, γνόντες ὅτι οἱ βάρβαροι τάς τε Θερμοπύλας εἷλον καὶ πρὸς τὴν 'Αττικὴν προσχωροῦσι, μάλιστα ἐφοβοῦντο.
3. ὁ Θεμιστοκλῆς, στρατηγὸς ὤν, ἀνέστη καὶ τοὺς 'Αθηναίους ἔπεισε μὴ εἴκειν τοῖς πολεμίοις.
4. οἱ 'Αθηναῖοι τάς τε γυναῖκας καὶ τοὺς παῖδας εἰς τὴν Σαλαμῖνα κομίσαντες, εἰς τὰς ναῦς εἰσέβησαν.
5. ὁ Ξέρξης, γνοὺς ὅτι ἐν νῷ ἔχουσιν ἀποφυγεῖν οἱ "Ελληνες, ἐβούλετο ἀναγκάσαι αὐτοὺς στῆναί τε καὶ πρὸς τῇ Σαλαμῖνι μάχεσθαι.
6. ἔκβηθι ἐκ τῆς νεώς, ὦ παῖ, καὶ στῆθι ἐν τῷ χώματι (*pier*).
7. ὁ ναύκληρος τὸν παῖδα ἐκέλευσεν ἀναστάντα ἐκβῆναι ἐκ τῆς νεώς.
8. αἱ γυναῖκες εἰς τὴν ἀγορὰν εἰσελθοῦσαι ἔστησαν πάντα θαυμάζουσαι.
9. ὁ 'Απόλλων ἐν τοῖς Δελφοῖς ἔφη· "γνῶθι σεαυτόν."
10. στῆτε, ὦ φίλοι, καὶ ἐμὲ μείνατε.

Exercise 15c

Translate into Greek, using second aorist verbs from page 184 with the prepositional prefixes εἰσ-, ἀνα-, and ἐκ-, as appropriate:

1. (After) going into the house, the women sat talking to one another.
2. Be silent, boy; stand up and help me.
3. Going into the temple, the priest stood and prayed to the god.
4. Climbing the mountain, we stood and looked at the city.
5. The old man told the boys to stand and listen.
6. Learning what had happened, I decided to go out of the house and look for father.
7. The women want to know why they must leave their homes behind.
8. Having learned what happened (*use present tense*), the women embarked on the ships.
9. The soldiers, whom Xerxes sent, climbed the mountain very quickly.
10. When they arrived at the top (**τὸ ἄκρον**), they saw the Greeks, who did not stand bravely but fled away.

Aeschylus' Persae

Aeschylus, the first of the three great Athenian writers of tragedy, had fought at the battle of Marathon and probably also at Salamis. He certainly saw the battle, and he has left us an eyewitness account of it. Eight years after the battle, he entered his play *The Persians* in the dramatic contest at the festival of Dionysus in 472 B.C. This is our earliest extant Greek tragedy, and it is unique in that it has an historical theme; all other extant tragedies draw their plots from myth. For Aeschylus, human events were interwoven with the divine; he saw the defeat and humiliation of Xerxes as the supreme example of *hubris* (human pride) punished by *Nemesis* (Divine Vengeance).

The scene of the play is Sousa, the Persian capital, where the Elders anxiously wait for news of Xerxes' expedition. Since he left, they have heard nothing, and their hearts are heavy with foreboding as they wonder what has happened to the host that went forth in pride to cast the yoke of slavery on Greece. As they speculate gloomily, they see Atossa, the Queen-mother, approaching. She tells them that ever since her son left, she has been troubled by dreams and that now she has had a dream of unmistakable significance: she saw Xerxes yoke two women to his chariot, one in Asian dress, the other in Greek. The Asian woman was proud of her harness and was obedient to the reins, but the Greek struggled, tore the harness from the chariot, threw off the bridle, and broke the yoke. When Atossa woke and went to the altar to pray for deliverance from evil, she saw another terrible omen: an eagle (the king of birds = Xerxes) flew to Apollo's altar, pursued by a falcon (= the Greeks), which clawed at its head, while it cowered unresisting.

As the Elders attempt to calm and comfort Atossa, a messenger is seen approaching in haste, who without preamble reveals the news they have dreaded: "Cities of all the lands of Asia, by one blow your great prosperity has been destroyed and the flower of the Persians is fallen and gone; the whole host has perished."

While Atossa is stunned to silence, the Elders lament wildly until the queen recovers and with quiet dignity asks the messenger how it could have happened since the Persians surely outnumbered the Greeks. The messenger replies (337–347, tr. Podlecki):

> Be sure of this, that in a matter of sheer numbers,
> The ships on our side would have conquered, for the Greeks'
> Entire total of ships was only three hundred ten. . . .
> But the multitude of ships in Xerxes' fleet—I know
> The facts—were no less than a thousand, those in speed
> Surpassing, two hundred seven. This is the total sum.
> Was it here you think we were surpassed when battle came?
> No, not by numbers, but some Spirit crushed the host,
> Threw in an evil fate against us in the scales.
> The gods are keeping the Goddess Pallas' city safe.

The messenger then describes the battle as follows (386–430, tr. Podlecki):

But when the white-horsed chariot of dawn appeared
And filled the entire earth with radiance to behold,
The first thing was a sound, a shouting from the Greeks,
A joyful song, and to it, making shrill response,
From the island rocks about there came an antiphony
Of echoes; fear stood next to each one of our men,
Tripped up in their hopes: for not as if in flight
Were the Greeks raising then a solemn paean-strain,
But rushing into battle with daring confidence;
A trumpet, too, blazed over everything its sound.
At once, with measured stroke of surging, sea-dipped oar,
They struck the brine and made it roar from one command,
And quickly all of them were visible to sight.
Their right wing first, in order just as they had been
Arranged, led off, and next the whole remaining force
Came out to the attack, and with the sight we heard
A loud voice of command: "O sons of Greeks, go on,
Bring freedom to your fatherland, bring freedom to
Your children, wives, and seats of your ancestral gods,
And your forebears' graves; now the struggle is for all."
Of course, on our side, too, a roar of Persian tongues
Went forth in answer; the moment would not brook delay.
Immediately ship struck its brazen-plated beak
On ship. The ramming was begun by a Greek ship
And it snapped off from one of the Phoenicians the whole
Curving stern, and men on both sides shot their spears.
At first the streaming Persian force withstood the shocks;
But when their crowd of ships was gathered in the straits,
And no assistance could be given one to another,
But they were being struck by their own brazen rams,
They kept on breaking all their equipage of oars,
And the ships of the Greeks, with perfect plan and order, came
Around them in a circle and struck, and hulls of ships
Were overturned; and the sea no longer was visible,
Filled as it was with shipwrecks and the slaughter of men.
The beaches, too, and the reefs around were filled with corpses.
Now every ship that came with the Persian armament
Was being rowed for quick escape, no order left.
And they kept striking us, deboning us, like tunnies
Or a catch of fish, with broken fragments of oars, or bits
Of flotsam from the wrecks; and all this time, moaning
And wailing held control of that area of sea,
Until the eye of black night took it away.
So great a crowd of ills, not even if I took
Ten days in order to tell, could I tell the tale in full.

Η ΕΝ ΤΗΙ ΣΑΛΑΜΙΝΙ ΜΑΧΗ (β)

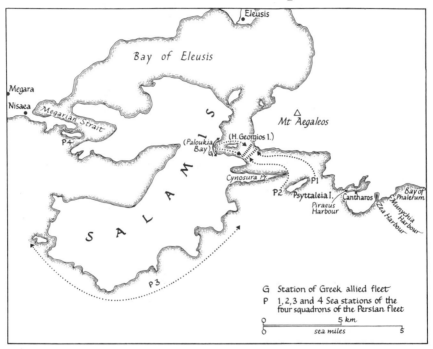

ἡ ἐν τῇ Σαλαμῖνι μάχη

Vocabulary

Verbs

ἀνέστην, ἀναστάς, I stood up

βλάπτω, ἔβλαψα, βλάψᾱς I harm

δηλόω, ἐδήλωσα, δηλώσᾱς I show

ἐλευθερόω, ἠλευθέρωσα, ἐλευθερώσᾱς I set free, free

ἐμπίπτω, ἐνέπεσον, ἐμπεσών (+ *dat.*) I fall upon, attack

ἐπιπλέω, ἐπέπλευσα, ἐπιπλεύσᾱς (+ *dat.* or + εἰς + *acc.*) I sail against

ναυμαχέω, ἐναυμάχησα, ναυμαχήσᾱς I fight by sea

πειράω, ἐπείρᾱσα, πειρᾱσᾱς (*active or middle*) I try, attempt

πιστεύω, ἐπίστευσα, πιστεύσᾱς I trust, am confident (in) (+ *dat.*), I believe (that)

συμπίπτω, συνέπεσον, συμπεσών (+ *dat.*) I clash with

Nouns

ὁ ἀγών, τοῦ ἀγῶνος struggle, contest

ἡ ἀρετή, τῆς ἀρετῆς excellence, virtue, courage

ὁ θόρυβος, τοῦ θορύβου uproar, din

ὁ κόσμος, τοῦ κόσμου good order

κόσμῳ in order

τὸ μέρος, τοῦ μέρους part

ὁ νεκρός, τοῦ νεκροῦ corpse

ἡ νίκη, τῆς νίκης victory

ἡ πατρίς, τῆς πατρίδος fatherland

ὁ πέπλος, τοῦ πέπλου robe, cloth

ὁ πρόγονος, τοῦ προγόνου ancestor

ἡ σπουδή, τῆς σπουδῆς haste, eagerness

ἡ τύχη, τῆς τύχης chance, luck, fortune

Adjectives

δεξιός, -ά, -όν right (i.e., on the right hand)

πεζός, -ή, -όν on foot

Adverb

πανταχοῦ everywhere

Proper Names

ὁ Αἰσχύλος, τοῦ Αἰσχύλου Aeschylus

ἡ Ἀσίᾱ, τῆς Ἀσίᾱς Asia (Minor)

Περσικός, -ή, -όν Persian

ὁ Σιμωνίδης, τοῦ Σιμωνίδου Simonides

"πᾶσαν οὖν τὴν νύκτα οἱ βάρβαροι ἔνθα καὶ ἔνθα ἤρεσσον τά τε στενὰ φυλάττοντες καὶ τοὺς ἔκπλους, οἱ δὲ Ἕλληνες ἡσύχαζον παρασκευαζόμενοι μάχεσθαι. ἐπεὶ δὲ πρῶτον ἐγένετο ἡ ἡμέρᾱ, προὔχώρουν οἱ βάρβαροι εἰς τὰ στενά, πιστεύοντες ὡς ῥᾳδίως μέλλουσι νικᾶν τοὺς Ἕλληνας, ἐξαίφνης δὲ βοὴν μεγίστην ἤκουσαν 5 ὥστε μάλιστα ἐφοβοῦντο. οἱ γὰρ Ἕλληνες, κόσμῳ χρώμενοι εἰς μάχην προὔχώρουν καὶ ἐπὶ τοὺς βαρβάρους πλέοντες τὸν παιᾶνα ἐβόων.

[ἔνθα καὶ ἔνθα this way and that   ὡς that   ἐξαίφνης suddenly   τὸν παιᾶνα the battle song]

"οὕτω δὲ ὁ Αἰσχύλος ὁ ποιητής, ὃς καὶ αὐτὸς τῇ μάχῃ παρῆν, τοὺς Ἕλληνας ποιεῖ ἐπὶ τοὺς βαρβάρους ἐπιπλέοντας·   10

τὸ δεξιὸν μὲν πρῶτον εὐτάκτως κέρας
ἡγεῖτο κόσμῳ, δεύτερον δ' ὁ πᾶς στόλος
ἐπεξεχώρει, καὶ παρῆν ὁμοῦ κλύειν
πολλὴν βοήν· 'ὦ παῖδες Ἑλλήνων, ἴτε,
ἐλευθεροῦτε πατρίδ', ἐλευθεροῦτε δὲ   15
παῖδας, γυναῖκας, θεῶν τε πατρῴων ἕδη,
θήκᾱς τε προγόνων· νῦν ὑπὲρ πάντων ἀγών.'

[ποιεῖ describes   τὸ δεξιὸν . . . κέρᾱς right wing   εὐτάκτως in an orderly manner   δεύτερον secondly   ἐπεξεχώρει came out against (them)   παρῆν it was possible   ὁμοῦ together, at the same time   κλύειν to hear   θεῶν (*pronounce as one syllable*)   πατρῴων ancestral   ἕδη shrines   θήκᾱς tombs (the quotation is from Aeschylus, *Persians* 399–405)]

"οὕτως οὖν οἱ Ἕλληνες τῷ Περσικῷ στρατῷ προσέβαλλον καὶ ἐν τοῖς στενοῖς συμπίπτοντες ἐναυμάχουν ὀλίγοι πρὸς πολλούς. οἱ δὲ βάρβαροι καίπερ πλείστᾱς ἔχοντες ναῦς οὐκ ἐδύναντο πάσαις ταῖς 20 ναυσὶν ἅμα χρῆσθαι. καὶ οἱ μὲν Ἕλληνες τὰς πρώτᾱς τῶν βαρβάρων ναῦς ἢ ἔβλαψαν ἢ κατέδῡσαν τοσαύτῃ σπουδῇ προσβάλλοντες ὥστε οἱ βάρβαροι μάλιστα φοβούμενοι ἐτρέποντο καὶ ἐπειρῶντο ἐκφυγεῖν. ἐνταῦθα δὴ πλεῖστος ἐγένετο θόρυβος. αἱ γὰρ τῶν βαρβάρων νῆες ἀλλήλαις ἐνέπῑπτον, αἱ μὲν ἐκ τῆς μάχης 25 πειρώμεναι ἐκφυγεῖν, αἱ δὲ εἰς τὴν μάχην προχωροῦσαι. τέλος δὲ πάντες οἱ βάρβαροι ἔφευγον οὐδενὶ κόσμῳ χρώμενοι, οἱ δὲ Ἕλληνες διώκοντες πλείστᾱς δὴ ναῦς κατέδῡσαν· καὶ πανταχοῦ μὲν ἦν ναυάγια, πανταχοῦ δὲ νεκροί, ὥστε τὴν θάλατταν οὐκέτι ἐξῆν ἰδεῖν. οὕτως οὖν ἐμάχοντο ἕως ἐγένετο ἡ νύξ. 30

[προσέβαλλον began to attack   κατέδῡσαν sank   ναυάγια shipwrecks]

"ἐν δὲ τούτῳ ὁ Ξέρξης ἐκαθίζετο ἐπὶ ὄχθῳ τινὶ ἐγγὺς τῆς θαλάττης τὴν μάχην θεώμενος· ἐπίστευε γὰρ ὡς ῥᾳδίως νῑκήσουσιν οἱ Πέρσαι· ἠγνόει γὰρ τὰ τῆς τύχης οὐδ᾽ ἔγνω τί ἐν νῷ ἔχουσιν οἱ θεοὶ ἀλλ᾽ αἰεὶ ὕβρει ἐχρῆτο.

[ὄχθῳ hill   νῑκήσουσιν would (will) win   ἠγνόει he was ignorant of   τὰ τῆς τύχης the (things) of chance, i.e., that chance rules human affairs   ὕβρει insolence, pride]

"γνοὺς δὲ ὅτι νῑκῶσι μὲν οἱ Ἕλληνες οἱ δὲ βάρβαροι 35 ἀποφεύγουσιν, ἀνέστη καὶ τοὺς πέπλους ἔρρηξεν. ἐν ἀπορίᾳ γὰρ μεγίστῃ ἦν· ἀπολέσᾱς γὰρ τὸ ναυτικὸν οὐκέτι ἐδύνατο σῖτον παρέχειν τῷ πεζῷ στρατῷ μεγίστῳ ὄντι. τοὺς μὲν οὖν στρατηγοὺς ἐκέλευσε τὸν πεζὸν στρατὸν ἄγειν κατὰ γῆν πρὸς τὴν Ἀσίᾱν, αὐτὸς δὲ ἀπέφυγεν ὀδῡρόμενος. 40

[ἔρρηξεν he tore   ἀπολέσᾱς having lost   ὀδῡρόμενος lamenting]

"οὕτως οὖν οἱ Ἕλληνες τοὺς Πέρσᾱς νῑκήσαντες τὴν Ἑλλάδα ἠλευθέρωσαν. καὶ δὴ καὶ ἐν τούτῳ τῷ ἔργῳ οἱ Ἀθηναῖοι πλείστᾱς τε ναῦς παρέσχον τῶν Ἑλλήνων καὶ πλείστην ἐδήλωσαν ἀρετήν, ὥστε ἔξεστιν ἀληθῶς λέγειν ὅτι οἱ Ἀθηναῖοι τὴν Ἑλλάδα ἔσωσαν, καὶ οὐχ ἥκιστα ὁ Θεμιστοκλῆς, ὃς στρατηγὸς ὢν Ἀθηναῖος μάλιστα αἴτιος ἦν 45 τῆς νίκης.

[καὶ δὴ καί and in particular, and what is more   ἥκιστα least]

τοῦτο τὸ ἐπίγραμμα τοῖς Ἀθηναίοις τοῖς ἐν τούτῳ τῷ πολέμῳ
ἀποθανοῦσιν ἔγραψεν ὁ Σιμωνίδης, ποιητὴς ὢν ἄριστος·

εἰ τὸ καλῶς θνήσκειν ἀρετῆς μέρος ἐστὶ μέγιστον,
    ἡμῖν ἐκ πάντων τοῦτ' ἀπένειμε τύχη.
Ἑλλάδι γὰρ σπεύδοντες ἐλευθερίᾱν περιθεῖναι
    κείμεθ' ἀγηράντῳ χρώμενοι εὐλογίᾳ."

50

[τὸ ἐπίγραμμα epigram   τὸ καλῶς θνήσκειν to die well (*this infinitive phrase is
the subject of the sentence*)   ἀπένειμε bestowed, gave   περιθεῖναι to place around,
bring, give   κείμεθ(α) we lie (in our graves)   ἀγηράντῳ ageless   εὐλογίᾳ
praise, eulogy]

Word Building

*In the following pairs of words, deduce the meaning of the nouns and the
adjective from the meaning of the verbs. Note the change in vowels from ε in the
verbs to o in the nouns and the adjective:*

1. λέγω   ὁ λόγος   4. μένω   ἡ μονή
2. τρέπω   ἡ τροπή   5. σπεύδω   ἡ σπουδή
3. πέμπω   ἡ πομπή   6. λείπω   λοιπός, -ή, -όν

Grammar

2. Contract Verbs in -o-

In the vocabulary list and reading passage above, you have seen
examples of two contract verbs with stems ending in -o- instead of in -ε-
or -α-. Verbs in -o- contract as follows:

Present Active

Indic.		*Imper.*	*Infin.*	*Particip.*
δηλό-ω>	δηλῶ		δηλό-ειν> δηλοῦν	
δηλό-εις>	δηλοῖς	δήλο-ε > δήλου		δηλό-ων > δηλῶν,
δηλό-ει>	δηλοῖ			δηλό-ουσα > δηλοῦσα,
δηλό-ομεν>	δηλοῦμεν			δηλό-ον > δηλοῦν
δηλό-ετε>	δηλοῦτε	δηλό-ετε > δηλοῦτε		
δηλό-ουσι(ν) >	δηλοῦσι(ν)			

Present Middle
(Shown here in contracted forms only)

δηλοῦμαι		δηλοῦσθαι	δηλούμενος, -η, -ον
δηλοῖ	δηλοῦ		
δηλοῦται			
δηλούμεθα			
δηλοῦσθε	δηλοῦσθε		
δηλοῦνται			

Imperfect Active

ἐ-δήλο-ον >	ἐδήλουν
ἐ-δήλο-ες >	ἐδήλους
ἐ-δήλο-ε >	ἐδήλου
ἐ-δηλό-ομεν >	ἐδηλοῦμεν
ἐ-δηλό-ετε >	ἐδηλοῦτε
ἐ-δήλο-ον >	ἐδήλουν

Imperfect Middle

ἐδηλο-ό-μην >	ἐδηλούμην
ἐδηλό-ε-σο >	ἐδηλοῦ
ἐδηλό-ε-το >	ἐδηλοῦτο
ἐδηλο-ό-μεθα >	ἐδηλούμεθα
ἐδηλό-ε-σθε >	ἐδηλοῦσθε
ἐδηλό-ο-ντο >	ἐδηλοῦντο

The following rules for these contractions may be observed:

1. ο + ε, ο, or ου > ου.
2. ο + ει, οι, or ῃ > οι.
3. ο + η or ω > ω.

There are only a few contract verbs in -ο-; examples are δηλόω, ἐλευθερόω, and δουλόω (I enslave).

Exercise 15d

Locate four examples of -ο- contract verbs in reading passage β in this chapter and identify the form of each.

3. Contract Nouns of the Second Declension

A few nouns of the second declension with stems ending in -οο- show the same process of contraction as is seen in the verbs above, e.g.:

	Singular			*Plural*		
Nom.	ὁ	νόο-ς >	νοῦς	οἱ	νόοι >	νοῖ
Gen.	τοῦ	νόου >	νοῦ	τῶν	νόων >	νῶν
Dat.	τῷ	νόῳ >	νῷ	τοῖς	νόοις >	νοῖς
Acc.	τὸν	νόο-ν >	νοῦν	τοὺς	νόους >	νοῦς
Voc.	ὦ	νόε >	νοῦ	ὦ	νόοι >	νοῖ

*   *   *

ΟΙ ΠΕΡΣΑΙ ΤΑΣ ΑΘΗΝΑΣ ΑΙΡΟΥΣΙΝ

Read the following passages (based on Herodotus 8.51–53) and answer the comprehension questions:

οἱ Πέρσαι αἱροῦσι ἔρημον τὸ ἄστυ, καί τινας εὑρίσκουσι τῶν Ἀθηναίων ἐν τῷ ἱερῷ ὄντας, ταμίας τε τοῦ ἱεροῦ καὶ πένητας ἀνθρώπους, οἳ φραξάμενοι τὴν Ἀκρόπολιν ἠμύνοντο τοὺς προσβάλλοντας. οἱ δὲ Πέρσαι καθιζόμενοι ἐπὶ τὸν ὄχθον τὸν ἐναντίον τῆς Ἀκροπόλεως, ὃν οἱ Ἀθηναῖοι καλοῦσι Ἀρειόπαγον, ἐπολιόρκουν.

[ἔρημον deserted   ταμίας stewards   πένητας poor   φραξάμενοι
barricading   ἐπὶ τὸν ὄχθον upon the hill   ἐναντίον (+ gen.) opposite
'Αρειόπαγον the Areopagus or Hill of Ares (the god of war)   ἐπολιόρκουν were
besieging]

1. When the Persians take the city, whom do they find in the temple?
2. What had these people done, and what were they doing?
3. How did the Persians situate themselves to besiege the Acropolis?

οἱ δὲ 'Αθηναῖοι, καίπερ κάκιστα πάσχοντες, οὐκ ἤθελον εἴκειν ἀλλὰ ἠμύνοντο,   5
ὥστε πολὺν χρόνον Ξέρξης ἠπόρει, οὐ δυνάμενος αὐτοὺς ἑλεῖν. τέλος δὲ οἱ Πέρσαι
οὕτως εἶλον· ἀνέβησαν γάρ τινες ὅπου ἀπόκρημνος ἦν ὁ χῶρος καὶ οὐκ ἐφύλασσον οἱ
'Αθηναῖοι ἀλλ' ἐπίστευον ὡς οὐδεὶς δύναται ταύτῃ ἀναβῆναι. ὡς δὲ εἶδον αὐτοὺς
ταύτῃ ἀναβεβηκότας ἐπὶ τὴν 'Ακρόπολιν, οἱ μὲν ἔρρῑπτον ἑαυτοὺς κατὰ τὸ τεῖχος
καὶ ἀπέθανον, οἱ δὲ εἰς τὸ ἱερὸν ἔφευγον. οἱ δὲ Πέρσαι πρῶτον μὲν τοὺς ἱκέτᾱς   10
ἀπέκτειναν, ἔπειτα δὲ τὸ ἱερὸν σῡλήσαντες ἐνέπρησαν πᾶσαν τὴν 'Ακρόπολιν.
[ἀπόκρημνος sheer   ὁ χῶρος the place   ὡς that   ἀναβεβηκότας having gone
up   ἔρρῑπτον threw   τοὺς ἱκέτᾱς the suppliants   σῡλήσαντες having
plundered   ἐνέπρησαν they set fire to]

4. How were the Athenians faring and what were their intentions?
5. Why was it possible for the Persians finally to scale the Acropolis?
6. What did the Athenians do when they saw the Persians coming up onto
    the Acropolis?
7. What did the Persians do that showed their ignorance of or lack of respect
    for customary forms of Greek behavior?

Exercise 15f

Translate into Greek:

1   When the Athenians learned that the Persians were advancing
    toward Attica, they sent messengers to Delphi (οἱ Δελφοί).
2. These, having gone into the temple, asked the god what the Athenians
    ought (δεῖ) to do.
3. The god, answering, said: "Athena cannot save you. The
    barbarians will take (αἱρήσουσι) Athens. Only the wooden
    (ξύλινος, -ον) wall will be (ἔσται) unsacked (ἀπόρθητος, -ον)."
4. The messengers wrote these words and having returned to Athens
    announced them to the people.
5. Themistocles stood up and said: "Hear, Athenians, what the oracle
    (τὸ χρηστήριον) means (λέγει); the ships of the Athenians are the
    wooden wall; these will save (σώσουσι) the city.
6. Saying this, he persuaded the Athenians not to yield to the barbarians
    but to fight by sea.

16

ΜΕΤΑ ΤΗΝ ΕΝ ΤΗΙ ΣΑΛΑΜΙΝΙ ΜΑΧΗΝ

(α)

τάς τε πυραμίδας ἐθεωρήσαμεν καὶ τὴν Σφίγγα καὶ ζῷα ἔκτοπα.

Vocabulary

Verbs

ἀφίσταμαι, ἀπέστην,
  ἀποστάς I revolt from
εἰσρέω I flow in
ἐπίσταμαι, (*imperfect*)
  ἠπιστάμην, ἐπιστάμενος I
  understand, know
θεωρέω, ἐθεώρησα,
  θεωρήσᾱς I watch, see
κατάκειμαι, (*imperfect*)
  κατεκείμην I lie down
καταλαμβάνω, κατέλαβον,
  καταλαβών I overtake,
  catch
κεῖμαι, (*imperfect*) ἐκείμην I
  lie
στρατεύω, ἐστράτευσα,
  στρατεύσᾱς (*active or
  middle*) I wage war, campaign

συναγείρω, συνήγειρα,
  συναγείρᾱς I gather
  (*transitive*); (*middle,
  intransitive*) I gather together
τελευτάω, ἐτελεύτησα,
  τελευτήσᾱς I end, die

Nouns

ὁ ἔνοικος, τοῦ ἐνοίκου
  inhabitant
ὁ ἵππος, τοῦ ἵππου horse
ὁ ποταμός, τοῦ ποταμοῦ river
ὁ σύμμαχος, τοῦ συμμάχου
  ally
ἡ συμφορά, τῆς συμφορᾶς
  misfortune, disaster

Adjectives

διακόσιοι, -αι, -α two
  hundred
ἑκατόν (*indeclinable*) a
  hundred

ἐλεύθερος, -ᾱ, -ον free
πόσος, -η, -ον how much?
  (plural) how many?

Adverbs
  οὐδαμοῦ nowhere
  πανταχόσε in every direction
  πολλαχόσε to many parts
  ὕστερον later

Expressions
  καὶ δὴ καί and in particular,
    and what is more
  κατ' οἶκον at home
  ποῦ γῆς; where (in the world)?

Proper Names
  For the proper names in this
    reading, see the vocabulary at
    the end of the book.

οὕτως οὖν περᾱ́νᾱς τὸν λόγον ὁ ναύτης κατέκειτο ἐπὶ τῷ καταστρώματι, ὁ δὲ Δικαιόπολις καὶ ὁ Φίλιππος ἐσῑ́γων, πάντα
θαυμάζοντες ἅπερ εἶπεν. τέλος δὲ ὁ Φίλιππος, "ὡς ἀνδρείως," ἔφη,
"ἐμάχοντο οἱ Ἕλληνες, ὡς λαμπρῶς τοῖς συμμάχοις ἡγοῦντο οἱ
Ἀθηναῖοι. σὺ δὲ τί ἐποίεις μετὰ τὸν πόλεμον; ἆρα ἔμπορος   5
γενόμενος ἐν ὁλκάσιν ἔπλεις;" ὁ δέ, "οὐχί," ἔφη, "οὐ γὰρ ἐτελεύτησεν
ὁ πόλεμος ἀλλὰ πολὺν ἔτι χρόνον ἔδει πρὸς τοὺς βαρβάρους
μάχεσθαι. πάσᾱς τε γὰρ τὰς νήσους καὶ πᾶσαν τὴν Ἰωνίαν εἶχον οἱ
βάρβαροι."

[περᾱ́νᾱς having finished   τῷ καταστρώματι deck   ὁλκάσιν merchant
ships]

ὁ δὲ Φίλιππος, "ἀλλὰ πόσον χρόνον ἔδει μάχεσθαι; ἆρα πολλαῖς   10
παρῆσθα μάχαις;"
  ὁ δὲ ναύτης ἀναστὰς καὶ αὐτῷ προσχωρήσᾱς, "μάλιστά γε, ὦ
παῖ," ἔφη, "πλείσταις τε μάχαις παρῆν καὶ πολλαχόσε τῆς γῆς ἔπλεον
μετὰ τῶν συμμάχων. αἰεὶ δὲ τοὺς βαρβάρους ἐνῑκῶμεν."
  ὁ δὲ Φίλιππος, "ἀλλὰ ποῦ γῆς ἐμάχεσθε;"   15
  ὁ δέ, "πρῶτον μὲν ἅμα ἦρι ἀρχομένῳ τοῖς Ἴωσι τὴν ἐλευθερίᾱν
κατηγάγομεν· πλεύσαντες γὰρ ἑκατὸν ναυσὶ πρὸς τὴν Σάμον καὶ τὸ
τῶν βαρβάρων ναυτικὸν εἰς τὴν Μυκάλην διώξαντες, ἐξέβημεν εἰς
τὴν γῆν καὶ τόν τε στρατὸν αὐτῶν ἐνῑκήσαμεν καὶ τὸ ναυτικὸν
διεφθείραμεν. οἱ δὲ Ἴωνες, ὡς ἠπίσταντο ὅτι νῑκῶμεν, ἀπὸ τῶν   20
Περσῶν ἀποστάντες ἡμῖν ἐβοήθουν· οὕτως οὖν ἐλεύθεροι αὖθις
ἐγένοντο. τῷ δὲ ἐπιγιγνομένῳ ἔτει πανταχόσε τοῦ Αἰγαίου πόντου
πλέοντες τοὺς βαρβάρους ἐξηλάσαμεν· τήν τε γὰρ Κύπρον
ἠλευθερώσαμεν καὶ πρὸς τὸν Πόντον πλεύσαντες τό τε Βυζάντιον
εἵλομεν καὶ ἄλλᾱς πόλεις πολλάς· οὐδαμοῦ γὰρ ἡμῖν ἀντέχειν   25
ἐδύναντο οἱ βάρβαροι.

[ἅμα ἦρι ἀρχομένῳ with the beginning of spring   κατηγάγομεν we brought back, restored   τῷ . . . ἐπιγιγνομένῳ ἔτει the next year]

"ὕστερον δέ, ὡς οἱ Πέρσαι στρατόν τε μέγιστον καὶ ναῦς διακοσίᾱς συναγείραντες εἰς τὸν Αἰγαῖον πόντον αὖθις εἰσβιάζεσθαι ἐπειρῶντο, ὁ Κίμων, στρατηγὸς ἄριστος ὤν, ἡμῖν ἡγούμενος κατέλαβεν αὐτοὺς παρὰ τῷ Εὐρυμέδοντι ποταμῷ καὶ ἐνίκησε κατὰ γήν τε καὶ   30 θάλατταν ἐν μάχῃ μεγίστῃ.

[εἰσβιάζεσθαι to force their way into]

"καὶ δὴ καὶ εἰς τὴν Αἴγυπτον ἐστρατεύσαμεν καὶ τοῖς ἐνοίκοις βοηθοῦντες τοὺς Πέρσᾱς ἐξηλάσαμεν. ἀνά τε γὰρ τὸν Νεῖλον ἐπλέομεν, ποταμὸν μέγιστον, ὃς πᾶσαν τὴν Αἴγυπτον τοῦ θέρους ἄρδει καὶ εἰς τὴν θάλατταν ἑπτάροος εἰσρεῖ· καὶ τὴν Μέμφιν εἵλομεν,   35 πόλιν μεγάλην ἐπὶ τῷ Νείλῳ κειμένην. ἓξ οὖν ἔτη ἐν τῇ Αἰγύπτῳ ἐμένομεν καὶ πολλὰ θαύματα εἴδομεν· οἱ γὰρ Αἰγύπτιοι πάντα ἔμπαλιν τοῖς ἄλλοις ἀνθρώποις ποιοῦσι καὶ νόμοις ἀλλοίοις χρῶνται. ἐν γὰρ τοῖς Αἰγυπτίοις αἱ μὲν γυναῖκες ἀγοράζουσιν, οἱ δὲ ἄνδρες κατ' οἶκον μένοντες ὑφαίνουσιν.   40

[τοῦ θέρους in the summer   ἄρδει waters   ἑπτάροος in seven channels   ἔτη years   θαύματα wonders   ἔμπαλιν opposite to (+ *dat.*)   νόμοις ἀλλοίοις different customs   ἀγοράζουσιν spend their time in the market place, do the shopping   ὑφαίνουσιν do the weaving]

"τάς τε οὖν πυραμίδας ἐθεωρήσαμεν, σήματα μέγιστα ὄντα τῶν βασιλέων τῶν ἀρχαίων, καὶ τὴν Σφίγγα, εἰκόνα δεινοτάτην, τὸ μὲν ἥμισυ γυναῖκα, τὸ δὲ ἥμισυ λέαιναν. καὶ δὴ καὶ ζῷα ἔκτοπα εἴδομεν, κροκοδίλους τε, οἳ πάντων θνητῶν ἐξ ἐλαχίστου μέγιστοι γίγνονται καὶ φοβερώτατοι, καὶ στρουθούς, ὄρνῑθάς τινας μεγίστους, οἳ   45 πέτεσθαι οὐ δύνανται ἀλλὰ τρέχουσιν οὐδὲν βραδύτερον ἢ οἱ ἵπποι. τέλος δὲ οἱ Πέρσαι, στρατὸν μέγιστον συναγείραντες, προσέβαλόν τε ἡμῖν καὶ ἐκ Μέμφεως ἐξήλασαν. οὕτως οὖν πρῶτον συμφορὰν μεγίστην ἐπάθομεν· διακοσίᾱς γὰρ ναῦς ἀπολέσαντες μόλις ἡμεῖς αὐτοὶ εἰς τὴν Κυρήνην ἐξεφύγομεν."   50

[σήματα tombs   ἀρχαίων old, ancient   εἰκόνα a statue   τὸ . . . ἥμισυ half λέαιναν lioness   ἔκτοπα out of the way, unusual   κροκοδίλους crocodiles πάντων θνητῶν of all living creatures   ἐξ ἐλαχίστου from the smallest φοβερώτατοι most fearsome   στρουθούς ostriches   ὄρνῑθας birds πέτεσθαι to fly   ἀπολέσαντες having lost]

Word Study

How are the following words derived from the Greek verb δύναμαι and the related noun δύναμις?

1. dynamic 2. dynamo 3. dynamite 4. dynasty

Grammar

1. The verbs δύναμαι, κεῖμαι, and ἐπίσταμαι

The following common deponent verbs add personal endings directly to the stem:

Stem: δυνα- be able

Present

Indicative	*Imperative*	*Infinitive*	*Participle*
δύνα-μαι		δύνα-σθαι	δυνά-μενος, -η, -ον
δύνα-σαι	δύνα-σο		
δύνα-ται			
δυνά-μεθα			
δύνα-σθε	δύνα-σθε		
δύνα-νται			

Stem: κει- lie

κεῖ-μαι		κεῖ-σθαι	κεί-μενος, -η, -ον
κεῖ-σαι	κεῖ-σο		
κεῖ-ται			
κεί-μεθα			
κεῖ-σθε	κεῖ-σθε		
κεῖ-νται			

Stem: ἐπιστα- understand, know

ἐπίστα-μαι		ἐπίστα-σθαι	ἐπιστά-μενος, -η, -ον
ἐπίστα-σαι	ἐπίστα-σο		
ἐπίστα-ται			
ἐπιστά-μεθα			
ἐπίστα-σθε	ἐπίστα-σθε		
ἐπίστα-νται			

Imperfect Indicative:

ἐ-δυνά-μην	ἐ-κεί-μην	ἠπιστά-μην
ἐ-δύνα-σο *or* ἐδύνω	ἔ-κει-σο	ἠπίστα-σο *or* ἠπίστω
ἐ-δύνα-το	ἔ-κει-το	ἠπίστα-το
ἐ-δυνά-μεθα	ἐ-κεί-μεθα	ἠπιστά-μεθα
ἐ-δύνα-σθε	ἔ-κει-σθε	ἠπίστα-σθε
ἐ-δύνα-ντο	ἔ-κει-ντο	ἠπίστα-ντο

Exercise 16a

In the reading passage at the beginning of this chapter, locate four examples of the verbs above or compounds of them, and identify each form fully.

Exercise 16b

Read aloud and translate:

1. ὦ ξεῖν', ἄγγειλον Λακεδαιμονίοις ὅτι τῇδε
     κείμεθα τοῖς κείνων ῥήμασι πειθόμενοι.
2. ἆρ' ἐπίστασθε διὰ τί οὐ δύνανται ἡμῖν βοηθεῖν οἱ σύμμαχοι;
3. ἡ γυνὴ οὐκ ἠπίστατο ὅτι ὁ ἀνὴρ ἐν ἐκείνῃ τῇ μάχῃ ἀπέθανεν.
4. αὕτη ἡ νῆσος οὕτως ἐπέκειτο τῇ ἠπείρῳ (*the mainland*) ὥστε ῥᾳδίως ἐκεῖσε διέβημεν.
5. ἐν οὐδεμίᾳ ναυμαχίᾳ ἐδύναντο οἱ βάρβαροι τοὺς Ἕλληνας νῑκῆσαι.
6. τῶν γυναικῶν αἱ πολλαὶ (*the majority*) τοῖς ἀνδράσι βοηθοῦσιν, δύο δὲ ἐν τῇ οἰκίᾳ κεῖνται διαλεγόμεναι ἀλλήλαις.
7. καίπερ ἄριστα μαχόμενοι, οὐκ ἐδύναντο οἱ Λακεδαιμόνιοι τοὺς βαρβάρους ἀμῦναι.
8. διὰ τί οὐκ ἐργάζῃ, ὦ νεᾱνίᾱ, ἀλλὰ οὕτως ἀργὸς (*idle*) κεῖσαι;
9. ἐπιστάμενοι ὅτι ὁ δεσπότης προσχωρεῖ, οἱ δοῦλοι, οἳ ἐν τῷ ἀγρῷ ἔκειντο, ἀνέστησαν καὶ εἰργάζοντο.
10. τοῦτο ἐπίστασο, ὅτι οὐ δύνασαι τοὺς θεοὺς ἐξαπατᾶν (*to deceive*).

Exercise 16c

Translate into Greek:

1. We cannot help you, for father told us to go to the field.
2. Not knowing why her husband had not returned (*use aorist*), the woman was very afraid.
3. The sailors who were lying under that tree stood up and hurried to the harbor.
4. Not being able to find the flocks, the young men climbed the mountain and looked for them all day.
5. No one knows why the woman left home and (having left home) went to the city.

The Athenian Empire

During the invasion of Xerxes, the loyal Greeks had accepted without question the leadership of Sparta by both land and sea; for she was still the dominant power in Greece. In spring of 479 B.C., the allied fleet, led by a Spartan general, was based at Delos and, invited by the Samians, sailed to Ionia, defeated the Persians at Mycale, and liberated the Ionians, who revolted from their Persian masters (see map, page 167). The following year the allies were led by Pausanias, the Spartan commander at Plataea. In a brilliant campaign he first liberated most of Cyprus from Persian rule and then sailed north and took Byzantium, the key to the Black Sea. Here he fell victim to *hubris*; he adopted Persian dress, intrigued with the Persian authorities, and alienated the allies by his outrageous and tyrannical behavior. In consequence, the allies appealed to the Athenians for protection, and Pausanias was recalled to Sparta and later executed.

Meanwhile the Athenians took over the leadership of the allies. Representatives met at Delos and agreed to form a voluntary league (the Delian League) to carry on the war against Persia under the leadership of Athens. Each member state was to provide ships or money in proportion to its means, of which an assessment was made. The representatives threw lumps of lead into the sea and swore to maintain the League until the lead swam.

The Athenian Empire

Led by Cimon, their Athenian general, the fleet of the League had a series of very successful campaigns, expelling the Persian garrisons wherever they remained and finally defeating them in the great battle of the Eurymedon River on the southern coast of Asia Minor when they tried to make a comeback (ca. 467 B.C.). As the Persian danger receded, some members became less willing to contribute ships or money. Around 469 B.C. the important island of Naxos seceded from the League; the allied fleet blockaded the island and forced it back into the League on terms that made it a subject of Athens. This was the first step of the Athenians on the road to empire.

As time went by, more and more members ceased to provide ships and contributed money instead, and soon only three large and wealthy islands (Lesbos, Chios, and Samos) were independent members contributing ships. The rest had become tributary allies, in whose internal affairs Athens began to interfere. In 454 B.C., a highly significant step was taken when the treasury of the League was transferred from Delos to Athens, ostensibly because the defeat of the Athenian expeditionary force in Egypt in 456 B.C. left the Aegean exposed to danger.

A number of inscriptions carved on stone have been found in Athens that throw much light on the development and organization of the Empire in these years. These include records of the annual tribute payed by each member from 454 B.C., when the treasury of the League was moved to Athens, until 415 B.C. We find that the Empire included nearly all the Aegean Sea and stretched from the coast of the Black Sea to the south of Asia Minor. In 449 B.C., the Athenians made peace with Persia; the purpose of the Delian League had come to an end. The following year the tribute list is very short; many members must have refused to pay. We then find a decree that introduced measures for tightening up the collection of the tribute, and the next year's tribute list is long; recalcitrant members had been forced to pay up. At the same time, evidence accumulates of Athenian interference in the internal affairs of League members. Uniform coinage, weights, and measures are imposed by decree; democracies are installed in some cities under the supervision of Athenian officials; garrisons of Athenian troops are stationed at some danger points; settlements of Athenian citizens are made on allied territory; and judicial cases involving an Athenian and an ally are referred to Athenian courts. All such measures infringed the sovereignty of "independent" allies, who were being reduced to the status of subjects in what the Athenians now openly called their Empire (ἡ ἀρχή).

These developments were inspired by Pericles, who dominated the Athenian democracy for nearly thirty years, until his death in 429 B.C. They were largely responsible for the great war between Athens and the Peloponnesian League led by Sparta, for the Peloponnesians not only feared the ever-growing power of Athens but also condemned the "enslavement" of fellow Greeks. The final ultimatum sent by Sparta to Athens said: "The Spartans want peace; and there would be peace, if you let the Greeks be independent." Even at Athens not all approved of the Empire, despite the economic and military advantages it brought. Not even Pericles himself sought moral justification

for it. In a speech to the people shortly before his death, he said: "The Empire
you hold is a tyranny, which you may think it was wrong to acquire, but it is
dangerous to give it up."

Athenian tribute list

This fragment records the tribute payed in 440/439 B.C. by the Hellespontine and
Thraceward districts of the Empire.   In the columns below the headings
(ΗΕΛΛΕΣΠΟΝΤΙΟΣ ΦΟΡΟΣ, ΑΠΟ ΘΡΑΙΚΕΣ ΦΟΡΟΣ) are listed on the left the amount of
tribute and on the right the name of the city concerned.

ΜΕΤΑ ΤΗΝ ΕΝ ΤΗΙ ΣΑΛΑΜΙΝΙ ΜΑΧΗΝ

(β)

τὸ Αἰτναῖον ὄρος εἶδον ποταμοὺς πυρὸς πρὸς τὸν οὐρανὸν ἔκβαλλον.

Vocabulary

Verbs

λῡπέω, ἐλύπησα, λῡπήσᾱς I
grieve, pain; (*middle*) I am
sad, sorrowful

πολιορκέω, ἐπολιόρκησα,
πολιορκήσᾱς I besiege

Nouns

ὁ βίος, τοῦ βίου life

ἡ εἰρήνη, τῆς εἰρήνης peace

τὸ ἔτος, τοῦ ἔτους year

ὁ θάνατος, τοῦ θανάτου
death

ὁ θῡμός, τοῦ θῡμοῦ spirit

αἱ σπονδαί, τῶν σπονδῶν
(*plural*) peace treaty

Adjectives

ἄξιος, -ᾱ, -ον (+ *gen.*) worthy
of

Expression

ἥκιστά γε (*the opposite of*
μάλιστά γε) least of all, not
at all

Proper Names

For the proper names in this
reading, see the vocabulary at
the end of the book.

ὁ δὲ Φίλιππος, "ἆρ' οὐ τοσαύτην συμφορὰν παθόντες τοῦ πολέμου ἐπαύσασθε;"

ὁ δὲ ναύτης, "ἥκιστά γε," ἔφη· "οὐδὲν γὰρ ἐδύνατο τὸν τῶν Ἀθηναίων θυμὸν καθαιρεῖν. δι' ὀλίγου οὖν ὁ Κίμων τῷ ναυτικῷ εἰς Κύπρον ἡγησάμενος τοὺς Πέρσας αὖθις ἐνίκησεν, αὐτὸς δὲ πόλιν   5
τινὰ πολιορκῶν ἀπέθανεν. ἡμεῖς οὖν λυπούμενοι οἴκαδε ἀπεπλεύσαμεν. τῷ δὲ ἐπιγιγνομένῳ ἔτει σπονδὰς ὁ δῆμος ἐποιήσατο τῷ βασιλεῖ. τοσαῦτα οὖν εἰργασάμεθα πρὸς τοὺς βαρβάρους μαχόμενοι. ἀγὼν οὖν μέγιστος πρόκειταί σοι, ὦ παῖ· δεῖ γάρ σε ἄξιον γίγνεσθαι τῶν πατέρων."   10

[καθαιρεῖν to reduce   τῷ . . . ἐπιγιγνομένῳ ἔτει the next year   εἰργασάμεθα we accomplished   πρόκειταί σοι lies before you]

ὁ δὲ Φίλιππος, "ἀληθῆ λέγεις, ὦ γέρον," ἔφη· "ἐὰν δὲ ἵλαος ᾖ ὁ θεός, ἐγὼ ἀνὴρ ἀγαθὸς γίγνεσθαι πειράσομαι, ἄξιος τῶν πατέρων. ἀλλὰ τί ἐποίεις σὺ ἐν τῇ εἰρήνῃ;"

[ἐὰν . . . ᾖ if . . . is]

ὁ δὲ γέρων, "οὐκέτι νεανίας ἦν ἐγώ," ἔφη, "οὐδὲ τοσαύτη ῥώμη ἐχρώμην ὥστε ἐν τῷ ναυτικῷ ἐρέσσειν. μισθοφορῶν οὖν ἐν ὁλκάσι   15
πολλαχόσε τῆς γῆς ἔπλεον. εἴς τε γὰρ τὴν Σικελίᾱν ἦλθον, οὗπερ τὸ Αἰτναῖον ὄρος εἶδον ποταμοὺς πυρὸς πρὸς τὸν οὐρανὸν ἔκβαλλον, καὶ εἰς τὴν Σκυθίᾱν ἔπλευσα, οὗπερ τοῦ χειμῶνος τοσαῦτά ἐστιν τὰ ψύχεα ὥστε πήγνυσθαι καὶ τὴν θάλατταν. νῦν δὲ μάλα γεραιὸς ὢν πλοῦς τινὰς μικροὺς ποιοῦμαι περὶ τὰς νήσους, καὶ θάνατον   20
εὔκολος προσδέχομαι."

[ῥώμη strength   μισθοφορῶν hiring myself out   οὗπερ where   τοῦ χειμῶνος in winter   τὰ ψύχεα the frosts   πήγνυσθαι freezes   πλοῦς voyages   εὔκολος contented   προσδέχομαι I await]

ὁ δὲ Φίλιππος, "πολλὰ μὲν εἶδες, ὦ γέρον," ἔφη, "ἐν μακρῷ τῷ βίῳ, πολλὰ δὲ καὶ ἔπαθες. οὐ γὰρ αὐτὸς ὁ Ὀδυσσεὺς πορρωτέρω ἐπλανᾶτο ἢ σύ."

[πορρωτέρω further   ἐπλανᾶτο wandered]

ὁ δὲ γέρων πρὸς τὴν γῆν βλέψᾱς ἀνέστη καί, "ἰδού," ἔφη, "ἤδη   25
πάρεσμεν εἰς τὸν λιμένα. χαίρετε οὖν. δεῖ γάρ με σπεύδειν καὶ τοῖς ἄλλοις ναύταις βοηθεῖν."

οὕτως εἰπὼν ἀπέβη πρὸς τὴν πρῷραν, οἱ δὲ ἔμενον πάντα ἐνθῡμούμενοι ἅπερ εἶπεν.

[τὴν **πρῷραν** the bow of the ship   **ἐνθῡμούμενοι** thinking about, pondering]

οἱ δ᾽ ὅτε δὴ λιμένος πολυβενθέος ἐντὸς ἵκοντο,   30
ἱστία μὲν στείλαντο, θέσαν δ᾽ ἐν νηὶ μελαίνῃ
καρπαλίμως, τὴν δ᾽ εἰς ὅρμον προέρεσσαν ἐρετμοῖς.

[**πολυβενθέος** (gen. sing.) very deep   **ἐντός** (+ gen.) within   **ἵκοντο** they arrived
στείλαντο they took down   **θέσαν** they put   **μελαίνῃ** black   **καρπαλίμως**
quickly   **τήν** it, i.e., the ship   **ὅρμον** anchorage   **προέρεσσαν ἐρετμοῖς** they
rowed . . . forward with the oars (the quotation is from *Iliad* 1.432, 3, and 5)]

ἐπεὶ οὖν ἡ ναῦς ὥρμει πρὸς τῷ χώματι, ἐξέβησαν οἱ ἄνθρωποι εἰς
τὴν γῆν. ἐκβάντες δὲ οἱ μὲν οἴκαδε ἔσπευδον, οἱ δὲ εἰς τὴν πόλιν
ἐβάδιζον οἰνοπώλιον ζητοῦντες.   35

[**ὥρμει** was lying at anchor, was moored   **τῷ χώματι** the pier   **οἰνοπώλιον**
wine-shop, inn]

Word Building

*The following adjectives, verbs, and nouns are all derived from the root of ὁ
θῡμός "spirit," using the prefixes ἀ- "not," εὐ- "good," and προ- "before,"
"forth" (often indicating readiness). Deduce the meaning of the following
compounds:*

1. ἄθῡμος, -ον   ἀθῡμέω   ἡ ἀθῡμίᾱ
2. εὔθῡμος, -ον   εὐθῡμέω   ἡ εὐθῡμίᾱ
3. πρόθῡμος, -ον   προθῡμέομαι   ἡ προθῡμίᾱ

Grammar

2. Two More Third Declension Nouns: ἡ ναῦς and ὁ βοῦς

The stems of ναῦς and βοῦς were originally ναϝ- and βοϝ-. The letter ϝ
(digamma) represented a *w* sound (compare Latin *navis* and *bovis*). This
sound and letter were lost in the development of the Greek language.

	Singular		*Plural*		*Singular*		*Plural*	
Nom.	ἡ	ναῦ-ς	αἱ	νῆ-ες	ὁ	βοῦ-ς	οἱ	βό-ες
Gen.	τῆς	νε-ώς	τῶν	νε-ῶν	τοῦ	βο-ός	τῶν	βο-ῶν
Dat.	τῇ	νη-ΐ	ταῖς	ναυ-σί(ν)	τῷ	βο-ΐ	τοῖς	βου-σί(ν)
Acc.	τὴν	ναῦ-ν	τὰς	ναῦ-ς	τὸν	βοῦ-ν	τοὺς	βοῦ-ς
Voc.	ὦ	ναῦ	ὦ	νῆ-ες	ὦ	βοῦ	ὦ	βό-ες

Exercise 16d

In each of the following phrases put the nouns and adjectives into the correct forms to agree with the article:

1. αἱ (μακρός) (ναῦς)
2. οἱ (ἀληθής) (λόγος)
3. τοῦ (σώφρων) (ποιητής)
4. τῷ (μέγας) (βοῦς)
5. τῆς (καλλίων) (πόλις)
6. (οὗτος) τὸν (νεανίας)
7. (οὗτος) τῆς (ναῦς)
8. (οὗτος) αἱ (γυνή)
9. τοῖς (σώφρων) (ἱερεύς)
10. τῇ (μείζων) (ναῦς)
11. τοῦ (μέγας) βασιλεύς
12. τοῖς (ψευδής) (μῦθος)
13. οἱ (μέγας) (βοῦς)
14. (ὅδε) τοῖς (τεῖχος)

3. More Numbers

You have already learned the cardinals 1–10 and the ordinals 1st–10th (see Chapter 8, Grammar 5). You should learn to recognize the following:

11	ἕνδεκα	11th	ἑνδέκατος, -η, -ον
12	δώδεκα	12th	δωδέκατος, -η, -ον
20	εἴκοσι	20th	εἰκοστός, -ή, -όν
100	ἑκατόν	100th	ἑκατοστός
1,000	χίλιοι, -αι, -α	1,000th	χιλιοστός, -ή, -όν
10,000	μύριοι, -αι, -α	10,000th	μυριοστός, -ή, -όν

13, etc.	τρεῖς καὶ δέκα, etc.
21, etc.	εἷς καὶ εἴκοσι, etc.

The numbers 30 to 90 are formed from the corresponding cardinal form + -κοντα (with some variations in spelling): τριάκοντα, τετταράκοντα, πεντήκοντα, ἑξήκοντα, ἑβδομήκοντα, ὀγδοήκοντα, ἐνενήκοντα.

The numbers 200 to 900 are formed from the corresponding cardinal forms + -κοσιοι, -αι, -α (with some variations in spelling): διακόσιοι, τριακόσιοι, τετρακόσιοι, πεντακόσιοι, ἑξακόσιοι, ἑπτακόσιοι, ὀκτακόσιοι, ἐνακόσιοι.

The following numerical adverbs should be learned: ἅπαξ once, δίς twice, τρίς three times. The others are formed by adding -ακις to the corresponding cardinal form (with some variations in spelling): τετράκις, πεντάκις, ἑξάκις, ἑπτάκις, ἐνάκις, δεκάκις.

* * *

Ο ΞΕΡΞΗΣ ΠΡΟΣ ΤΗΝ ΑΣΙΑΝ ΑΝΑΧΩΡΕΙ

Read the following passage (adapted from Herodotus 8.118) and answer the comprehension questions below:

After the defeat at Salamis, Xerxes accompanied his army on the retreat northwards. In Thessaly he left a large army under Mardonius to renew the attack the following year. Herodotus gives two versions of the rest of his journey home, of which this is the second.

ἔστι δὲ καὶ ὅδε ἄλλος λόγος, ὅτι ἐπεὶ ὁ Ξέρξης ἀπελαύνων ἐξ Ἀθηνῶν ἀφίκετο εἰς Ἠϊόνα, οὐκέτι κατὰ γῆν ἐπορεύετο ἀλλὰ τὴν μὲν στρατίᾱν Ὑδάρνει ἐπιτρέπει ἀπάγειν εἰς τὸν Ἑλλήσποντον, αὐτὸς δὲ εἰς ναῦν εἰσβὰς ἔπλει εἰς τὴν Ἀσίᾱν. πλέοντι δὲ αὐτῷ ἄνεμος μὲν μείζων ἐγίγνετο, ἡ δὲ θάλασσα ἐκύμαινεν. ἡ δὲ ναῦς πλείστους φέρουσα ἀνθρώπους τῶν Περσῶν, οἳ τῷ Ξέρξῃ ἠκολούθουν, ἐν κινδύνῳ ἦν. 5
ὁ δὲ βασιλεὺς μάλα φοβούμενος τὸν κυβερνήτην ἤρετο εἴ τις ἔστι σωτηρίᾱ αὐτοῖς. ὁ δὲ εἶπεν· "ὦ δέσποτα, οὐκ ἔστιν οὐδεμία σωτηρίᾱ, ἐὰν μὴ ἀπαλλάγωμέν τινων τῶν πολλῶν ἐπιβατῶν."

[ἀπελαύνων marching away   Ἠϊόνα Eion, a town in Thrace   τὴν . . . στρατίᾱν the army   Ὑδάρνει to Hydarnes   ἐπιτρέπει entrusts   ἀπάγειν to lead back   τὸν Ἑλλήσποντον the Hellespont   ἐκύμαινεν was becoming rough ἠκολούθουν (+ *dat.*) were following, accompanying   τὸν κυβερνήτην the steersman   σωτηρίᾱ salvation   ἐὰν μή unless   ἀπαλλάγωμεν get rid of (+ *gen.*) ἐπιβατῶν passengers]

1. In this second version of the story of Xerxes' return to Asia, what did he do with his army and what did he do himself?
2. What happened during the voyage?
3. What did Xerxes ask his helmsman?
4. On what did the helmsman say their salvation depended?

καὶ Ξέρξης ταῦτα ἀκούσᾱς εἶπεν· "ὦ ἄνδρες Πέρσαι, νῦν δεῖ ὑμᾶς δηλοῦν εἰ τὸν βασιλέᾱ φιλεῖτε· ἐν ὑμῖν γάρ, ὡς δοκεῖ, ἔστιν ἡ ἐμὴ σωτηρίᾱ." ὁ μὲν ταῦτα 1
εἶπεν, οἱ δὲ αὐτὸν προσκυνοῦντες ἔρρῑψαν ἑαυτοὺς εἰς τὴν θάλασσαν, καὶ ἡ ναῦς ἐπικουφισθεῖσα οὕτω δὴ ἔσωσε τὸν βασιλέᾱ εἰς τὴν Ἀσίᾱν. ὡς δὲ ἐξέβη εἰς τὴν γῆν, ὁ Ξέρξης ἐποίησε τοῦτο· ὅτι μὲν ἔσωσε τὸν βασιλέᾱ, χρῡσοῦν στέφανον τῷ κυβερνήτῃ ἔδωκεν, ὅτι δὲ Περσῶν πολλοὺς διέφθειρεν ἀπέταμε τὴν κεφαλὴν αὐτοῦ.

[προσκυνοῦντες bowing down to   ἔρρῑψαν they threw   ἐπικουφισθεῖσα lightened   ὅτι because   χρῡσοῦν στέφανον a golden crown   ἔδωκεν he gave ἀπέταμε he cut off]

5. What does Xerxes say that the Persians must now show?
6. Upon whom does Xerxes say his salvation depends?
7. What two things do the Persians do?
8. What is the result of their action?

9. Why did Xerxes give his helmsman a golden crown?
10. Why did he cut off his head?

Temple of Athena Nike on the Acropolis
The Athenians built this temple in 427–424 B.C. to commemorate their victories in
the Persian Wars

Exercise 16e

Translate into Greek:

1. After the battle, Xerxes and his generals stayed a few days in Attica
    and (then) set out (*use aorist active*) toward Boeotia.
2. The king ordered Mardonius (ὁ Μαρδόνιος) to stay in Thessaly (ἡ
    Θεσσαλίᾱ) during the winter and at the beginning of spring (ἅμα
    ἦρι ἀρχομένῳ) to advance against the Peloponnesus.
3. When they arrived in Thessaly, Mardonius (on the one hand)ʹ
    selected (ἐξελέγετο) the best soldiers, (on the other hand) Xerxes
    leaving them there marched as quickly as possible to the Hellespont.
4. We cannot trust the other story that they tell about the return (ὁ νόστος)
    of Xerxes.
5. Those who know the truth say that he returned to Asia by land and
    arrived at the Hellespont in forty-five days (*use genitive*).

REFERENCE GRAMMAR

1. SYLLABLES AND ACCENTS

A Greek word has as many syllables as it has vowels and diphthongs, e.g.: ἄν-θρω-πος.

In dividing words into syllables, single consonants go with the following vowel (note -πος in ἄν-θρω-πος above); a group of consonants that cannot stand at the beginning of a word is divided between two syllables (note how the consonants νθρ are divided in ἄν-θρω-πος above); and double consonants are divided between syllables, e.g., θά-λατ-τα.

The final syllable is called the *ultima*, the next to the last, the *penult*, and the third from the end, the *antepenult*. These terms are useful in discussing the placement of accents.

A syllable is said to be long (1) if it contains a long vowel or diphthong or (2) if it contains a short vowel followed by two or more consecutive consonants or by ζ, ξ, or ψ. Exceptions to these rules are the diphthongs αι and οι, which are regarded as short when they stand as the final element in a word (except in the optative mood, to be studied in Book II). Note that η and ω are long vowels, ε and ο are short vowels, and α, ι, and υ may be either long or short—when long they are marked with a macron in this book.

For the three types of accents, see Introduction, page x. The acute accent can stand on any of the last three syllables of a word; the circumflex can stand on either of the last two syllables; and the grave can stand only on the ultima. The grave accent replaces an acute on the ultima when that word is followed immediately by another word with no intervening punctuation, except when the following word is an enclitic (see below).

The accent on a verb is *recessive*, i.e., it is placed as far toward the beginning of the word as is allowed by the rule in d1 below. The accent of a noun, pronoun, adjective, or participle is *persistent*, i.e., it remains as it is in the nominative case unless forced to change by one of the rules in d1 and d2 below. The placement of the accent in the nominative must be learned by observation, e.g.: ἄν-θρω-πος, ὀ-λί-γος, κα-λός.

Placement of accents

a. On the antepenult
    Only an acute accent may stand on the antepenult, e.g.: ἄν-θρω-πος.
b. On the penult
    If the penult is accented, it will have a circumflex if it contains a diphthong or a long vowel and if the vowel or diphthong of the final syllable is short, e.g.: οἶ-κος, οἶ-κοι. Otherwise, it will have an acute, e.g.: ἀν-θρώ-που, πό-νου.
c. On the ultima
    If the ultima is accented, its accent will be an acute (changed to a grave as noted above) or a circumflex (by special rules, particularly in contract verbs).

d. Shifts and changes of accent
   1. The acute cannot stand on the antepenult if the vowel of the ultima is long. Therefore, ἄν-θρω-πος becomes ἀν-θρώ-που in the genitive case.
   2. Since the circumflex can stand on the accented penult only if the vowel or diphthong of the ultima is short, the circumflex on οἶ-κος changes to an acute in the genitive case (οἴ-κου).

Enclitics

Enclitics lean upon the preceding word, and the two words taken together are accented to some extent as if they were one word. Enclitics met in Book I of *Athenaze* include the short forms of the personal pronouns (μου, μοι, με; σου, σοι, σε); the indefinite pronoun and adjective τις, τι; the indefinite adverbs που, πως, ποτέ, ποθέν, and ποι; the particle γε; the conjunction τε; and the forms of εἰμί and φημί in the present tense (except for the second person singular).

a. An acute accent on the ultima of a word preceding an enclitic does not change to a grave, and the enclitic has no accent, e.g.:
   ἀγρός τις
   ἀγροί τινες.
b. If a circumflex stands on the ultima of a word preceding an enclitic, the enclitic has no accent, e.g.:
   ἀγρῶν τινων
c. A word with an acute on its penult does not change its accent when followed by an enclitic, but a disyllabic enclitic will require an accent on its ultima (an acute accent if the ultima is short and a circumflex if it is long), e.g.:
   πόνος τις
   ἀνθρώπου τινός
   ἀνθρώπων τινῶν
   The acute on the ultima of the enclitic will change to a grave if the enclitic is followed by another word with no intervening punctuation.
d. A word with an acute on its antepenult will need to add an acute to its ultima to support an enclitic, e.g.:
   ἄνθρωπός τις
   ἄνθρωποί τινες
   The enclitics need no accents.
e. If a word has a circumflex on its penult, an acute accent is added to its ultima to support a following enclitic, e.g.:
   οἶκός τις
   οἶκοί τινες
f. If an enclitic is followed by another enclitic, the first receives an accent but the second does not, e.g.:
   δυνατόν ἐστί σοι
   If an enclitic is followed by more than one enclitic, all but the last receive acute accents, e.g.:
   δυνατόν ἐστί σοί ποτε
g. The form ἐστι(ν) receives an acute acent on its penult when it stands at the beginning of its sentence or clause, when it follows οὐκ, or when it means "there is" or "it is possible," e.g.:
   οὐκ ἔστιν ἄνθρωπος

Proclitics

Proclitics are words of a single syllable that normally do not have accents,
e.g., οὐ and εἰ. When followed by enclitics, they must be accented, e.g.:

εἴ τις
οὔ τις

Elision

For elision between words and for elision or dropping of the final vowel of a
prepositional prefix added to a verb beginning with a vowel, see pages 45 and 149.

2. THE DEFINITE ARTICLE

See page 40.

	Singular			*Plural*		
	M	**F**	**N**	**M**	**F**	**N**
Nom.	ὁ	ἡ	τό	οἱ	αἱ	τά
Gen.	τοῦ	τῆς	τοῦ	τῶν	τῶν	τῶν
Dat.	τῷ	τῇ	τῷ	τοῖς	ταῖς	τοῖς
Acc.	τόν	τήν	τό	τούς	τάς	τά

Note that the genitive and dative cases have circumflex accents in all forms,
singular and plural.

3. DECLENSIONS OF NOUNS

For the general concept of three declensions of nouns in Greek, see pages 33
and 70–71. The three declensions may be distinguished as follows:

First (or ᾱ) declension: stems end in ᾱ (changed in Attic Greek to η in the
singular, except after ε, ι, and ρ), e.g.:
    ἡ κρήνη: stem κρηνη-
    ἡ οἰκίᾱ: stem οἰκιᾱ-
    ὁ δεσπότης,: stem δεσποτη-
    ὁ νεᾱνίᾱς: stem νεᾱνιᾱ-
(A few nouns are irregular in that the nominative, accusative, and vocative
singular show ᾰ, e.g., ἡ θάλαττᾰ.)

Second (or ο) declension: stems end in ο (a few in οο or εο), e.g.,:
    ὁ ἀγρός: stem ἀγρο-
    τὸ δένδρον: stem δένδρο-
    ὁ νοῦς: stem voo-
    τὸ κανοῦν: stem κανεο-
Third (or consonant) declension: stems end in a consonant or in the vowels ι
or υ, e.g.:
    ὁ παῖς: stem παιδ-
    ἡ πόλις: stem πολι-
    τὸ ἄστυ: stem ἀστυ-

4. NOUNS OF THE FIRST DECLENSION

Six types of nouns of the first declension may be distinguished; the following serve as examples:

Feminine (see pages 32–34):
1. ἡ κρήνη
2. ἡ οἰκίᾱ
3. ἡ θάλαττᾰ (genitive τῆς θαλάττης, dative τῇ θαλάττῃ)
4. ἡ μάχαιρᾰ (genitive τῆς μαχαίρᾱς, dative τῇ μαχαίρᾳ)

Masculine (see page 38):
5. ὁ δεσπότη-ς
6. ὁ νεᾱνίᾱ-ς
   The letter ς is the nominative masculine singular ending added to the stem.

Feminine

		Singular		*Plural*
1.	**Nom.**	ἡ	κρήνη	αἱ	κρῆναι
	Gen.	τῆς	κρήνης	τῶν	κρηνῶν
	Dat.	τῇ	κρήνῃ	ταῖς	κρήναις
	Acc.	τὴν	κρήνην	τὰς	κρήνᾱς
	Voc.	ὦ	κρήνη	ὦ	κρῆναι
2.	**Nom.**	ἡ	οἰκίᾱ	αἱ	οἰκίαι
	Gen.	τῆς	οἰκίᾱς	τῶν	οἰκιῶν
	Dat.	τῇ	οἰκίᾳ	ταῖς	οἰκίαις
	Acc.	τὴν	οἰκίᾱν	τὰς	οἰκίᾱς
	Voc.	ὦ	οἰκίᾱ	ὦ	οἰκίαι
3.	**Nom.**	ἡ	θάλαττᾰ	αἱ	θάλατται
	Gen.	τῆς	θαλάττης	τῶν	θαλαττῶν
	Dat.	τῇ	θαλάττῃ	ταῖς	θαλάτταις
	Acc.	τὴν	θάλαττᾰν	τὰς	θαλάττᾱς
	Voc.	ὦ	θάλαττᾰ	ὦ	θάλατται
4.	**Nom.**	ἡ	μάχαιρᾰ	αἱ	μάχαιραι
	Gen.	τῆς	μαχαίρᾱς	τῶν	μαχαιρῶν
	Dat.	τῇ	μαχαίρᾳ	ταῖς	μαχαίραις
	Acc.	τὴν	μάχαιρᾰν	τὰς	μαχαίρᾱς
	Voc.	ὦ	μάχαιρᾰ	ὦ	μάχαιραι

Masculine

		Singular		*Plural*
5.	**Nom.**	ὁ δεσπότης	οἱ	δεσπόται
	Gen.	τοῦ δεσπότου	τῶν	δεσποτῶν
	Dat.	τῷ δεσπότῃ	τοῖς	δεσπόταις
	Acc.	τὸν δεσπότην	τοὺς	δεσπότᾱς
	Voc.	ὦ δέσποτα	ὦ	δεσπόται

Singular

		Singular		*Plural*
6.	**Nom.**	ὁ νεᾱνίᾱς	οἱ	νεᾱνίαι
	Gen.	τοῦ νεᾱνίου	τῶν	νεᾱνιῶν
	Dat.	τῷ νεᾱνίᾳ	τοῖς	νεᾱνίαις
	Acc.	τὸν νεᾱνίᾱν	τοὺς	νεᾱνίᾱς
	Voc.	ὦ νεᾱνίᾱ	ὦ	νεᾱνίαι

Note that all first declension nouns, whether feminine or masculine, have the same endings in the plural. The rules for the singular are as follows:
a.   If the nominative ends in -η (feminine) or -ης (masculine), all cases (except the genitive and vocative of masculine nouns) show the η in the singular.
b.   Normally if the final vowel of the stem is preceded by ε, ι, or ρ, the stem will end in ᾱ instead of η, and the ᾱ is retained in all the singular endings (except the genitive singular of masculine nouns, which is always -ου).
c.   If the nominative ends in ᾰ, the genitive and dative singular end in -ης and -ῃ, unless the ᾰ is preceded by ε, ι, or ρ, in which case the genitive and dative singular end in -ᾱς and -ᾳ.

First declension nouns with an acute accent on the final syllable (e.g., ἡ ἀρχή) have a circumflex accent on the genitive and dative, singular and plural, e.g.: τῆς ἀρχῆς, τῇ ἀρχῇ, τῶν ἀρχῶν, ταῖς ἀρχαῖς.

All first declension nouns, no matter where the accent falls in the nominative case, have a circumflex accent on the ending of the genitive plural, e.g.: ἡ κρήνη, gen. pl. τῶν κρηνῶν.

5.   NOUNS OF THE SECOND DECLENSION

Five types of nouns of the second declension may be distinguished (the first three have stems ending in o, the last two in oo and εo); the following serve as examples:

Masculine (see pages 27–28):

		Singular		*Plural*
1.	**Nom.**	ὁ ἀγρός	οἱ	ἀγροί
	Gen.	τοῦ ἀγροῦ	τῶν	ἀγρῶν
	Dat.	τῷ ἀγρῷ	τοῖς	ἀγροῖς
	Acc.	τὸν ἀγρόν	τοὺς	ἀγρούς
	Voc.	ὦ ἀγρέ	ὦ	ἀγροί

Feminine (see page 52):

	Singular		Plural	
2. *Nom.*	ἡ	ὁδός	αἱ	ὁδοί
Gen.	τῆς	ὁδοῦ	τῶν	ὁδῶν
Dat.	τῇ	ὁδῷ	ταῖς	ὁδοῖς
Acc.	τὴν	ὁδόν	τὰς	ὁδούς
Voc.	ὦ	ὁδέ	ὦ	ὁδοί

Other feminine nouns of the second declension are ἡ θεός, ἡ νῆσος, ἡ παρθένος, and many names of towns, e.g., ἡ Κόρινθος and ἡ Σάμος.

Neuter (see pages 27–28):

	Singular		Plural	
3. *Nom.*	τὸ	δένδρον	τὰ	δένδρα
Gen.	τοῦ	δένδρου	τῶν	δένδρων
Dat.	τῷ	δένδρῳ	τοῖς	δένδροις
Acc.	τὸ	δένδρον	τὰ	δένδρα
Voc.	ὦ	δένδρον	ὦ	δένδρα

Second declension nouns with an acute accent on the final syllable (e.g., ὁ ἀγρός and ἡ ὁδός) have a circumflex accent on the genitive and dative, singular and plural.

Contract (Masculine and Neuter):

ὁ νοῦς (see page 192)

	Singular			Plural		
4. *Nom.*	ὁ	νόο-ς >	νοῦς	οἱ	νόοι >	νοῖ
Gen.	τοῦ	νόου >	νοῦ	τῶν	νόων >	νῶν
Dat.	τῷ	νόῳ >	νῷ	τοῖς	νόοις >	νοῖς
Acc.	τὸν	νόο-ν >	νοῦν	τοὺς	νόους >	νοῦς
Voc.	ὦ	νόε >	νοῦ	ὦ	νόοι >	νοῖ

5. τὸ κανοῦν (rare; not formally presented in this course; for an example, see 9β:6)

6.   NOUNS OF THE THIRD DECLENSION

Four types of nouns of the third declension may be distinguished; the following serve as examples:

Type 1: Consonant Stems:
ὁ παῖς (παιδ-) (see page 71)
τὸ ὄνομα (ὀνοματ-) (see page 71)
ὁ χειμών (χειμων-) (see page 78)

	Singular			*Plural*

Stem: παιδ-

Nom.	ὁ	παῖς	οἱ	παῖδ-ες
Gen.	τοῦ	παιδ-ός	τῶν	παίδ-ων
Dat.	τῷ	παιδ-ί	τοῖς	παιδ-σί(ν) > παισί(ν)
Acc.	τὸν	παῖδ-α	τοὺς	παῖδ-ας
Voc.	ὦ	παῖ	ὦ	παῖδ-ες

Stem: ὀνοματ-

Nom.	τὸ	ὄνομα	τὰ	ὀνόματ-α
Gen.	τοῦ	ὀνόματ-ος	τῶν	ὀνομάτ-ων
Dat.	τῷ	ὀνόματ-ι	τοῖς	ὀνόματ-σι(ν) > ὀνόμασι(ν)
Acc.	τὸ	ὄνομα	τὰ	ὀνόματ-α
Voc.	ὦ	ὄνομα	ὦ	ὀνόματ-α

Stem: χειμων-

Nom.	ὁ	χειμών	οἱ	χειμῶν-ες
Gen.	τοῦ	χειμῶν-ος	τῶν	χειμών-ων
Dat.	τῷ	χειμῶν-ι	τοῖς	χειμῶν-σι(ν) > χειμῶσι(ν)
Acc.	τὸν	χειμῶν-α	τοὺς	χειμῶν-ας
Voc.	ὦ	χειμών	ὦ	χειμῶνες

The case endings (singular: –, -ος, -ι, -ἄ; plural: -ες, -ων, -σι, -ἄς) are added to the stem. The only difficulty arises in the dative plural, where changes occur when the final consonant of the stem is followed by the ending, which begins with a consonant. The rules for these changes are as follows:

a.   If the stem ends in a labial (π, φ, or β), the result is ψι, e.g.: φλέψ, φλεβ-ός, dative plural φλεψί.

b.   If the stem ends in a dental (δ, θ, ν, or τ), drop the last consonant of the stem, e.g.: παῖς, παιδ-ός, dative plural παισί.

c.   If the stem ends in a guttural (κ, γ, or χ), the result is ξι, e.g.: κῆρυξ, κήρῡκ-ος, dative plural κήρῡξι.

d.   If the stem ends in λ or ρ, add the ending -σι to the stem with no change, e.g.: ῥήτωρ, ῥήτορ-ος, dative plural ῥήτορσι.

e. If the stem ends in -οντ, the result is -ουσι, e.g., λέων, λέοντ-ος, dative
    plural λέουσι. (Beware of the resemblance of this form to the third person
    plural present indicative active of verbs.)

These rules also apply to third declension adjectives, the stems of which end
in consonants, e.g.: σώφρων, σώφρον-ος, dative plural σώφροσι. They also
apply to participles, e.g.: λύων, λύοντ-ος, dative plural λύουσι.

All of these dative plural endings may take a movable ν, e.g.: λύουσιν.

It may be noted that third declension nouns with monosyllabic stems, e.g.,
παιδ-, usually have an acute accent on the genitive and dative singular and
plural: παιδός, παιδί, παίδων (exception!), παισί(ν). Otherwise, the accent of
third declension nouns is usually persistent.

Type 2: Stems in -εσ-:

τὸ τεῖχος (τειχεσ-) (see page 164)
ἡ τριήρης (τριηρεσ-) (see page 164)

	Singular		*Plural*		
Nom.	τὸ	τεῖχος	τὰ	τείχε-α >	τείχη
Gen.	τοῦ	τείχε-ος > τείχους	τῶν	τειχέ-ων >	τειχῶν
Dat.	τῷ	τείχε-ι > τείχει	τοῖς	τείχεσ-σι(ν) >	τείχεσι(ν)
Acc.	τὸ	τεῖχος	τὰ	τείχε-α >	τείχη

The σ of the stem drops between the vowel of the stem and the vowel of the
ending, allowing the ε of the stem to contract with the vowels of the endings.
The nouns τὸ κράτος, τὸ ὄρος, and τὸ πλῆθος are declined like τὸ τεῖχος.

	Singular		*Plural*	
Nom.	ἡ	τριήρης	αἱ	τριήρε-ες > τριήρεις
Gen.	τῆς	τριήρε-ος > τριήρους	τῶν	τριηρέ-ων > τριήρων
Dat.	τῇ	τριήρει	ταῖς	τριήρεσ-σι > τριήρεσι.
Acc.	τὴν	τριήρε-α > τριήρη	τὰς	τριήρεις
Voc.	ὦ	τριῆρες	ὦ	τριήρε-ες > τριήρεις

Type 3: Stems Ending in Vowels:

ἡ πόλις (πολι-) (see page 113)
τὸ ἄστυ (ἀστυ-) (see page 113)
ὁ βασιλεύς (βασιλευ-) (see page 108)
ἡ ναῦς (ναυ- originally ναϝ-; note that the stem also appears as νε- and
    νη-) (see page 204)
ὁ βοῦς (βου- originally βοϝ-) (see page 204)

	Singular		*Plural*	
Nom.	ἡ	πόλι-ς	αἱ	πόλε-ες > πόλεις
Gen.	τῆς	πόλε-ως	τῶν	πόλε-ων
Dat.	τῇ	πόλε-ι	ταῖς	πόλε-σι(ν)
Acc.	τὴν	πόλι-ν	τὰς	πόλεις
Voc.	ὦ	πόλι	ὦ	πόλε-ες > πόλεις

A large number of nouns formed from verbs decline like πόλις, e.g.: ἡ ποίησις "making," "creation", "composition." They are all feminine. See page 134.

Note that nouns with stems in ι have their accusative singular in ν instead of α.

Note that in the genitive and dative singular and throughout the plural the stem ends in ε instead of ι and that the ε contracts with the ες nominative plural ending. The accusative plural form is borrowed from the nominative plural.

Nouns declined like πόλις originally had a genitive singular ending in -ηος (πόληος), showing the usual -ος ending for the genitive singular of third declension nouns. In the course of time the quantities of the last two vowels were reversed by a process known as *metathesis*, and the word was spelled πόλεως. The accent remained on the first syllable, in violation of the rule that the third syllable from the end cannot be accented if the final syllable is long. The genitive plural, by analogy, has its accent on the same syllable, also in violation of the rule.

Note the contractions in some of the forms.

	Singular		*Plural*	
Nom.	τὸ	ἄστυ	τὰ	ἄστε-α > ἄστη
Gen.	τοῦ	ἄστε-ως	τῶν	ἄστε-ων
Dat.	τῷ	ἄστε-ι	τοῖς	ἄστε-σι(ν)
Acc.	τὸ	ἄστυ	τὰ	ἄστε-α > ἄστη
Voc.	ὦ	ἄστυ	ὦ	ἄστε-α > ἄστη

Note that the stem ends in ε in the genitive and dative singular and throughout the plural, with contractions occuring in the nominative and accusative plural.

	Singular		*Plural*	
Nom.	ὁ	βασιλεύ-ς	οἱ	βασιλῆς
Gen.	τοῦ	βασιλέ-ως	τῶν	βασιλέ-ων
Dat.	τῷ	βασιλέ-ι (> εῖ)	τοῖς	βασιλεῦ-σι(ν)
Acc.	τὸν	βασιλέ-ᾱ	τοὺς	βασιλέ-ᾱς
Voc.	ὦ	βασιλεῦ	ὦ	βασιλῆς

A small number of nouns decline like βασιλεύς; they are all masculine and designate some occupation, e.g., ὁ ἱερεύς "priest"; ὁ χαλκεύς "bronze smith."

	Singular		*Plural*	
Nom.	ἡ	ναῦ-ς	αἱ	νῆ-ες
Gen.	τῆς	νε-ώς	τῶν	νε-ῶν
Dat.	τῇ	νη-ΐ	ταῖς	ναυ-σί(ν)
Acc.	τὴν	ναῦ-ν	τὰς	ναῦ-ς
Voc.	ὦ	ναῦ	ὦ	νῆ-ες

	Singular		**Plural**	
Nom.	ὁ	βοῦ-ς	οἱ	βό-ες
Gen.	τοῦ	βο-ός	τῶν	βο-ῶν
Dat.	τῷ	βο-ΐ	τοῖς	βου-σί(ν)
Acc.	τὸν	βοῦ-ν	τοὺς	βοῦ-ς
Voc.	ὦ	βοῦ	ὦ	βό-ες

Note that the stem also appears as βο-.

As with nouns with stems in ι, these nouns (ναῦς and βοῦς) have their accusative singular in ν.

The nominative singular and the accusative plural of ναῦς and βοῦς are spelled the same; in context they will often be distinguished by accompanying definite articles.

Type 4: Stems with Three Forms of Gradation (ηρ, ερ, and ρ)

See page 92 for the following examples:

ὁ ἀνήρ (ἀνηρ-, ἀνερ-, and ἀνδρ-)
ὁ πατήρ (πατηρ-, πατερ-, and πατρ-)
ἡ μήτηρ (μητηρ-, μητερ-, and μητρ-)
ἡ θυγάτηρ (θυγατηρ-, θυγατερ-, and θυγατρ-)

These nouns show long vowel, short vowel, and zero grade stems. The accents of πατήρ, μήτηρ, and θυγάτηρ are the same except in the nominative singular.

ὁ	ἀνήρ	ὁ	πατήρ	ἡ	μήτηρ	ἡ	θυγάτηρ
τοῦ	ἀνδρός	τοῦ	πατρός	τῆς	μητρός	τῆς	θυγατρός
τῷ	ἀνδρί	τῷ	πατρί	τῇ	μητρί	τῇ	θυγατρί
τὸν	ἄνδρα	τὸν	πατέρα	τὴν	μητέρα	τὴν	θυγατέρα
ὦ	ἄνερ	ὦ	πάτερ	ὦ	μῆτερ	ὦ	θύγατερ
οἱ	ἄνδρες	οἱ	πατέρες	αἱ	μητέρες	αἱ	θυγατέρες
τῶν	ἀνδρῶν	τῶν	πατέρων	τῶν	μητέρων	τῶν	θυγατέρων
τοῖς	ἀνδράσι(ν)	τοῖς	πατράσι(ν)	ταῖς	μητράσι(ν)	ταῖς	θυγατράσι(ν)
τοὺς	ἄνδρας	τοὺς	πατέρας	τὰς	μητέρας	τὰς	θυγατέρας
ὦ	ἄνδρες	ὦ	πατέρες	ὦ	μητέρες	ὦ	θυγατέρες

7. ADJECTIVES AND PARTICIPLES OF THE FIRST AND SECOND
    DECLENSIONS

    Adjectives (see pages 38–39)

	Singular			*Plural*		
	M.	*F.*	*N.*	*M.*	*F.*	*N.*
Nom.	καλός	καλή	καλόν	καλοί	καλαί	καλά
Gen.	καλοῦ	καλῆς	καλοῦ	καλῶν	καλῶν	καλῶν
Dat.	καλῷ	καλῇ	καλῷ	καλοῖς	καλαῖς	καλοῖς
Acc.	καλόν	καλήν	καλόν	καλούς	καλάς	καλά
Voc.	καλέ	καλή	καλόν	καλοί	καλαί	καλά

Note that adjectives such as καλός that have an acute accent on the final
syllable have circumflex acccents in the genitive and dative, singular and
plural, in all genders.

Note that adjectives with ε, ι, or ρ preceding -ος have feminine endings that
show ᾱ instead of η in the singular (like the noun ἡ οἰκίᾱ), e.g., ῥᾴδιος, ῥᾳδίᾱ,
ῥᾴδιον and ἐλεύθερος, ἐλευθέρᾱ, ἐλεύθερον. Note that since the α is long the
accent shifts toward the end of the word:

	Singular			*Plural*		
	M.	*F.*	*N.*	*M.*	*F.*	*N.*
Nom.	ῥᾴδιος	ῥᾳδίᾱ	ῥᾴδιον	ῥᾴδιοι	ῥᾴδιαι	ῥᾴδια
Gen.	ῥᾳδίου	ῥᾳδίᾱς	ῥᾳδίου	ῥᾳδίων	ῥᾳδίων	ῥᾳδίων
Dat.	ῥᾳδίῳ	ῥᾳδίᾳ	ῥᾳδίῳ	ῥᾳδίοις	ῥᾳδίαις	ῥᾳδίοις
Acc.	ῥᾴδιον	ῥᾳδίᾱν	ῥᾴδιον	ῥᾳδίους	ῥᾳδίᾱς	ῥᾴδια
Voc.	ῥᾴδιε	ῥᾳδίᾱ	ῥᾴδιον	ῥᾴδιοι	ῥᾴδιαι	ῥᾴδια

A fair number of first and second declension adjectives, including all
compound adjectives (including those with α-privative; see page 148), have no
separate feminine form, e.g.: ἔρημος, -ον, ἵλαος, -ον, and ἀναίτιος, -ον.

Participles (see pages 84–85, 86, and 191)
λῡ-ό-μενος

	Masculine	*Feminine*	*Neuter*
Nom.	λῡόμενος	λῡομένη	λῡόμενον
Gen.	λῡομένου	λῡομένης	λῡομένου
Dat.	λῡομένῳ	λῡομένη	λῡομένῳ
Acc.	λῡόμενον	λῡομένην	λῡόμενον
Nom.	λῡόμενοι	λῡόμεναι	λῡόμενα
Gen.	λῡομένων	λῡομένων	λῡομένων
Dat.	λῡομένοις	λῡομέναις	λῡομένοις
Acc.	λῡομένους	λῡομένᾱς	λῡόμενα

φιλε-ό-μενος > φιλούμενος

Nom.	φιλούμενος	φιλουμένη	φιλούμενον
Gen.	φιλουμένου	φιλουμένης	φιλουμένου
Dat.	φιλουμένῳ	φιλουμένῃ	φιλουμένῳ
Acc.	φιλούμενον	φιλουμένην	φιλούμενον
Nom.	φιλούμενοι	φιλούμεναι	φιλούμενα
Gen.	φιλουμένων	φιλουμένων	φιλουμένων
Dat.	φιλουμένοις	φιλουμέναις	φιλουμένοις
Acc.	φιλουμένους	φιλουμένᾱς	φιλούμενα

τῑμα-ό-μενος > τῑμώμενος

Nom.	τῑμώμενος	τῑμωμένη	τῑμώμενον

δηλο-ύ-μενος > δηλούμενος

Nom.	δηλούμενος	δηλουμένη	δηλούμενον

For the first and second aorist middle participles, see pages 142 and 129:

Nom.	λῡσάμενος	λῡσαμένη	λῡσάμενον
Nom.	γενόμενος	γενομένη	γενομένον

8. ADJECTIVES OF IRREGULAR DECLENSION

The adjectives μέγας, μεγάλη, μέγα and πολύς, πολλή, πολύ (see page 39) have the endings of first and second declension adjectives except in the masculine and neuter nominative and accusative singular forms, where shorter stems are used (μεγα- instead of μεγαλο- and πολυ- instead of πολλο-).

	M.	F.	N.	M.	F.	N.
Nom.	μέγας	μεγάλη	μέγα	μεγάλοι	μεγάλαι	μεγάλα
Gen.	μεγάλου	μεγάλης	μεγάλου	μεγάλων	μεγάλων	μεγάλων
Dat.	μεγάλῳ	μεγάλῃ	μεγάλῳ	μεγάλοις	μεγάλαις	μεγάλοις
Acc.	μέγαν	μεγάλην	μέγα	μεγάλους	μεγάλᾱς	μεγάλα
Voc.	μέγας	μεγάλη	μέγα	μεγάλοι	μεγάλαι	μεγάλα
Nom.	πολύς	πολλή	πολύ	πολλοί	πολλαί	πολλά
Gen.	πολλοῦ	πολλῆς	πολλοῦ	πολλῶν	πολλῶν	πολλῶν
Dat.	πολλῷ	πολλῇ	πολλῷ	πολλοῖς	πολλαῖς	πολλοῖς
Acc.	πολύν	πολλήν	πολύ	πολλούς	πολλάς	πολλά
Voc.	none					

9. ADJECTIVES OF THE THIRD DECLENSION

Adjectives with stems in -ov-:

σώφρων, σῶφρον, (genitive) σώφρον-ος (see page 78)

	Singular		*Plural*	
	M. & F.	**N.**	**M. & F.**	**N.**
Nom.	σώφρων	σῶφρον	σώφρον-ες	σώφρον-α
Gen.	σώφρον-ος	σώφρον-ος	σωφρόν-ων	σωφρόν-ων
Dat.	σώφρον-ι	σώφρον-ι	σώφρον-σι >	σώφρον-σι >
			σώφροσι(ν)	σώφροσι(ν)
Acc.	σώφρον-α	σῶφρον	σώφρον-ας	σώφρον-α
Voc.	σῶφρον	σῶφρον	σώφρον-ες	σώφρον-α

The endings are added directly to the stem; in the dative plural the ν of the stem drops. Compare the discussion of third declension consonant stem nouns above.

The irregular comparative adjectives (see page 171), such as ἀμείνων, ἄμεινον, are declined like σώφρων, σῶφρον, but have some alternative forms that will be presented in Book II.

Adjectives with stems in -εσ-:

ἀληθής, ἀληθές (stem ἀληθεσ-), genitive αληθέ(σ)-ος > ἀληθοῦς. (See page 164)

	Masc./Fem.		*Neut.*	
Nom.	ἀληθής		ἀληθές	
Gen.	ἀληθέ-ος >	ἀληθοῦς	ἀληθέ-ος >	ἀληθοῦς
Dat.	ἀληθέ-ι >	ἀληθεῖ	ἀληθέ-ι >	ἀληθεῖ
Acc.	ἀληθέ-α >	ἀληθῆ	ἀληθές	
Nom.	ἀληθέ-ες >	ἀληθεῖς	ἀληθέ-α >	ἀληθῆ
Gen.	ἀληθέ-ων >	ἀληθῶν	ἀληθέ-ων >	ἀληθῶν
Dat.	ἀληθέσ-σι(ν) >	ἀληθέσι(ν)	ἀληθέσ-σι(ν) >	ἀληθέσι(ν)
Acc.	ἀληθεῖς		ἀληθέ-α >	ἀληθῆ

As with third declension nouns with stems in -εσ- discussed above, the σ of the stem drops out before the endings, allowing the vowels to contract.

10. ADJECTIVES AND PARTICIPLES OF MIXED DECLENSION

Adjectives
πᾶς, πᾶσα, πᾶν (see page 92–93).

	Masculine	*Feminine*	*Neuter*
Nom.	πᾶς	πᾶσα	πᾶν
Gen.	παντ-ός	πάσης	παντ-ός
Dat.	παντ-ί	πάσῃ	παντ-ί
Acc.	πάντ-α	πᾶσαν	πᾶν
Nom.	πάντ-ες	πᾶσαι	πάντ-α
Gen.	πάντ-ων	πασῶν	πάντ-ων
Dat.	πάντ-σι(ν) > πᾶσι(ν)	πάσαις	πάντ-σι(ν) > πᾶσι(ν)
Acc.	πάντ-ας	πάσᾱς	πάντ-α

Here the masculine and neuter have third declension forms, and the feminine has first declension forms. Here the feminine endings are like those of ἡ θάλαττα, with η appearing in the genitive and dative. Note that as with θάλαττα the final α of πᾶσα is short (this is apparent from the accent of the word).]

ταχύς, ταχεῖα, ταχύ

	Masculine	*Feminine*	*Neuter*
Nom.	ταχύ ς	ταχεῖα	ταχύ
Gen.	ταχέ-ος	ταχείᾱς	ταχέ-ος
Dat.	ταχεῖ	ταχείᾳ	ταχεῖ
Acc.	ταχύ-ν	ταχεῖαν	ταχύ
Nom.	ταχεῖς	ταχεῖαι	ταχέ-α
Gen.	ταχέ-ων	ταχειῶν	ταχέ-ων
Dat.	ταχέ-σι(ν)	ταχείαις	ταχέ-σι(ν)
Acc.	ταχεῖς	ταχείᾱς	ταχέ-α

Participles
The present active participle is also of mixed declension and ends in short α in the feminine nominative singular:

	Masculine	*Feminine*	*Neuter*
εἰμί (see page 99):			
Nom.	ὤν	οὖσα	ὄν
Gen.	ὄντος	οὔσης	ὄντος
Dat.	ὄντι	οὔσῃ	ὄντι
Acc.	ὄντα	οὖσαν	ὄν

Nom.	ὄντες	οὖσαι	ὄντα
Gen.	ὄντων	οὐσῶν	ὄντων
Dat.	οὖσι(ν)	οὔσαις	οὖσι(ν)
Acc.	ὄντας	οὔσᾱς	ὄντα

λύω (see page 100):

Nom.	λῡ́-ων	λῡ́-ουσα	λῦ-ον
Gen.	λῡ́-οντος	λῡ-ούσης	λῡ́-οντος
Dat.	λῡ́-οντι	λῡ-ούσῃ	λῡ́-οντι
Acc.	λῡ́-οντα	λῡ́-ουσαν	λῦ-ον

Nom.	λῡ́-οντες	λῡ́-ουσαι	λῡ́-οντα
Gen.	λῡ-όντων	λῡ-ουσῶν	λῡ-όντων
Dat.	λῡ́-ουσι(ν)	λῡ-ούσαις	λῡ́-ουσι(ν)
Acc.	λῡ́-οντας	λῡ-ούσᾱς	λῡ́-οντα

φιλέω (see page 100):

Nom.	φιλῶν	φιλοῦσα	φιλοῦν
Gen.	φιλοῦντος	φιλούσης	φιλοῦντος
Dat.	φιλοῦντι	φιλούσῃς	φιλοῦντι
Acc.	φιλοῦντα	φιλοῦσαν	φιλοῦν

Nom.	φιλοῦντες	φιλοῦσαι	φιλοῦντα
Gen.	φιλούντων	φιλουσῶν	φιλούντων
Dat.	φιλοῦσι	φιλούσαις	φιλοῦσι
Acc.	φιλοῦντας	φιλούσᾱς	φιλοῦντα

τῑμάω (see page 100):

Nom.	τῑμῶν	τῑμῶσα	τῑμῶν
Gen.	τῑμῶντος	τῑμῶσης	τῑμῶντος
Dat.	τῑμῶντι	τῑμώσῃ	τῑμῶντι
Acc.	τῑμῶντα	τῑμῶσαν	τῑμῶν

Nom.	τῑμῶντες	τῑμῶσαι	τῑμῶντα
Gen.	τῑμώντων	τῑμωσῶν	τῑμώντων
Dat.	τῑμῶσι	τῑμώσαις	τῑμῶσι
Acc.	τῑμῶντας	τῑμώσᾱς	τῑμῶντα

δηλόω (see page 191; declined like φιλῶν above; we give only the nominative):   δηλῶν   δηλοῦσα   δηλοῦν

λύω (first aorist; see page 142):

Nom.	λῡ́σᾱς	λῡ́σᾱσα	λῦσαν
Gen.	λῡ́σαντ-ος	λῡσάσης	λῡ́σαντ-ος
Dat.	λῡ́σαντ-ι	λῡσάσῃ	λῡ́σαντ-ι
Acc.	λῡ́σαντ-α	λῡ́σᾱσαν	λῦσαν

Nom.	λύσαντ-ες	λύσᾱσαι	λύσαντ-α
Gen.	λῡσάντ-ων	λῡσᾱσῶν	λῡσάντ-ων
Dat.	λύσᾱσι(ν)	λῡσάσαις	λύσᾱσι(ν)
Acc.	λύσαντ-ας	λῡσάσᾱς	λύσαντ-α

λαμβάνω (second aorist; see page 128)

Nom.	λαβ-ών	λαβ-οῦσα	λαβ-όν
Gen.	λαβ-όντος	λαβ-ούσης	λαβ-όντος
Dat.	λαβ-όντι	λαβ-ούσῃ	λαβ-όντι
Acc.	λαβ-όντα	λαβ-οῦσαν	λαβ-όν

Nom.	λαβ-όντες	λαβ-οῦσαι	λαβ-όντα
Gen.	λαβ-όντων	λαβ-ουσῶν	λαβ-όντων
Dat.	λαβ-οῦσι(ν)	λαβ-ούσαις	λαβ-οῦσι(ν)
Acc.	λαβ-όντας	λαβ-ούσᾱς	λαβ-όντα

11. COMPARISON OF ADJECTIVES

See pages 170–171.

Positive	Comparative	Superlative
ἀνδρεῖος	ἀνδρειότερος	ἀνδρειότατος
χαλεπός	χαλεπώτερος	χαλεπώτατος

Note: as in the example just above, the o at the end of the stem of the positive is lengthened to ω if the syllable preceding it is regarded as short (e.g., contains a short vowel).

| ἀληθής | ἀληθέστερος | ἀληθέστατος |
| σώφρων | σωφρονέστερος | σωφρονέστατος |

Many of the most common adjectives have irregular comparatives in -ιων or -ων (masc. and fem.) and -ιον or -ον (neuter) and superlatives in -ιστος, -η, -ον, (see page 171), e.g.:

ἀγαθός, -ή, -όν	ἀμείνων, ἄμεινον	ἄριστος, -η, ον
κακός, -ή, -όν	κακίων, κάκιον	κάκιστος, -η, -ον
καλός, -ή, -όν	καλλίων, κάλλιον	κάλλιστος, -η, -ον
μέγας, μεγάλη, μέγα	μείζων, μεῖζον	μέγιστος, -η, -ον
ὀλίγος, -η, -ον	ἐλάττων, ἔλαττον	ὀλίγιστος, -η, -ον
πολύς, πολλή, πολύ	πλείων/πλέων, πλεῖον, πλέον	πλεῖστος, -η, -ον

The comparatives ending in -ιων or -ων and -ιον or -ον decline like σώφρων, σῶφρον (see page 78), but they have some alternative forms that will be presented in Book II.

For the use of comparative and superlative adjectives in sentences, see page 172.

12. DEMONSTRATIVE ADJECTIVES

οὗτος, αὕτη, τοῦτο this (see page 178)

	Singular			Plural		
	Masc.	*Fem.*	*Neuter*	*Masc.*	*Fem.*	*Neuter*
Nom.	οὗτος	αὕτη	τοῦτο	οὗτοι	αὗται	ταῦτα
Gen.	τούτου	ταύτης	τούτου	τούτων	τούτων	τούτων
Dat.	τούτῳ	ταύτῃ	τούτῳ	τούτοις	ταύταις	τούτοις
Acc.	τοῦτον	ταύτην	τοῦτο	τούτους	ταύτας	ταῦτα

Declined in the same way is τοσοῦτος, τοσαύτη, τοσοῦτο "so great"; (*plural*) "so many," "so great."

ἐκεῖνος, ἐκείνη, ἐκεῖνο that (see page 179):

	Singular			Plural		
	Masc.	*Fem.*	*Neuter*	*Masc.*	*Fem.*	*Neuter*
Nom.	ἐκεῖνος	ἐκείνη	ἐκεῖνο	ἐκεῖνοι	ἐκεῖναι	ἐκεῖνα
Gen.	ἐκείνου	ἐκείνης	ἐκείνου	ἐκείνων	ἐκείνων	ἐκείνων
Dat.	ἐκείνῳ	ἐκείνῃ	ἐκείνῳ	ἐκείνοις	ἐκείναις	ἐκείνοις
Acc.	ἐκεῖνον	ἐκείνην	ἐκεῖνο	ἐκείνους	ἐκείνᾱς	ἐκεῖνα

Note that the neuter nominative and accusative singular of this and the above adjectives end in -o instead of -ov.

ὅδε, ἥδε, τόδε this here (formed from the definite article plus -δε; see page 179):

	Singular			Plural		
	Masc.	*Fem.*	*Neuter*	*Masc.*	*Fem.*	*Neuter*
Nom.	ὅδε	ἥδε	τόδε	οἵδε	αἵδε	τάδε
Gen.	τοῦδε	τῆσδε	τοῦδε	τῶνδε	τῶνδε	τῶνδε
Dat.	τῷδε	τῇδε	τῷδε	τοῖσδε	ταῖσδε	τοῖσδε
Acc.	τόνδε	τήνδε	τόδε	τούσδε	τάσδε	τάδε

Note that οὗτος, ἐκεῖνος, and ὅδε are used with the definite article and stand outside the definite article-noun group, that is, in the predicate position, e.g.: αὗται αἱ γυναῖκες "these women."

13. THE ADJECTIVE αὐτός

	Masculine	Feminine	Neuter
Nom.	αὐτός	αὐτή	αὐτό
Gen.	αὐτοῦ	αὐτῆς	αὐτοῦ
Dat.	αὐτῷ	αὐτῇ	αὐτῷ
Acc.	αὐτόν	αὐτήν	αὐτό

Nom.	αὐτοί	αὐταί	αὐτά
Gen.	αὐτῶν	αὐτῶν	αὐτῶν
Dat.	αὐτοῖς	αὐταῖς	αὐτοῖς
Acc.	αὐτούς	αὐτάς	αὐτά

For the use of this adjective as a pronoun in the genitive, dative, and accusative cases, see pages 50–51 and see below under Personal Pronouns. For its use as an adjective, see page 51.

As an adjective, αὐτός is intensive and may emphasize the subject of the sentence or modify a noun in any case, e.g.:

αὐτὸς αἴρει τὸν λίθον.
He *himself* lifts the stone.

ἡ παρθένος **αὐτὴ** προσῆλθε πρὸς τὴν κρήνην.
The girl *herself* approached the spring.

εἶδον **αὐτὴν** τὴν παρθένον προσιοῦσαν πρὸς τὴν κρήνην.
I saw the girl *herself* approaching the spring.

The adjective here stands in the predicate position *outside* the article-noun group.

When the adjective stands in the attributive position *between* the article and its noun, it means *same*, e.g.:

ἡ **αὐτὴ** παρθένος προσῆλθε πρὸς τὸν οἶκον.
The *same* girl approached the house.

14. THE INTERROGATIVE ADJECTIVE

For the interrogative adjective τίς, τί "what?" "which?" see page 79. This adjective always has an acute accent on the first syllable.

Stem: τιν-

	Singular		*Plural*	
	M. & F.	**N.**	**M. & F.**	**N.**
Nom.	τίς	τί	τίν-ες	τίν-α
Gen.	τίν-ος	τίν-ος	τίν-ων	τίν-ων
Dat.	τίν-ι	τίν-ι	τίν-σι > τίσι	τίν-σι > τίσι
Acc.	τίν-α	τί	τίν-ας	τίν-α

εἰς **τίνα** νῆσον πλέομεν;
To *what* island are we sailing?

15.   THE INDEFINITE ADJECTIVE

For the indefinite adjective τις, τι, "a certain," "a," "an," see page 79. This adjective is enclitic.

Stem: τιν-

	Singular		**Plural**	
	M. & F.	**N.**	**M. & F.**	**N.**
Nom.	τις	τι	τιν-ές	τιν-ά
Gen.	τιν-ός	τιν-ός	τιν-ῶν	τιν-ῶν
Dat.	τιν-ί	τιν-ί	τιν-σί > τισί	τιν-σί > τισί
Acc.	τιν-ά	τι	τιν-άς	τιν-ά

Πλέουσί ποτε εἰς νῆσόν **τινα** μῑκράν.
Once they sail to *a certain* little island.

16.   PERSONAL PRONOUNS

	1st Person Singular			**1st Person Plural**	
Nom.	ἐγώ		I	ἡμεῖς	we
Gen.	ἐμοῦ	μου	of me	ἡμῶν	of us
Dat.	ἐμοί	μοι	to *or* for me	ἡμῖν	to *or* for us
Acc.	ἐμέ	με	me	ἡμᾶς	us

	2nd Person Singular			**2nd Person Plural**	
Nom.	σύ		you	ὑμεῖς	you
Gen.	σοῦ	σου	of you	ὑμῶν	of you
Dat.	σοί	σοι	to *or* for you	ὑμῖν	to *or* for you
Acc.	σέ	σε	you	ὑμᾶς	you

See page 50. The unaccented forms are unemphatic and enclitic.

There is no 3rd person pronoun; in the genitive, dative, and accusative cases, forms of αὐτός "self" are used in its place (see pages 50–51):

	Masculine		**Feminine**		**Neuter**	
G.	αὐτοῦ	of him *or* it	αὐτῆς	of her *or* it	αὐτοῦ	of it
D.	αὐτῷ	to *or* for him *or* it	αὐτῇ	to *or* for her *or* it	αὐτῷ	to it
A.	αὐτόν	him *or* it	αὐτήν	her *or* it	αὐτό	i t
G.	αὐτῶν	of them	αὐτῶν	of them	αὐτῶν	of them
D.	αὐτοῖς	to *or* for them	αὐταῖς	to *or* for them	αὐτοῖς	to *or* for them
A.	αὐτούς	them	αὐτάς	them	αὐτά	them

17. REFLEXIVE PRONOUNS

	First Person		*Second Person*	
	Masculine	*Feminine*	*Masculine*	*Feminine*
G.	ἐμαυτοῦ	ἐμαυτῆς	σεαυτοῦ	σεαυτῆς
D.	ἐμαυτῷ	ἐμαυτῇ	σεαυτῷ	σεαυτῇ
A.	ἐμαυτόν	ἐμαυτήν	σεαυτόν	σεαυτήν
G.	ἡμῶν αὐτῶν	ἡμῶν αὐτῶν	ὑμῶν αὐτῶν	ὑμῶν αὐτῶν
D.	ἡμῖν αὐτοῖς	ἡμῖν αὐταῖς	ὑμῖν αὐτοῖς	ὑμῖν αὐταῖς
A.	ἡμᾶς αὐτούς	ἡμᾶς αὐτάς	ὑμᾶς αὐτούς	ὑμᾶς αὐτάς

	Third Person		
	Masculine	*Feminine*	*Neuter*
G.	ἑαυτοῦ	ἑαυτῆς	ἑαυτοῦ
D.	ἑαυτῷ	ἑαυτῇ	ἑαυτῷ
A.	ἑαυτόν	ἑαυτήν	ἑαυτό
G.	ἑαυτῶν	ἑαυτῶν	ἑαυτῶν
D.	ἑαυτοῖς	ἑαυταῖς	ἑαυτοῖς
A.	ἑαυτούς	ἑαυτάς	ἑαυτά

See pages 72–73.

18. THE RECIPROCAL PRONOUN

The pronoun ἀλλήλων "of one another" (introduced in Chapter 13) is used only in the following cases and only in the plural:

	Masculine	*Feminine*	*Neuter*
G.	ἀλλήλων	ἀλλήλων	ἀλλήλων
D.	ἀλλήλοις	ἀλλήλαις	ἀλλήλοις
A.	ἀλλήλους	ἀλλήλας	ἄλλληλα

διελέγοντο **ἀλλήλοις.**
They were talking with *one another*.

19. POSSESSIVES

Possessive Adjectives:	*Singular*	*Plural*
First Person	ἐμός, -ή, -όν my, mine	ἡμέτερος, -ᾱ, -ον our
Second Person	σός, -ή, -όν your	ὑμέτερος, -ᾱ, -ον your

See pages 51–52.

Possessive Pronouns:

Third Person	αὐτοῦ his *or* its	αὐτῶν their
	αυτῆς her *or* hers *or* its	αὐτῶν their
	αὐτοῦ its	αὐτῶν their

See pages 51–52.

The genitive of the reflexive pronoun may be used to show possession.

Note the placement of the genitives with respect to the noun-article group in the following examples:

φιλεῖ τὸν πατέρα **αὑτοῦ**. He loves *his* father.
(I.e., someone else's father; the genitive of αὑτός stands in the predicate position outside the article-noun group.)

φιλεῖ τὸν **ἑαυτῆς** πατέρα. She loves *her own* father.
(literally, "the father of herself"; the genitive of the reflexive pronoun stands in the attributive position between the article and the noun.)

20.   THE INTERROGATIVE PRONOUN

For the interrogative pronoun τίς, τί "who?" "what?" see page 79. Its forms are the same as those of the interrogative adjective (see above) and are not repeated here; it always has an acute accent on the first syllable.

τίνες ἐστέ;
Who are you?

21.   THE INDEFINITE PRONOUN

For the indefinite pronoun τις, τι "someone," "something," "anyone," "anything," see page 79. This pronoun is enclitic, and it has the same forms as the indefinite adjective (see above).

ἆρ' ὁρᾷς **τινὰ** ἐν τῷ ἄντρῳ;
Do you see *anyone* in the cave?

22.   THE RELATIVE PRONOUN

For the relative pronouon ὅς, ἥ, ὅ, "who," "which," "that," etc., see pages 162–163. Distinguish these forms carefully from those of the definite article (see page 40).

	Singular			*Plural*		
	Masc.	*Fem.*	*Neut.*	*Masc.*	*Fem.*	*Neut.*
Nom.	ὅς	ἥ	ὅ	οἵ	αἵ	ἅ
Gen.	οὗ	ἧς	οὗ	ὧν	ὧν	ὧν
Dat.	ᾧ	ᾗ	ᾧ	οἷς	αἷς	οἷς
Acc.	ὅν	ἥν	ὅ	οὕς	ἅς	ἅ

Relative pronouns introduce relative clauses, and the pronouns agree with their antecedents in gender and number and take their case from their use in their own clause, e.g.:

οὗτος ὁ ἄνθρωπος, **ὅν** ἐν τῇ νηὶ φέρομεν, κακός ἐστιν.
This man, *whom* we are carrying in the ship, is bad.
(The relative pronoun is masculine and singular because its antecedent, ἄνθρωπος, is masculine and singular; it is accusative because it is the direct object of φέρομεν in its own clause.)

23. FORMATION OF ΛDVERBS

Adverbs regularly have the same spelling and accent as the genitive plural of the corresponding adjective, but with the final ν changed to ς (see page 39):

Adjective καλός (genitive plural καλῶν) > adverb καλῶς
Adjective σώφρων (genitive plural σωφρόνων) > adverb σωφρόνως
Adjective ἀληθής (genitive plural ἀληθῶν) > adverb ἀληθῶς
Λdjective ταχύς (genitive plural ταχέων) > adverb ταχέως

24. COMPARISON OF ADVERBS

For the comparative adverb the neuter singular of the comparative adjective is used, and for the superlative the neuter plural of the superlative adjective (see pages 171–172), e.g.:

ἀνδρείως	ἀνδρειότερον	ἀνδρειότατα
χαλεπῶς	χαλεπώτερον	χαλεπώτατα
ἀληθῶς	ἀληθέστερον	ἀληθέστατα
σωφρόνως	σωφρονέστερον	σωφρονέστατα

For common irregular adverbs, see page 172.

εὖ	ἄμεινον	ἄριστα
κακῶς	κάκῑον	κάκιστα
πόλυ	πλέυν	πλεῖστα
μάλα	μᾶλλον	μάλιστα

For the use of comparative and superlative adverbs in sentences, see page 172.

25. INTERROGATIVE AND INDEFINITE ADVERBS

For the corresponding forms of some of the common interrogative and indefinite adverbs, see page 180.

Interrogative		*Indefinite*	
ποῦ;	where?	που	somewhere, anywhere
πόθεν	where from?	ποθέν	from somewhere
ποῖ	where to?	ποι	to somewhere
πότε	when?	ποτέ	at some time, ever
πῶς	how?	πως	somehow, in any way

26. NUMBERS

For the cardinal and ordinal numbers from one to ten, see page 93. For more numbers, see page 205.

The Greek numbers from one to twenty are:

1	εἷς, μία, ἕν	11	ἕνδεκα
2	δύο	12	δώδεκα
3	τρεῖς, τρία	13	τρεῖς (τρία) καὶ δέκα or τρεισκαίδεκα
4	τέτταρες, τέτταρα	14	τέτταρες (τέτταρα) καὶ δέκα
5	πέντε	15	πεντεκαίδεκα
6	ἕξ	16	ἑκκαίδεκα
7	ἑπτά	17	ἑπτακαίδεκα
8	ὀκτώ	18	ὀκτωκαίδεκα
9	ἐννέα	19	ἐννεακαίδεκα
10	δέκα	20	εἴκοσι(ν)

Other numbers

21	εἷς καὶ εἴκοσι
100	ἑκατόν
1,000	χίλιοι, -αι, -α
10,000	μύριοι, -αι, -α

Forms:

	M.	**F.**	**N.**
Nom.	εἷς	μία	ἕν
Gen.	ἑν-ός	μιᾶς	ἑν-ός
Dat.	ἑν-ί	μιᾷ	ἑν-ί
Acc.	ἕν-α	μίαν	ἕν

The word οὐδείς, οὐδεμία, οὐδέν or μηδείς, μηδεμία, μηδέν (*pronoun / adjective*) "no one," "no," is declined exactly like εἷς, μία, ἕν (see page 93).

	M. F. N.	**M. F.**	**N.**	**M. F.**	**N.**
Nom.	δύο	τρεῖς	τρία	τέτταρες	τέτταρα
Gen.	δυοῖν	τριῶν	τριῶν	τεττάρων	τεττάρων
Dat.	δυοῖν	τρισί(ν)	τρισί(ν)	τέτταρσι(ν)	τέτταρσι(ν)
Acc.	δύο	τρεῖς	τρία	τέτταρας	τέτταρα

The ordinals ("first," "second," "third," etc.) are as follows:

1st	πρῶτος, -η, -ον	6th	ἕκτος, -η, -ον
2nd	δεύτερος, -ᾱ, -ον	7th	ἕβδομος, -η, -ον
3rd	τρίτος, -η, -ον	8th	ὄγδοος, -η, -ον
4th	τέταρτος, -η, -ον	9th	ἔνατος, -η, -ον
5th	πέμπτος, -η, -ον	10th	δέκατος, -η, -ον

11th   ἑνδέκατος, -η, -ον
12th   δωδέκατος, -η, -ον
20th   εἰκοστός, -ή, -όν
100th   ἑκατοστός
1,000th   χῑλιοστός, -ή, -όν
10,000th   μῡριοστός, -ή, -όν

The ordinals are declined as first and second declension adjectives.

27. PREPOSITIONS

The following list includes all of the prepositions that have occurred in the readings in Book I. Prepositions generally have a range of meanings that must be learned by observation of their use in context. In the following list asterisks mark those prepositions and meanings that should be thoroughly learned by the completion of Book I.

ἅμα (+ *dat.*)
    together with, with: ἅμα τῷ παιδί (5a:22)
*ἀνά (+ *acc.*)
    *up: ἀνὰ τὴν ὁδόν (5a:4)
*ἀπό (+ *gen.*)
    *from: ἀπὸ τοῦ ἄστεως (4α:20)
*διά (+ *gen.*)
    *through: δι' ὀλίγου (= "soon," 5α:8)
*διά (+ *acc.*)
    *because of: διὰ τί (3α:5)
*ἐγγύς (+ *gen.*)
    *near: ἐγγὺς τῆς οἰκίας (9 tail reading:8)
*εἰς (+ *acc.*)
    *into: εἰς τὸν ἀγρόν (2β:3)
    *to: εἰς τὴν κρήνην (4 tail reading:1)
    *at (with verbs such as ἀφικνέομαι): εἰς τὴν νῆσον (6α:14)
    onto: εἰς τὴν γῆν (16β:33–34)
    for: εἰς πολλὰς ἡμέρᾱς
*ἐκ, ἐξ (+ *gen.*)
    *out of: ἐκ τοῦ ἀγροῦ (1β:2), ἐξ ἔργων (8α:16)
*ἐν (+ *dat.*)
    *in: ἐν ταῖς 'Αθήναις (1α:1–2)
    *on: ἐν τῇ ὁδῷ (4β:9)
    among: ἐν τοῖς δούλοις (11 tail reading: 5)
ἐντός (+ *gen.*)
    within: λιμένος πολυβενθέος ἐντός (16β:30)
*ἐπί (+ *dat.*)
    at: ἐπὶ τῇ θύρᾳ (9 tail reading:10)
    *upon, on: ἐπὶ τῇ γῇ (5β:15)
*ἐπί (+ *acc.*)
    *at, against: ἐπ' αὐτόν (5β:7–8)

*onto (with ἀναβαίνω): ἐπὶ ἄκρᾱν τὴν ἀκτήν (7 tail reading:4)
   upon: ἐπὶ τὸν ὄχθον (15 tail reading:3)
κατά (+ *acc.*)
   *down: κατὰ τὴν ὁδόν (5 tail reading:5)
   distributive: κατ' ἔτος (= "each year," 6α:5)
   *by: κατὰ θάλατταν (11α:38)
   on: κατὰ τοῦτο τοῦ ὄρους (14 tail reading:6)
   at: κατ' οἶκον (16α:30)
μετά (+ *gen.*)
   *with: μετὰ τῶν ἑταίρων (6α:11)
μετά (+ *acc.*) (of time and place)
   *after: μετὰ τὸ δεῖπνον (3β:7)
   *after: μετὰ αὐτούς (5α:10)
ὄπισθεν (+ *gen.*)
   behind: ὄπισθεν τοῦ ἱεροῦ (9α:35)
παρά (+ *acc.*)
   *to (of persons only): παρὰ ἰᾱτρόν τινα (11α:3–4)
   along, past: παρὰ τὴν Σικελίᾱν (10 tail reading: 2)
περί (+ *acc.*)
   *around: περὶ Τροίᾱν (7α:8)
πλήν (+ *acc.*)
   except: πλὴν ἑνός (8 tail reading:7)
πρό (+ *gen.*)
   *before (of time or place): πρὸ τῆς νυκτός (10β:3)
πρός (+ *dat.*)
   *at: πρὸς τῇ κρήνῃ (4:title)
   *near, by: πρὸς τῇ ὁδῷ (5 tail reading:9)
πρός (+ *acc.*)
   *to, toward: πρὸς τὸ ἕρμα (1β:3)
   *against: πρὸς τοὺς λίθους (11β:3–4)
   upon: πρὸς τὸν τοῦ Δικαιοπόλιδος πόδα (3α:17)
σύν (+ *dat.*)
   with: σὺν θεῷ (12β:30–31)
ὑπέρ (+ *gen.*)
   *on behalf of, for: ὑπὲρ σοῦ (7 tail reading:2)
   over, above: ὑπὲρ Θερμοπυλῶν (14 tail reading, title)
ὑπέρ (+ *acc.*)
   over: ὑπὲρ τὸ ὄρος (14 tail reading:1)
ὑπό (+ *gen.*)
   under: ὑπὸ τῶν οἰῶν (7β:31–32)
ὑπό (+ *dat.*)
   *under: ὑπὸ τῷ δένδρῳ (1β:5)
ὑπό (+ *acc.*)
   under (with verbs of motion): ὑπὸ τὸ ζυγόν (2β:8)

28. VERBS: PRESENT TENSE

a. Regular verbs, e.g., λύω.
   For the forms of λύω, see pages 4, 11, 22, 32, 57, 84, 100, and 119.
   For the middle voice, its meanings, and forms, see pages 56–58.
   For deponent verbs, see pages 56–57.
   Some deponent verbs add endings directly to their stems, and no
   contractions take place (see page 197), e.g., δύνα-μαι, δύνα-σαι, etc. (See
   below.)
   For sets of active and middle voice forms, see page 119.

Indicative	*Imperative*	*Infinitive*	*Participle*

λύω: Active Voice

λύω		λύειν	λύων, λύουσα,
λύεις	λῦε		λῦον
λύει			
λύομεν			
λύετε	λύετε		
λύουσι(ν)			

λύω: Middle Voice

λύομαι		λύεσθαι	λυόμενος, -η,
λύῃ or λύει	λύου		-ον
λύεται			
λυόμεθα			
λύεσθε	λύεσθε		
λύονται			

Note the following:

i.   The active endings -ω, -εις, -ει, ομεν, -ετε, -ουσι(ν) show person,
     number and mood (indicative; see page 11). The middle endings -μαι,
     -σαι, -ται, -μεθα, -σθε, -νται show person and number.
ii. The letter ν (movable ν) is added to the end of the third person plural
     when this form of the verb is followed by a word beginning with a vowel
     (with no punctuation between the two words) or when it comes at the end
     of a sentence.
iii. In the layout of the forms of the middle voice (page 57) note that the
     vowels ο and ε stand between λῡ- and the endings. These are called
     thematic or *variable* vowels, and they regularly alternate in the pattern
     as seen here: ο, ε, ε, ο, ε, ο. Compare, for example, the present
     indicative active forms ending in -ω, -εις, -ει, -ομεν, -ετε, -ουσι,
     which are the result of combinations of this thematic vowel with the
     personal endings.
iv. Note the contraction in the second person singular of the middle voice:
     λύ-ε-σαι > λύῃ. The intervocalic σ drops out, the ε and α contract to η,
     and the ι becomes a subscript. Sometimes this contracted ending is
     written ει. Likewise, in the imperative λύ-ε-σο > λύου.

b.   Contract Verbs in -ε-, -α-, and -ο-

For the forms of the contract verbs in -ε-, see pages 4, 11, 12, 22, 58, 85, and 100. For the full set of forms, see page 120 and below.

For a summary of the way vowels contract in -ε- contract verbs, see page 32. In the set of forms for the middle voice (page 58) note the presence of the thematic vowel, which can here be easily isolated from the personal endings, and note the dropping of intervocalic σ in the second person singular and the singular imperative.

For the forms of the contract verbs in -α-, see pages 44, 85–86, and 100. For the full set of forms, see page 120 and below.

For a summary of the way vowels contract in -α- contract verbs, see page 44.   In the set of forms for the middle voice (page 86) note the presence of the thematic vowel, which can here be easily isolated from the personal endings, and note the dropping of intervocalic σ in the second person singular and the singular imperative.

For the forms and the rules of contraction for verbs with stems in -ο-, see pages 191–192 and below.

φιλέω: Active Voice

φιλῶ		φιλεῖν	φιλῶν, φιλοῦσα,
φιλεῖς	φίλει		φιλοῦν
φιλεῖ			
φιλοῦμεν			
φιλεῖτε	φιλεῖτε		
φιλοῦσι(ν)			

φιλέω: Middle Voice

φιλοῦμαι		φιλεῖσθαι	φιλούμενος, -η,
φιλῇ or φιλεῖ	φιλοῦ		-ον
φιλεῖται			
φιλούμεθα			
φιλεῖσθε	φιλεῖσθε		
φιλοῦνται			

τῑμάω: Active Voice

τῑμῶ		τῑμᾶν	τῑμῶν, τῑμῶσα,
τῑμᾷς	τίμα		τῑμῶν
τῑμᾷ			
τῑμῶμεν			
τῑμᾶτε	τῑμᾶτε		
τῑμῶσι(ν)			

τῑμάω: Middle Voice

τῑμῶμαι		τῑμᾶσθαι	τῑμώμενος, -η,
τῑμᾷ	τῑμῶ		-ον
τῑμᾶται			
τῑμώμεθα			
τῑμᾶσθε	τῑμᾶσθε		
τῑμῶνται			

δηλόω: Active Voice

δηλῶ   δηλοῦν   δηλῶν, δηλοῦσα,
δηλοῖς   δήλου   δηλοῦν
δηλοῖ
δηλοῦμεν
δηλοῦτε   δηλοῦτε
δηλοῦσι(ν)

δηλόω: Middle Voice

δηλοῦμαι   δηλοῦσθαι   δηλούμενος, -η,
δηλοῖ   δηλοῦ   -ον
δηλοῦται
δηλούμεθα
δηλοῦσθε   δηλοῦσθε
δηλοῦνται

29. THE IMPERFECT TENSE

The imperfect tense is always formed from the same stem as the present; see pages 153–154. Compare the formation of the second aorist (pages 126–127). The imperfect and the second aorist have the same augment, thematic vowels, and endings, but they are based on different stems; compare, for example ἐ-λάμβαν-ο-ν (imperfect) and ἔ-λαβ-ο-ν (aorist).

For the imperfect of contract verbs in -ε- and -α-, see page 154 and for -ο-contract verbs, see page 192.

For the imperfect of the verb εἰμί, see page 142.

The imperfect differs from the aorist indicative in aspect; while the imperfect looks on the action of the verb as a process, the aorist regards it as an event. See page 155.

Imperfect Active

ἔ-λ ῡ-ο-ν	I was loosening, I loosened
ἔ-λ ῡ-ε-ς	you were loosening, you loosened
ἔ-λ ῡ-ε(ν)	he/she was loosening, he/she loosened
ἐ-λ ῡ́-ο-μεν	we were loosening, we loosened
ἐ-λ ῡ́-ε-τε	you were loosening, you loosened
ἔ-λ ῡ-ο-ν	they were loosening, they loosened

Imperfect Middle

ἐ-λ ῡ-ό-μην	I was ransoming
ἐ-λ ῡ́-ε-σο > ἐλ ῡ́ου	you were ransoming
ἐ-λ ῡ́-ε-το	he/she was ransoming
ἐ-λ ῡ-ό-μεθα	we were ransoming
ἐ-λ ῡ́-ε-σθε	you were ransoming
ἐ-λ ῡ́-ο-ντο	they were ransoming

Contract verbs follow the rules given above for the formation of the imperfect tense and the rules for contraction given on pages 32, 44, and 192:

Active

ἐφίλουν	ἐτίμων	ἐδήλουν
ἐφίλεις	ἐτίμας	ἐδήλους
ἐφίλει	ἐτίμα	ἐδήλου
ἐφιλοῦμεν	ἐτῑμῶμεν	ἐδηλοῦμεν
ἐφιλεῖτε	ἐτῑμᾶτε	ἐδηλοῦτε
ἐφίλουν	ἐτίμων	ἐδήλουν

Middle

ἐφιλούμην	ἐτῑμώμην	ἐδηλούμην
ἐφιλοῦ	ἐτῑμῶ	ἐδηλοῦ
ἐφιλεῖτο	ἐτῑμᾶτο	ἐδηλοῦτο
ἐφιλούμεθα	ἐτῑμώμεθα	ἐδηλούμεθα
ἐφιλεῖσθε	ἐτῑμᾶσθε	ἐδηλοῦσθε
ἐφιλοῦντο	ἐτῑμῶντο	ἐδηλοῦντο

30. THE FIRST AORIST

For the formation of the first aorist, see pages 140–141.

For the augment (syllabic or temporal) of imperfects and of first and second aorists, see pages 135 and 149.

First Aorist Active   First Aorist Middle

Indicative

ἔ-λῡ-σα	I loosened	ἐ-λῡ-σά-μην	I ransomed
ἔ-λῡ-σας	you loosened	ἐ-λύ-σα-σο > ἐλύσω	you ransomed
ἔ-λῡ-σ-ε(ν)	he/she loosened	ἐ-λύ-σα-το	he/she ransomed
ἐ-λύ-σα-μεν	we loosened	ἐ-λῡ-σά-μεθα	we ransomed
ἐ-λύ-σα-τε	you loosened	ἐ-λύ-σα-σθε	you ransomed
ἔ-λῡ-σα-ν	they loosened	ἐ-λύ-σα-ντο	they ransomed

Imperative

λῦ-σον	loosen!	λῦ-σαι	ransom!
λύ-σα-τε	loosen!	λύ-σα-σθε	ransom!

Infinitive

λῦ-σαι	to loosen	λύ-σα-σθαι	to ransom

Participle

λύ-σᾱς, λύ-σᾱσα, λῦ-σαν   λῡ-σά-μενος, λῡ-σα-μένη, λῡ-σά-μενον

               loosening or   ransoming or

               having loosened   having ransomed

Note the changes that take place when the σα termination is added to stems that end in the following categories of consonants (see page 141):

    labials: β, π, or φ + σα > ψα

    gutturals: γ, κ, or χ + σα > ξα

dentals: δ, ζ, θ, or τ + σα > σα
    N.B. Verbs with double τ have guttural stems, e.g., πράττω (stem πράγ-, see page 141).
    Stems that end in liquids have different formations. For the first aorist of liquid verbs, see page 149. There is often a change of stem, and only α rather than σα is added as the termination, e.g., μένω, (aorist) ἔμεινα.
    Contract verbs lengthen their final stem vowel and then add the σα (see page 141), e. g., φιλέω, (aorist) ἐφίλησα.
    Some verbs show irregular first aorists (see page 149), e.g., δοκεῖ, (aorist) ἔδοξε (instead of ἐδόκησε).
    For aspect and the difference in meaning of the various moods of the aorist, see page 128.

31.   THE SECOND AORIST

    For the formation of the second aorist, see pages 126–127. Note that the forms contain the thematic vowels.

Second Aorist Active		*Second Aorist Middle*	
Present. λαμβάνω		Present: γίγνομαι	
Aorist stem: λαβ-		Aorist stem: γεν-	
Indicative			
ἔ-λαβ-ο-ν	I took	ἐ-γεν-ό-μην	I became
ἔ-λαβ-ε-ς	you took	ἐ-γέν-ε-σο > ἐγένου	you became
ἔ-λαβ-ε(ν)	he/she took	ἐ-γέν-ε-το	he/she/it became
ἐ-λάβ-ο-μεν	we took	ἐ-γεν-ό-μεθα	we became
ἐ-λάβ-ε-τε	you took	ἐ-γέν-ε-σθε	you became
ἔ-λαβ-ο-ν	they took	ἐ-γέν-ο-ντο	they became
Imperative			
λαβ-έ	take!	γενοῦ	become!
λαβ-έτε	take!	γέν-ε-σθε	become!
Infinitive			
λαβ-εῖν	to take	γεν-έ-σθαι	to become
Participle			
λαβ-ών, λαβ-οῦσα,		γεν-ό-μενος, γεν-ο-μένη,	
λαβ-όν	taking or having taken	γεν-ό-μενον	becoming or having become

    For the augment (syllabic or temporal) of imperfects and of first and second aorists, see pages 135 and 149.
    For a list of some important verbs that have a second rather than a first aorist, see page 129; for a list of all verbs with second aorists that occur in the vocabularies of Book I, see page 244. Some verbs have both a first and a second

aorist; there is no difference in meaning between the first and second aorist forms.

Some verbs have aorists that are formed from completely different roots (see pages 134–135), e.g., ἔρχομαι, (aorist) ἦλθον.

Some verbs have athematic second aorists (see page 184 and below), e.g., βαίνω, (aorist) ἔβην.

For aspect in the aorist, see page 128.

32. ATHEMATIC SECOND AORISTS

See page 184

βαίνω, stems βη-/βα-   γιγνώσκω, stems γνω-/γνο-
I step, walk, go   I get to know, learn

Indic.	*Imper.*	*Infin.*	*Partic.*	*Indic.*	*Imper.*	*Infin.*	*Partic.*
ἔβην		βῆναι	βάς,	ἔγνων		γνῶναι	γνούς,
ἔβης	βῆθι		βᾶσα,	ἔγνως	γνῶθι		γνοῦσα,
ἔβη			βάν	ἔγνω			γνόν
ἔβημεν				ἔγνωμεν			
ἔβητε	βῆτε			ἔγνωτε	γνῶτε		
ἔβησαν				ἔγνωσαν			

stems στη-/στα-
stand

ἔστην		στῆναι	στάς,
ἔστης	στῆθι		στᾶσα,
ἔστη			στάν
ἔστημεν			
ἔστητε	στῆτε		
ἔστησαν			

33. THE VERB εἰμί

For the forms of the verb εἰμί, see pages 4, 11, 12, 22, 32, 99, and 120.

Indic.	*Imper.*	*Infin.*	*Partic.*
εἰμί		εἶναι	ὤν, οὖσα, ὄν
εἶ	ἴσθι		
ἐστί(ν)			
ἐσμέν			
ἐστέ	ἔστε		
εἰσί(ν)			

For the imperfect, see page 142:

ἦν	I was	ἦμεν	we were
ἦσθα	you were	ἦτε	you were
ἦν	he/she/it was	ἦσαν	they were

34. THE VERBS δύναμαι, κεῖμαι, and ἐπίσταμαι

The following common deponent verbs add personal endings directly to the stem (see page 197):

Stem: δυνα- be able

Present

Indicative	*Imperative*	*Infinitive*	*Participle*
δύνα-μαι		δύνα-σθαι	δυνά-μενος, -η, -ον
δύνα-σαι	δύνα-σο		
δύνα-ται			
δυνά-μεθα			
δύνα-σθε	δύνα-σθε		
δύνα-νται			

Stem: κει- lie

κεῖ-μαι		κεῖ-σθαι	κεί-μενος, -η, -ον
κεῖ-σαι	κεῖ-σο		
κεῖ-ται			
κεί-μεθα			
κεῖ-σθε	κεῖ-σθε		
κεῖ-νται			

Stem: ἐπιστα- understand, know

ἐπίστα-μαι		ἐπίστα-σθαι	ἐπιστά-μενος, -η, -ον
ἐπίστα-σαι	ἐπίστα-σο		
ἐπίστα-ται			
ἐπιστά-μεθα			
ἐπίστα-σθε	ἐπίστα-σθε		
ἐπίστα-ντο			

Imperfect Indicative:

ἐ-δυνά-μην	ἐ-κεί-μην	ἠπιστά-μην
ἐ-δύνα-σο *or* ἐδύνω	ἔ-κει-σο	ἠπίστα-σο *or* ἠπίστω
ἐ-δύνα-το	ἔ-κει-το	ἠπίστα-το
ἐ-δυνά-μεθα	ἐ-κεί-μεθα	ἠπιστά-μεθα
ἐ-δύνα-σθε	ἔ-κει-σθε	ἠπίστα-σθε
ἐ-δύνα-ντο	ἔ-κει-ντο	ἠπίστα-ντο

35. IMPERSONAL VERBS

Impersonal verbs are used in the third person singular with an implied impersonal "it" as subject, see page 118.
Impersonal verb plus accusative and infinitive:
δεῖ ἡμᾶς πρὸ τῆς νυκτὸς ἐκεῖσε παρεῖναι.
It is necessary for us to be there before night.
We must be there before night.
Impersonal verb plus dative and infinitive:
ἆρ᾽ ἔξεστιν ἡμῖν αὔριον ἐπανιέναι;
Is it possible for us to return tomorrow?
May we return tomorrow?   Can we return tomorrow?

36. USES OF THE ARTICLE

Greek sometimes uses the definite article where we would not use an article in English (see page 5), e.g.:
ὁ Δικαιόπολις αὐτουργός ἐστιν.
Dicaeopolis is a farmer.
The article + δέ is often used at the beginning of a clause to indicate a change of subject (see pages 44 and 109–110), e.g.:
ὁ δεσπότης τὸν δοῦλον καλεῖ· ὁ δὲ οὐ πάρεστιν.
The master calls the slave, *but he* is not present.
The article + a participle form a noun phrase that may be translated by a noun or a relative clause in English (see page 110), e.g.:

ὁ ἱερεὺς ὁ τὴν θυσίαν ποιούμενος   οἱ τρέχοντες
the priest who is making the sacrifice   the runners

37. USES OF THE CASES

a. Nominative
    1. Subject of a finite verb (see page 5), e.g.:
        ὁ ἄνθρωπος γεωργεῖ τὸν κλῆρον.
        The man cultivates the farm.
    2. Complement with the linking verb εἰμί and verbs of becoming such as γίγνομαι (see page 5), e.g.:
        ὁ κλῆρός ἐστιν **ὀλίγος**.
        The farm is *small*.
        οἱ δὲ εὐθὺς **σύες** γίγνονται.
        And immediately they become *pigs*
b. Genitive
    1. Genitive of possession (see page 109), e.g.:
        ὁ **τοῦ παιδὸς** κύων
        the *boy's* dog (or) the dog *of the boy*
        Note that the word in the genitive case is here in the attributive position between the article and the noun. It may also be placed after the repeated article, e.g.:
        ὁ κύων ὁ **τοῦ παιδός**
    2. Genitive with adjectives, such as αἴτιος and ἄξιος, e.g.:
        δεῖ γάρ σε ἄξιον γίγνεσθαι **τῶν πατέρων**.
        You must become worthy *of your ancestors (fathers)*.

3. Genitive of the whole or partitive genitive, (see page 109) e.g.:
   τῶν παρόντων πολλοί many of those present
4. Genitive of time within which (see page 165), e.g.:
   νυκτός in the night   πέντε ἡμερῶν within five days
5. Genitive of comparison (see page 172), e.g.:
   ὁ ἀνὴρ μείζων ἐστὶ **τοῦ παιδός**.
   The man is bigger *than the boy*.
6. Genitive with prepositions, often expressing ideas of place from which
   (see page 109), e.g.:
   ἀπὸ τοῦ ἄστεως
   from the city
7. Genitive with certain verbs (see page 109), e.g.:
   ὁ Θησεὺς τῇ ἀριστερᾷ **λαμβάνεται τῆς κεφαλῆς** τοῦ θηρίου.
   Theseus *takes hold of the head* of the beast with his left hand.
   The following verbs in the vocabulary lists of Book I are used with the
   genitive case:
   ἀκούω I hear (a person talking; the accusative is used for the
           thing heard)
   ἔχομαι I hold onto
   λαμβάνομαι I seize, take hold of

c. Dative
   For the uses of the dative case, see pages 64–65, 165, and 172:
1. Indirect object, e.g.:
   οὕτω τῷ **Μῑνωταύρῳ** σῖτον παρέχουσιν.
   In this way they give *the Minotaur* food.
   In this way they give food *to the Minotaur*.
2. Dative of possession, e.g.:
   ἔστιν **αὐτῷ** παῖς τις ὀνόματι Θησεύς.
   He has a child named Theseus.
   (literally: There is *for him* a child by name Theseus.)
3. Dative of respect, e.g.:
   ὀνόματι Θησεύς
   Theseus *by name*
4. Dative of means or instrument, e.g.:
   τῇ ἀριστερᾷ λαμβάνεται τῆς κεφαλῆς τοῦ θηρίου.
   Theseus seizes the head of the beast *with his left hand*.
5. Dative of time when, e.g.:
   τῇ τρίτῃ ἡμέρᾳ ἀφῑκόμεθα.
   We arrived *on the third day*.
6. Dative of degree of difference with comparatives, e.g.:
   ὁ ἀνὴρ **πολλῷ** μείζων ἐστὶ τοῦ παιδός.
   The man is *much* bigger (bigger *by much*) than the boy.
7. Dative with prepositions, especially those that indicate the place where
   someone or something is or something happens , e.g.:
   παρὰ τῇ κρήνῃ
   By the spring

8. Dative with certain verbs, e.g.:

ἕπεσθέ **μοι** ἀνδρείως.

Follow *me* bravely.

The following verbs in the vocabulary lists of Book I are used with the dative case:

ἀντέχω I resist
βοηθέω I help
διαλέγομαι I talk to, converse with
εἴκω I yield
ἐμπῑπτω I fall into, fall on
ἕπομαι I follow
εὔχομαι I pray to
ἡγέομαι I lead
μάχομαι I fight with
ὀργίζομαι I grow angry at
πείθομαι I obey
πιστεύω I trust, am confident in
προσβάλλω I attack
προσέρχομαι I approach
προσχωρέω I go toward, approach
συμπῑπτω I clash with
τέρπομαι I enjoy
χράομαι I use, enjoy

d. Accusative

1. Direct object of many verbs (see page 5), e.g.:

ὁ ἄνθρωπος γεωργεῖ **τὸν κλῆρον**.

The man cultivates *the farm*.

2. Duration of time (see page 165), e.g.:

τρεῖς ἡμέρᾱς ἐμείναμεν.

We stayed *for three days*.

3. Accusative with prepositions, especially with those expressing motion toward a place (*place to which*) (see page 5), e.g.:

πρὸς τὸν οἶκον βαδίζει.

He/she walks toward his/her house.

4. Adverbial, e.g.:

μέγα βοᾷ.

He shouts *loudly*.

38. AGREEMENT

Definite articles and adjectives agree with the nouns they go with in gender, number, and case (see page 5), e.g.:

ὁ καλὸς ἀγρός   ὁ ἀληθὴς μῦθος   ἡ ἀληθὴς γνώμη

The definite article will indicate the gender, number, and case of the noun with which it goes; this helps identify the forms of unfamiliar nouns (see page 40).

Normally subjects and verbs agree in number (i.e., a singular subject takes a singular verb, and a plural subject, a plural verb), but in Greek neuter plural subjects regularly take singular verbs (see page 44), e.g.:

τὰ μῆλα ἐν τῷ ἀγρῷ μένει.   The flocks remain in the field.

Teacher and pupil

39. WORD ORDER

It is the endings of words and not the order in which they are placed that builds the meaning of a Greek sentence. Word order in Greek is therefore more flexible than in English and can be manipulated to convey emphasis. See page 5.

Attributive and Predicate Position

For the attributive and predicate position of adjectives, see page 52. For the predicate position of possessive genitives of αὐτός, see page 52. For the predicate position of demonstrative adjectives, see page 179. For the attributive position of the possessive genitive of nouns, see page 109.

40. USES OF PARTICIPLES

The article + a participle forms a noun phrase, which may be translated by a noun or a relative clause in English (see page 110), e.g.:

οἱ τοὺς χοροὺς θεώμενοι
those who are watching the dances

LIST OF VERBS

The following verbs with second aorists have appeared in the vocabulary lists in Book I. We give the present tense, the aorist stem, and the aorist indicative. Sometimes stems undergo complex linguistic changes.

Present	*Stem*	*Aorist*
ἄγω	ἀγαγ-	ἤγαγον
αἱρέω*	ἑλ-	εἶλον
ἀποθνήσκω	θαν-	ἀπ-έθανον
ἀφ-ικνέομαι	ἱκ-	ἀφῑκόμην
βαίνω	βη-/βα-	ἔβην
βάλλω	βαλ-	ἔβαλον
γίγνομαι	γεν-	ἐγενόμην
γιγνώσκω	γνω-/γνο-	ἔγνων
ἔρχομαι*	ἐλθ-	ἦλθον
ἐρωτάω	ἐρ-	ἠρόμην
ἐσθίω*	φαγ-	ἔφαγον
εὑρίσκω	εὑρ-	ηὗρον
ἔχω	σχ-	ἔσχον
κάμνω	καμ-	ἔκαμον
λαμβάνω	λαβ-	ἔλαβον
λέγω*	εἰπ-	εἶπον
λείπω	λιπ-	ἔλιπον
μανθάνω	μαθ-	ἔμαθον
ὁράω*	ἰδ-	εἶδον
πάσχω	παθ-	ἔπαθον
πῑνω	πῑ-	ἔπιον
πῑπτω	πεσ-	ἔπεσον
φέρω	ἐνεγκ-	ἤνεγκον (also first aorist ἤνεγκα)
φεύγω	φυγ-	ἔφυγον

*Verbs marked with asterisks form their aorists from a completely different stem from that seen in the present tense.

The following verbs are irregular in the formation of their first aorist:

αἴρω	ἀρ-	ἦρα
δοκεῖ	δοκ-	ἔδοξε
ἐλαύνω	ἐλα-	ἤλασα
καίω	καυ-	ἔκαυσα
καλέω	καλε-	ἐκάλεσα
μάχομαι	μαχε-	ἐμαχεσάμην
πλέω	πλευ-	ἔπλευσα
σκοπέω	σκεπ-	ἐσκεψάμην

GREEK TO ENGLISH VOCABULARY

Note: the numbers in parentheses indicate the chapters in which words appear in the vocabulary lists or grammar sections. Nouns are listed with the nominative case first, then the genitive, and then the definite article.

A

ἀγαθός, ἀγαθή, ἀγαθόν good (5, 14)

'Αγαμέμνων, 'Αγαμέμνονος, ὁ Agamemnon (7)

ἀγγέλλω, ἤγγειλα I announce (14)

ἄγγελος, ἀγγέλου, ὁ messenger (4)

ἄγε, (plural) ἄγετε come on! (9)

ἀγορᾱ, ἀγορᾶς, ἡ agora, city center, marketplace (8)

ἄγριος, ἀγρίᾱ, ἄγριον savage, wild, fierce (5)

ἀγρός, ἀγροῦ, ὁ field (1)

ἄγω, ἤγαγον I lead, take (2, 13)
ἄγε, (plural) ἄγετε come on! (9)

ἀγών, ἀγῶνος, ὁ struggle, contest (15)

ἀδελφός, ἀδελφοῦ, ὁ brother (11)

ἀδύνατος, ἀδύνατον impossible

'Αθήναζε to Athens (12)

'Αθῆναι, 'Αθηνῶν, αἱ Athens (6)

'Αθηναῖος, 'Αθηναίᾱ, 'Αθηναῖον Athenian (1)
οἱ 'Αθηναῖοι the Athenians

'Αθήνη, 'Αθήνης, ἡ Athena, daughter of Zeus (9)

'Αθήνησι at Athens

Αἰγαῖος πόντος, Αἰγαίου πόντου, ὁ Aegean Sea

Αἰγεύς, Αἰγέως, ὁ Aegeus, king of Athens (6)

Αἰγύπτιοι, Αἰγυπτίων, οἱ Egyptians

Αἴγυπτος, Αἰγύπτου, ἡ Egypt

αἰεί always (4)

αἴξ, αἰγός, ὁ or ἡ goat

Αἴολος, Αἰόλου, ὁ Aeolus

αἱρέω, εἷλον I take (7, 11)

αἴρω, ἦρα I lift; (with reflexive pronoun) I get up (1)

Αἰσχύλος, Αἰσχύλου, ὁ Aeschylus (15)

αἰτέω, ἤτησα I ask, ask for (11)

αἴτιος, αἰτίᾱ, αἴτιον responsible, to blame, responsible for (+ gen.) (3)

Αἰτναῖον ὄρος, Αἰτναίου ὄρους, τό Mount Etna

ἀκίνητος, ἀκίνητον motionless

ἀκούω, ἤκουσα (+ gen. of person, acc. of thing) I listen, hear (4)

'Ακρόπολις, 'Ακροπόλεως, ἡ Acropolis, the citadel of Athens (8)

ἄκρος, ἄκρᾱ, ἄκρον top (of) (5)
ἄκρον τὸ ὄρος the top of the mountain/hill (5)

ἀκτή, ἀκτῆς, ἡ promontory

ἀληθής, ἀληθές true (13)
ἀληθῆ, ἀληθῶν, τά the truth (13)

ἀλλά but (1)
οὐ μόνον . . . ἀλλὰ καί not only . . . but also (15)

ἀλλαντοπώλης, ἀλλαντοπώλου, ὁ sausage-seller

ἀλλήλων of one another (13)

ἄλλος, ἄλλη, ἄλλο other, another (4)

ἅμα together, at the same time (13)

ἄμαξα, ἁμάξης, ἡ wagon

ἀμείνων, ἄμεινον better (14)

ἀμύνω, ἤμῡνα (active) I ward off X (acc.) from Y (dat.); (middle) I ward off, defend myself (against + acc.) (13)

ἀνά (+ acc.) up (5)

ἀναβαίνω, ἀνέβην I go up, get up; I climb, go up onto (+ ἐπί "onto" + acc.) (9)

ἀναγκάζω, ἠνάγκασα I compel (15)

ἀνάστηθι stand up!

ἀναχωρέω, ἀνεχώρησα I retreat, withdraw (14)

ἀνδρεῖος, ἀνδρείᾱ, ἀνδρεῖον brave (3)

  ἀνδρείως bravely

ἄνεμος, ἀνέμου, ὁ wind (13)

ἀνέστην I stood up (15)

ἀνήρ, ἀνδρός, ὁ man, husband (4)

ἄνθρωπος, ἀνθρώπου, ὁ man, human being, person (1)

ἀντέχω, ἀντέσχον (+ dat.) I resist (14)

ἄντρον, ἄντρου, τό cave

ἄξιος, ἀξίᾱ, ἄξιον (+ gen.) worthy of (16)

ἅπᾱς, ἅπᾱσα, ἅπαν all, every, whole (14)

ἄπειμι, ἄπην I am away; (+ gen.) am away from (5)

ἀπέκτονε he/she has killed

ἀπελαύνω, ἀπήλασα I drive away

ἀπέρχομαι, ἀπῆλθον I go away (6)

ἀπό (+ gen.) from (4)

ἀποθνῄσκω, ἀπέθανον I die (11)

ἀποκρίνομαι, ἀπεκρῑνάμην I answer (7)

ἀποκτείνω, ἀπέκτεινα I kill (6)

ἀπόλλῡμι, ἀπώλεσα I lose, destroy

ἀποπέμπω, ἀπέπεμψα I send away

ἀποπλέω, ἀπέπλευσα I sail away

ἀπορέω, ἠπόρησα I am at a loss (12)

ἀπορίᾱ, ἀπορίᾱς, ἡ perplexity, difficulty, the state of being at a loss (15)

ἀποφεύγω, ἀπέφυγον I flee (away) (6)

ἆρα (introduces a question) (4)

Ἄργος, Ἄργου, ὁ Argus (name of a dog) (5)

ἀργός, ἀργή, ἀργόν lazy

ἀργύριον, ἀργυρίου, τό silver, money (11)

ἀρετή, ἀρετῆς, ἡ excellence, virtue, courage (15)

Ἀριάδνη, Ἀριάδνης, ἡ Ariadne, daughter of King Minos (6)

ἀριστερά, ἀριστερᾶς, ἡ left hand (9)

ἄριστος, ἀρίστη, ἄριστον best, very good, noble (9, 14)

ἄροτος, ἀρότου, ὁ plowing

ἀροτρεύω, ἠρότρευσα I plow (3)

ἄροτρον, ἀρότρου, τό plow (2)

Ἀρτεμίσιον, Ἀρτεμισίου, τό Artemisium (14)

ἀρχή, ἀρχῆς, ἡ beginning, empire (13)

Ἀσίᾱ, Ἀσίᾱς, ἡ Asia (Minor) (15)

Ἀσκλήπιος, Ἀσκληπίου, ὁ Asclepius, the Greek god of healing (11)

ἀσκός, ἀσκοῦ, ὁ bag

ἄστυ, ἄστεως, τό city (8)

ἀτραπός, ἀτραποῦ, ἡ path

Ἀττική, Ἀττικῆς, ἡ Attica (14)

αὖθις again (3)

αὔλιον, αὐλίου, τό sheepfold

αὐξάνω, ηὔξησα I increase (9)

αὔριον tomorrow (11)

αὐτήν her, it

αὐτό it (3)

αὐτόν him, it (1, 3)

αὐτός, αὐτή, αὐτό (intensive adjective) -self, -selves; (pronoun) him, her, it, them (5)

αὐτουργός, αὐτουργοῦ, ὁ farmer (1)

ἀφικνέομαι, ἀφῑκόμην I arrive, arrive at (+ εἰς + acc.) (6, 11)

ἀφίσταμαι, ἀπέστην I revolt from (16)

Ἀχαιοί, Ἀχαιῶν, οἱ Achaeans, Greeks (7)

B

βαδίζω, ἐβάδισα I walk, go (1)

βαίνω, ἔβην I step, walk, go (2, 15)

βάλλω, ἔβαλον I throw, put, pelt (7)

βάρβαρος, βαρβάρου, ὁ barbarian (13)

βασιλεύς, βασιλέως, ὁ king (6)

βασιλεύω I rule, rule over (+ gen.) (6)

βέβαιος, βεβαίᾱ, βέβαιον firm (13)

βίος, βίου, ὁ life (16)

βλάπτω, ἔβλαψα I harm (15)

βλέπω, ἔβλεψα I look, see (2)

βοάω, ἐβόησα I shout (5)

βοή, βοῆς, ἡ shout (10)

βοηθέω, ἐβοήθησα (+ dat.) I help (2, 6)

Βοιωτίᾱ, Βοιωτίᾱς, ἡ Boeotia (14)

βότρυες, βοτρύων, οἱ grapes
βούλομαι, (imperfect) ἐβουλόμην I
want, wish (6)
βοῦς, βοός, ὁ ox (2)
βραδέως slowly (2)
Βρόμιος, Βρομίου, ὁ Thunderer (an
epithet of Dionysus) (9)
Βυζάντιον, Βυζαντίου, τό
Byzantium
βωμός, βωμοῦ, ὁ altar (8)

Γ
γάρ (postpositive) for (1)
γε (postpositive enclitic) at least, indeed
(restrictive or intensive) (6)
γέγονε he/she/it has become, is
γεραιός, γεραιά, γεραιόν old (12)
γέρων, γέροντος, ὁ old man (9)
γέφυρα, γεφύρας, ἡ bridge
γεωργέω I farm
γῆ, γῆς, ἡ land, earth, ground (4)
κατὰ γῆν on land (14)
ποῦ γῆς; where (in the world)? (16)
γίγας, γίγαντος, ὁ giant
γίγνομαι I become, happen (6)
γίγνεται he/she/it becomes; it
happens (6)
γιγνώσκω, ἔγνων I get to know, learn
(5, 15)
γράφω, ἔγραψα I write (14)
γυνή, γυναικός, ἡ woman, wife (4)

Δ
δακρύω, ἐδάκρυσα I cry, weep (11)
δέ (postpositive) and, but (1)
δέ (see μέν . . . δέ . . .)
δεῖ (+ acc. and infinitive) it is necessary
(10)
δεῖ ἡμᾶς παρεῖναι we must be
there (10)
δεινός, δεινή, δεινόν terrible (6)
δεινά terrible things
δεινῶς terribly, frightfully
δειπνέω, ἐδείπνησα I eat
δεῖπνον, δείπνου, τό dinner (3)
δέκα ten (8)
δέκατος, δεκάτη, δέκατον tenth
(8)
δένδρον, δένδρου, τό tree (2)
δεξιά, δεξιᾶς, ἡ right hand (9)

δεξιός, δεξιά, δεξιόν right (i.e., on
the right hand) (15)
δεσμωτήριον, δεσμωτηρίου, τό
prison
δεσπότης, δεσπότου, ὁ master (2)
δεῦρο here (3)
δεύτερος, δευτέρα, δεύτερον
second (8)
δέχομαι, ἐδεξάμην I receive (6)
δή (postpositive) indeed, in fact
(emphasizes that what is said is obvious
or true) (6)
δηλόω, ἐδήλωσα I show (15)
δῆμος, δήμου, ὁ the people (9)
διά (+ gen.) through (9)
διαβαίνω, διέβην I cross
διαβιβάσαι to take across, transport
διακόσιοι, διακόσιαι, διακόσια
two hundred (16)
διαλέγομαι, (imperfect) διελεγόμην
(+ dat.) I talk to, converse with (8)
διὰ τί; why? (2)
διαφθείρω, διέφθειρα I destroy (15)
διέρχομαι, διῆλθον I come through,
go through (14)
Δικαιόπολις, Δικαιοπόλεως, ὁ
Dicaeopolis (1)
δι' ὀλίγου soon (5)
Διόνυσος, Διονύσου, ὁ Dionysus
(8)
διώκω, ἐδίωξα I pursue (5)
δοκεῖ, ἔδοξε (+ dat. and infinitive) it
seems (good) (11)
δοκεῖ μοι it seems good to me, I
decide, I think it best (11)
ὡς δοκεῖ as it seems (13)
δοῦλος, δούλου, ὁ slave (2)
δουλόω, ἐδούλωσα I enslave
δραμεῖν (aorist infinitive of τρέχω)
δραχμή, δραχμῆς, ἡ drachma (11)
δύναμαι, (imperfect) ἐδυνάμην I
- am able, can (12)
δυνατός, δυνατή, δυνατόν possible
(3)
δύο two (7)

Ε
ἕβδομος, ἑβδόμη, ἕβδομον
seventh (8)
ἐγγύς (+ gen.) near (13)

ἐγείρω, ἤγειρα I wake (someone) up;
(*middle, intransitive*) I wake up (8)
ἐγώ I (2)
ἐθέλω, ἠθέλησα I wish, am willing
(4)
οὐκ ἐθέλω I refuse (4)
εἰ if (11)
εἰ μή unless
εἴκω, εἶξα (+ *dat.*) I yield (15)
εἰκών, εἰκόνος, ἡ statue
εἰπέ, (*plural*) εἴπετε tell! (7)
εἰπεῖν to say, tell (7)
εἶπον I, they told
εἴ πως if somehow, if perhaps
εἰρήνη, εἰρήνης, ἡ peace (16)
εἷς, μία, ἕν one (7)
εἰς (+ *acc.*), into, to, at, onto, for (2)
εἰσάγω, εἰσήγαγον I lead in, take in
(2, 11)
εἰσβαίνω, εἰσέβην I go in, come in
εἰς ναῦν εἰσβαίνω I go on board
ship, embark
εἰσβάντες having embarked
εἰσελαύνω, εἰσήλασα I drive in
εἴσελθε, (*plural*) εἰσέλθετε come in!
εἰσέρχομαι, εἰσῆλθον I go in, come
in
εἰσηγέομαι, εἰσηγησάμην (+ *dat.*) I
lead in
εἰσιέναι to go in
εἰς καιρόν at just the right time
εἰσκαλέω, εἰσεκάλεσα I call in
εἴσοδος, εἰσόδου, ἡ entrance
εἰσπλέω, εἰσέπλευσα I sail into
εἰσρέω I flow in (16)
εἰσφέρω, εἰσήνεγκα *or* εἰσήνεγκον
I bring in
ἐκ (+ *gen.*) out of (3)
ἑκατόν (*indeclinable*) a hundred (16)
ἐκβαίνω, ἐξέβην I step out, come out
(2)
ἐκβαίνω ἐκ τῆς νεώς I disembark
ἐκβάλλω, ἐξέβαλον I throw out
ἐκεῖ there (6)
ἐκεῖνος, ἐκείνη, ἐκεῖνο that,
(*plural*) those (13)
ἐκεῖσε to there (8)
ἐκκαλέω, ἐξεκάλεσα I call out
ἐκπέμπω, ἐξέπεμψα I send out
ἐκπίπτω, ἐξέπεσον I fall out

ἐκπλέω, ἐξέπλευσα I sail out
ἔκπλους, ἔκπλου, ὁ escape route
ἕκτος, ἕκτη, ἕκτον sixth (8)
ἐκ τοῦ ὄπισθεν from the rear
ἐκφέρω, ἐξήνεγκα *or* ἐξήνεγκον I
carry out
ἐκφεύγω, ἐξέφυγον I flee (out)
ἐλάττων, ἔλαττον smaller, (*plural*)
fewer (14)
ἐλαύνω, ἤλασα I drive (2)
ἐλεῖν (*aorist infinitive of* αἱρέω)
ἐλευθερίᾱ, ἐλευθερίᾱς, ἡ freedom
(13)
ἐλεύθερος, ἐλευθέρᾱ, ἐλεύθερον
free (16)
ἐλευθερόω, ἠλευθέρωσα I set free,
free (15)
ἐλθέ, (*plural*) ἐλθέτε come! (2)
ἐλθεῖν (see ἔρχομαι)
ἕλκω, (*imperfect*) εἷλκον I drag
Ἑλλάς, Ἑλλάδος, ἡ Hellas,
Greece (13)
Ἕλλην, Ἕλληνος, ὁ Greek,
(*plural*) the Greeks (14)
Ἑλλήσποντος, Ἑλλησπόντου, ὁ
Hellespont
ἐλπίζω, ἤλπισα I hope, expect (14)
ἐμαυτοῦ, σεαυτοῦ, ἑαυτοῦ of
myself, of yourself, of him-, her-,
itself, etc. (7)
ἐμβαίνω, ἐνέβην I come into, get into
ἐμός, ἐμή, ἐμόν my, mine (5)
ἐμπίπτω, ἐνέπεσον (+ *dat.*) I fall
upon, attack (15)
ἐμποδίζω I obstruct
ἔμπορος, ἐμπόρου, ὁ merchant (12)
ἐν (+ *dat.*) in, on, among (3)
ἐναντίος, ἐναντίᾱ, ἐναντίον
opposite
ἔνατος, ἐνάτη, ἔνατον ninth (8)
ἔνειμι I am in
ἐνθάδε here, to this place (7)
ἐν μέσῳ (+ *gen.*) between (14)
ἐννέα nine (8)
ἐν νῷ ἔχω (+ *infinitive*) I have in
mind, intend (4)
ἔνοικος, ἐνοίκου, ὁ inhabitant (16)
ἐν ταῖς Ἀθήναις in Athens (1)
ἐνταῦθα then, there, here (5)
ἐνταῦθα δή at that very moment,
then (5)

ἐν ... τούτῳ meanwhile (8)

ἐν ᾧ while (8)

ἐξ (*before words beginning with vowels*) = ἐκ (8)

ἕξ six (8)

ἐξάγω, ἐξήγαγον I lead out

ἐξαιρέω, ἐξεῖλον I take out

ἐξελαύνω, ἐξήλασα I drive out

ἐξελθών coming out, having come out

ἐξέρχομαι, ἐξῆλθον (+ ἐκ + *gen.*) I go out of, come out of (6)

ἔξεστι(ν) (+ *dat. and infinitive*) it is allowed, possible (10)

ἔξεστιν ἡμῖν ἐπανιέναι we are allowed to return, we may return, we can return (10)

ἐξηγέομαι, ἐξηγησάμην I relate (12)

ἑορτή, ἑορτῆς, ἡ festival (4)

ἐπαίρω, ἐπῆρα I lift up, raise; (*with reflexive pronoun*), I get up

ἐπάνελθε, (*plural*) ἐπανέλθετε come back!

ἐπανέρχομαι, ἐπανῆλθον I come back, return, return to (+ εἰς or πρός + *acc.*) (9)

ἐπανιέναι to come back, return, return to (+ εἰς or πρός + *acc.*) (9)

ἐπεί when (3)

ἔπειτα then (2)

ἐπί (+ *dat.*) at , upon, on; (+ *acc.*) at, against, onto (5, 9)

Ἐπίδαυρος, Ἐπιδαύρου, ἡ Epidaurus (11)

ἐπίκειμαι (+ *dat.*) I lie near, lie off (of islands with respect to the mainland)

ἐπιπέμπω, ἐπέπεμψα I send against, send in (14)

ἐπιπλέω, ἐπέπλευσα (+ *dat. or* + εἰς + *acc.*) I sail against (15)

ἐπίσταμαι, (*imperfect*) ἠπιστάμην I understand, know (16)

ἕπομαι, (*imperfect*) εἱπόμην (+ *dat.*) I follow (8)

ἑπτά seven (8)

ἐράω (+ *gen.*) I love

ἐργάζομαι, εἰργασάμην I work, accomplish (8)

ἔργον, ἔργου, τό work, deed (8)

ἐρέσσω, ἤρεσα I row (13)

ἐρέτης, ἐρέτου, ὁ rower

ἔρχομαι, ἦλθον I come, go (6, 11)

ἐρωτάω, ἠρόμην I ask (12)

ἐσθίω, ἔφαγον I eat (9)

ἑσπέρᾱ, ἑσπέρᾱς, ἡ evening (8)

ἔστην I stood

ἐστί(ν) he/she/it is (1)

ἔστω let it be so! all right!

ἑταῖρος, ἑταίρου, ὁ comrade, companion (6)

ἔτι still (3)

ἕτοιμος, ἑτοίμη, ἕτοιμον ready (9)

ἔτος, ἔτους, τό year (16)

εὖ well (12, 14)

Εὔβοια, Εὐβοίᾱς, ἡ Euboea (14)

εὖ γε good! well done! (8)

εὐθύς immediately (10)

εὐμενῶς kindly

εὑρίσκω, ηὖρον I find (7)

Εὐρύλοχος, Εὐρυλόχου, ὁ Eurylochus

Εὐρυμέδων ποταμός, Εὐρυμέδοντος ποταμοῦ, ὁ the Eurymedon River

εὔχομαι, ηὐξάμην I pray, pray to (+ *dat.*) (8)

ἔφη he/she said (11)

ἔφασαν they said

Ἐφιάλτης, Ἐφιάλτου, ὁ Ephialtes (14)

ἔχω, (*imperfect*) εἶχον, ἔσχον I have, hold; (*middle* + *gen.*) I hold onto (4)

ἕως until (14)

Z

Ζεύς, ὁ, τοῦ Διός, τῷ Διί, τὸν Δία, ὦ Ζεῦ Zeus, king of the gods (3, 8)

ζητέω, ἐζήτησα I seek, look for (5)

ζῷον, ζῴου, τό animal

H

ἤ or, (*with comparatives*) than (12, 14)

ἤ ... ἤ either ... or (12)

ἡγέομαι, ἡγησάμην (+ *dat.*) I lead (6)

ἤδη already, now (2)

ἥκιστά γε (*the opposite of* μάλιστά γε) least of all, not at all (16)

ἥκω I have come (5)

ἥλιος, ἡλίου, ὁ sun (1)

ἡμεῖς we (5)

ἡμέρᾱ, ἡμέρᾱς, ἡ day (6)

ἡμέτερος, ἡμετέρᾱ, ἡμέτερον our (5)

ἡμίονος, ἡμιόνου, ὁ mule (12)

ἡσυχάζω, ἡσύχασα I keep quiet (13)

Θ

θάλαττα, θαλάττης, ἡ sea (7)
  κατὰ θάλατταν by sea (14)

θάνατος, θανάτου, ὁ death (16)

θαυμάζω, ἐθαύμασα I wonder at, am amazed, admire (5)

θεάομαι, ἐθεᾱσάμην I see, watch, look at (8)

θέᾱτρον, θεᾱτρου, τό theater

Θεμιστοκλῆς, Θεμιστοκλέους, ὁ Themistocles (15)

θεός, θεοῦ, ἡ goddess (9)
  θεός, θεοῦ, ὁ god (8)

Θερμοπύλαι, Θερμοπυλῶν, αἱ Thermopylae (14)

θεωρέω, ἐθεώρησα I watch, see (16)

θηρίον, θηρίου, τό beast

Θησεύς, Θησέως, ὁ Theseus, son of King Aegeus (6)

θόρυβος, θορύβου, ὁ uproar, din (15)

θυγάτηρ, θυγατρός, ἡ daughter (4)

θῡμός, θῡμοῦ, ὁ spirit (16)

θύρᾱ, θύρᾱς, ἡ door (8)

Ι

ῑᾱτρεύω, ῑᾱτρευσα I heal

ῑᾱτρός, ῑᾱτροῦ, ὁ doctor (11)

ἰδεῖν (aorist infinitive of ὁράω)

ἰδού look! (4)

ἰέναι to go (7)

ἱερεῖον, ἱερείου, τό sacrificial victim (9)

ἱερεύς, ἱερέως, ὁ priest (9)

ἱερόν, ἱεροῦ, τό temple (9)

ἴθι δή go on! (5)

ἴθι, (plural) ἴτε go! (5)

ἵλαος, ἵλαον propitious (9)

ἵππος, ἵππου, ὁ horse (16)

ἴσθι, (plural) ἔστε be!

ἱστία, ἱστίων, τά sails (13)

ἰσχῡρός, ἰσχῡρά, ἰσχῡρόν strong (1)

Ἴωνες, Ἰώνων, οἱ Ionians

Ἰωνίᾱ, Ἰωνίᾱς, ἡ Ionia

Κ

καθεύδω I sleep (2)

καθ' ἡμέρᾱν every day

καθίζω (transitive) I make someone sit down; (intransitive) I sit; (middle, intransitive) I sit down (1, 8)

καί and, also, too (1)
  καί . . . καί both . . . and (5)
  καὶ δὴ καί and in particular, and what is more (16)

καίπερ (+ participle) although (12)

καιρός, καιροῦ, ὁ time, right time (4)

καίω, ἔκαυσα I kindle, burn; (middle, intransitive) I burn, am on fire (9)

κάκιστος, κακίστη, κάκιστον worst (14)

κακίων, κάκιον worse (14)

κακός, κακή, κακόν bad (12, 14)
  κακόν τι something bad
  κακῶς badly (14)

καλέω, ἐκάλεσα I call (2)

κάλλιστος, καλλίστη, κάλλιστον most beautiful, very beautiful (9, 14)

καλλίων, κάλλιον more beautiful (14)

καλός, καλή, καλόν beautiful (1, 14)

καλῶς well (10)
  καλῶς ἔχω I am well (11)

κάμνω, ἔκαμον I am sick, tired (9)

κασσίτερος, κασσιτέρου, ὁ tin

κατά (+ acc.), down, on (5)
  κατὰ γῆν by land (14)
  κατὰ θάλατταν by sea (11)

καταβαίνω, κατέβην I come down, go down

καταβάλλω, κατέβαλον I throw down, drop

κατάκειμαι, (imperfect) κατεκείμην I lie down (16)

καταλαμβάνω, κατέλαβον I overtake, catch (16)

καταλείπω, κατέλιπον I leave behind, desert (12)

καταπῑπτω, κατέπεσον I fall down

κατάρᾱτος, κατάρᾱτον cursed

κατ' οἶκον at home (16)

κεῖμαι, (imperfect) ἐκείμην I lie (16)

κεῖνος = ἐκεῖνος

κελεύω, ἐκέλευσα I order, tell (someone to do something) (7)

κεφαλή, κεφαλῆς, ἡ head (10)

κῆπος, κήπου, ὁ garden

κῆρυξ, κήρῡκος, ὁ herald (9)

Κίμων, Κίμονος, ὁ Cimon

κίνδῡνος, κινδῡνου, ὁ danger (9)

Κίρκη, Κίρκης, ἡ Circe

κλῆρος, κλήρου, ὁ farm

Κνωσσός, Κνωσσοῦ, ἡ Knossos (6)

κολάζω, ἐκόλασα I punish

κομίζω, ἐκόμισα I bring, take (11)

κόπτω, ἔκοψα I strike, knock on (a door) (11)

κόρη, κόρης, ἡ girl

Κόρινθος, Κορίνθου, ἡ Corinth (14)

κόσμος, κόσμου, ὁ good order (15)
κόσμῳ in order (15)

κρήνη, κρήνης, ἡ spring (4)

Κρήτη, Κρήτης, ἡ Crete (6)

κυβερνήτης, κυβερνήτου, ὁ steersman

Κύκλωψ, Κύκλωπος, ὁ Cyclops (one-eyed monster) (7)

κῦμα, κύματος, τό wave (13)

κῡμαίνω I become rough

Κύπρος, Κύπρου, ἡ Cyprus

Κυρήνη, Κυρήνης, ἡ Cyrene

κύων, κυνός, ὁ or ἡ dog (5)

κωμάζω, ἐκώμασα I revel

Λ

λαβύρινθος, λαβυρίνθου, ὁ labyrinth (6)

λαγώς, λαγώ, ὁ hare

Λακεδαιμόνιοι, Λακεδαιμονίων, οἱ the Lacedaemonians, Spartans (14)

λαμβάνω, ἔλαβον I take; (middle + gen.) I seize, take hold of (2, 11)

λαμπρός, λαμπρά, λαμπρόν bright, brilliant (13)

λανθάνομαι, ἐλαθόμην (+ gen.) I forget

λέγω, εἶπον I say, tell, speak (1, 11)

λείπω, ἔλιπον I leave (3)

λέων, λέοντος, ὁ lion

Λεωνίδης, Λεωνίδου, ὁ Leonidas (14)

λίθινος, λιθίνη, λίθινον of stone

λίθος, λίθου, ὁ stone (3)

λιμήν, λιμένος, ὁ harbor (12)

λῑμός, λῑμοῦ, ὁ hunger

λίνον, λίνου, τό thread

λόγος, λόγου, ὁ word, story (11)

λύκος, λύκου, ὁ wolf (5)

λῡπέω, ἐλύπησα I grieve, pain; (middle) I am sad, sorrowful (16)

λύω I loosen (3)

M

μακρός, μακρά, μακρόν long, large (1)

μάλα very (4, 14)

μάλιστα very much, especially (4)
μάλιστά γε certainly, indeed (12)

μᾶλλον more, rather
μᾶλλον ἤ rather than

μανθάνω, ἔμαθον I learn, understand (11)

μάχαιρα, μαχαίρᾱς, ἡ knife

μάχη, μάχης, ἡ battle (13)

μάχομαι, ἐμαχεσάμην I fight, fight with (+ dat.) (6)

μέγας, μεγάλη, μέγα big (3, 14)
μέγα greatly, loudly (12)

μέγιστος, μεγίστη, μέγιστον very big, biggest (7, 14)

μεθύω I am drunk

μείζων, μεῖζον bigger (14)

μέλᾱς, μέλαινα, μέλαν black

Μέλιττα, Μελίττης, ἡ Melissa, daughter of Dicaeopolis and Myrrhine (4)

μέλλω (+ infinitive) I am about to, am destined to, intend to (7)

Μέμφις, Μέμφεως, ἡ Memphis

μέν ... δέ ... on the one hand ... on the other hand ... (2)

μένω, ἔμεινα I stay, wait; (transitive) I wait for (3)

μέρος, μέρους, τό part (15)

μέσος, μέση, μέσον middle (of) (9)
ἐν μέσῳ (+ gen.) between

μετά (+ gen.) with, (+ acc.) after (6, 14)

μή (with imperative) don't (2)
εἰ μή unless

μηδείς, μηδεμία, μηδέν (used
   instead of οὐδείς with imperatives and
   infinitives) no one, nothing, no (13)
μηκέτι (+ imperative) don't . . . any
   longer; (+ infinitive) no longer (3, 15)
μῆλα, μήλων, τά (plural) flocks (5)
μήτηρ, μητρός, ἡ mother (4)
μῑκρός, μῑκρά, μῑκρόν small (1)
Μῑνώταυρος, Μῑνωταύρου, ὁ
   Minotaur (6)
Μίνως, Μίνωος, ὁ Minos, king of
   Crete (6)
μισθός, μισθοῦ, ὁ reward, pay (11)
μνῆμα, μνήματος, τό monument
μόλις with difficulty, scarcely,
   reluctantly (4)
μόνος, μόνη, μόνον alone, only
   (15)
   μόνον only (15)
   οὐ μόνον . . . ἀλλὰ καί not
   only . . . but also (15)
μόσχος, μόσχου, ὁ calf
μῦθος, μύθου, ὁ story (5)
Μυκαλή, Μυκαλῆς, ἡ Mycale
Μυρρίνη, Μυρρίνης, ἡ Myrrhine,
   wife of Dicaeopolis (4)
μυχός, μυχοῦ, ὁ far corner

N
ναύαρχος, ναυάρχου, ὁ admiral
   (15)
ναύκληρος, ναυκλήρου, ὁ ship's
   captain (12)
ναυμαχέω, ἐναυμάχησα I fight by
   sea (15)
ναῦς, νεώς, ἡ ship (6)
ναύτης, ναύτου, ὁ sailor (12)
ναυτικόν, ναυτικοῦ, τό fleet (13)
νεᾱνίᾱς, νεᾱνίου, ὁ young man (8)
Νεῖλος, Νείλου, ὁ Nile
νεκρός, νεκροῦ, ὁ corpse (15)
νῆσος, νήσου, ἡ island (6)
νῑκάω I defeat, win (10)
νίκη, νίκης, ἡ victory (15)
   Νίκη, Νίκης, ἡ Nike, the goddess
   of victory (9)
νοσέω, ἐνόσησα I am sick, ill (11)
νοστέω, ἐνόστησα I return home
νοῦς, νοῦ, ὁ mind (15)
   ἐν νῷ ἔχω I have in mind, intend
   (4)

νύμφη, νύμφης, ἡ nymph
νύξ, νυκτός, ἡ night (6)
νῦν now (5)

Ξ
Ξανθίᾱς, Ξανθίου, ὁ Xanthias (2)
ξένος, ξένου, ὁ foreigner (7)
   ξεῖνος = ξένος
Ξέρξης, Ξέρξου, ὁ Xerxes (14)
ξίφος, ξίφους, τό sword

O
ὄγδοος, ὀγδόη, ὄγδοον eighth (8)
ὅδε, ἥδε, τόδε this, (pl.) these (14)
ὁ δέ and he
ὀβολός, ὀβολοῦ, ὁ obol (11)
ὁδός, ὁδοῦ, ἡ road, way, journey (4)
Ὀδυσσεύς, Ὀδυσσέως, ὁ
   Odysseus (7)
οἴκαδε homeward, to home (4)
οἰκέω, ᾤκησα I live, dwell (1)
οἰκίᾱ, ἡ house, home, dwelling (5)
οἴκοι at home (8)
οἶκος, οἴκου, ὁ house, home,
   dwelling (1)
   κατ' οἶκον at home (16)
οἴμοι alas! (11)
οἶνος, οἴνου, ὁ wine (7)
οἶς, οἰός, ὁ or ἡ sheep
ὀκνέω, ὤκνησα I shirk
ὀκτώ eight (8)
ὀλίγιστος, ὀλιγίστη, ὀλίγιστον
   smallest, (plural) fewest (14)
ὀλίγος, ὀλίγη, ὀλίγον small,
   (plural) few (14)
ὁλκάς, ὁλκάδος, ἡ merchant ship
ὅμῑλος, ὁμίλου, ὁ crowd (12)
ὅμως nevertheless (8)
ὄνομα, ὀνόματος, τό name (7)
   ὀνόματι by name, called (7)
ὄπισθεν (adverb or preposition + gen.)
   behind
ὁπλίτης, ὁπλίτου, ὁ hoplite (14)
ὅπου where (14)
ὁράω, εἶδον I see (5, 11)
ὀργίζομαι I grow angry (at + dat.) (13)
ὀρθός, ὀρθή, ὀρθόν straight, right,
   correct (12)
ὁρμάω, ὥρμησα I set in motion, set
   out, start, rush; (middle, intransitive) I
   set out, start, rush (7)

ὄρος, ὄρους, τό mountain, hill (5)

ὅς, ἥ, ὅ who, whose, whom, which, that (13)

ὅσπερ, ἥπερ, ὅπερ (emphatic forms) who, whose, whom, which, that (13)

ὅτε when (13)

ὅτι that (5)

οὐ, οὐκ, οὐχ not (1)

οὐ μόνον . . . ἀλλὰ καί not only . . . but also (15)

οὐδαμοῦ nowhere (16)

οὐδέ and . . . not, nor, not even (5)

οὐδείς, οὐδεμία, οὐδέν (pronoun) no one, nothing; (adjective) no (7)

οὐκέτι no longer (3)

οὖν (postpositive) and so (1)

οὐρανός, οὐρανοῦ, ὁ sky, heaven (9)

οὔτε . . . οὔτε neither . . . nor (5)

οὗτος, αὕτη, τοῦτο this, (plural) these (14)

οὕτω(ς) so, thus (2, 6)

οὐχί (an emphatic form of οὐ, οὐκ, οὐχ) not, no! (6)

ὀφθαλμός, ὀφθαλμοῦ, ὁ eye (7)

Π

παῖς, παιδός, ὁ or ἡ boy, girl, child (3)

πανήγυρις, πανηγύρεως, ἡ festival

πάντα everything

πανταχόσε in every direction (16)

πανταχοῦ everywhere (15)

πάππας, πάππου, ὁ father, papa (6)

πάππος, πάππου, ὁ grandfather (5)

παρά (+ acc.) to (11)

παραγίγνομαι, παρεγενόμην I arrive (14)

παραπλέω, παρέπλευσα I sail along, sail past

παρασκευάζω, παρεσκεύασα I prepare (7)

πάρειμι, (imperfect) παρῆν I am present, am here, am there; I am present at (+ dat.) (2)

παρέχω, παρέσχον I provide, give (6)

παρθένος, παρθένου, ἡ maiden, girl (6)

Παρθένος, Παρθένου, ἡ the Maiden, the goddess Athena (9)

Παρθενών, Παρθενῶνος, ὁ the Parthenon, temple of Athena on the Acropolis in Athens (8)

πᾶς, πᾶσα, πᾶν all, every (7)

πάσχω, ἔπαθον I suffer, experience (5, 11)

πατήρ, πατρός, ὁ father (3)

πατρίς, πατρίδος, ἡ fatherland (15)

παύω, ἔπαυσα I stop; (middle, intransitive) I stop (+ participle), cease from (+ gen.) (7)

πεζός, πεζή, πεζόν on foot (15)

πείθομαι (+ dat.) I obey (6)

πείθω, ἔπεισα I persuade (4)

Πειραιεύς, Πειραιῶς, ὁ Piraeus, the port of Athens (11)

πειράω, ἐπείρασα (active or middle) I try, attempt (15)

Πελοπόννησος, Πελοποννήσου, ἡ the Peloponnesus (14)

πέμπτος, πέμπτη, πέμπτον fifth (8)

πέμπω, ἔπεμψα I send (6)

πέντε five (8)

πέπλος, πέπλου, ὁ robe, cloth (15)

περί (+ acc.) around (7)

Πέρσαι, Περσῶν, οἱ the Persians (14)

Περσικός, Περσική, Περσικόν Persian (15)

πεσεῖν (aorist infinitive of πίπτω)

πίνω, ἔπιον I drink (9)

πίπτω, ἔπεσον I fall (3)

πιστεύω, ἐπίστευσα I trust, am confident (in) (+ dat.), I believe (15)

πλεῖστος, πλείστη, πλεῖστον most, very great, (plural) very many (12, 14)

πλείων/πλέων (alternative forms for either masculine or feminine), πλέον (neuter) more (12, 14)

πλέω, ἔπλευσα I sail (6)

πλῆθος, πλήθους, τό number, multitude (14)

πληρόω, ἐπλήρωσα I fill

πόθεν; from where? (7, 14)

ποθέν (enclitic) from somewhere (14)

ποῖ; where to? (14)

ποι (enclitic) to somewhere (14)

ποιέω, ἐποίησα I make, do (4)

ποιητής, ποιητοῦ, ὁ poet (8)
πολέμιος, πολεμίᾱ, πολέμιον hostile, enemy (14)
πολέμιοι, πολεμίων, οἱ the enemy (14)
πόλεμος, πολέμου, ὁ war (14)
πολιορκέω, ἐπολιόρκησα I besiege (16)
πόλις, πόλεως, ἡ city (7)
πολίτης, πολίτου, ὁ citizen (8)
πολλάκις many times, often (6)
πολλαχόσε to many parts (16)
πολύς, πολλή, πολύ much, (plural) many (1, 3, 14)
πομπή, πομπῆς, ἡ procession (9)
πονέω, ἐπόνησα I work (1)
πόνος, πόνου, ὁ toil, work (1)
Πόντος, Πόντου, ὁ Pontus, the Black Sea
πορεύομαι I go, walk, march, journey (6)
Ποσειδῶν, Ποσειδῶνος, ὁ Poseidon (13)
πόσος, πόση, πόσον how much? (plural) how many? (16)
ποταμός, ποταμοῦ, ὁ river (16)
πότε; when? (9, 14)
    ποτέ (enclitic) at some time, ever (10, 14)
ποῦ; where? (5, 14)
    που (enclitic) somewhere, anywhere (14)
ποῦ γῆς; where (in the world)? (16)
πούς, ποδός, ὁ foot
πρᾱττω, ἔπρᾱξα I do, fare (14)
πρό (+ gen.) before (of time or place) (10)
πρόγονος, προγόνου, ὁ ancestor (15)
πρός (+ dat.) at, near, by, (+ acc.), to, toward, against, upon (1, 4, 11)
προσβάλλω, προσέβαλον (+ dat.) I attack (14)
προσέρχομαι, προσῆλθον (+ dat. or πρός + acc.) I approach (11)
προσπλέω, προσέπλευσα I sail toward
προστρέχω, προσέδραμον I run toward
προσχωρέω, προσεχώρησα (+ dat.) I go toward, approach (3)

τῇ προτεραίᾳ on the day before (14)
προχωρέω, προεχώρησα (or προὐχώρησα) I go forward, come forward, advance (6)
πρῶτος, πρώτη, πρῶτον first, (as noun in plural) leaders (5)
πρῶτον first (4)
    τὸ πρῶτον at first
πύλαι, πυλῶν, αἱ (plural) double gates, pass (6, 14)
πῦρ, πυρός, τό fire (7)
πυραμίς, πυραμίδος, ἡ pyramid
πῶς; how? (7, 14)
    πως (enclitic) somehow, in any way (14)
    πῶς ἔχεις; How are you? (11)

Ρ

ῥάβδος, ῥάβδου, ὁ wand
ῥᾴδιος, ῥᾳδίᾱ, ῥᾴδιον easy (4)
ῥᾴθῡμος, ῥᾴθῡμον lazy (4)
ῥῆμα, ῥήματος, τό word
ῥόπαλον, ῥοπάλου, τό stake

Σ

Σαλαμίς, Σαλαμῖνος, ἡ Salamis (13)
Σάμος, Σάμου, ἡ Samos
σῑγάω, ἐσῑγησα I am silent (9)
Σικελίᾱ, Σικελίᾱς, ἡ Sicily
Σιμωνίδης, Σιμωνίδου, ὁ Simonides (15)
σῖτος, σῑτου, ὁ grain, food (1)
σκοπέω, ἐσκεψάμην I look at, examine, consider (11)
σκότος, σκότου, ὁ darkness
Σκυθίᾱ, Σκυθίᾱς, ἡ Scythia
σός, σή, σόν your (singular) (5)
σοφός, σοφή, σοφόν skilled, wise, clever (11)
Σπαρτιάτης, Σπαρτιάτου, ὁ Spartan (14)
σπείρω I sow
σπέρμα, σπέρματος, τό seed
σπεύδω, ἔσπευσα I hurry (2)
σπονδή, σπονδῆς, ἡ libation (10)
    σπονδαί, σπονδῶν, αἱ (plural) peace treaty (16)
σπουδή, σπουδῆς, ἡ haste, eagerness (15)
στέλλω, ἔστειλα I take down (sails)

στενά, στενῶν, τά (plural) narrows, straits, mountain pass (13)

στενάζω I groan (4)

στενός, στενή, στενόν narrow (14)

στοά, στοᾶς, ἡ colonnade

στόλος, στόλου, ὁ expedition, army, fleet (14)

στρατεύω, ἐστράτευσα (active or middle) I wage war, campaign (16)

στρατηγός, στρατηγοῦ, ὁ general (15)

στρατιώτης, στρατιώτου, ὁ soldier (14)

στρατός, στρατοῦ, ὁ army (14)

στρογγύλος, στρογγύλη, στρογγύλον round

σύ you (singular) (3)

συμβάλλω, συνέβαλον I join battle with (14)

σύμμαχος, συμμάχου, ὁ ally (16)

συμπίπτω, συνέπεσον (+ dat.) I clash with (15)

συμφορά, συμφορᾶς, ἡ misfortune, disaster (16)

συναγείρω, συνήγειρα I gather (transitive); (middle, intransitive) I gather together (16)

συνέρχομαι, συνῆλθον I come together (14)

συφεός, συφεοῦ, ὁ pigsty

Σφίγξ, Σφιγγός, ἡ Sphinx

σῴζω, ἔσωσα I save (6)

σώφρων, σῶφρον wise, prudent, well-behaved (7)

T

ταύτῃ this way

ταχέως quickly (4)

τάχιστα very quickly, most quickly (12)

ὡς τάχιστα as quickly as possible (12)

ταχύς, ταχεῖα, ταχύ quick, swift (13)

τε ... καί or τε καί both ... and (3)

τεῖχος, τείχους, τό wall (12)

τεκόντες, τεκόντων, οἱ (plural) parents (10)

τελευτάω, ἐτελεύτησα I end, die (16)

τέλος in the end, finally (8)

τέμενος, τεμένους, τό sacred precinct

τέρπομαι I enjoy myself; I enjoy (+ dat. or participle) (9)

τέταρτος, τετάρτη, τέταρτον fourth (8)

τέτταρες, τέτταρα four (8)

τῇδε here

τῇ ὑστεραίᾳ on the next day (8)

τῇ προτεραίᾳ on the day before (14)

τί; what? (4)

τῑμάω, ἐτίμησα I honor (6)

τις (indefinite pronoun, enclitic) someone, something, anyone, anything; (indefinite adjective, enclitic) a certain, a, some (7)

τίς; (interrogative pronoun) who? (interrogative adjective) which ... ? what ... ? (7)

τλήμων, τλήμονος poor, wretched

τοσοῦτος, τοσαύτη, τοσοῦτο so great, (plural) so many, so great (3)

τότε then (12)

τραγῳδίᾱ, τραγῳδίᾱς, ἡ tragedy

τρεῖς, τρία three (8)

τρέπω, ἔτρεψα I turn; (middle, intransitive) I turn myself, turn (10)

τρέχω, ἔδραμον I run (5)

τριᾱκόσιοι, τριᾱκόσιαι, τριᾱκόσια three hundred

τριήρης, τριήρους, ἡ trireme (13)

τρίτος, τρίτη, τρίτον third (8)

Τροίᾱ, Τροίᾱς, ἡ Troy (7)

τύπτω I strike (6)

τυφλός, τυφλή, τυφλόν blind (11)

τύχη, τύχης, ἡ chance, luck, fortune (15)

τῷ ὄντι in truth (13)

Y

ὑδρίᾱ, ὑδρίᾱς, ἡ water jar (4)

ὕδωρ, ὕδατος, τό water (10)

ὑλακτέω I bark

ὑμεῖς you (plural) (5)

ὑμέτερος, ὑμετέρᾱ, ὑμέτερον your (plural) (5)

ὑμνέω, ὕμνησα I hymn, praise

ὑπέρ (+ gen.) on behalf of, for, above (8)

ὑπηρέτης, ὑπηρέτου, ὁ attendant (5)

ὑπό (+ dat.), under (5)

ὑστεραίᾳ (see τῇ ὑστεραίᾳ)

ὕστερον later (16)

Φ

φαίνομαι I appear (12)

Φάληρον, Φαλήρου, τό Phalerum, the old harbor of Athens (14)

φᾱσί(ν) (postpositive enclitic) they say (6)

Φειδίᾱς, Φειδίου, ὁ Pheidias, the great Athenian sculptor (9)

φέρω, ἤνεγκα or ἤνεγκον I carry, (of roads) lead (1)

φεῦ (often used with gen. of cause) alas! (10)

φεύγω, ἔφυγον I flee, escape (5)

φησί(ν) (postpositive enclitic) he/she says (3)
  φᾱσί(ν) (postpositive enclitic) they say (6)

φιλέω, ἐφίλησα I love (1)

Φίλιππος, Φιλίππου, ὁ Philip (3)

φίλος, φίλη, φίλον dear, friendly; (as noun) friend (4)

φλυᾱρέω I talk nonsense

φοβέομαι, (imperfect) ἐφοβούμην I fear, am afraid of (something or someone), am frightened, am afraid (6)

φοβερός, φοβερά̄, φοβερόν terrifying

φράζω, ἔφρασα I tell (of) (14)

φροντίζω, ἐφρόντισα I worry, care (12)

φυλάττω, ἐφύλαξα I guard (5)

φυγή, φυγῆς, ἡ flight, (15)

X

χαῖρε, (plural) χαίρετε greetings! (4)

χαίρω I rejoice (1)
  χαίρειν κελεύω I bid farewell (12)

χαλεπός, χαλεπή, χαλεπόν difficult (1)

χειμών, χειμῶνος, ὁ storm, winter (7)

χείρ, χειρός, ἡ hand (8)

χορός, χοροῦ, ὁ dance, chorus (4)

χράομαι, ἐχρησάμην (+ dat.) I use, enjoy (14)

χρόνος, χρόνου, ὁ time (1)

Ψ

ψευδής, ψευδές false (13)
  ψευδῆ, ψευδῶν, τά lies (13)

Ω

ὦ Ζεῦ O Zeus (3)

ὠθίζομαι I push

ὤν, οὖσα, ὄν being

ὤνια, ὠνίων, τά wares

ὡς (adverb) how; (conjunction) as, when, that (6, 13, 14)
  ὡς δοκεῖ as it seems (13)
  ὡς τάχιστα as quickly as possible (12)

ὥσπερ just as (8)

ὥστε so that, that (5)

ὠφελέω, ὠφέλησα I help, benefit (11)

ENGLISH TO GREEK VOCABULARY

Note: This English to Greek vocabulary is provided merely as a reminder of approximate Greek equivalents of English words. For further information about the Greek words, you must consult the Greek to English vocabulary and the readings and grammar sections in the various chapters of this book.

A
a τις
able, I am δύναμαι
about to, I am μέλλω
accomplish, I
  ἐργάζομαι
Achaeans Ἀχαιοί
Acropolis Ἀκρόπολις
admiral ναύαρχος
admire, I θαυμάζω
advance, I προχωρέω
Aegean Sea Αἰγαῖος
  πόντος
Aegeus Αἰγεύς
Aeolus Αἴολος
Aeschylus Αἰσχύλος
afraid (of), I am
  φοβέομαι
after μετά
again αὖθις
against ἐπί, πρός
Agamemnon
  Ἀγαμέμνων
agora ἀγορά
alas! οἴμοι, φεῦ
all ἅπας, πᾶς
all right! ἔστω
allowed, it is ἔξεστι(ν)
ally σύμμαχος
alone μόνος
already ἤδη
also καί
altar βωμός
although καίπερ
always αἰεί
amazed, I am θαυμάζω
among ἐν
ancestor πρόγονος
and δέ, καί

and . . . not οὐδέ
and so οὖν
angry (at), I grow
  ὀργίζομαι
animal ζῷον
announce, I ἀγγέλλω
another ἄλλος
answer, I ἀποκρίνομαι
anyone/anything τις/τι
anywhere που
appear, I φαίνομαι
approach, I
  προσέρχομαι,
  προσχωρέω
Argus Ἄργος
Ariadne Ἀριάδνη
army στόλος, στρατός
around περί
arrive (at), I
  ἀφικνέομαι,
  παραγίγνομαι
Artemisium
  Ἀρτεμίσιον
as ὡς
Asclepius Ἀσκλήπιος
Asia (Minor) Ἀσία
ask, I αἰτέω, ἐρωτάω
as quickly as possible ὡς
  τάχιστα
at εἰς, ἐπί, πρός
at first τὸ πρῶτον
Athena Ἀθήνη,
  Παρθένος
Athenian Ἀθηναῖος
Athenians Ἀθηναῖοι
Athens Ἀθῆναι
Athens, at Ἀθήνησι
Athens, in ἐν ταῖς
  Ἀθήναις

Athens, to Ἀθήναζε
at least γε
at some time ποτέ
attack, I ἐμπίπτω,
  προσβάλλω
attempt, I πειράω,
  πειράομαι
attendant ὑπηρέτης
at that very moment
  ἐνταῦθα δή
Attica Ἀττική
away (from), I am
  ἄπειμι

B
bad κακός
bag ἀσκός
barbarian βάρβαρος
bark, I ὑλακτέω
battle μάχη
be! ἴσθι
beast θηρίον
beautiful καλός
beautiful, more
  καλλίων
beautiful, most/very
  κάλλιστος
become, I γίγνομαι
become, he/she/it has
  γέγονε
before πρό
beginning ἀρχή
behind ὄπισθεν
being ὤν
benefit, I ὠφελέω
besiege, I πολιορκέω
be so!, let it ἔστω
best ἄριστος

better ἀμείνων
between ἐν μέσῳ
bid farewell, I χαίρειν
  κελεύω
big μέγας
bigger μείζων
big, very/biggest
  μέγιστος
black μέλᾱς
Black Sea, the Πόντος
blame, to (adj.) αἴτιος
blind τυφλός
Boeotia Βοιωτίᾱ
both . . . and καί . . .
  καί or τε . . . καί
boy παῖς
brave ἀνδρεῖος
bravely ἀνδρείως
bridge γέφῡρα
bright λαμπρός
brilliant λαμπρός
bring, I κομίζω
bring in, I εἰσφέρω
brother ἀδελφός
burn, I καίω
but ἀλλά, δέ
by πρός
by land κατὰ γῆν
by sea κατὰ θάλατταν
Byzantium Βυζάντιον

C
calf μόσχος
call, I καλέω
called ὀνόματι
call in, I εἰσκαλέω
call out, I ἐκκαλέω
campaign, I στρατεύω
can, I δύναμαι
captain: see ship's
  captain
care, I φροντίζω
carry, I φέρω
carry out, I ἐκφέρω
catch, I καταλαμβάνω
cave ἄντρον
cease from, I παύομαι
certain, a τις
certainly μάλιστά γε
chance τύχη
child παῖς

chorus χορός
Cimon Κίμων
Circe Κίρκη
citizen πολίτης
city ἄστυ, πόλις
city center ἀγορᾷ
clash with, I συμπίπτω
clever σοφός
climb, I ἀναβαίνω
cloth πέπλος
colonnade στοά
come, I ἔρχομαι
come! ἐλθέ
come back, I
  ἐπανέρχομαι
come back! ἐπάνελθε
come back, to ἐπανιέναι
come down, I
  καταβαίνω
come forward, I
  προχωρέω
come, I have ἥκω
come in, I εἰσβαίνω,
  εἰσέρχομαι
come in! εἴσελθε
come on! ἄγε
come out (of), I ἐκβαίνω,
  ἐξέρχομαι
come together, I
  συνέρχομαι
coming out ἐξελθών
companion ἑταῖρος
compel, I ἀναγκάζω
comrade ἑταῖρος
confident in, I am
  πιστεύω
consider, I σκοπέω
contest ἀγών
converse with, I
  διαλέγομαι
Corinth Κόρινθος
corpse νεκρός
correct ὀρθός
courage ἀρετή
Crete Κρήτη
cross, I διαβαίνω
crowd ὅμιλος
cry, I δακρύω
cursed κατάρᾱτος
Cyclops Κύκλωψ
Cyprus Κύπρος

Cyrene Κυρήνη

D
dance χορός
danger κίνδῡνος
darkness σκότος
daughter θυγάτηρ
day ἡμέρᾱ
day before, on the τῇ
  προτεραίᾳ
day, on the next τῇ
  ὑστεραίᾳ
dear φίλος
death θάνατος
decide, I δοκεῖ μοι
deed ἔργον
defeat, I νῑκάω
defend myself (against),
  I ἀμύνομαι
desert, I καταλείπω
destined to, I am μέλλω
destroy, I ἀπόλλῡμι,
  διαφθείρω
Dicaeopolis
  Δικαιόπολις
die, I ἀποθνῄσκω,
  τελευτάω
difficult χαλεπός
difficulty ἀπορίᾱ
difficulty, with μόλις
din θόρυβος
dinner δεῖπνον
Dionysus Διόνῡσος
direction, in every
  πανταχόσε
disaster συμφορά
disembark ἐκβαίνω ἐκ
  τῆς νεώς
do, I ποιέω, πράττω
doctor ἰᾱτρός
dog κύων
don't μή
don't . . . any longer
  μηκέτι
door θύρᾱ
down κατά
drachma δραχμή
drag, I ἕλκω
drink, I πίνω
drive, I ἐλαύνω
drive away, I ἀπελαύνω

drive in, I εἰσελαύνω
drive out, I ἐξελαύνω
drop, I καταβάλλω
drunk, I am μεθύω
during (*use acc. of
  duration of time*)
dwell, I οἰκέω
dwelling οἰκίᾱ, οἶκος

E
eagerness σπουδή
earth γῆ
easy ῥᾴδιος
eat, I δειπνέω, ἐσθίω
Egypt Αἴγυπτος
Egyptians Αἰγύπτιοι
eight ὀκτώ
eighth ὄγδοος
either . . . or ἤ . . . ἤ
embark, I εἰς ναῦν
  εἰσβαίνω
end, I τελευτάω
enemy πολέμιος
enemy, the πολέμιοι
enjoy (myself), I
  τέρπομαι
enjoy, I χράομαι
enslave, I δουλόω
entrance εἴσοδος
Ephialtes Ἐφιάλτης
Epidaurus Ἐπίδαυρος
escape, I φεύγω
escape from, I ἐκφεύγω
escape route ἔκπλους
especially μάλιστα
Euboea Εὔβοια
Eurylochus Εὐρύλοχος
Eurymedon River, the
  Εὐρυμέδων
evening ἑσπέρᾱ
ever ποτέ
every ἅπᾱς, πᾶς
every day καθ' ἡμέρᾱν
everything πάντα
everywhere πανταχοῦ
examine, I σκοπέω
excellence ἀρετή
expect, I ἐλπίζω
expedition στόλος
experience πάσχω
eye ὀφθαλμός

F
fall, I πίπτω
fall down, I καταπίπτω
fall (of evening)
  γίγνεται
fall on, I ἐμπίπτω
fall out, I ἐκπίπτω
fall upon, I ἐμπίπτω
false ψευδής
far corner μυχός
fare, I πρᾱ́ττω
farm κλῆρος
farm, I γεωργέω
farmer αὐτουργός
father πάππας, πατήρ
fatherland πατρίς
fear, I φοβέομαι
festival ἑορτή,
  πανήγυρις
few (*plural of* ὀλίγος)
fewer (*plural of*
  ἐλάττων)
fewest (*plural of*
  ὀλίγιστος)
field ἀγρός
fierce ἄγριος
fifth πέμπτος
fight (with), I μάχομαι
fight by sea, I ναυμαχέω
fill, I πληρόω
finally τέλος
find, I εὑρίσκω
fire πῦρ
fire, I am on καίομαι
firm βέβαιος
first πρῶτος
first, at πρῶτον
five πέντε
flee, I φεύγω
flee (away), I ἀποφεύγω
flee (out), I ἐκφεύγω
fleet ναυτικόν, στόλος
flight φυγή
flocks μῆλα
flow in, I εἰσρέω
follow, I ἕπομαι
food σῖτος
foot πούς
foot, on πεζός
for γάρ, εἰς, ὑπέρ
foreigner ξένος

forget, I λανθάνομαι
four τέτταρες
fourth τέταρτος
free, I ἐλευθερόω
free ἐλεύθερος
freedom ἐλευθερίᾱ
friend φίλη, φίλος
friendly φίλος
frightened, I am
  φοβέομαι
frightfully δεινῶς
from ἀπό

G
garden κῆπος
gates, double πύλαι
gather (together), I
  συναγείρω
general στρατηγός
get into, I ἐμβαίνω
get (myself) up, I (*see
  αἴρω, ἐπαίρω*)
get up, I ἀναβαίνω
giant γίγᾱς
girl κόρη, παῖς,
  παρθένος
give, I παρέχω
go, I βαδίζω, βαίνω,
  ἔρχομαι, πορεύομαι
go! ἴθι
go away, I ἀπέρχομαι
go down, I καταβαίνω
go forward, I προχωρέω
go in, I εἰσβαίνω,
  εἰσέρχομαι
go in, to εἰσιέναι
go on! ἴθι δή
go on board ship, I εἰς
  ναῦν εἰσβαίνω
go out of, I ἐκβαίνω,
  ἐξέρχομαι
go through, I διέρχομαι
go, to ἰέναι
go toward, I προσχωρέω
go up (onto), I ἀναβαίνω
goat αἴξ
god θεός
goddess θεός
good ἀγαθός
good! εὖ γε
good order κόσμος

grain σῖτος
grandfather πάππος
grapes βότρυες
greatly μέγα
Greece Ἑλλάς
Greek(s) Ἕλλην(ες)
Greeks Ἀχαιοί
greetings! χαῖρε
grieve, I λῡπέω
groan, I στενάζω
ground γῆ
grow angry, I
    ὀργίζομαι
guard, I φυλάττω

H
hand χείρ
happen, I γίγνομαι
harbor λιμήν
hare λαγώς
harm, I βλάπτω
haste σπουδή
have, I ἔχω
he, and ὁ δέ
head κεφαλή
heal, I ἰᾱτρεύω
hear, I ἀκούω
heaven οὐρανός
Hellas Ἑλλάς
Hellespont
    Ἑλλήσποντος
help, I βοηθέω, ὠφελέω
her αὐτήν
herald κῆρυξ
here δεῦρο, ἐνθάδε,
    ἐνταῦθα, τῇδε
here, I am πάρειμι
herself (see ἐμαυτοῦ)
hill ὄρος
him αὐτόν
himself (see ἐμαυτοῦ)
hold, I ἔχω
hold (a festival), I ποιέω
hold onto, I ἔχομαι
home οἰκίᾱ, οἶκος
home, at κατ' οἶκον,
    οἴκοι
home, to οἴκαδε
homeward οἴκαδε
honor, I τῑμάω
hope, I ἐλπίζω

hoplite ὁπλίτης
horse ἵππος
hostile πολέμιος
house οἰκίᾱ, οἶκος
how ὡς
how? πῶς;
How are you? πῶς ἔχεις
how many (plural of
    πόσος)
how much πόσος
human being ἄνθρωπος
hundred, a ἑκατόν
hunger λῑμός
hurry, I σπεύδω
husband ἀνήρ
hymn, I ὑμνέω

I
I ἐγώ
I am εἰμί
if εἰ
if perhaps, if somehow εἰ
    πως
ill, I am νοσέω
immediately εὐθύς
impossible ἀδύνατος
in ἐν
in, I am ἔνειμι
in Athens ἐν ταῖς
    Ἀθήναις
increase, I αὐξάνω
indeed γε, δή,
    μάλιστά γε
in every direction
    πανταχόσε
in the end τέλος
in fact δή
in the field ἐν τῷ ἀγρῷ
inhabitant ἔνοικος
intend, I ἐν νῷ ἔχω,
    μέλλω
into εἰς
Ionia Ἰωνίᾱ
Ionians Ἴωνες
is, he/she/it ἐστί(ν)
island νῆσος
it αὐτήν, αὐτό, αὐτόν
itself (see ἐμαυτοῦ)

J
jar, water ὑδρίᾱ

join battle with, I
    συμβάλλω
journey, I πορεύομαι
journey ὁδός
just as ὥσπερ

K
kill, I ἀποκτείνω
killed, he/she has
    ἀπέκτονε
kindle, I καίω
kindly εὐμενῶς
king βασιλεύς
knife μάχαιρα
knock on (a door), I
    κόπτω
Knossos Κνωσσός
know, I ἐπίσταμαι
know, get to, I γιγνώσκω

L
labyrinth λαβύρινθος
Lacedaemonians, the
    Λακεδαιμόνιοι
land γῆ
land, on or by κατὰ γῆν
large μακρός
later ὕστερον
lazy ἀργός, ῥᾴθυμος
lead (of roads), I φέρω
lead, I ἄγω, ἡγέομαι
leaders (plural of
    πρῶτος)
lead in, I εἰσάγω,
    εἰσηγέομαι
lead out, I ἐξάγω
learn, I γιγνώσκω,
    μανθάνω
least of all ἥκιστά γε
leave, I λείπω
leave behind, I
    καταλείπω
left hand ἀριστερά
Leonidas Λεωνίδης
libation σπονδή
lie, I κεῖμαι
lie down, I κατάκειμαι
lie near, I ἐπίκειμαι
lie off, I ἐπίκειμαι
lies ψευδῆ
life βίος

lift, I αἴρω
lift up, I ἐπαίρω
lion λέων
listen, I ἀκούω
live, I οἰκέω
long μακρός
long (of time) πολύς
look, I βλέπω
look! ἰδού
look at, I θεάομαι,
   σκοπέω
look for, I ζητέω
loosen, I λύω
lose, I ἀπόλλῡμι
loss, I am at a ἀπορέω
loss, state of being at a
   ἀπορίᾱ
loudly μέγα
love, I ἐράω, φιλέω
luck τύχη

M
maiden παρθένος
make, I ποιέω
man ἀνήρ, ἄνθρωπος
man, young νεᾱνίᾱς
many πολλοί
many times πολλάκις
march, I πορεύομαι
market place ἀγορά
master δεσπότης
may ἔξεστι(ν)
me με
meanwhile ἐν . . .
   τούτῳ
Melissa Μέλιττα
Memphis Μέμφις
merchant ἔμπορος
merchant ship ὁλκάς
messenger ἄγγελος
middle (of) μέσος
mind νοῦς
mind, have in, I ἐν νῷ
   ἔχω
mine ἐμός
Minos Μίνως
Minotaur Μῑνώταυρος
misfortune συμφορά
money ἀργύριον
monument μνῆμα

more μᾶλλον,
   πλείων/πλέων
more, and what is καὶ
   δὴ καί
most μάλιστα,
   πλεῖστος
mother μήτηρ
motion, set in, I ὁρμάω
motionless ἀκίνητος
mountain ὄρος
mountain pass στενά
Mount Etna Αἰτναῖον
   ὄρος
much πολύς
mule ἡμίονος
multitude πλῆθος
must δεῖ
my ἐμός
Mycale Μυκαλή
Myrrhine Μυρρίνη
myself (see ἐμαυτοῦ)

N
name ὄνομα
name, by ὀνόματι
narrow στενός
narrows στενά
near ἐγγύς, πρός
necessary, it is δεῖ
neither . . . nor
   οὔτε . . . οὔτε
nevertheless ὅμως
next day, on the τῇ
   ὑστεραίᾳ
night νύξ
Nike Νίκη
Nile Νεῖλος
nine ἐννέα
ninth ἔνατος
no μηδείς, οὐδείς,
   οὐδέν, οὐχί
noble ἄριστος
no longer μηκέτι,
   οὐκέτι
no one μηδείς, οὐδείς
nor οὐδέ
not οὐ, οὐκ, οὐχ,
   οὐχί
not, and οὐδέ
not at all ἥκιστά γε
nothing μηδέν, οὐδέν

not only . . . but also οὐ
   μόνον . . . ἀλλὰ
   καί
now ἤδη, νῦν
nowhere οὐδαμοῦ
number πλῆθος
nymph νύμφη

O
obey, I πείθομαι
obol ὀβολός
obstruct, I ἐμποδίζω
Odysseus Ὀδυσσεύς
often πολλάκις
old γεραιός
old man γέρων
on ἐν, ἐπί, κατά,
   πρός
on behalf of ὑπέρ
on the next day τῇ
   ὑστεραίᾳ
on the one hand . . . on the
   other hand . . .
   μέν . . . δέ . . .
one εἷς
one another, of
   ἀλλήλων
only μόνον, μόνος
onto εἰς, ἐπί
opposite ἐναντίος
or ἤ
order, I κελεύω
order, in κόσμῳ
other ἄλλος
our ἡμέτερος
out of ἐκ
out of the field ἐκ τοῦ
   ἀγροῦ
overtake, I
   καταλαμβάνω
ox βοῦς

P
pain, cause, I λῡπέω
papa πάππας
parents τεκόντες
part μέρος
Parthenon Παρθενών
particular, and in καὶ
   δὴ καί

parts, to many
  πολλαχόσε
pass πύλαι
path ἀτραπός
pay μισθός
peace εἰρήνη
peace treaty σπονδαί
Peloponnesus, the
  Πελοπόννησος
pelt, I βάλλω
people, the δῆμος
perplexity ἀπορίᾱ
Persian Περσικός
Persians, the Πέρσαι
person ἄνθρωπος
persuade, I πείθω
Phalerum Φάληρον
Pheidias Φειδίᾱς
Philip Φίλιππος
pigsty σῦφεός
Piraeus Πειραιεύς
place, to this ἐνθάδε
plow, I ἀροτρεύω
plow ἄροτρον
plowing ἄροτος
poet ποιητής
Pontus Πόντος
poor τλήμων
Poseidon Ποσειδῶν
possible δυνατός
possible, it is ἔξεστι(ν)
praise, I ὑμνέω
pray (to), I εὔχομαι
precinct, sacred τέμενος
prepare, I
  παρασκευάζω,
  παρασκευάζομαι
present (at), I am
  πάρειμι
priest ἱερεύς
prison δεσμωτήριον
procession πομπή
promontory ἀκτή
propitious ἵλαος
provide, I παρέχω
prudent σώφρων
punish, I κολάζω
pursue, I διώκω
push, I ὠθίζομαι
put, I βάλλω
pyramid πυραμίς

Q

quick ταχύς
quickly ταχέως
quickly, very/most
  τάχιστα
quiet, keep, I ἡσυχάζω

R

raise, I ἐπαίρω
rather μᾶλλον
rather than μᾶλλον ἤ
ready ἕτοιμος
rear, from the ἐκ τοῦ
  ὄπισθεν
receive, I δέχομαι
refuse, I οὐκ ἐθέλω
rejoice, I χαίρω
relate, I ἐξηγέομαι
reluctantly μόλις
resist, I ἀντέχω
responsible (for) αἴτιος
retreat, I ἀναχωρέω
return (to), I
  ἐπανέρχομαι
return home, I νοστέω
return, to ἐπανιέναι
revel, I κωμάζω
revolt from, I
  ἀφίσταμαι
reward μισθός
right δεξιός, ὀρθός
right hand δεξιά
right time καιρός
right time, just at the εἰς
  καιρόν
river ποταμός
road ὁδός
robe πέπλος
rough, I become
  κυμαίνω
round στρογγύλος
route, escape ἔκπλους
row, I ἐρέσσω
rower ἐρέτης
rule, I βασιλεύω
run, I τρέχω
run toward, I
  προστρέχω
rush, I ὁρμάω

S

sad, I am λῡπέομαι
said, he/she ἔφη
said, they ἔφασαν
sail, I πλέω
sail against, I ἐπιπλέω
sail along, I παραπλέω
sail away, I ἀποπλέω
sail into, I εἰσπλέω
sail out, I ἐκπλέω
sail past, I παραπλέω
sail toward, I προσπλέω
sailor ναύτης
sails ἱστία
Salamis Σαλαμίς
same time, at the ἅμα
Samos Σάμος
sausage-seller
  ἀλλαντοπώλης
savage ἄγριος
save, I σῴζω
say, I λέγω
say, to εἰπεῖν
say, they φᾱσί(ν)
says, he/she φησί(ν)
scarcely μόλις
Scythia Σκυθίᾱ
sea θάλαττα
sea, by κατὰ θάλατταν
second δεύτερος
see, I βλέπω, θεάομαι,
  θεωρέω, ὁράω
seed σπέρμα
seek, I ζητέω
seems, as it ὡς δοκεῖ
seems (good), it δοκεῖ
seems good to me, it μοι
  δοκεῖ
seize, I λαμβάνομαι
self, -selves αὐτός
send, I πέμπω
send against, I
  ἐπιπέμπω
send away, I ἀποπέμπω
send in, I ἐπιπέμπω
send out, I ἐκπέμπω
servants θεράποντες
set free, I ἐλευθερόω
set out, I ὁρμάω,
  ὁρμάομαι
seven ἑπτά

seventh ἕβδομος
sheep οἶς
sheepfold αὔλιον
ship ναῦς
ship, merchant ὁλκάς
ship's captain
    ναύκληρος
shirk, I ὀκνέω
shout, I βοάω
shout βοή
show, I δηλόω
Sicily Σικελίᾱ
sick, I am κάμνω,
    νοσέω
silent, I am σῑγάω
silver ἀργύριον
Simonides Σιμωνίδης
sit, I καθίζω,
    καθίζομαι
sit down, (make
    someone), I καθίζω
six ἕξ
sixth ἕκτος
skilled σοφός
sky οὐρανός
slave δοῦλος
sleep, I καθεύδω
slowly βραδέως
small μῑκρός, ὀλίγος
smaller ἐλάττων,
    μῑκρότερος
smallest μῑκρότατος,
    ὀλίγιστος
so οὕτω(ς)
so great τοσοῦτος
so many (plural of
    τοσοῦτος)
so that ὥστε
soldier στρατιώτης
some τις
somehow πως
someone/something
    τις/τι
something bad κακόν τι
somewhere που
somewhere, from ποθέν
somewhere, to ποι
soon δι' ὀλίγου
sorrowful, I am
    λῡπέομαι
sow, I σπείρω

Spartan Σπαρτιᾱτης
Spartans, the
    Λακεδαιμόνιοι
speak, I λέγω
Sphinx Σφίγξ
spirit θῡμός
spring κρήνη
stake ῥόπαλον
stand/stood (see ἔστην,
    page 184)
stand up! ἀνάστηθι
start, I ὁρμάω
statue εἰκών
stay, I μένω
steersman κυβερνήτης
step, I βαίνω
step out, I ἐκβαίνω
still ἔτι
stone λίθος
stone, of λίθινος
stood ἔστην
stood up ἀνέστην
stop, I παύω
stop! παῦε
stop (doing), I παύομαι
storm χειμών
story λόγος, μῦθος
straight ὀρθός
straits στενά
strike, I κόπτω, τύπτω
strong ἰσχῡρός
struggle ἀγών
suffer, I πάσχω
sun ἥλιος
swift ταχύς
sword ξίφος

T
take, I ἄγω, αἱρέω,
    κομίζω, λαμβάνω
take across, to
    διαβιβάσαι
take down (sails), I
    στέλλω
take hold of, I
    λαμβάνομαι
take in, I εἰσάγω
take out, I ἐξαιρέω
talk nonsense, I
    φλῡαρέω
talk to, I διαλέγομαι

tell, I λέγω
tell, to εἰπεῖν
tell (of), I φράζω
tell (someone to do
    something), I κελεύω
tell! εἰπέ
temple ἱερόν
ten δέκα
tenth δέκατος
terrible δεινός
terrible things δεινά
terribly δεινά, δεινῶς
terrifying φοβερός
than ἤ
that ἐκεῖνος
that ὅς, ὅσπερ, ὅτι,
    ὥστε
theater θέᾱτρον
them (see αὐτός)
Themistocles
    Θεμιστοκλῆς
then ἐνταῦθα (δή),
    ἔπειτα, τότε
there ἐκεῖ, ἐνταῦθα
there, I am πάρειμι
there, to ἐκεῖσε
Thermopylae
    Θερμοπύλαι
Theseus Θησεύς
things (use neuter plural
    of adjective)
think it best, I δοκεῖ μοι
third τρίτος
this, these ὅδε, οὗτος
those ἐκεῖνος
thread λίνον
three τρεῖς
three hundred
    τριᾱκόσιοι
through διά
throw, I βάλλω
throw down, I
    καταβάλλω
throw out, I ἐκβάλλω
Thunderer Βρόμιος
thus οὕτω(ς)
time χρόνος
time, (right) καιρός
tin κασσίτερος
tired, I am κάμνω
to εἰς, παρά, πρός

to blame (*adj.*) αἴτιος
together ἅμα
toil πόνος
told, I, they εἶπον
tomorrow αὔριον
too καί
top (of) ἄκρος
top of the mountain/hill
  ἄκρον τὸ ὄρος
toward πρός
tragedy τραγῳδίᾱ
transport, to
  διαβιβάσαι
tree δένδρον
trireme τριήρης
Troy Τροίᾱ
true ἀληθής
trust, I πιστεύω
truth ἀληθῆ
truth, in τῷ ὄντι
try, I πειράω,
  πειράομαι
turn, I τρέπω
turn (myself), I
  τρέπομαι
two δύο
two hundred διακόσιοι

U
under ὑπό
understand, I
  ἐπίσταμαι,
  μανθάνω
unless εἰ μή
until ἕως
up ἀνά
upon ἐπί, πρός
uproar θόρυβος
us ἡμῶν, ἡμῖν, ἡμᾶς
use, I χράομαι

V
very μάλα
very big μέγιστος
very good ἄριστος
very great πλεῖστος
very many (*plural of*
  πλεῖστος)

very much μάλιστα
victim, sacrificial
  ἱερεῖον
victory νίκη
virtue ἀρετή

W
wage war, I στρατεύω
wagon ἅμαξα
wait (for), I μένω
wake (someone) up, I
  ἐγείρω
walk, I βαδίζω,
  βαίνω, πορεύομαι
wall τεῖχος
wand ῥάβδος
want, I βούλομαι
war πόλεμος
ward off, I ἀμύνω
wares ὤνια
watch, I θεάομαι,
  θεωρέω
water ὕδωρ
wave κῦμα
way ὁδός
way, in any πως
way, this ταύτῃ
we ἡμεῖς
weep, I δακρύω
well εὖ, καλῶς
well-behaved σώφρων
well done! εὖ γε
well, I am καλῶς ἔχω
what? τί; τίς;
when ἐπεί, ὡς, ὅτε,
  πότε;
where ὅπου, ποῦ;
where?, from πόθεν;
where (in the world)?
  ποῦ γῆς;
where to? ποῖ;
which? τί; τίς;
while ἐν ᾧ
who? τίς;
who, whose, whom,
  which, that ὅς, ὅσπερ
whole ἅπᾱς
why? διὰ τί;

wife γυνή
wild ἄγριος
willing, I am ἐθέλω
win, I νῑκάω
wind ἄνεμος
wine οἶνος
winter χειμών
wise σοφός, σώφρων
wish, I βούλομαι,
  ἐθέλω
with μετά
withdraw, I ἀναχωρέω
wolf λύκος
woman γυνή
wonder (at), I θαυμάζω
word λόγος, ῥῆμα
work ἔργον, πόνος
work, I ἐργάζομαι,
  πονέω
worry, I φροντίζω
worse κακίων
worst κάκιστος
worthy (of) ἄξιος
wretched τλήμων
write, I γράφω

X
Xanthias Ξανθίᾱς
Xerxes Ξέρξης

Y
year ἔτος
yield, I εἴκω
you (*plural*) ὑμεῖς
you (*singular*) σύ
young man νεᾱνίᾱς
your (*plural*) ὑμέτερος
your (*singular*) σός
yourself, of σεαυτοῦ

Z
Zeus Ζεύς
Zeus, O ὦ Ζεῦ

INDEX

Numbers in boldface refer to illustrations.

CREDITS

Front cover and pages 2, 9, 61, 86, 104, 105, 108, and 176: Alison Frantz, Princeton. Frontispiece and pages vii, 8, 10, 16, 20, 26, 30, 37, 42, 48, 54, 62, 66, 68, 76, 82, 90, 106, 112, 116, 124, 132, 138, 146, 151, 152, 168, 182, 194, 202, and 243: Drawings by Catherine Balme. Page xiii: From *These Were the Greeks* by H. D. Amos and A. G. P. Lang, © 1979 by Dufour Editions, Inc. Page 6: Antikenmuseum Berlin, Staatliche Museen Preußischer Kulturbesitz. Page 7: From *Aristophanic Comedy* by K. J. Dover, © 1972 by B. T. Batsford, Ltd. Page 13: Photograph copyright of the Fitzwilliam Museum, Cambridge. Page 15 (top): From *The Oxford History of the Classical World* ed. by J. Boardman, J. Griffin, and O. Murray, © 1985 by Oxford University Press (Berlin, Staatliche Museen; after *Antike Denkmäler* I, p. 8.7). Pages 15 (bottom), 35, 41, and 111: All rights reserved, The Metropolitan Museum of Art. Pages 24, 102, 156, and 167: Acknowledgment is due to Michael Grant and George Weidenfeld & Nicolson Limited for permission to reproduce the maps on pages 24, 102, 156, and 167 taken from *Ancient History Atlas*. Page 46: National Archaeological Museum, Athens. Pages 59, 74, 75, 89, 114, 122, 144, and 175: Reproduced by courtesy of the Trustees of the British Museum. Pages 88 and 159: Courtesy of The Oriental Institute of The University of Chicago. Page 96 (top): From *A History of the Ancient World* by Chester G. Starr, © 1965 by Oxford University Press. Pages 96 (bottom) and 105: Courtesy of the Royal Ontario Museum, Toronto, Canada. Page 102 (bottom): American School of Classical Studies at Athens. Page 115: Archäologisches Museum, Frankfurt am Main. Page 130: Deutsches Archäologisches Institut, Athens. Pages 148 and 160: By Raymond V. Schoder, S.J., © Loyola University of Chicago. Pages 186–187: From *The Persians by Aeschylus*, tr. Anthony J. Podlecki, © 1970 by Prentice-Hall, Inc. Page 188: From *The Athenian Trireme* by J. S. Morrison and J. F. Coates, © 1986 by Cambridge University Press. Page 199: From *The Oxford History of the Classical World* ed. by J. Boardman, J. Griffin, and O. Murray, © 1985 by Oxford University Press. Page 201: From *The Oxford History of the Classical World* ed. by J. Boardman, J. Griffin, and O. Murray, © 1985 by Oxford University Press (after J. Kirchner, *Imagines Inscriptionum Atticarum*, 1935, pl. 15).